D1232290

Anthropology and Global Counterinsurgency

ANTHROPOLOGY
and **GLOBAL**
COUNTERINSURGENCY

EDITED BY JOHN D. KELLY,

BEATRICE JAUREGUI,

SEAN T. MITCHELL, AND

JEREMY WALTON

The University of Chicago Press :: Chicago & London

JOHN D. KELLY is professor of anthropology at the University of Chicago.

BEATRICE JAUREGUI is visiting fellow at the Center for the Advanced Study of India.

SEAN T. MITCHELL is visiting assistant professor of anthropology at Vanderbuilt University.

JEREMY WALTON is assistant professor of religion at New York University.

The University of Chicago Press, Chicago 60637
The University of Chicago Press, Ltd., London
© 2010 by The University of Chicago
All rights reserved. Published 2010
Printed in the United States of America

19 18 17 16 15 14 13 12 11 10   1 2 3 4 5

ISBN-13: 978-0-226-42993-9   (cloth)
ISBN-13: 978-0-226-42994-6   (paper)
ISBN-10: 0-226-42993-8   (cloth)
ISBN-10: 0-226-42994-6   (paper)

Library of Congress Cataloging-in-Publication Data

Anthropology and global counterinsurgency / John D. Kelly ... [et al.].
    p. cm.
    Includes bibliographical references and index.
    ISBN-13: 978-0-226-42993-9 (cloth : alk. paper)
    ISBN-10: 0-226-42993-8 (cloth : alk. paper)
    ISBN-13: 978-0-226-42994-6 (pbk. : alk. paper)
    ISBN-10: 0-226-42994-6 (pbk. : alk. paper)   1. Political anthropology—United
States. 2. War and society—United States. 3. Counterinsurgency—United States.
4. United States—Foreign relations. 5. United States—Military policy.
    GN560.U6A58 2010
    306.2′70973—dc22
                                                                    2009029074

♾ The paper used in this publication meets the minimum requirements of the American
National Standard for Information Sciences—Permanence of Paper for Printed Library
Materials, ANSI Z39.48-1992.

CONTENTS

Introduction: Culture, Counterinsurgency, Conscience   *1*
:: John D. Kelly, Beatrice Jauregui, Sean T. Mitchell,
and Jeremy Walton

SECTION 1

Categories of Conflict and Coercion: The Blue in Green and
the Other   *17*
:: Beatrice Jauregui

1   Bluing Green in the Maldives: Countering Citizen Insurgency
by "Civil"-izing National Security   *23*
:: Beatrice Jauregui

2   Phantom Power: Notes on Provisionality in Haiti   *39*
:: Greg Beckett

3   The Categorization of People as Targets of Violence:
A Perspective on the Colombian Armed Conflict   *53*
:: Paola Castaño

4   Seeing Red: Mao Fetishism, Pax Americana, and
the Moral Economy of War   *67*
:: John D. Kelly

SECTION 2

Ethnographic Experiences of American Power in the Age of
the War on Terror   *85*
:: Jeremy Walton and Sean T. Mitchell

5   Paranoid Styles of Nationalism after the Cold War:
Notes from an Invasion of the Amazon   *89*
:: Sean T. Mitchell

6   Hungry Wolves, Inclement Storms: Commodified Fantasies of
        American Imperial Power in Contemporary Turkey   *105*
        : : Jeremy Walton

7   Rwandan Rebels and U.S. Federal Prosecutors: American Power,
        Violence, and the Pursuit of Justice in the Age of the War on Terror   *117*
        : : Elizabeth Garland

8   Weapons, Passports, and News: Palestinian Perceptions of U.S.
        Power as a Mediator of War   *125*
        : : Amahl Bishara

9   The Cold War Present: The Logic of Defense Time   *137*
        : : Mihir Pandya

SECTION 3
        Counterinsurgency, Past and Present: Precedents to the Manual   *149*
        : : Jeremy Walton and Beatrice Jauregui

10   The Uses of Anthropology in the Insurgent Age   *153*
        : : Dustin M. Wax

11   Small Wars and Counterinsurgency   *169*
        : : James L. Hevia

12   Repetition Compulsion? Counterinsurgency Bravado in Iraq
        and Vietnam   *179*
        : : Kurt Jacobsen

13   Counterinsurgency, *The Spook*, and Blowback   *193*
        : : Joseph Masco

SECTION 4
        The U.S. Military and U.S. Anthropology   *209*
        : : Sean T. Mitchell and John D. Kelly

14   An Anthropologist among the Soldiers: Notes from the Field   *215*
        : : Marcus B. Griffin

15   Indirect Rule and Embedded Anthropology: Practical,
        Theoretical, and Ethical Concerns   *231*
        : : Roberto J. González

16   Soft Power, Hard Power, and the Anthropological "Leveraging"
        of Cultural "Assets": Distilling the Politics and Ethics of
        Anthropological Counterinsurgency   *245*
        : : David H. Price

17 Yes, Both, Absolutely: A Personal and Professional Commentary on Anthropological Engagement with Military and Intelligence Organizations   *261*
:: Kerry Fosher

SECTION 5
Constructions and Destructions of Conscience   *273*
:: John D. Kelly

18 The Cultural Turn in the War on Terror   *279*
:: Hugh Gusterson

19 Cultural Sensitivity in a Military Occupation: The U.S. Military in Iraq   *297*
:: Rochelle Davis, with Dahlia El Zein and Dena Takruri

20 The "Bad" Kill: A Short Case Study in American Counterinsurgency   *311*
:: Jeffrey Bennett

21 The Destruction of Conscience and the Winter Soldier   *327*
:: Kevin Caffrey

22 No Better Friend, No Worse Enemy: History, Memory, and the Conscience of a Marine   *343*
:: Christopher T. Nelson

Reference List   *355*
List of Contributors   *381*
Index   *385*

Culture, Counterinsurgency, Conscience

:: JOHN D. KELLY, BEATRICE JAUREGUI, SEAN T. MITCHELL,
and JEREMY WALTON ::

Political anthropology finds itself at a challenging, potentially productive crossroads. The wars in Afghanistan and Iraq have placed new stress on the relationships among anthropology, governance, and war. In response to the prolonged violence of wars officially begun in 2001 and 2003, segments in the United States military have taken a new interest in culture and ethnography. Hoping to revitalize counterinsurgency theory and practice, the post-Rumsfeld Department of Defense has called for a new kind of intelligence gathering, what General David Petraeus called "knowledge of the cultural 'terrain'" (Petraeus 2006, 7). Simultaneously, for political anthropologists, global war and governance have emerged as significant objects of ethnographic and theoretical study. This book explores anthropology's relationship to the United States' global projection of its power, while simultaneously mounting an anthropological inquiry into the nature of that power and of the changing world in which it operates.

During World War II, anthropology was among the social science disciplines with the most Ph.D.s in U.S. government service. But at the war's end, which is to say, after the United States deployed atomic weapons against civilian populations in two Japanese cities, anthropologists left government service at an astonishing rate. As Margaret Mead famously put it, "the social scientists . . . took their marbles and went home" (Yans-McLaughlin 1986, 214). Since then, and until very recently, only a small minority of anthropologists has worked for U.S. institutions of war and governance—institutions that are increasingly objects of anthropological study.

This book is a professional and scholarly response to these dual developments: the recent engagement of some sectors of American anthropology with parts of the American defense establishment, on the one hand, and a new analytic focus by American anthropology on military power, on the other. We believe ethnography is a key tool that will help us deepen understanding of contemporary war, American power, and the structures and logics of security, both domestic and international. In other words, we seek ethnographic understanding of global responses to recent deployments and actions of the U.S. military, in comparison with other forms of coercion and compellance, intervention and nonintervention. Reading U.S. military theorists, we seek to understand the redirection of attention to culture in the broad context of military responses to U.S. military failures (and opportunities). And we examine, in particular, the renewal of counterinsurgency as a focal concern in the U.S. military, that is, the idea that a central task for the U.S. military is to forcefully oppose insurgent political movements in nation-states worldwide. As U.S. military strategists connect insurgency with culture, in their planning of counterinsurgency warfare, we turn an anthropological lens on this connection and on the nature of violence and order in the current era.

We expect the primary audience for this book to come from the world of anthropology. However, we intend it to reach a wider audience as well, including military professionals and other scholars of military theory, practice, history, and culture. It is time for serious conversation about the purposes, metrics for success and failure, and even the advisability of U.S. military institutionalization of global counterinsurgency. We also hope that this volume might find its way to every reader interested in the fundamental political questions that are involved here—a wide range of questions about security, on the one hand, and about integrity, responsibility, freedom, and conscience in a liberal state and fraught world state system, on the other. Considered in this light, our enterprise has to find its way in already vast literatures. Important post–cold war public and scholarly discussions of the ethics, politics, and advisability of U.S. global military deployments began long before the military articulated its counterinsurgency doctrines of the early twenty-first century. These discussions have involved historians, political scientists, philosophers, and career military officers, as well as journalists and polemicists of many persuasions. However, it is only recently that these discussions have relied upon anthropological means and insights.

In fact, this public and scholarly conversation began before the attacks of

September 11, 2001, and even before the end of the cold war, spurred by such critical events as U.S. sponsorship of counterinsurgency warfare in Central America during the 1980s; the invasion of Grenada and the bombing of the U.S. Marine barracks in Beirut (both in 1983); the "Black Hawk down" and firefights while "nation building" in Mogadishu (1993); and the preemptive cruise missile strike on al-Qaeda camps in Afghanistan and an alleged bin Laden chemical weapons factory in the Sudan, the intervention called Operation Infinite Reach, by the military under Bill Clinton (1998). An orienting dilemma became whether to improve U.S. military interventions or to curtail them. Consider the contrast between the influential arguments of Colin Powell in the pages of *Foreign Affairs* (1992/1993) and those of Chalmers Johnson in *Blowback* (2000)—a book pushed onto bestseller lists by public interest after 9/11. The embrace of anthropology in counterinsurgency doctrines has taken place in the midst of these often contentious debates about the ways and means of U.S. military deployment. Does the United States have another rendezvous with destiny, as Powell contended, an opportunity to lead and reshape the world for the better? Or has the vast U.S. deployment of military force during and after the cold war made the world more dangerous, as Johnson argued? This book offers contrasting perspectives on these questions. The authors gathered here are not of one mind about what is to be done or by whom. However, all these authors share in a major goal of this volume: to incorporate ethnography into these debates.[1]

Anthropologists and Global Counterinsurgency

Anthropology's influence on global military affairs will follow only from its insights and its ability to bring those insights to plural audiences. This volume demonstrates the power of ethnography to illuminate the complexities underlying contemporary order and disorder at national and global scales. Whatever the advisability of collaboration of anthropologists with a widely extended U.S. military (and this volume has many occasions to debate this point), we do not believe that anthropology's influence should be merely, or even principally, internal to U.S. military and government agencies. We strongly believe in the importance of an independent anthropology, one that can help both intellectuals and a broad public. Indeed, for this reason this volume gathers a variety of anthropologists doing and advocating different types of anthropological work within a variety of institutions. We therefore envisage a broad readership, both within the United States and outside of it, of people concerned about the nature of order and violence in the current era.

That said, there is no doubt that the volume will be of particular interest to professional anthropologists. To that audience, as well as to scholars in related social sciences, the immediate question is, what is to be done in response to the overtures intrinsic to the "cultural turn" in the U.S. military?[2] Particular responses are called for. The U.S. military already has operational relationships with social scientists of many kinds, but now important voices within it call for a closer partnership with anthropology. The manifold connections of political science and economics and, to a lesser degree, sociology with governments and militaries make their issues of engagement different from those of anthropology. Advising the state is a significant part of the constitutive mission of major subfields in each of these social science disciplines. Even so, anthropology has not been alone in its internal conflict over participation in the early twenty-first-century wars of the United States. Psychology also found itself in an acute dilemma during the wars in Iraq and Afghanistan as researchers and clinicians debated the ethics of professional psychologists advising military and military-sponsored interrogators (especially during torture). How are psychologists to draw the line between therapeutic uses of psychology to improve the mental health of subjects of interrogation and the deliberate use of psychological techniques (from talking cures to drugs) to break down subjects and gather intelligence? In September 2008, prompted by professional groups such as the Psychologists for Social Responsibility, the American Psychological Association (APA) passed a referendum banning APA member psychologists from participating in U.S. detention facilities or acting in violation of international law or the U.S. Constitution.

The debates in psychology overlap with but differ from those involving anthropology. The intelligence context and the ethical concern for the well-being of the research subject are the same, a topic addressed and enforced by federal law and association bylaws in each case. But, while psychology has had to react to a history of direct complicity of some psychologists in interrogation violence, anthropology's debates are more nebulous, embedded as much in prospective plans for the cultural turn of the U.S. military as in actual military deployments and uses of anthropology and anthropologists (see also Griffin, this volume). And in these matters, anthropology—as is typical of the discipline—seeks to reconsider the specificities and ambiguities of its own mission in the world as many anthropologists seek also to define a path of scholarly and political action.

The cultural turn in the U.S. military began to manifest publicly in 2006. This turn is reviewed in greater detail in many of these essays; here we offer some orienting signposts: the initial release in 2006 of the U.S. Army *Field Manual 3-24: Counterinsurgency;* the introduction into occupied territories in 2007 of Human Terrain Teams (HTTs); and the announcement in 2008 of the Minerva Project.[3] Unusually theoretical for a field manual, the 2006 *Field Manual 3-24: Counterinsurgency* advocates reliance upon anthropological concepts and methods to reorient counterinsurgency efforts. With millions of copies downloaded (U.S. Army 2007, xxi), and a print edition published by the University of Chicago Press in 2007, this "manual" is clearly oriented to a public audience, in addition to its actual military one. In autumn 2007, great publicity attended the revelation that HTTs had been deployed by the U.S. Army as part of a larger program called the Human Terrain System (HTS) to provide cultural guidance in occupied territories. The teams include anthropologists and linguists—or at least personnel the military designates as anthropologists and linguists. And the 2008 Minerva Project initiative was created to sponsor new large-scale research in anthropology and other fields of social science and cultural scholarship, with multimillion-dollar grants for research projects selected by the military.

By autumn 2007, professional anthropologists in the United States began to rally against the new military ventures. A new group, the Network of Concerned Anthropologists, mounted strong protests against involvement in military occupations and everything associated with them. In October 2007, the Executive Committee of the American Anthropological Association (AAA) expressed official disapproval of the HTS program on ethical grounds focused on professional responsibilities to informants. Its Ad Hoc Commission on the Engagement of Anthropology with U.S. National Security and Intelligence Communities issued its report before the November-December 2007 Annual Meeting, recommending significant revisions to strengthen the AAA's ethical code. The business meeting at those 2007 Annual Meeting revealed overwhelming support among the AAA's rank and file for an ethical code that would be even tougher on participation in counterinsurgency and intelligence work than the one recommended by the committee. This debate continues as this book goes to press, but the larger issues have only begun to be addressed.

Origins of This Volume

This volume is, to a significant degree, the product of one professional workshop's deep interest in these matters. The workshop entitled "Science, Technology, Society and the State" (STSS) at the University of Chicago is ordinarily a clearinghouse for connecting the range of issues raised in science and technology studies (STS) to the issues and agendas of political anthropology. Its mission, most broadly, is better definition of the relationships between knowledge and the state. Founded in 2002 by professors John D. Kelly and Tanya Luhrmann and then student Tara Schwegler, the first years of the workshop were devoted to comparing the reception and use of STS theory in different domains of the cultural sciences, especially as they included matters of state policy.[4]

The STSS workshop has from its inception addressed issues of interest in the intersecting subsets of anthropology, STS, political science, cultural studies, and sociology. But as it turned its agenda toward counterinsurgency, its discussions gained a new political urgency. This shift did not make the scholarship any less intellectually complex than in the workshop's previous discussions of early twentieth-century media or seventeenth-century scientific concept building. However, the politics of counterinsurgency brought many issues of immediate public significance to the workshop's discussions. In response to the October 2007 press coverage announcing the HTS program and the outcry from the Network of Concerned Anthropologists, on November 26, 2007, the STSS workshop sponsored a roundtable discussion, "Military Ethnographers?" in advance of the wider discussions at the AAA Annual Meeting. Five months later, it sponsored a conference entitled "Anthropology and Global Counterinsurgency" from April 25 to 27, 2008. Nineteen of the twenty-one papers read at that conference are completed, collected, and reproduced here; one author could not contribute to this volume, and another, who had committed his conference essay elsewhere, provided a new essay.[5]

Another significant point of origin for this volume was a panel organized for the 2007 AAA Annual Meeting, "Mapping a Space among Criticism, Consumption and Complicity: Ethnographic Experiences of American Power vis-à-vis the 'War on Terror,'" which is discussed at greater length later in this introduction. The confluence of concerns in these different projects helped us connect our interest in the production and institutionalization of anthropological knowledge to a consideration of the insights that anthropology can provide on the post–cold war world order. This collective effort suggests the intense interest among political anthropologists in this deliberation and, we believe, hints at new directions for anthropological research. Indeed, we intend for this conference and volume to be the first step in a new project for political anthropological research on the world of Pax Americana.

Pax Americana and Political Anthropology

Recent decades have been the best of times and the worst of times for the subdiscipline of political anthropology and for the idea of an anthropology of politics. On the one hand, the centrality in anthropology of postcolonial theory and the comprehensive discussion of nationalism and, more recently, transnationalism have put political issues into the analysis of more and more cultural and social phenomena. Under the continuing influence of critical philosophies, philologies, and sociologies—from Elias, Foucault, and Bourdieu to Said, Zizek, Agamben, and Latour—anthropologists have begun to find politics everywhere. This has crumbled the walls of the domain establishing the particular institutions of interest to a political anthropology. In the relative peace of Pax Americana following World War II, studies of war and peace took second place to political studies of powers of life, from biopower to governmentality to neoliberal economic orders. Even the study of national politics became a study of the culture of modernity and alternate modernities, and ethnographers attempted to delineate and represent increasingly sublime ideological objects, finding often the deepest politics there (Kelly 2002). This is not to say that anthropologists stopped studying violence and war.[6] But it was only with the attacks of September 11, 2001, the U.S. invasions and occupations of the early twenty-first century, and the emergence of the cultural turn within the U.S. military that war and violence, especially on a geopolitical scale, have become such central concerns of political anthropology.

Many of the authors in this volume are active participants in the Network of Concerned Anthropologists. They suggest that current times require a sort of "counter-counterinsurgency" from political anthropology. This image, following as a trope in a sequence of debates in anthropology about "anti-antirelativism" and "anti-antipositivism" and other negations of negations, provides its own compelling vision of a political anthropology that speaks truth to power. This vision stands in obvious contrast to that of counterinsurgency's planners and participants, a group that also includes anthropologists. These planners and participants, as Masco argues in this volume, see counterinsurgency as the necessary response to trouble at large, rendering all nonstate actors as potential threats and imagining sinister designs while deploying machineries of suppression. Without denying that the contemporary world does possess real threats that warrant real responses, nevertheless, in counter-counterinsurgency's compelling romance, political anthropology finds its purpose in the defense of "the damned of the earth"—to recall the famous book title of colonial critic Frantz Fanon, usually mistranslated from the French as "the wretched of the earth."[7]

This volume advocates a political anthropology that includes both proponents of counter-counterinsurgency and proponents of participation in the military's cultural turn. We believe that political anthropology must be centered on scholarship that brings ethnographic techniques and insights into discussions of war, peace, and American power. And we hope to provide an intellectual venue of the highest creativity and rigor. To us, this means not merely extended conversation about what anthropology can and should do but increasing exemplification of anthropology actually doing what it can. We sponsor and provoke ethnographic discussion of the world of Pax Americana, in relationship to its theories, its imaginaries, its dicta as experienced, and its unintended consequences. We consider many parts of the U.S. military by way of ethnographic analysis of their consequences—consequences for the others in the world, for the United States, and, not least, for soldiers themselves. We advocate a political anthropology that provides not what the U.S. military leadership wants but what we believe it and the world need: more acute and diverse perspectives and better information about what exactly is going on.

The participants in this volume and the conference, workshop, and panel behind it include sociologists, historians, and political scientists interested in culture and counterinsurgency; but they are mostly anthropologists, in quest of an effective political anthropology. Some are ex-soldiers; some are anthropologists who work for the military; some are sponsors of petitions against anthropological involvement in counterinsurgency; some are scholars who study the U.S. and other militaries and their effects worldwide. Not everyone necessarily agrees with the implications of Max Weber's famous discussions of science and of politics as callings—or "vocations"—that exist in separate spheres (Weber 1958b, 1958c). But we want Weber's concept of the line between science and politics to energize this project. Science, ultimately, has to leave it to other agencies to decide what is to be done. What is to be done and how we shall live are, as Weber put it, Tolstoy's questions (Weber 1958b, 1958c). As Weber argued, the answers to these questions depend on value judgments that are in turn mediated by human culture. No science can answer these questions by its own will to truth. Weber agreed with Tolstoy, and we agree with Weber, that there is no hope for the positivist dream (and to some the nightmare) of sciences that can replace the need for political value judgments.

As Weber argued against Tolstoy, science has a crucial role, not in solving problems but in clarifying them. Here, we agree, is one of the most important things that science can seek to provide. Many social sciences can play a role in clarifying political dilemmas; political anthropology can provide real ethnography. A political anthropology can help us—an "us" of various kinds and scales, of various histories, trajectories, and possibilities—to know our political past, present, and our options for possible futures. Like the world that it investigates, this political anthropology will be plural. And it will be united by rigorous and comparative attention to empirical detail. Science cannot render political value judgments, but for good judgments on any large scale, it is now necessary. The authors gathered in this volume *do* make their own value judgments and *do* debate them here; but the primary goal of this volume—and of this political anthropology—is not value judgments as such, but fine-grained knowledge of a complex and dangerous world, knowledge that might make good value judgments possible.

The World Made Safe for What?

While we see no prospect for straightforwardly scientific solutions to political problems, we align ourselves with the deliberate and politically motivated tendency of anthropologists to clarify their objects from a critical vantage, always as if exterior, the tendency to make the familiar strange and to critically reconsider its forms, powers, means, and ends. To see the self as others do is part of this orienting impulse, as is the quest to supplement the better-known top-down self-understandings of the powerful with bottom-up and outside-in reconsiderations and reflections. This clarifying, critical, bottom-up, and outside-in vantage is what distinguishes, for example, the discussion in section 1 of the "Blue in Green" from myriad discussions of civil-military relations in political science circles. Taken in its entirety, we view this volume as an argument for the importance of this ethnographic vantage to our understanding of contemporary politics on a global scale. The papers exemplify the kinds of criticism that ethnography can arrange, even of political ends themselves.

To illuminate another important dilemma in the political ends of American military interventions, consider the contrast between two important intellectual responses to Woodrow Wilson's famous assertion of U.S. political ends. When Wilson appeared before the U.S. Congress to ask for a declaration of war on April 2, 1917, he provided a new justification for American military intervention. Against prior calls (from Wilson and others) for nonintervention and nonalignment, the once president of the American Political Science Association and then president of the United States told the U.S. Congress that "the world must be made safe for democracy." Wilson's injunction marked a sea change in the imaginaries orienting U.S. power and its relation to the world. The Gettysburg Address had posited an imaginary of the United States as tenuous project and exception, the very possibility of which was thrown into doubt by a Civil War that tested "whether any nation so conceived and so dedicated [could] long endure." Wilson, instead, made of this exception a blueprint for a peaceful and prosperous world future. Decades after Wilson's presidency, during another World War and its aftermath, in the emerging world of the United Nations, intellectuals recalled Wilson's vision with critical acuteness and varied points of critique.

Anthropologists Clyde Kluckhohn and Ruth Benedict coined and promoted a significant revision to Wilson's injunction. They argued that the tough minded know and respect the existence of cultural differences and seek "a world made safe for differences" (Benedict 1946, 15). Decades later, political theorist Leo Strauss expressed his skepticism about the possibility of global reform, and his concern for the danger it could pose, by declaring the need "to make the world safe for the Western democracies" (1964, 4). Safe for difference or safe for the institutions of the West? Benedict and Strauss each sought to modify Wilson's one-size-fits-all imaginary of symmetrical democratic nation-states. On philosophical grounds, and in light of the unparalleled universalism that he saw as intrinsic to Western values, Strauss sought not to challenge but to protect the West's political self-understanding and to shield its institutions and accomplishments. On anthropological grounds, on the other hand, and in light of anthropology's knowledge of the complexity and diversity of human institutions, Kluckhohn and Benedict were more skeptical of the West's potential for narcissism. They sought edifying challenges to Western self-understanding and protection for human knowledge and institutions beyond the dreams of Western philosophies.

Of course, Benedict and Strauss are only two voices from two disciplines among the many that have debated the future of U.S. power and military intervention since World War II. The issues they raise complicate but also clarify the central question of the recent intervention debates: Colin Powell's rendezvous with destiny or Chalmers Johnson's perils of blowback? Strauss's concern to protect the heritage and promote the destiny of the Western liberal democracies resonates with Powell's idea of a new U.S. rendezvous with destiny. Many would align Benedict's cautionary tale with Johnson's. However, Benedict did not, like Johnson, call for a general retreat from "forward positions" for U.S. military power. When she wrote about nation building and social engineering, she was more interested in contesting the ends than the means, especially the ethnocentric ends of global Westernization. Benedict sought a world made safe for differences, a United Nations that could protect social and cultural difference around the globe. Here, precisely, is where a Straussian might fear overreach and entanglement, emphasizing Strauss's concern rather to protect what he saw as already transcendently valuable, the Western democracies. Such a Straussian would be more afraid of blowback. Global counterinsurgency doctrines are motivated by fears of difference *and* by fears of blowback. They tend to promote no clear vision of political ends whatsoever, beyond enforced peace. But whether to intervene and how to intervene entail the question of why to intervene. As ethnography repeatedly shows us, counterinsurgency interventions raise basic questions about the ends as well as the means.

Whether Benedict's premise of a world with cultures "safely" distinct from one another is still viable—whether it ever was—enormously complicates the goal she and Kluckhohn sought to set. Nevertheless, we think it is almost inevitable, and certainly reasonable, for anthropologists to continue their own deliberate, political as well as scientific, quests toward goals closer to the goal of Kluckhohn and Benedict than to that of Leo Strauss. A Straussian anthropology—that is, an anthropology seeking to specify why other societies do not have the greatness of the West—is conceivable in prospect but rare in practice and thin in findings. It almost necessarily oversimplifies real cultural complexity; and beyond that, its own romanticism leans against spending extensive time outside the West. By these lights, anything learned beyond the West would likely be something low and valueless. So it is not surprising that all the anthropologists in this volume, whatever position they take on the political issues engaged, follow political and scientific vectors discernibly closer to the call for a tough-minded pursuit of a world safe for differences. In its very design, in fact, as a whole, our book seeks to delineate key contexts for understanding the current deployments of U.S. military power in this light.

In Sum: Toward an Anthropology of the World of Pax Americana

This volume pursues a political anthropology that seeks to uncover the culturally mediated rationalities that underlie global counterinsurgency and the larger world of order and violence in the era of Pax Americana. As is demonstrated by Gonzalez (2004) such inquiry is already well begun. We hope it will continue, and we call for more ethnography analyzing contemporary order and violence in all its materiality and complexity. This volume is intended to demonstrate that ethnography can take a significant role in discussions of Pax Americana. It can and should become a central tool in research on global violence and security. For historians of anthropology, it is striking how little the British anthropologists had to say about British power in the era of Pax Britannica. Ironically, in recent decades, American historical anthropologists have made the long-gone European empires an important focus of their scholarship. Let us not wait this time for the Owl of Minerva to spread its wings at dusk. It is time for ethnography to become a key analytic force in research on the world of Pax Americana and for this ethnography to become a central focus of the new political anthropology.

Outline of the Sections

The volume begins with essays examining the organization and institutionalization of order and violence in the age of global counterinsurgency. In three separate contexts—the Maldives, Haiti, and Colombia—ethnographically informed scholars examine the institutional line that Beatrice Jauregui has described as "the Blue in Green," the moving borderline necessary for all states but variously configured between policing powers (Blue) and military capacities and deployments (Green). This section then concludes with reconsideration of the planning of global counterinsurgency as an expansive effort to define political violence as Green (or, as it turns out, Red) and to use Green, military means to extend peace even in foreign civil spaces.

The second section also mounts an empirical interrogation of contemporary order and violence. The focus is not on dilemmas for the state's supposed monopoly on legitimate violence, as it is in the preceding section, but on the lights cast variously by non-American observers on a ubiquitous American power that is not always so well illuminated. In this section, participants in a panel (organized by Sean T. Mitchell and Jeremy Walton) at the 2007 Annual Meeting of the AAA, along with several other scholars, were invited to discuss "Ethnographic Experiences of American Power in the Age of the 'War on Terror.'" We are pleased to be able to include an additional paper written by Elizabeth Garland—who had participated in that AAA session but was unable to join us in Chicago for the April conference on "Anthropology and Global Counterinsurgency." Papers here examine fears of imagined U.S. invasion plans in places as disparate as urban Turkey and rural Brazil, and they consider, in local context, actual encounters with both Green and Blue U.S. military power in the Middle East and Africa. This section finishes with a classically anthropological reconsideration of the War on Terror, from the outside point of view, in this case the view of the southern California defense industries, whose corporate orientations and long clock for development projects force an inadvertent and material translation of counterinsurgency into terms not its own.

The third and fourth sections focus the discussion on counterinsurgency as such. The third section begins with acute reconsiderations of the past and present of U.S. and British counterinsurgency enterprises. It then turns to an analysis of the politics of "repetition compulsion" in contemporary counterinsurgency, delineating the return of doctrines not so much repressed as discarded for their failures. Finally, section 3 addresses counterinsurgency planners' own imaginaries, as they are refracted in cinema and reappropriated by military agents. Collectively, the essays that constitute this section review the history of anthropological participation in U.S. military engagements, especially in World War II and Vietnam. They also review the history of anthropological critique in World War II and Vietnam and its consequences, and several of these authors voice clear conclusions about the advisability of anthropological participation in counterinsurgency operations.

This central question becomes the primary focus of the book's fourth section. Here some leading voices in the recent anthropological debates over direct engagement by scholars with the military discuss the issues and draw what they see as the most important lines of distinction. Two of the authors in this section are against and two are in favor of anthropological participation in at least some U.S. military institutions. Here we are pleased to add the only paper in the volume not by a participant in the conference or the panels and workshops that preceded it; as Marcus Griffin's account of his participation in the HTS program makes clear, he was in Iraq while we were in Chicago.

Finally, in keeping with our intention to do what political anthropology can, and not only to discuss what it should, the book does not finish with this moment in ongoing debate. Instead, we conclude with papers that answered the call to discuss construction and destruction of conscience in the contemporary U.S. military in Iraq and Afghanistan. The first two papers here review in fine detail what the U.S. military currently tries to accomplish by instrumentalizing knowledge of culture and teaching deployed troops about the culture of noncombatants in the territories the troops occupy. The volume concludes with three essays reconsidering and updating a path-breaking discussion of destruction of conscience in Vietnam written by Marshall Sahlins in 1966. We complete this first foray into a political anthropology of the world of Pax Americana with ethnographic inquiries into the effects of deployed American force on the conscience of the U.S. soldiers themselves.

Thanks are owed to a long list of individuals and institutions for helping to fund and host the conference underlying this volume and for participating variously in the planning, staging, and consolidating of its scholarship. In particular we would like to thank the Center for International Studies, the Center for the Study of Communication and Society, the Department of Anthropology, the Norman Wait Harris Fund, and the Marion R. and Adolph J. Lichtstern Fund, all parts of the University of Chicago, for providing the funding that made it possible to call forth these papers to conference and begin this project. We would also like to thank, in particular, Sandra Hagen, the Faculty Affairs Administrator of the Department of Anthropology, University of Chicago; Fione Dukes, Faculty Services Representative of the University of Chicago Local Business Center; and Anne Ch'ien, the Student Affairs Administrator in the Department of Anthropology, University of Chicago, for their tireless and effective administrative support for the endeavor. In addition, the conference would not have been possible were it not for the support and encouragement of Kathy Morrison, Director, and Steven Wilkinson, Acting Director, of the University's Center for International Studies. Our thanks are also owed to Beth Iams Wellman for her hard work compiling the index to this volume. We would also like to thank Marshall Sahlins for the many roles he played in the roundtable, conference, and volume planning and preparation. This enterprise owes a great deal to all of these people and many others for their support and participation.

A final note about funding: the University of Chicago funded the conference and the workshop behind it, and the AAA sponsored the annual meeting that launched one of the panels, represented here as a section of the book. No direct funding was sought or obtained from the U.S. military. Ironically, participants with positions in the U.S. military had to navigate dilemmas concerning what they could and could not take from the University of Chicago. There is something worth reconsidering there too. Our project need not end with what legal scholar Roberto Unger has called the political philosophy of Pontius Pilate (2007, 115), washing our hands of involvement with each other; but it does begin there. In keeping with classic concerns for academic freedom, we intend to keep the Pax Americana project free of funding from the U.S. military, including Minerva funding. But we also want to provide seats at the table for serious scholars of Pax Americana from every quarter.

:: **NOTES** ::

1. Other established axes of political and intellectual debate are also relevant to the critical evaluation of the counterinsurgency project that has been launched by the U.S. military, and here we name some more of them. Dilemmas in the modeling of globalization might be marked, for example, by announcements of a new kind of capitalism (Greider 1998; Klein 2007) versus "the end of history" (Fukuyama 1989) or by the extreme anxieties of Samuel Huntington and his geography of threats and conflicts (1996) versus the optimism of Akira Iriye (2002) about the social, cultural, and political powers of an emerging "global community." Separately, the Iriye-Huntington comparison might also mark another extreme, Iriye's patient attention to historical fact and empirically attentive conceptual development versus Huntington's reliance on anecdote, stereotype, and emotional imagery. Next, the dilemmas of intervention themselves can also be portrayed differently if put in the context of longer U.S. histories and other state and military histories. Here one might contrast, for example, Philip Bobbitt's 2002 treatise on the centrality of military victory in the "long war" for nation-states with James Carroll's 2006 cautionary tale about actual U.S. military policy and practice since the building of the Pentagon in 1943. While neither Bobbitt nor Carroll declare laws of history, Bobbitt's strong sense of evolutionary political forces rewarding the bold, wise, and aggressive, contrasts strongly with Carroll's skeptical sense that disaster follows from grand deployments and aggressive arrogance and that wisdom lies in reconsiderations attentive to actual outcomes. Two more points worth noting: Bobbitt's is one of the earliest relevant uses of the concept of long war, but he used it in a sense distinguishable from President George W. Bush and others: not as a new war after the cold war, against ubiquitous and dangerous global insurgencies, but as an "epochal war fought to determine whether the nineteenth-century imperial constitutional order would be replaced by nation-states" (2002, 805), which Bobbitt dates from 1914 to 1990. He finds that "the Long War of the nation-state is over" (2002, 805) and that it was "the US policy

of containment that successfully ended that war" (2002, 802). Second, Bobbit distinguishes the strategies and deployments of U.S. military power from those of "empires" (cf. Kelly, this volume), in contrast to a large literature describing American empire and/or U.S. imperialism, including authors against U.S. empire (for example, Harvey 2005, Khalidi 2004), authors for it (N. Fergusson 2004), and authors resigned to its inevitability (Bacevich 2004). Readers interested in the empire question and the relation of the war in Iraq to prior conflicts, might see also Calhoun, Cooper, and Moore (2006), Sifry and Cerf (2003), and Gardner and Young (2008).

2. The cultural turn has not characterized the entire U.S. military but emerged, in dissenting sectors of the U.S. military, as the wars in Iraq and Afghanistan became much longer, more violent, and more complicated than Donald Rumsfeld's (2001–2006) Department of Defense had advertised. The turn has been institutionalized through the appointment of Rumsfeld's successor Robert Gates and through the rise of General David Petraeus (for scholarly discussions, see Jager 2007 and Gusterson, this volume).

3. As we submit final drafts of these essays to press, the week of the inauguration of President Barack Obama in January 2009, the next milestone in this U.S. military project has emerged: the *US Government Counterinsurgency Guide* (or *COIN Guide*). The drafting of the guide was led by the Interagency Counterinsurgency Initiative (ICI) of the State Department's Bureau of Political-Military Affairs. Its release has signaled the far-reaching strategic aims and doctrines that groups within the Bush administration have sought to bequeath to their heirs. With its cosigning by the departments of State and Defense and contributions by at least seven other government departments and agencies—from USAID and the Department of Justice, to the Departments of Agriculture and Transportation—the new *COIN Guide* demonstrates a new level of interagency cooperation between civil and military organs. And the ICI logo itself gestures toward a COIN strategy of unprecedented reach and integration, with its pledge, "Whole-of-Government, Whole-of-Society," surrounding silhouettes of a red-colored man and woman in suits flanking a blue-colored soldier in front of a globe, all working together to push down into the corner a black-colored insurgent. The papers in this volume were all written before this latest development.

4. For those interested, we offer here a somewhat fuller intellectual history of the workshop. It was founded on the premise that scholars of the state, especially ethnographers of actual state-society relationships, might have insights into the power of knowledge unavailable within studies of STS. For example, the proposition that "knowledge is power and power is knowledge" would be more interesting, and more testable, from the perspective of study of actual knowledge and its history in actual states and societies. The workshop quickly became interested in the uneven scholarly trajectories in studies of different kinds of knowledge in practice. In its first years, the workshop compared the challenge of STS for emergent theories of biopolitics and bioethics (in human development, medical anthropology, and environmental studies) to the utility of STS for studies of semiotic technologies, language, law, and the state (in linguistics and linguistic anthropology), where the nature-culture line was much less salient than legal questions in the constitution of unambiguously artificial, invented, new kinds of information in cyberspace (compare, for example, Haraway 1997 with Lessig 1999). It also discussed economics as a technology-delivering science and markets as built environments. In discussions of more recent years, the workshop turned increasingly toward a fourth distinct area in which STS scholarship was provoking important questions about knowledge, power, and the state: military knowledge and power. Here the workshop issues overlapped with John Kelly's course on "Military Theory and Practice" (first taught in spring 2003) and codirector Joseph Masco's courses on "Big Science and the Birth of the National Security State" (first taught in autumn 2001), "Science Studies I: Military Science and War" (first taught in 2003), and "The Anthropology of Security" (first taught in winter 2004). As the workshop has come to model it, military technologies have, again, their own material politics and provide means to material changes that are not merely dependent on legal, biological, or market forces and relations. Focus on military knowledge and power reopened basic questions about changing conditions

of possibility in what Foucault had bracketed as "power over death," allegedly superceded by the politics of "power over life."

5. One index of the professional domains and boundaries that have shaped this collection is the interesting pattern of response of scholars invited to the conference on "Anthropology and Global Counterinsurgency." Experts on counterinsurgency in the military were invited, and all refused the invitation. Anthropologists involved in the discussions within the discipline not only accepted invitations but actively suggested other potential invitees. In between were the professional anthropologists working for the military, two of whom accepted our invitations. The persons in this last group are now in high demand for ethical and intellectual debates throughout the discipline and outside it, and they report real fatigue in attempting to meet all requests to articulate and support their minority opinion. We suspect that in declining invitations to the April 2008 conference, the counterinsurgency experts correctly read the tidal forces within the anthropological profession. We wish that everyone invited had come and are thankful to those who displayed the courage of their convictions by attending. They not only enlivened but also extended the intellectual conversation.

6. For important examples of continuing anthropology of war, peace, and military matters, see Duffield (2001), Gill (2004), Lutz (2001), Nordstrom (1997), and Ferguson and Whitehead (2000). Studies of violence, fear and policing have been more common, notably including Caldeira (2000), Das (1990), Siegel (1998), Tambiah (1997), Taussig (1991), and many works by Jean Comaroff and John L. Comaroff (see, for example, Comaroff and Comaroff 2003, 2006a–d).

7. See Fanon (1976). Thanks also to Marston Morgan for pointing out this mistranslation, which follows the original English rendering of "*Les damnés de la terre*" in the first line of "The Internationale."

SECTION 1

CATEGORIES OF CONFLICT AND COERCION
The Blue in Green and the Other

:: BEATRICE JAUREGUI ::

There is a common assumption, an unreflecting belief, that it is somehow
"natural" for the armed forces to obey the civil power. Therefore instances
which show civilian control to have broken down are regarded, if at all, as
isolated disturbances, after which matters will again return to "normal."

Samuel E. Finer (2002 [1962], 5)

Among proponents of liberal democracy there exists a
general consensus that ultimately peace and public order
should be secured by an institutional means of coercion
that is controlled by a civil rather than a military authority (Bruneau and Tollefson 2006; Easton 2006; Feaver 2005; Welch 1976;
Huntington 1957). By extension, if military intervention has been
authorized in a situation of conflict, there tend to be widespread
calls and promises for an eventual demilitarization or "reduction
to policing" of a state's primary means of security. One of the more
recent examples of this tendency is the fact that after three years of
ongoing combat and counterinsurgency operations in Iraq, General
George W. Casey, Jr., and other senior commanders of the United
States Army deemed 2006 the "Year of the Police" in order to demonstrate to the world the U.S. commitment to "[h]elp[ing] the
Iraqi people build a new Iraq, with a constitutional and representative government that respects political and human rights, and with
sufficient security forces both to maintain domestic order and to

prevent Iraq from becoming a safe haven for terrorists" (U.S. Department of Defense 2006, 1; see also Deflem and Sutphin 2006; Schmitt 2006).

The globally hegemonic paradigm that all roads *must* lead eventually to a government with civil means of coercion, even while order is being secured by a military body, is here represented under the analytical rubric of the "Blue in Green."[1] The Blue—a hue which often colors purposely visible police uniforms, as well as the United Nations (UN) flag and peacekeeper helmets—symbolizes the ideal pacific order of civil-legal security, upheld by its claim to transparency and accountability to "the people." The Green—a color commonly worn by army and other military personnel for both ceremonial and camouflage purposes—represents the "necessary evil" of martial force required during war or a state of emergency. Importantly, Blue and Green are not merely ideal-juridical categories but also practiced concepts, manifest in social institutions. According to the Blue *in* Green paradigm of security and statecraft, the (secondary color) Green ought to be always already permeated by, and ultimately reducible to, the (primary color) Blue. Advocates of democracy naturalize discrete spheres of Blue ("rule of law") and Green ("fog of war") and lend a moral supremacy and everyday legitimacy to institutions of coercion falling under the former category. But history makes clear that these spheres do not merely exist in contiguity but bleed into and out of each other in comparative and particularistic ways. And the continual and complex shifting of categories of conflict and legitimate coercion demonstrates how the Blue in Green is colored by treacherous contradictions and troublesome implications.[2]

The paradoxes of securing a democratic order through potential or actual violence have a long genealogy in "Western" political theory. In Platonic philosophy, the citizens serve the state while "just rule" occurs through public debates and policies that reflect the moral virtue of civil leaders operating in accord with the generalized will of the people (Plato 2008 [ca. 360 B.C.E.]). The Machiavellian counterpoint, however, argues that the state serves the citizens and that its success requires a prince with a "flexible disposition" who leads a military comprised of soldiers with *virtù* to do whatever is "necessary" at any and all times to protect and promote civic life (Machiavelli 2008 [1513], 2001 [1521]). This same century-spanning tension between civil supremacy and military security is legible in Michel Foucault's inversion of Carl von Clausewitz's maxim that "war is merely the continuation of policy [politics] by other means" (Clausewitz 1989 [1832], 87) to "politics is the continuation of war by other means" (Foucault 2003 [1976], 15).[3]

Historically, leaders of liberal democratic and republican states conceptually and rhetorically have tended to favor Platonic "just rule" by a civil government and the Clausewitzian axiom, while institutionally adopting Machiavellian militarized "flexibility" and the Foucauldian axiom. This structural paradox of civil-ized military governance, which is the central contradiction of the Blue in Green paradigm of security, was particularly stark during the era of European colonialism in the eighteenth and nineteenth centuries and continued through the era of decolonization. The social fact of this paradox has not gone unnoticed by twentieth-century historians (see, e.g., Miller 1994; Gottman 1986 [1943]) and has been theorized from various angles by a wide range of philosophers of sovereignty and violence: from Hannah Arendt (1951), Walter Benjamin (1968 [1942], 1978 [1922]), and Carl Schmitt (1985 [1922]) to Giorgio Agamben (1998 [1995]) and Jacques Derrida (1991). Beyond igniting scholarly inquiry and critique, the challenges of simultaneously staking a claim to civil ends while utilizing military means remain a daily empirical and operational problem. This is particularly true for persons charged with strategizing security measures on the ground, whether planning police crowd control for a political protest or intervening in a war-ravaged region of the world. Indeed, an enormous literature—spanning scholarly explanations, journalistic descriptions, and policy prescriptions—has grown around questions of the experience, efficacy, and advisability of UN peacekeeping missions, with titles including the likes of *Blue Geopolitics* and *Soldiers for Peace* (e.g., Hillen 2000; Benton 1996; Pirnie and Simons 1996; Fisas 1995; for a comparative anthropological analysis of the "cultural side of peacekeeping" itself, see Rubinstein 2008).

In the twenty-first century, the content and form of both global economic integration and international power relations are rapidly changing. In explaining and evaluating this ever-shifting political economic complex, some scholars theorize the UN/U.S.-led global order as an updated imperial structure, while others argue that we need new categories and conceptual frameworks, since there no longer exists an "empire" in the historical sense of expansive territorial invasion and direct, or even indirect, rule by an occupying colonial power (cf. Gonzalez, this volume; Kelly 2003; Hardt and Negri 2001; see also note 1 in the Introduction to this volume). But while there are differing theoretical schools of postcoloniality, most would agree on some general trends. First, for the most part, naked capitalist colonizations and civilizing missions have morphed into campaigns to "bring democracy and freedom" to subjugated peoples. Moreover, the colonial occupation and conventional warfare that marked the nineteenth and early twentieth centuries have been supplanted by more "irregular" forms of international war and intervention. In any case, while current delineations and rationalizations of the means and forms of warfare, and the rules of engagement, may differ in both content and form from those of times past, the intractable paradoxes of the "force of law" and "legitimate coercion by violence" remain. Ultimately, through various forms of a "logic of necessity" (cf. Hussain 2003), both civil police violence and various forms of "military intervention" or "use of force" (Haass 1999) may be rearticulated and legitimated as the securing of peace and civil order in the name of the democratic rule of law. This is the Blue in Green paradigm of security and statecraft writ large.[4]

Configurations and conceptualizations of that which constitutes a Weberian state monopoly on legitimate violence (of either the Blue or Green ideal type) undoubtedly vary across time and space. And the deliberate drawing of lines between Blue and Green spheres—and, inter alia, the production of admixtures or even entirely new spheres—is historically and culturally contingent. Counterinsurgency theories are a good example, and hardly the only example, of such admixture. The chapters in this first section of the volume contextualize our studies of counterinsurgency by ethnographic pursuit of Blue in Green problematics more generally. Each chapter illustrates the contingency of the line between the Blue and the Green as it manifests in various moments and places, and also demonstrates what is at stake when the Blue in Green is invoked, or *re*voked "temporarily" as a means to validate campaigns to (re)establish order.

In the first chapter, I describe some labor pains of the birth of a national police force in the Maldives to demonstrate how counterinsurgency strategies may take counterintuitive forms—in this case, the form of a program of democratization through demilitarization. Next, Greg Beckett explains UN intervention efforts in Haiti as a function of the "phantom power" of the U.S. to define the line between Green and Blue outside its own borders and to install and depose state leaders by strategically deploying categories of a "failed state" or a "state of emergency." Then Paola Castaño elucidates some of the theoretical and practical contradictions and dangers of the categorizations of civilians and combatants in the armed conflict in Colombia by both state government and nonstate actors (i.e., guerilla and paramilitary organs). Following these three ethnographic accounts of attempts to institutionalize, legalize, legitimize, and monopolize violence against alleged insurgents and enemies, John D. Kelly reads the works of past and present military theorists, statesmen, and social scientists to produce a genealogy of counterinsurgency doctrine and practice. In the tradition of Kantian critique, Kelly integrates an interrogation of the Blue in Green paradigm of security and statecraft with an examination of the "relative peace" of the post–World War II U.S.-dominated global order, or Pax Americana, to find a political role for anthropologists in the contemporary moment.

Foucauldian analyses do well to observe that power is always already dispersed and institutionalized; however, stating this fact as an end in itself is not enough. In addition to conceptual terms that are more clear and nuanced than "power" (this author prefers, for example, the precision of Weber's "legitimate coercion by violence" and "means of coercion"), what we need to develop and deploy are comparative, contextualized, and culturally informed accounts of the dispersion and institutionalization of coercive authority. In this vein, each of the chapters in this section questions what is revealed, and what is occluded, by shifts of the line between Blue and Green, and more generally by shifts of categories of conflict and coercion and their relation specifically to programs of counterinsurgency. And all of the chapters compel us to rethink what the hegemony of the Blue in Green may mean, both for current structures of local and global governance and for the future of international order and violence more generally. While some theorists note an evolving role for the military, and its expansion into domains of law enforcement, development, humanitarian aid, and even governance itself (e.g., Ankersen 2008; Gupta 2003; Koonings and Kruijt 2002), there remain many gray areas (cf. Duffield 2001, who critiques the changing role of militaries as part of the emergence of a dialectical relationship of security and development policies, which is arguably the most recent and complex iteration of the Blue in Green to date). Indeed, there is an expanding accumulation of more controversial categories of coercion, such as private security services, paramilitaries, alleged links between nongovernmental organizations and terrorism, organized and disorganized crime, holy war, revolution, and, above all, insurgency and counterinsurgency. In this context, we should ask, How do more recent strategies of counterinsurgency resemble and differ from previous ones? How, by whom, and for what are lines of civil and military spheres being drawn in specific instances of conflict and calm? How does theorizing global politics with such questions in mind reframe ongoing debates about the U.S.-led campaigns in the so-called War on Terror? And how should anthropologists specifically, and other social scientists more generally, engage with military organizations and the state? The ensuing analyses aim to provide some foundation for new answers to these and related questions.

:: **NOTES** ::

1. The Blue in Green argument grew out of a paper I wrote in spring 2003, which was inspired by a course organized at the University of Chicago by John D. Kelly on "Military Theory and Practice." My utmost thanks go to him for critical and encouraging reviews of later drafts and for conversations over the years that helped to refine the idea.

2. Certainly, the world over, a wide variety of colors camouflage, decorate, and generally identify public (and increasingly, private) security forces. Some military branches wear blue, and some police forces wear green. Other state security organizations don khaki, black, white, and a host of other hues. The color scheme chosen to delineate the ideal typical Blue in Green paradigm reflects the hegemonic standard of the UN world as currently dominated by the United States. This globalized paradigm reflects the inevitable paradoxes immanent to legitimation of authority to deploy coercion in a liberal democracy. No state leader and no state representative wearing any uniform color is exempt from participating, voluntarily or by conscription, in a far-reaching discourse of securing order that is fraught with these paradoxes.

3. This is not the place to provide a nuanced genealogy or critical analysis of what all Foucault meant to do with this inversion of Clausewitz. For now, suffice it to say that although both thinkers were speaking of war categorically and philosophically, contrary to a Clausewitzian conception of war in the conventional sense, Foucault was theorizing what he deemed a "permanent state of war" that defines not merely modernity but all of humanity, in all times. Foucault argued that this permanent state of war—not of every man against every man, but of every race against every race—had been elided by Hobbesian notions of sovereignty and political will (cf. Foucault 2003 [1976], especially lectures 5 [February 4, 1976] and 11 [March 17, 1976]; and Hobbes 1968 [1651], especially *Of Man,* chapter 13, "Of the NATURALL [*sic*] CONDITION of Mankind as Concerning Their Felicity, and Misery," and *Of Commonwealth,* chapter 30, "Of the OFFICE of the Soveraign [*sic*] Representative").

4. Of course, there exist forms of government legitimated by principles other than civil-legal democracy—usually, although not necessarily, internally to a state. These forms include, although are not limited to, royal monarchy, religious law, socialist counsel, or leadership by a charismatic executive (many of which often appear to outsiders or adversaries as authoritarian or dictatorial government). But the empirical studies mounted in this section of the volume examine ideologies and practices of legal means of coercion that develop in a context of globally hegemonic ideals of liberal democratic rule of law.

1

Bluing Green in the Maldives

Countering Citizen Insurgency by "Civil"-izing
National Security

:: BEATRICE JAUREGUI ::

In the Maldives, September 2004 saw the division of the unified
National Security Service (NSS) into separate military and civil
police components. The NSS, which was eventually renamed the
National Defence Force (NDF) in April 2006, remained under the
Ministry of Defence, while the new Maldives Police Service (MPS)
became a separate organization under the Ministry of Home Affairs. The birth of the MPS was a direct, if partial, response to recurrent popular uprisings protesting the regime of then president
Maumoon Abdul Gayoom.

As the cornerstone of a broad agenda for national legal reform, the founding of a civil police was intended to signify to the
Maldivian people—and just as importantly, to the international
community—that the Maldivian state's control of the means of coercion manifests in a nonmilitary body. In so doing, the reigning
authorities hoped to exhibit their adherence to liberal democratic
values and thereby legitimize their sovereign authority through a
praxis of what I call the Blue in Green paradigm of security and
statecraft (Jauregui, Introduction to section 1, this volume). The
particular manner in which the Blue in Green suffuses governance
in the Maldives today gives rise to (1) contradictory views about
which species of law and bureaucracy grow out of democratic reforms and (2) counterinsurgency strategies that, paradoxically, call
for the demilitarization of national security.

Domestic "Insurgency" and the Politics of Security:
Ethnographic and Historical Background

The island nation of the Republic of the Maldives is, in terms of population (approximately 380,000 in 2008), both the smallest country in Asia and the smallest Islamic country in the world. Sunni Islam in the Maldives generally takes a relatively moderate form—similar to that practiced in much of India, Indonesia, or Turkey—and is inextricably linked with people's sense of nation-hood. The country, famed as one of the world's premier island paradise desti-nations, is exalted by foreign travelers for its stunning coral reefs, luxurious beaches, and breath-taking seascapes. The first tourist resorts opened across the archipelago soon after the fall of the last sultanate and the inauguration of a new republic in 1968; and the tourism industry is now the primary sector of the economy, making up almost 30 percent of the country's gross domes-tic product (GDP), far ahead of the next most important national industry, fishing.

Sometimes sardonically called "the CEO of the Maldives," President Mau-moon Abdul Gayoom, who came to power in 1978, made it his mission to promote the Maldives as an unparalleled holiday resort. At the time of this writing, Gayoom had just been voted out of power in the country's first dem-ocratic elections and replaced by Mohamed ["Anni"] Nasheed. Prior to this historic shift of power, Gayoom had never been officially opposed by another candidate in thirty years. However, this lack of electoral opposition did not equate to ubiquitous contentment with such a long-standing reign by one man, his crony-istic cabinet, and a *majlis* ('parliament') alleged to be stacked in his favor. There were three attempted coups against the Gayoom government, in 1980, 1983, and 1988, respectively. The last—plotted by disgruntled Mal-divian businessmen and some eighty Sri Lankan mercenaries—resulted in the death of fourteen people and was considered serious enough that then prime minister of India Rajiv Gandhi sent paratroopers and a frigate to help suppress the rebellion in the small neighboring country.

This incident, in combination with other evidence of increasing agitation by various groups against his government, led President Gayoom to grow in-creasingly apprehensive about internal revolts potentially buttressed by exter-nal adversaries. So he made efforts to augment the resources and personnel of the NSS, which he had founded during his first term as president as the sole security force in the Maldives. This multifunctional paramilitary organization eventually grew from a size of approximately 1,000 in the 1980s to more than 3,500 by the turn of the twenty-first century. The NSS came to be notorious and greatly feared for its harsh treatment of anyone thought to be engaged in antigovernment or criminal activity. An unofficial study estimates the number of custodial deaths in the Maldives since 1978 to be twenty-six; and according to an unnamed consultant on constitutional reform, the Maldives has had the highest proportion of its population arrested and charged of any country in the world.[1]

Whatever the actual numbers, the fact remains that relatively little attention was paid by the international community to human rights abuses under what many call the dictatorship of Gayoom, until an incident in September 2003. When a nineteen-year-old inmate, Evan Naseem, was beaten to death at Maafushi prison, the largest detention center in the country, fellow inmates revolted out of fear and anger. In the ensuing showdown, three persons were killed, and seventeen others, including one security guard, suffered gunshot injuries (Presidential Commission, Republic of the Maldives 2003). When news of Naseem's death reached the capital island of Malé, crowds of people already agitated by what they felt were the national government's oppressive policies became outraged, and some protestors vandalized public buildings and set fire to police stations and government vehicles. President Gayoom imposed a curfew and declared the republic's first official state of emergency, which lasted for more than one month. These events drew the attention of international media and human rights organizations and spurred the solidification of a growing group of Gayoom detractors into the Maldivian Democratic Party (MDP), which ultimately became the main opposition to the president's Dhivehi Rayyithunge Party (DRP), or Maldivian People's Party.[2]

From exile in the neighboring island nation of Sri Lanka, the MDP leadership officially announced the founding of their party in November 2003. Back in the Maldives, voices of opposition to the regime continued to grow louder. In response, on June 9, 2004, President Gayoom declared that he would put forth a sweeping reform agenda to constitute a more transparent and democratic government. Among other promised changes, it was announced that citizens would, for the first time, be granted the opportunity to hold open political debates. However, as soon as these public fora became functional, vitriolic criticism of the government spewed forth, and Gayoom was so dismayed at the sound and fury that he revoked this new allowance after just a few months. Meanwhile, MDP and other reformist activists were blacklisted and routinely arrested and detained by the NSS for questioning.

On August 12, 2004, a vigil held in Malé at *Jumhooree Maidan* ('Republican Square') to protest indefinite detentions transformed over some thirty hours into a mass demonstration of people demanding not only release of the prisoners but also the resignation of President Gayoom. It is reported by some protestors that several pro-Gayoom persons infiltrated the crowd and began acting out violently. Whoever the culprits were, this disturbance gave the NSS a "legitimate" reason to use force, and they ultimately released tear gas and beat and severely injured many protestors. The incident was reported in state-controlled local media as merely a small crowd of rotten apples engaging in patently illegal activity, and a second state of emergency was imposed for two months. Locals came to refer to the event as Black Friday.

After the MDP chairman—and as of October 2008, the new president—Anni (Mohamed Nasheed) was arrested in August 2005 for staging a sit-in at *Jumhooree Maidan* in further protest of the Gayoom regime, and in remembrance of Black Friday, unrest spread to other atolls (groups of islands) outside of Malé. In the meantime, Gayoom professed to be moving forward with his democratic reform agenda. This agenda included an entire overhaul of criminal law, which proceeded via intensive consultation with legal experts from the United States and involved drafting an entirely new Maldivian penal code, in a unique and controversial attempt to "codify Shar'ia" in a "modern" civil legal form (see Robinson 2006; Robinson et al. 2007; An-Na'im 2007). The process eventually culminated in a new police act and even a new constitution, which was ratified by Gayoom on August 5, 2008, and ushered in with a speech by him declaring that this new era of governance would be based on the principles of modern liberal democracy and the principles of Islam.

But in the four years prior to these reform "results," which ultimately included the voting out of Gayoom and voting in of Nasheed as president, the Gayoom government struggled to demonstrate its sincere adherence to a program of democratization. To prove its progress, just two weeks after Black Friday, the Gayoom government announced that it was going to split off from the NSS an entirely separate civil police. With great ceremony, on September 1, 2004, the Maldivian government held a grand public event signifying a "renaissance" in governmental security through the birth of a national police organization. Many Maldivian citizens with whom I have spoken interpreted this reorganization as a post haste dog-and-pony show by the government merely to "appear reform minded" to both Maldivians and the international community in the wake of Black Friday. These detractors claimed that the purported change really led to nothing more than old wine in new bottles—or more to the point, the same tyrants in different costumes. However, while I conducted ethnographic fieldwork in Malé in 2007, while Gayoom was still well entrenched in the presidency, commissioned officers (COs) in the new police service informed me that, in fact, plans and operations to form a civil police had begun in March 2004, five months prior to the events of Black Friday.[3]

COs told me that for the half year prior to the September 2004 uniform change ceremony, the Change Maintenance Committee had been expending an extraordinary amount of time and resources on activities related to founding a civil police organization. These activities included conducting research into the structure of other police departments across the globe, signing memoranda of understanding with some of these departments and their training academies, drawing up programs of operation and training that would be "community oriented," and designing the new uniform. Although I asked, it was never made clear to me what initially inspired the formation of this committee. It seems most likely, however, that the events surrounding Evan Naseem's death in 2003 were a significant factor.

Notably, many of the COs interviewed emphasize the conscious choice of the word "service" over "force" in naming the new organization the MPS. This clearly was supposed to connote the civil nature of the national police as distinct from the military. Some police admit, however, that there was quite a bit of debate among planners regarding the necessity and advisability of this choice (cf. Comaroff and Comaroff 2006a). This is only one of myriad internal conflicts still plaguing the neophyte organization. Indeed, as I interviewed serving and former police and military officers of various ranks, it became clear that there was no firm consensus regarding the utility and legitimacy of the separation of military and civil security institutions.

Even following the election of a new president, it is fair to say that there is no definitive interpretation of the still emerging effects of the division. As the Maldives continues to democratize and integrate into a globalized political economy that is still dominated by U.S. power and interests and by United Nations (UN) ideologies of peace and stability, it must manage the inevitable tensions of balancing liberty and rights with security and order. These tensions both produce and are reproduced by a peculiarly local, but neither new nor unique, "culture war" regarding how best to organize national security.[4] Some argue that a military organization should take the lead in securing order, particularly in the event of mass demonstrations. However, others believe that if the country is to become truly modern and democratic, then the military and the civil police should be completely separate. Moreover, persons in this latter group tend to believe that the civil police should direct order-keeping operations by following a "community policing" model.[5] The debates continue in both discourse and practice. But while the "keep-'em-separated" perspective seems to be winning, there are many moments in which the dividing line between (Green) martial and (Blue) civil becomes blurry, shifts situationally, or seems to disappear altogether.

Chains of Command and Twists in Democratic Reform

There are myriad formal-legal and informal-illegal facets to the globally integrated tourism and domestic consumption sectors of the Maldivian economy
that mount challenges to national security. One problem in this realm that
appears to be increasing exponentially is drug trafficking. Several MPS officers have told me that the supply of drugs coming into the country—allegedly
aided by "corrupt customs officials in India"[6]—passes primarily through personnel of the Department of Penitentiary and Rehabilitation Service (DPRS).
These reproachful police officers aver that DPRS personnel sell or give the illicit paraphernalia to prison inmates (along with other contraband like mobile
phones, radios, and other electronics), which then exacerbates crime. "They
[DPRS] are not even police," chides one MPS officer, "but they are completely
corrupt, and make us [police] look bad." Indeed, he is not alone in believing
that the police in the Maldives get a disproportionately "bad rap" because of
such conflations.

Of course, this poor public image and its concomitant conflations have
a history. When the police were but a small wing of the NSS, many people
considered all security officers to be Gayoom's goons, a sort of private militia
for the president. When I spoke with MPS officers, some would admit that
this was not far from the truth and that the people's fear and loathing today
is understandable since, "mistakes [had] been made in the past" ("mistakes"
like torturing detainees and then, accidentally or intentionally, killing some
of them). They would also acknowledge that, even after programmatic reform
and the founding of the MPS, police would still ultimately have to answer to
the president. Thus a full changeover from the "military mind-set" had not yet
occurred, and, therefore, remarks one officer resignedly, "the people do not
like us; they are scared of us." Some MPS officers, especially leaders of the reorganization of the police, argue that it is precisely the continuing association
between them and "the military" (then NSS, now NDF) that is the bête noir
of their public image. One CO who has been integral to the restructuring of
the police—and who affirms that his studies in the United Kingdom and the
United States convinced him wholeheartedly that the police and the military
should be completely separate—explains, "The military mind-set is that you
shoot to kill the enemy. Police must understand that the people are not the
enemy." However, this same CO follows up the previous statement by saying,
somewhat mysteriously and performatively, "Of course this is only true if you
are pro-democracy. If you are a dictator, then the people *are* the enemy."

While a proudly post-NSS cluster of officers argues that the conflation
of the police and the military is the main problem, other officials partly dis-

agree. This latter group claims that it is not an association with the military but rather the epithet of "police" itself that incites negative feelings from the public. One CO laments that "[p]ast wrongdoings by NSS personnel became known as 'police atrocities' . . . and so now, even though we are brainwashing the former military mind-set out of, and the new police mind-set into, our new personnel, the people still think that anyone called 'police' is bad." Many in this latter group also assert that, in fact, now that the police and military have been separated, common people voice more support for the military as protectors of the nation and see the police as bullies in blue, who daily harass and oppress people in the name of "the law"—a law that is, in actual fact, the president's command. Notably, this claim of a respectable military vis-à-vis a reprehensible police seemed to bear out in discussions I have had with several citizens in Malé who are not associated with the government.

This alleged promilitary/antipolice sentiment is quite ironic, not only in light of attempts being made by police to clarify their "civil" character and community-oriented approach, but also because of the fact that NDF personnel actually express feeling marginalized since the creation of the police. When these NDF officers were part of the pre-2004 NSS, they were the only security force in the country and therefore commanded a lot of authority and respect. When President Gayoom's reform agenda foregrounded the police as the new protectors of the national populace, those remaining in the military came to feel sidelined and put on the back burner. These allegations that military personnel became peripheral auxiliaries to a core of police abide in stark contrast with the fact that, as of 2005, the percentage of the GDP of the Maldives devoted to military expenditures was listed as 5.5 percent, one of the fifteen highest percentages in the world and more than twice that of any nation-state with a comparable GDP. This fact is particularly striking since there is no real imminent national threat of any sort, with the exception of rising water levels from global warming (which, some claim, will completely submerge the low-lying island nation under the Indian Ocean in the next several decades). It is also peculiar in light of the following statement from the Central Intelligence Agency Factbook: "The Maldives National Defense Force (MNDF), with its small size and with little serviceable equipment, is inadequate to prevent external aggression and is primarily tasked to reinforce the Maldives Police Service (MPS) and ensure security in the exclusive economic zone (2008)."[7]

In keeping with this statement, it is thus understandable why many NDF military officers would complain of feeling relatively disenfranchised. And yet, simultaneously, many MPS police officers deem themselves victims of "citizens' brutality" (Rashid 2005). They consider their new status as something akin to that of routinized sacrificial lambs or, perhaps worse, as politicized and increasingly faulty tools of the government executive. During the course of my fieldwork in 2007, many MPS officers of all ranks and levels of experience—and, not surprisingly, especially those who trained as NSS prior to the 2004 division—expressed feelings that the new civil police is comprised of a substance that is essentially inadequate.

One noncommissioned officer (NCO) who had been on the job prior to the MPS splitting off told me that the new police recruits are "inexperienced, improperly trained, and have much less discipline than we [former NSS officers] do." Another police officer of the same rank agrees: "I lost 20 kg when I was training [as NSS], and these new recruits get to take a three-month vacation. Training is all academic now, there is no emphasis on physical discipline . . . and it shows in their work as police." These more seasoned officers are, notably, in their early and midtwenties, as is approximately 70 percent of the newly recruited MPS at the time of this writing. (Thus it really is a neophyte police force, in several ways.) This revelation of an experience by serving police officers, of decadence in the personnel and purpose that constitute the police, means that the internal critiques of the new structure of security are not merely a matter of a "superiority complex" or "sour grapes" on the part of now-sidelined military officers. There are other, more deep-seated problems plaguing the transformation.

The concerns of some MPS officers with the developing police organization are not limited to the waning of discipline and potency. As bad or worse, they say, are the ambiguities of command that have been introduced by the reformed laws, concomitant with the opening up to the public of political debate. (Note that until an edict by President Gayoom in 2005, political parties other than his own were technically illegal in the Maldives.) The NCO who contended that the new training scheme is a "vacation" for young recruits also said that the deterioration in government security reflected in the new police organization is part and parcel of a larger "loosening of the reins," and an increase of "leniency . . . political games and other bullshit" in the reform-oriented Gayoom regime. It would seem that he is on the verge of a "too much democracy" argument. But then, when I ask him to expound, he says that even the laws themselves are not enforced with any regularity or calculability, as they would be in a "proper democratic government" (cf. Weber 1958a on "modern" bureaucracy). He contends that this unpredictability is true whether it is a matter of trafficking of drugs and alcohol or enforcing traffic speed limits. (Zooming motorcycles are a growing menace in Malé, which houses over 100,000 people in an area of only 1.5 square kilometers, making it one of the most densely populated places on earth.) This officer also relates that, unsurprisingly, people who are well-connected have always received, and still do receive, special treatment. "If I arrest someone known to have committed a crime, and later find out he is Mr. So-and-So Minister's son, I can get put into solitary confinement for doing my job and arresting him." This is certainly not a simple issue of "too much democracy." Indeed, there are processes at work that are not fully elucidated by arguments that some people simply prefer military dictatorships or other oppressive regime forms to the muddled freedoms of democracy.

The disenchantment with ambiguities of command is echoed by an NCO in another division who says that since the country's democratic reforms began in 2004, it has become more and more difficult for security personnel to know when and how to intervene, especially in situations of public demonstrations. "Before, it was easy. Public meetings and gatherings were illegal, so it would always be clear what to do: stop it from continuing. But now, things are becoming more opened up, and uncertainty has come along with the new laws." He goes on to say, "Really, it is just not very clear to anyone what the law is. We [police] are taught the rules, but we are still dependent upon direct orders." The predictable response to the question, "Who gives the orders?" is "the president [Gayoom]."

Police officers are relating a sensibility that when the president began presenting himself as more democratic, his orders became more erratic and [potentially] despotic. Sometimes, they would say, Gayoom would give an order to disperse an "unlawful assembly" by any means necessary, while at other times, for various and often unclear reasons, he would try to appear inviting of public debate and "let it go." There is no small amount of irony here that when government officials would adhere and appeal to democracy and the rule of law, they would apparently end up acting even *more* inconsistently, arbitrarily, and perhaps even ruthlessly—read "undemocratically"—than when the structure of state order keeping was less equivocally authoritarian. It would seem that a performance of liberal civility by a government that is in flux, and in fear of being toppled by autochthonous rebellion, has backfired. Moreover, it would seem that we may, like many of the MDP activists and other critics, dismiss the Gayoom government's reform agenda as a ruse intended to cloak a dictator in the robes of a democratic leader.

And yet, further articulations by MPS personnel demonstrate that the reality is far more complicated than national-legal smoke and mirrors. Whatever the true motives driving the creation of the MPS may have been, and however tight the president's control over sovereign command remained following the restructuring of security to an allegedly more democratic form, an undeniable and ongoing organizational overhaul was, and still is, occurring. And through analysis of this genuine transformation, it begins to become clear how a Blue in Green paradigm of security renders internally contradictory democratic orders as well as counterintuitive forms of counterinsurgency.

Blue in Green Counterinsurgency

What became clear as the sunlit sea to me was that whatever uniform a security force officer in the Maldives wears, most citizens are color blinded by fear and loathing. Moreover, the lines between Blue and Green are made all the more blurry when one considers that at the time of my fieldwork, many police personnel still slept in the military barracks, and there existed photographic evidence of "joint operations" by police personnel (especially the Special Operations Command unit of the MPS) and military soldiers (NDF/NSS) against public demonstrations. There are also allegations from several independent sources—from within and outside the government—of occasional uniform swapping between the MPS and NDF by order of the [Gayoom] government. It is claimed that this occurred at least once during a public demonstration in 2006. Thus, there are credible assertions and assumptions that in the Maldives, Blue and Green are, indeed, interchangeable not just in theory but also in practice.

This interchangeability of Blue and Green is predictable in light of what many officials, both civil and military, would conceive as an isomorphism between much common criminality and political opposition to the government. Indeed, members of the MDP opposition to (now former) President Gayoom would tell me that they had been charged with crimes as benign as running a red light so that the authorities would be able to keep them under surveillance and harass them by forcing them to attend court hearings that might lead to imprisonment. Thus, persons considered "the enemy" by the Gayoom government could be censured and censored by means of labeling them as "criminals" and enacting exemplary punishment.

The trials and travails of Jennifer ("Jenny") Latheef present an ideal example and one of the more (in)famous ones since Amnesty International deemed her a prisoner of conscience in 2005.[8] She is the daughter of MDP cofounder Mohammad Latheef, who was self-exiled in Sri Lanka for several years following the protests in the wake of Evan Naseem's death. Jenny remained in Malé, and her unflagging participation in prodemocracy demonstrations was deemed "terrorism" by the Gayoom government. In October 2005, she received a ten-year prison sentence. Due to pressure from international actors, primarily nongovernmental organization (NGO) activists, Jenny was eventually pardoned by President Gayoom in August 2006. During an interview in

2007, she informed me that she was refusing to accept the pardon because it would leave her with a criminal record, which would bar her from continuing to lead the Native Operators on Rights organization she had founded to gather and disseminate information on human rights abuses in the Maldives. However, she ultimately decided to accept the pardon.

On the other side, police personnel, especially those trained as NSS, have complained that while a halting program of reform continues to confuse everyone about what "the law" in the Maldives really is, crime and unemployment have been on the rise, and the frequency and intensity of political demonstrations and incidents of unrest have been increasing and causing them a great deal of grief. Some officials have even expressed fears of their country soon degenerating into civil war, which lends support to an argument that the Gayoom government was devising reform policies on a "counterinsurgency begins at home" sort of logic. That said, the regime was generally careful to avoid describing domestic disturbances with terms like "insurgency" and "terrorism," preferring instead to use expressions such as "civil unrest." And with the exception of Jenny Latheef and several others, detainees and suspects would tend to be charged less often with terrorism and more often with everything from disobeying orders and creating disharmony to treason, or (the most prevalent) "unknown" (Maldivian Democratic Party 2007).

As is well-known, categories like insurgency and terrorism are closely associated with the current face of the enemy in the global War on Terror—that is, Islamic extremism. While some national governments would make conscious overtures to associate an "enemy of the state" with this so-called war (see, for example, Castaño, this volume), the Gayoom government appeared to purposely downplay such associations, most likely for fear of scaring away the country's core economic base—foreign and primarily Western travelers. However, many people allege that Islamic extremist activity has been on the rise in the Maldives, especially over the last five to ten years. Authorities in the Gayoom government would vehemently deny such charges, even though the country was faced in September 2007 with its first homemade bomb explosion—which injured more than a dozen foreign tourists—and in January 2008 with its first assassination attempt by a man shouting "*Allahu Akbar*" (Arabic for "God is great") while thrusting a knife wrapped in the national flag at President Gayoom. Both of these incidents were attributed to the designs of Islamic extremists. And significantly, the 2005 legalization of alternative political parties in the Maldives allowed not only for the continued existence of the main opposition of the MDP but also for the increased visibility, and arguably increased legitimacy, of more conservative Islamic parties such as the *Adaulat* (Justice) Party and the Islamic Democratic Party.

The Maldivian government's security policies and practices under Gayoom were not explicitly deemed "counterinsurgency" in the conventional sense. However, the data regarding Gayoom's various means of suppressing increasing opposition to his regime indicate that the former president had long feared an insurgency from within that would topple his rule. Thus, it is understandable that he would try to retain power using a variety of means, including experiments with strategies that appeared to heed increasingly loud and clear calls for a new (liberal democratic) government. Gayoom's fear of overthrow was not unfounded, obviously; but fortunately, it seems that in the end, the revolution desired was accompanied through the most democratic of means—free and fair elections. Fortunately, and for some perhaps ironically, the reforms Gayoom set in motion appear to have had the effect that was the stated intention: liberalizing and democratizing the Maldives.

What is of interest here, however, is the fact that what was framed as a project of liberal democratic reform was clearly, to a large extent, driven by an objective to quell internal political instability or potential citizen insurgency. This not only produced heated theoretical and practical challenges regarding how security should be reorganized but also had counterintuitive effects on the institution of policing, rendering it (seemingly) less democratic—or, at least, more contradictory and hypocritical—than it had been under a more autocratic type of government. Those following Agamben's *Homo Sacer* (1998) would probably argue that this fits perfectly with Agamben's claim that there is a contiguity between democracy and totalitarianism arising from the structural logic of modern governance as sovereignty over bare life. However, that is not the claim being made here, nor do I think such an ominous politics of despair is the right direction to take. What is at issue here is not an ultimate conflation of democracy and despotism as originating in the law as violence, but an inevitable paradox at the heart of liberal democratic praxis, namely, the ever shifting—and sometimes blurring or even disappearing—line between Blue and Green force, as configured by historical contingency, political particularisms, and cultural hybridities.

The process and politics of governmental reform in the Maldives, and in particular the development of the MPS, may be read in several ways: (1) as a project of police modernization and professionalization through the building of a community policing sensibility; (2) as a process of at best hybridization and at worst homogenization of national governance with hegemonic global discourses of what the civil police and the military are for; (3) as a sincere effort by an increasingly despised administration to demonstrate its responsiveness to the concerns of the people and to remake the nation through democratization, or (4) as a desperate and disingenuous maneuver by an authoritarian leader who is clinging to power. The ethnographic analysis here presents some evidence that all of these processes—even those that seem to contradict each other—are simultaneously at play, to varying degrees at various moments. This is one "logical" outcome of putting into practice the Blue in Green paradigm of securing a democratic order today: a regime that aims to counter insurgency by "civil"-izing national security.

Historically, counterinsurgency programs have foregrounded a military-led operation of fighting "the enemy within" by attaining and using intimate knowledge of both the enemy's strategies and tactics and the specific theater's geographical terrain. (And now, as detailed by various authors in this volume, such programs espouse the value of knowledge of the "human terrain" as well.) The birth of the MPS reveals in a unique way how some security strategists and governing authorities seek to suppress internal unrest, and to instate or-der, through precisely the opposite form, that is, through demilitarization, or a Bluing of the Green. Compare this with the organizational praxis of colo-nial military administrator Simon Galliéni, who served in French Indo-China with Hubert Lyautey (cf. Kelly, this volume). Galliéni wrote,

> The soldier is primarily a soldier as long as may be necessary for the submission of populations which have not yet been subdued. But, once peace is achieved, he puts down his weapons. He *becomes an administrator* ... At first these adminis-trative functions may seem incompatible with the concepts certain people have formed about military men. However, *this is the real role of the colonial officer,* and of his devoted and intelligent collaborators, the noncommissioned and private officers he commands. It is also a delicate function, requiring greater diligence, effort and high personal qualities, since *reconstruction is far more difficult than destruction* ... During the period following the conquest, the part of the troops is *reduced to policing,* a function which is soon taken over by special troops, the military and civilian police. (Gottman 1986 [1943], 244, emphasis added)

A comparison of the labor and growing pains of the MPS in the twenty-first century with something as seemingly distant as a reformer's approach to the French colonization of Southeast Asia and Northern Africa in the nine-teenth century, may seem far-fetched. However, I would argue that reading together the theories and practices of colonial administrations, counterinsur-gency programs, and instances of the "civil-ization" of security apparatuses throws into relief how problematic the Blue in Green paradigm has been throughout history and remains today. Importantly, such a comparison across time and space does not discount historical contingencies and political par-ticularities; in fact, it calls for analysts to account for precisely these sorts of variations. Moreover, it reveals that even seemingly progressive programs of national-legal democratic reform may be not only analogous with, but also *integrated* with, political ideologies and institutional technologies that drive more obviously militarized forms of counterinsurgency. We may thus compare the Maldivian case not only with older imperial designs but also with newer forms of power projection and foreign occupation—not least with the current U.S.-led campaigns in Iraq and Afghanistan. Understanding these historical and conceptual relationships demonstrates the necessity and significance of accounting for alternative forms of counterinsurgency (here conceived as an analytical category, not as a particular military doctrine or modus operandi). These alternative forms do not necessarily manifest in a military mode and in fact may not even require military operationalization at all. Such an understanding compels us to question further a wide range of other political-legal programs that put into practice a globally hegemonic Blue in Green paradigm of security and statecraft.

:: NOTES ::

I am grateful to Greg Beckett, John D. Kelly, Sean T. Mitchell, and Jeremy Walton for their reviews of earlier drafts of this chapter. I would also like to thank the participants at the April 25–27, 2008, Conference on Anthropology and Global Counterinsurgency at the University of Chicago for their incisive questions and comments on the version presented there.

1. Dr. Mohamed Munavvar, who was attorney general under President Gayoom's government from 1993 to 2003 (and, after being sacked, was affiliated with the MDP opposition) eventually made a public apology, during which he is said to have admitted that during his decade of service alone, some 45,000 people—almost one-sixth of the entire population—were arrested and charged with some crime. Since there has been so much censorship of information and so little publicly available evidence for many of these claims, the reports related here are primarily anecdotal. However, they are widely testified to and given considerable credence through documents such as the 2007 "State of Human Rights in the Maldives," by the Law and Society Trust, published in Colombo, Sri Lanka. The U.S. State Department and many international NGOs have also begun to pay close attention, as evidenced by country reports on human rights in the Maldives (see, for example, U.S. Department of State 2007 and Amnesty International 2007).

2. Space constraints disallow a full and proper ethnographic and historical treatment of the myriad factors and actors that coalesced to make up the growing opposition to President Gayoom's regime. Suffice it to say that while ideological challenges became the discursive forerunner—with Gayoom critics staking a claim to democratic governance as the necessary successor to (his) dynastic/despotic power—the ethnographic inquiry I have conducted up to this point led to disclosures by interlocutors of other types and forms of opposition. These seem to stem primarily from personal vendettas and conflicts deriving from kinship ties and ethnoreligious fractures and

identifications. A more traditional anthropological account of these dynamics is beyond the scope of this essay, but I hope to engage it elsewhere.

3. Unless referring to a public statement or event, in order to protect the confidentiality of interlocutors who are government officials, I will not only refrain from naming persons but also will distinguish someone's status only as either CO or NCO rather than as a more detailed rank such as sergeant. The MPS is so small that identification of individuals is dangerously facile.

4. In another version of this paper, I discuss in more detail how this culture war not only manifests different views about interaction of Maldivian and Western cultural forms but also intersects with categorical conflations of disgruntled youth, rising criminality, and increasing political instability in the Maldives. Regarding other historical culture wars, or perhaps "ideology of 'order' wars," over the integration or separation of police and military apparatuses, particularly in colonial South Asia, see Jauregui (2004).

5. For further readings on U.S. and international debates regarding community policing see Skogan (2003) and Brogden and Nijhar (2005). For readings specifically addressing questions of democratic policing in transitional and developing countries and developing democracies, see Pino and Wiatrowski (2006) and Hinton (2008), respectively.

6. For further discussion of local logics of corruption and security in India, see Jauregui (forthcoming).

7. This statement resides in the same section of the Central Intelligence Agency Factbook as the measure of military expenditure as a percentage of GDP (U.S. Central Intelligence Agency 2008). It remains to be seen how or if this figure will change under the new administration of President Mohamed "Anni" Nasheed. One would hypothesize that it will go down dramatically if the MDP leader fulfills promises of "true democratic reform"; but this question will only be answered in the future.

8. Note that the man who finally succeeded Gayoom as president, Anni, was imprisoned by the Gayoom government more than twenty times (British Broadcasting Corporation 2008).

2

Phantom Power

Notes on Provisionality in Haiti

:: GREG BECKETT ::

On January 1, 2004, Haiti celebrated its Bicentennial of Independence amidst a protracted political crisis that pitted then president Jean-Bertrand Aristide and his Fanmi Lavalas (FL) party against two groups calling for his resignation: a coalition of political parties called the Democratic Convergence (CD) and a union of civil society organizations called the Group 184. Throughout 2003 and early 2004, both groups refused a power-sharing deal and insisted the only solution to the crisis was the removal of Aristide, whom they accused of executive absolutism and of using armed gangs to terrorize and intimidate his opponents. The situation came to a head when a pro-Aristide gang called the Cannibal Army turned against him and joined with former members of the military and the police to launch what they called a "popular rebellion."

With the rebels marching on the capital, Aristide was flown out of Haiti on February 29, 2004, in what he later characterized as a "kidnapping" at the hands of the United States military. Within days, the political opposition named a provisional government charged with the task of managing new elections. The United States, Canada, and France backed the provisional government, and the United Nations sent a stabilizing mission (MINUSTAH) with a mandate to "support the Transition Government [and] to ensure a secure and stable environment within which the constitutional and political process in Haiti can take place" (United Nations 2005).

While the interim government handed over power to a newly elected government in 2006, the United Nations (UN) mission remains in Haiti.[1]

Known locally as the "Blue Helmets" (*casques bleus*), the UN peacekeeping force fits uneasily within the ideal-typical categories of the "Blue" and the "Green." On the one hand, it represents the peaceful order of a civil-legal force staffed by highly visible and accountable agents; on the other hand, its operatives dress in fatigues, patrol foreign national territory, and carry heavy firepower. In this sense, the Blue Helmets nicely illustrate what Beatrice Jauregui (this volume) calls the "Blue in Green" ideology so central to the contemporary liberal-democratic order for they represent clearly a paradigm that insists the transition to democracy end with the installation of civilian government and civil-legal rather than military-dictatorial rule.[2] Yet if the UN mission has sought to stabilize the country, rebuild the state, and restore civil security, then it has done so by invoking a state of exception—glossed in this case as "state failure"—that authorized the intervention of an emergency power meant to restore the juridicopolitical order and recapture the means of coercion through the violation of national sovereignty and the exercise of force.[3]

The UN mission has received mixed reviews. While some see it as necessary to the return of stability and security, there is growing sentiment that the mission has become permanent and that it represents nothing less than a foreign occupation. Those who feel this way have begun to refer to it as the "Third U.S. Occupation," thereby casting it as part of a long history of direct military intervention by the United States. Some even suggest that members of MINUSTAH were complicit in the wave of criminal and political violence that engulfed Port-au-Prince after Aristide's departure (see Kolbe and Huston 2006; Lindsay 2006; Schuller 2008). For their part, the UN and the interim government blamed the violence on criminal-political gangs linked to Aristide, and between 2004 and 2006 they sought to curb the violence through military-style raids in the city's slums, where both the gangs and most of Aristide's supporters live. Whether motivated by political allegiance to Aristide, or simply fighting for their lives, many of these "gangs" fought back, attacking UN soldiers and Haitian police officers directly.

Known locally as the *Chimès* (chimera or "ghosts"), these gangs, which used such names as the Cannibal Army, the Red Army, or the Little Machete Army, were reportedly formed by Aristide to serve as an armed wing of the FL. By 2004, their very existence had become a hotly contested issue, and in this sense, the name given them in public discourse—"ghosts"—is telling. Linked to the intimidation and assassination of journalists and members of the anti-Aristide opposition, the Chimès were widely feared (see Fatton 2002). They were both a visible sign of the dispersal of the means of violence across the social field and a haunting marker of the state's spectral presence in people's everyday lives. Members of such groups were frequently well-known in the garrison communities under their control. When they appeared at public demonstrations before the 2004 coup, they wore all-black outfits with black ski masks covering their faces. Concealed and anonymous, they represented an abstraction of violence and the opacity of force. The continued existence of the Chimès and other armed actors throughout the provisional period of 2004–2006 was a significant challenge to the Blue in Green paradigm and called the possibility of a transition to a civil-legal order into question. Highly visible yet cloaked from public scrutiny, these phantom forces challenged the monopoly of the means of violence claimed by the UN mission and the interim government and troubled the foundations of liberal democracy.

A full discussion of the Chimès is beyond the scope of this chapter. Here I want to focus instead on the presence of another phantom power—namely, the spectral role of the U.S. military in Haiti. While the U.S. military is noticeably absent from MINUSTAH, which is being led by Brazil, Chile, and Argentina, it has become commonplace in Port-au-Prince to note that the United States was really behind the intervention. There is good reason to believe this. For example, when the rebels took over Gonaïves and Cap Haïtien in February 2004, Aristide appealed to the international community for help. As the rebels approached the capital, however, then U.S. ambassador James Foley made it clear to Aristide that the United States would not protect him. The State Department also blocked the Steel Corporation, a San Francisco–based firm under contract to provide private security for Aristide, from sending additional personnel (Dupuy 2007, 172).

Why? On what basis did the U.S. government block the defense of a democratically elected government? As Johanna Mendelson Forman (2004) notes, the United States "routinely seeks to uphold democratically elected governments rather than allowing them to be overthrown by rebels or dissidents. The case of Haiti may represent a situation where a visceral dislike of a political leader may ultimately have hastened his departure." In what follows, I explore the phantom presence of U.S. power in Haiti through a consideration of the February 29, 2004, coup and the provisional period that followed in its wake.

The Modern Coup d'État

While there remains some dispute about the events that led up to Aristide's departure in 2004, the general outline of the story is by now well documented (see Blumenthal 2004; Caroit 2003, 2004; Chomsky, Farmer, and Goodman 2004; Dupuy 2007; Polgreen and Weiner 2004; Regan 2003). It began with the death of Amiot Mètayer, the leader of the pro-Aristide Cannibal Army. In response to his death, presumably at the hands of the national police (who were under pressure from the U.S. Embassy and the Organization of American States Special Mission in Haiti to curb gang violence), the members of the Cannibal Army broke with the government and took control of the coastal city of Gonaïves, destroying police stations, the courthouse, and the mayor's office in the process (Trujillo 2004). Over the next six months, the Cannibal Army changed its name to the Gonaïves Resistance Front for the Overthrow of Jean-Bertrand Aristide. The gang soon joined forces with a contingent of ex-army and police, and together the new "rebel" group launched a series of attacks on several cities in the northern provinces. By late February the rebels were marching on the capital, having declared their intention to take power by force and to remove Aristide "one way or another" (see Arthur 2003, 2004; Caroit 2003, 2004; Dupuy 2007; Polgreen and Weiner 2004).

The foreign media portrayed the rebels as a "ragtag" group disgruntled with Aristide. In reality, it was a well-trained, well-armed, and well-financed group composed of a strange—but hardly accidental—mixture of former allies of Aristide and former members of the Haitian army, the police, and various paramilitary groups. Its leaders included two prominent members of a defunct paramilitary death squad responsible for the assassination of hundreds, if not thousands, of Aristide supporters during the 1991–94 "de facto" period, when a military junta controlled the country. The most visible rebel leader was a man named Guy Philippe, a former police chief fired for plotting a coup in 2000 and suspected of leading a series of raids on the National Palace, the police academy, rural police stations, and a hydroelectric dam between 2001 and 2003 (Dupuy 2007, 165; see also Arthur 2003; Cala 2003; Chomsky et al. 2004; Reeves 2003). The rebels also included former officers and soldiers from the disbanded Haitian army, some of whom still wore army uniforms. This prompted Aristide's government to argue that the so-called rebels were in fact a well-armed and well-trained paramilitary group engaged in a coup d'état (see Chomsky et al. 2004, 43,165). In retrospect, it is clear that the rebel group acted as a military force and that it did so in the traditional mode of a political army—by claiming the right to use extraconstitutional but legitimate force to intervene in national politics, not to take power for its own sake, but rather to defend the nation from an internal threat, the so-called totalitarian drift (*dérive totalitaire*) of Aristide.[4]

For his part, Aristide called upon the international community to lend military support to his small, dispersed, and poorly armed police force in order to fight the rebels, which he described as an illegitimate and criminal force. In the end, his government did not receive either diplomatic or military support, and on February 29, 2004, Aristide was flown out of Haiti and into exile aboard a U.S. military plane. His departure marked the end of a political career that, for better or worse, had come to embody the hopes and aspirations of the democratic era for many Haitians. Some scholars have also suggested that it signaled "the end of an era of nation-building that demonstrates that the United States, and the international community in general, are unwilling to demonstrate full commitment in a place where winning the peace might have been possible" (Mendelson Forman 2004). Indeed, it was not merely a lack of full commitment but a radical reversal on the part of the international community, which had just ten years earlier launched a multilateral military intervention (led by the United States) to restore Aristide to power after a military coup forced him out. What had changed in the intervening years?

Perhaps one of the most decisive changes was the dramatic reversal of Aristide's support among the elite and middle classes in Haiti. As noted above, the political opposition formed an alliance called the Democratic Convergence (CD), whose only platform was the rejection of Aristide's presidency and the rule of the FL party. By 2003, a growing civil society opposition, headed by the Group 184, was mounting weekly protests in Port-au-Prince calling for Aristide to step down. One of their main concerns was Aristide's use of armed gangs to intimidate, silence, and terrorize any opposition. Within this broader context, the existence of the Chimès provided the basis for two related but distinct claims. First, the political opposition pointed to the Chimès as evidence that Aristide had violated the constitution and was establishing a new dictatorship. In response, the opposition thus began to call for Aristide's removal, declaring that extraconstitutional means were needed to defend the constitution and the nation. There was, however, no army to intervene (the traditional mechanism in Haiti). Second, the international community pointed to the Chimès as evidence of the break down of the rule of law. When a portion of the gangs broke with the government and launched an armed rebellion, foreign observers declared Haiti a failed state and called for an international intervention. In so doing, the opposition and the international community were both calling into question the newly established procedures of electoral democracy. Against his supporters' claims that Aristide should be able to serve out his full term, the opposition framed Aristide as a dictator and argued for the necessity of overthrowing the government precisely to restore democratic rule and constitutional order.[5]

This overthrow is, in effect, exactly what happened, although the manner in which it occurred was significantly different from previous declarations of such "revolutionary" moments, in which the army has taken power in order to "save" the constitutional order (Dumas 1994; Légitime 2002; Trouillot 1990). The intervention of a political army in times of crisis is a well-established pattern in Haiti. For example, the army intervened, and even ruled for a period, in 1946, 1950, and in 1956–57. The army also took power after the fall of the Duvalier regime in 1986 and effectively ruled the country (through several military councils and two civilian governments backed by the army) from 1986 to 1990. In 1990, just seven months into Aristide's first presidential term, the army again stepped in and replaced a democratically elected and constitutional government with an extraconstitutional military junta. Yet, in 2004, there was no Haitian army to intervene, as Aristide had disbanded it by presidential decree shortly before the end of his first term, in a move to put an end to the coup d'état in Haiti.[6]

There were, however, two groups that could intervene in the political crisis. One of these was the international community, especially regional governments that, working through the Organization of American States (OAS), sought to resolve the crisis by mediating between the government and the opposition. In August 2003, Aristide agreed to a power-sharing plan in which he would give up much of his own power as president and work with opposition leaders to form a government of consensus. The diplomatic solution did not work, however, as both U.S. officials (including Ambassador James Foley and Assistant Secretary of State for Western Hemispheric Affairs, Roger Noriega) and the CD backed out of the talks. There was much speculation that the United States was encouraging the opposition to block any solution that would allow Aristide to remain in power (Blumenthal 2004; Chomsky et al. 2004). This seems borne out by the fact that by late 2003, the CD and the Group 184 were publicly calling for Aristide's removal as the first condition to any deal (Dupuy 2007, 174). While the opposition and the international community exerted enormous pressure on Aristide, they were only able to intervene indirectly in the crisis. This brings me to the second group that was capable of intervening to resolve the crisis—namely, the insurgent forces that launched what they called a "popular rebellion" in order to remove Aristide and restore a constitutional government.

It is now clear that the rebels *did* stage a coup and that they had direct or indirect support from both the opposition in Haiti and the U.S. government (Dupuy 2007, 173; see also Blumenthal 2004; Chomsky et al. 2004). While the CD and the Group 184 formally denied any involvement with the rebels, they later lauded them as "freedom fighters" and argued that the "popular uprising" offered clear evidence that "the people" were unhappy with Aristide and that he was incapable of governing the country. The key to this claim lay in the representation of Aristide's government as a failed state.

State Failure as State of Emergency

No one has more clearly outlined the theory of state failure than Robert Rotberg. In several recent edited volumes, Rotberg (2003, 2004a, 2004b) and others have argued the value of comparative study for defining state failure, predicting its occurrence, and categorizing its many forms. Rotberg (2004b) has, for example, offered a general definition of state failure (states fail when they can no longer provide "political goods" to their citizens, especially the political good of security) and a taxonomy of weak, failed, and collapsed states. Writing before the 2004 coup, Rotberg classified Haiti as "enduringly frail," and he predicted that the country, "always . . . on the edge of failure," would "remain weak, but without failing" (2004b, 20; see also Gélin-Adams and Malone 2003). It is important to view this classification within the wider context of international relations theory, since the designation of "state failure" has been used recently to justify foreign intervention.

State failure emerged as a central concept in international relations theory in the 1990s, when the "peace dividend" heralded by the end of the cold war turned instead into the seemingly chronic instability and collapse of nation-states. Deemed a breeding ground for anarchy and violence, failed states are said to pose security threats well beyond their borders (Kasfir 2004; Zartman 1995). Rotberg, for example, argues that "in a modern era when national states constitute the building blocks of world order, the violent disintegration and palpable weakness" of even a single state threatens "the very foundation of that system" (2004b, 1). In short, failed states are a matter of international or global security. Within this classificatory scheme, however, a weak state, even a chronically weak and poor one, does not demand the same kind of response from the international community as do failed or collapsed states.

In 2004, however, it seems that the armed insurgency provided enough justification to edge Haiti into the "failed" category. The rebels were, after all, a prime example of the kind of internal violence that challenges a state's ability to govern and to uphold the rule of law. In Rotberg's formulation, for example, "Nation-states fail when they are consumed by internal violence and cease delivering political goods to their inhabitants. Their governments lose credibility, and the continuing nature of the particular nation-state itself becomes questionable and illegitimate in the hearts and minds of its citizens" (2004b, 1). Whatever the intensity of this internal violence might be, it is the fact that it is directed against the existing government and that it is used as part of a bid to seize power that is central to this diagnosis:

> Citizens depend on states and central governments to secure their persons and free them from fear. Unable to establish an atmosphere of security nationwide, and often struggling to project power and official authority, the faltering state's failure becomes obvious even before, or as, rebel groups and other contenders arm themselves, threaten the residents of central cities, and overwhelm demoralized government contingents, as in Liberia, Nepal, and Sierra Leone. (Rotberg 2004b, 6)

By early 2004 the U.S. government and media seemed ready to classify Haiti as a failed state. Vice President Dick Cheney, for example, hinted that Aristide had "worn out his welcome" (see Chomsky et al. 2004), and the head of U.S. Southern Command said of Haiti shortly after Aristide's removal, "We simply can't have these failed states. If we are not careful you will have a Rwanda type of human catastrophe in the middle of the advanced world" (Hernandez 2004). With the designation of failure came, too, the call for intervention. Christopher Anderson thus quotes a senior U.S. State Department official as saying in March 2004 that "[s]hort of running the country ourselves, we can't fix it" (2004, 38).

Of course, the United States *has* run the country in the past, specifically during the U.S. Occupation of 1915–34 (see Schmidt 1971).[7] Many in Haiti also refer to the U.S.-led multilateral military intervention in 1994 that restored Aristide to power after the 1990 coup as a "second U.S. occupation" (Ives 1995). There are parallels between both of those earlier periods and the provisional period of 2004–2006, but it bears noting that one of the defining characteristics of the current moment is the lack of direct U.S. military or administrative involvement. What is clear, however, is that the declaration of Haiti as a failed state in 2004 authorized a foreign humanitarian and military intervention. What is also clear is that the state failure paradigm is remarkably similar to the development and democratization paradigm of the post–World War II era of decolonization. During decolonization, the dominant mode of political intervention was nation building (Kelly and Kaplan 2001). Under the state failure paradigm, the new logic focuses not on economic development and the formation of national institutions but rather on *state-building*—that is, on strengthening the apparatuses of government and "building capacity," especially through the strengthening of the rule of law (Rose-Ackerman 2004).

The response to state failure, under this new logic, is to reestablish the rule of law and place political authority in state institutions. Yet this can only come through the application of force and the violation of law, in the form of foreign or international military and humanitarian interventions. This amounts to nothing less than the declaration, on the international political stage, of a political emergency. In this sense, the forced removal of Aristide and the formation of a provisional government were both grounded in the twin concepts of state failure and the state of exception. Indeed, the former is a new variant of the latter, in which the international community claims the right to violate national sovereignty and constitutional law in order to restore law through armed intervention. Just as the emergency or state of exception justified the suspension of the law in order to preserve the constitutional state (Schmitt 2005; see also Agamben 1998, 2005; McCormick 1997), state failure becomes an emergency that necessitates a radical, extralegal, and international intervention in order to preserve the interstate system. Perhaps then the 2004 uprising might better be seen not as a coup or a rebellion but rather as a well-orchestrated performance of state failure that authorized the unconstitutional seizure of the state by the political opposition and the invasion of a foreign military force disguised as a peacekeeping mission.

It remains to consider the way in which the emergency was declared, and the form of intervention its declaration called forth. Even before Aristide's departure, the U.S. government had a small military force on the ground to protect the embassy and other U.S. interests. It was these same U.S. forces that escorted Aristide out of the country (or, in his words, "kidnapped" him—see Chomsky et al. 2004). Within days of his departure, the UN deployed a Multinational Interim Force (MIF) made up of soldiers from Canada, France, the United States, and several Latin American countries. In June, the MIF was replaced by MINUSTAH, a multinational peacekeeping force headed by Brazil (Caroit 2004; Dupuy 2007; Lindsay 2006; UN 2005). The international community—led by the governments of the United States, Canada, and France—also immediately supported a proposal from the Group 184 to establish an interim government. The accepted proposal authorized the Group 184's selection of a seven-member Council of Sages.[8] Its main task was to designate a new prime minister, and on March 9 the council nominated Gérard Latortue, a Haitian economist then living in South Florida. His appointment was supported by the UN and the OAS, and the council proceeded to help form the rest of the interim government (Dupuy 2005, 2007, 172–73).[9]

The founding of the provisional period thus proceeded through two related but distinct mechanisms: (1) the authorization of a foreign military intervention and (2) the formation of an interim government charged with stabilizing the country and preparing a new set of elections that would restore constitutional order. These two mechanisms were intimately bound up with one another, although analytically we can say that each corresponded to a different locus of power and a different claim about legitimate authority and the means of force and coercion. The first relied on the moment of decision and the pronouncement of the emergency, which Carl Schmitt (2005) deemed so central to sovereign power. The second relied on the selection of agents granted the capacity to take up emergency powers and govern in a time of crisis. This distinction is crucial, because those who decide the exception must enable an emergency power that will, at a later date, give up that power so that a constitutional order can be restored (McCormick 1997). In the Haitian case, both the interim government and the countries selected to lead the UN mission seemed to have been chosen on the basis of their perceived neutrality in terms of Haitian national politics. For example, Heraldo Muñoz, the Chilean ambassador to the UN, speaking of the role of Latin American countries in MINUSTAH, noted that "[o]ne of the good things about Brazil and Chile and Argentina is that we had no vested interests—no geopolitical, ideological nor historical interests in Haiti—so we could have freer hands to try to focus solely on creating conditions for stability" (Lindsay 2006, 33). In a similar vein, it was quickly noted that the interim government was composed mainly of "technocrats," that is, of career bureaucrats who were deemed to have no ideological commitments to the political conflict in Haiti.[10] As Michel Laguerre (2005) aptly notes, many members of the interim government were expressly chosen from the diaspora, again because they were seen by the United States as removed from the political factionalism of pro- and anti-Aristide groups. There was thus a concerted effort to ensure that the interim government was not composed of (or at any rate not solely composed of) members of the anti-Aristide coalition, since it was assumed that such groups would not easily hand over power in new presidential elections. In short, the interim government acted in the emergency, and its members seem to have been chosen on the basis of their perceived willingness to hand over power after elections, but the decision came ultimately from the international community, and primarily from the United States.

Conclusion

What then can the Haitian case tell us about the operation of U.S. power in the contemporary moment? My central claim here is that while the 2004 coup and the resultant UN mission represent what may be understood as an internecine political struggle in Haiti or the operation of a global "police force" working to instill liberal democracy, it is also an important example of the operation of what I call "phantom power"—that is, the strategic use of political armies and the declaration of an emergency by a power that is removed from or beyond the reach of the national sovereign. In this sense, the declaration of state failure after February 29, 2004, was crucial to the legitimization of a certain kind of intervention, one that fit well within both the long-standing framework of U.S. military power in the Caribbean and Latin America and the more recent security paradigm driving global governance in the liberal democratic moment.

While the so-called third U.S. occupation of Haiti may be part of a long experiment with various forms of military and economic hegemony by the United States, it is important to distinguish the current U.S. and UN entanglement in Haiti from imperial or colonial forms of rule. As John Kelly (2003) has argued, the United States is not, and has not typically been, an empire. Rather, the United States has sought a robust program of economic and military integration throughout Latin America and the Caribbean, one that often has supported the national revolutions of many countries (although it rarely, if ever, supported Haiti in this capacity). This is more clearly seen after World War II, when Pax Americana proceeded through decolonization, development, and democratization. The nation-building efforts of the United States, however, were clearly part of a wider project based on the expansion of military power, economic integration, and the subordination of regional markets to U.S. capital. This project has often been couched in terms of U.S. strategic interests, making direct and indirect military occupations into defensive occupations, that is, into matters of U.S. national security.

Does the model of nation building and decolonization fit the Haitian case? And if so, what does it have to do with the Blue in Green paradigm, with its strange mixture of civil security and military (or paramilitary) force? In one sense, it seems that the existence of chimerical agents, whether in the form of rebel forces like the Cannibal Army/Resistance Front or political gangs like the Chimès, can be used to justify global Blue policing interventions. At the same time, we must also confront the haunting absence/presence in Haiti of a particular type of international Blue in Green force capable of declaring an exception and authorizing the suspension of the law, namely, the nexus of UN Blue Helmets as intervening agents on the ground and the phantom presence of U.S. military might and global dominance.

While the UN and the interim government ruled during the provisional period, it was the tacit support of armed insurgents by the United States in 2004 that was the decisive turning point. In this case, the United States allowed a revolutionary political army to seize power by refusing to intervene to defend a democratically elected government. Why? Whether it is the U.S.

military on the ground (as it was in 1915 and 1994) or not, one of the principal mechanisms of U.S. power in Haiti, and elsewhere, has historically been the use of political armies. Indeed, it is possible that a key mode of Pax Americana is not just nation building but also the formation, training, and arming of expressly national but "Americanized" armies inculcated with a particular ideology of national defense that is, at one and the same time, an ideology of the defense of U.S. economic, political, and strategic interests. The Haitian case shows then just how much political armies and a political discourse on state failure are foundational to the project of global governance and liberal democracy in the current moment.

:: **NOTES** ::

Acknowledgements: This essay is based on a paper first presented at the "Anthropology and Global Counterinsurgency" conference held at the University of Chicago, April 25–27, 2008. That conference was organized by John Kelly, Beatrice Jauregui, Sean Mitchell, and Jeremy Walton, and this essay has benefited greatly by comments from the organizers and conference participants. I would like to thank especially John Kelly, who has helped me rethink U.S.-Haitian relations in numerous ways, and Michelle Beckett, Bea Jauregui, and Sean Mitchell, each of whom provided insightful comments and needed criticism. This essay is based on research conducted in Port-au-Prince, Haiti, between June 2002 and September 2006. Partial funding for this research was provided by the Social Sciences and Humanities Research Council of Canada (award number 752-2001-0195) and by a Doolittle-Harrison Fellowship from the University of Chicago and a Leiffer Fellowship from the Department of Anthropology at the University of Chicago.

1. Many foreign observers have begun to call for a permanent mission. One such observer summarized this view when he declared that what Haiti needs is a "good, old fashioned trusteeship" headed by a "multilateral force with a 25-year mandate to rebuild the country year by year" (Riordan Roett, cited in Soderland 2006, 95; see also Bachelet 2004; Bohning 2004).

2. On this point I am indebted to Beatrice Jauregui, whose insightful comments on an earlier draft of this chapter forced me to think more carefully and critically about this matter.

3. While it is possible to see the declaration of state failure as mere context for the decision to intervene, I believe that the discursive formation of the state failure paradigm (and the broader discourse of global security in the contemporary moment) is itself a mode of power. I am here building on Giorgio Agamben's (1998, 2005) elaboration of Carl Schmitt's (2005) political theory in order to suggest that the international order is based on a set of legal and political discourses that allow, in certain cases, for one state to invade another in a way that is extrajudicial but nevertheless tolerated and made legal by an appeal to necessity (or the "state of emergency"). I thus argue it is precisely the declaration of state failure that sanctions the ability of one or more states to violate the sovereignty of another in order to uphold the global order, since this declaration authorizes—that is, makes legal—a mode of power or force that in normal cases (i.e., nonemergencies, or merely weak states) would appear as explicitly illegal (as, for example, an act of war or invasion).

4. For an insightful discussion of political armies in Latin America, see Koonings and Kruijt (2002).

5. If this sounds like Carl Schmitt's famous discussion of dictatorship and the state of exception, it is no accident. Several leaders of the Group 184 and the CD were open about their thinking on this matter. One such leader, for example, repeatedly told me that what Haiti needs is a "political theology" and directly and indirectly made reference to Schmitt's political philosophy on numerous occasions. For a discussion of the state of exception, see Schmitt (2005). See also Agamben (1998, 2005), Benjamin (1978), Derrida (1991), and McCormick (1997).

6. The Haitian Constitution of 1987 expressly states there is to be both a civilian police force and an armed forces. Some sectors of the opposition have noted that the removal of the army by presidential decree is in violation of the constitution. In recent years, there have been calls for the return of the army, and some former officers have lobbied the government for back wages. For a detailed discussion of the legal and constitutional arguments surrounding these issues, see the reports by the Commission Citoyenne de Réflexion sur les Forces Armées (2005, 2006).

7. During the occupation, the United States created and trained a new Haitian army, called the *Garde d'Haïti,* later renamed the *Forces Armées d'Haïti* (McCrocklin 1956). It was this army in particular that intervened in national politics repeatedly, until it was abolished by Aristide.

8. The council was ostensibly composed of representatives from a cross section of the political spectrum, although there were no representatives of either peasant or Protestant groups, and while there was one member from FL, the council later recommended barring the FL from any new elections.

9. Boniface Alexander was later chosen to serve as president in the interim government, but the government was headed by, and strongly associated with, Latortue. Indeed, as the Council of Sages and the Group 184 repeatedly noted, the constitution sets limits on the executive powers of the president and charges the prime minister, who is elected by the assembly, with much of the administrative duties of government. The decision to focus on the position of the prime minister then seems designed to counter the established tradition of the abuses of presidential power and the "drift" into authoritarian rule.

10. In practice, this was clearly not the case. Many of those in the interim government were from the CD and the Group 184, including the ministers of foreign affairs, justice, social affairs, and commerce and tourism, and there were no members from Aristide's FL party (Dupuy 2007, 175).

3

The Categorization of People as Targets of Violence

A Perspective on the Colombian Armed Conflict

:: PAOLA CASTAÑO ::

This paper offers an analysis of the Colombian armed conflict through the lens of the categorization of the civilian population. The goal is to analyze the increasingly blurry distinction between combatants and civilians and how the normalized use of the categories of "cooperant," "informant," and "collaborator" by both the government and the illegal armed actors configures the treatment and targeting of civilians.[1] The illegal armed actors are constituted primarily by two groups: (1) the *guerrilla* of the Revolutionary Armed Forces of Colombia (FARC) and the National Liberation Army (ELN) and (2) the paramilitaries, mainly the United Self Defenses of Colombia (AUC). The conflict in Colombia plays itself out not only in these groups' direct confrontations with the National Armed Forces but also in their logistical advancements based on the labeling, and then coopting or targeting, of civilian populations.

In this essay, my objective is to open a few analytical windows on this problem, some of which I will continue to pursue ethnographically in my current fieldwork in Colombia about the victims of the armed conflict. In the first part, I characterize how the categorization of the noncombatants operates in everyday life in zones controlled by some of these armed groups. In the second part, I describe how the current government of Alvaro Uribe Velez has redefined the conflict as a "terrorist threat" and has put the issue of cooperation of the civilians with the army at the center of his project and made this cooperation a normative ideal for Colombians. The third part looks at the way in which some statistics and "numbers of the conflict" have a strategic meaning as mechanisms to stabilize these categorizations. I conclude with some reflections and puzzles about the study of the logics of violence in this context.

The "Logic of Violence" against Noncombatants in the Colombian Armed Conflict

In general terms, the long-standing internal armed conflict in Colombia has been characterized as having less to do with the abuses of an almighty state and more as a function of a society that is "abandoned" to its own dynamic of opposed forces (Pecaut 1988). Indeed, the emergence of the FARC and the paramilitaries has been explained not so much as "state failure" (cf. Beckett, this volume), but rather mostly in terms of the "absence of the state" (Palacios 1995; González, Bolívar, and Vásquez 2003). Leaving aside the ambitious, and sometimes oversimplifying, explanatory aims of these statements, what is clear is that these groups operate as networks of power imposing their control over certain territories. What is also clear is that they use—with diverse intensities and tactics[2]—a strategy of threat and protection to enhance their power over the civilian population.

Violence in Colombia occurs between social actors who live in the same local worlds and who know, or think they know, each other. The question, therefore, is how people engage in "the tasks of daily living, inhabiting the world in the full recognition that perpetrators, victims, and witnesses come from the same social space" (Das and Kleinman 2000, 2). Beyond theoretical and practical distinctions of civil police and military forces (cf. Jauregui, this volume), the distinction on the ground between civilians and combatants is anything but obvious. And in such situations, where different types of violence, and variance in the means of and motives for violence, do not follow stable demarcating lines, the slightest disparity between persons acquires the greatest importance. People are forced to live by a set of categorizations and are compelled to make distinctions about the interactions, words, and spaces that are forbidden owing to the threat of a certain armed actor.

Following Stathis Kalyvas, a framework to understand the logic of violence in irregular wars does not need to make assumptions about the underlying preferences of the vast majority of the population and need make "only minimal assumptions about behavioral support, in which complex, ambiguous, and shifting behavior by the majority is assumed, along with strong commitment by a small minority" (Kalyvas 2006, 87). The problem here, therefore, is not to conceptualize support only in attitudinal terms, in terms of genuine loyalties or strategic arrangements, as if all of this could be revealed from "observed behavior" (Kalyvas 2006, 91–93). Rather, our task is to see how these dynamics of categorization operate on the ground before making assumptions about persons' beliefs.

A very illuminating and complex ethnographic approach in this regard is made by anthropologist Patricia Madariaga in her study of daily life in a small town controlled by the paramilitary in Urabá.[3] This work addresses the ways in which the control exercised by this armed group on the basis of coercion implies that the inhabitants must develop a series of adaptations, knowledges, and strategies to get by: "Thinking about violence as an element in daily life implies that we need to stop conceiving it as something having an extraordinary nature, to understand the way in which in certain contexts it no longer belongs to the realm of the extraordinary and is part of the realm of the expectable . . ." (Madariaga 2006, 3). Therefore, and this is central for the purposes of this analysis, in this space, the distinction between civilians and combatants or between victims and victimizers becomes extraordinarily problematic. Madariaga acknowledges this problem when she asserts that "it would be useless to try to introduce it into a research whose subjects do not define themselves as victims and do not situate the paramilitary as perpetrators, even when juridically that is the case" (Madariaga 2006, 63).

It is clear that the identification problem, that is, the inability to tell friend from enemy, is fundamental for understanding the character of irregular wars (Kalyvas 2006, 89). The fear of resembling or becoming a collaborator, a helper, or an informer is a constant, because the armed groups repeatedly cite informing as a justification to level accusations of collaboration with their opponents. In this context, the capacity of the citizens to distinguish among the paramilitary, the *guerrilla,* and the cooperants or helpers of either side relies on a particular set of practical skills summarized in the expression "we just know." Small indicators, gestures, ways of ascertaining the presence of concealed weapons: these are all part of the practices of categorization by which many people in Colombia have to live every day. Another significant aspect is the terminology itself. The words *"guerrilla"* or "paramilitary" are hardly used in these contexts. Instead, people use a set of labels such as "them," voiced in a certain tone or with a certain gesture to refer to particular armed actors.

Across Colombia, cities, towns, and the countryside have been carved into localized, often fluid spheres of influence controlled by one armed group or another. This shifting map of the control of space encompasses what may be called an "order for war." In many zones, the *guerrilla* and paramilitary groups set the borderlines of territories, "solve" family conflicts, impose what they call "general norms of social coexistence," and apply punishments that can include forms of communitarian work but also torture and execution (see Molano 2001).

An example from a woman in Urabá illuminates this regulatory role of the paramilitary in this region:

> When my ex-husband started coming home drunk and making scandals in front of the house, the person who lived with me went and told the *paracos* (paramilitary): "look, my friend has a problem" and they went and talked to him. They solve common problems like this: bad neighbors who play loud music, or the son who does not study and spends the whole day out on the street. The same, if someone owes you a lot of money you give them a percentage so they can go and recover it, you give them ten percent and they make them pay you. (Madariaga 2006, 37)

The fundamental tension here is between a predatory and a regulative presence of these armed actors. In their argument about "law and disorder in the postcolony," John and Jean Comaroff help to shed light on an analogous tension in a different setting (namely, former colonies, which may or may not be characterized as war-torn but are often deemed weak or failed states):

> Under such conditions . . . criminal violence does not so much repudiate the rule of the law or the licit operations of the market as appropriate their forms— and recommission their substance. Its perpetrators create parallel modes of production and profiteering, sometimes even of governance and taxation, thereby establishing simulacra of social order. (Comaroff and Comaroff 2006b, 5)

However, the central concern of all the actors involved is the fundamentally volatile character of this "order." Some people believe that there is a reliable distinction between those who get targeted for being cooperants of the other side and those who "stay quiet" under the paramilitary and are safe. Says one informant, "They do not go around killing anybody, when you are killed it is because they know who you are and what you did" (Madariaga 2006, 55). Another person states:

> They investigate, and do follow-ups. When they kill someone, people already say: "he must have been involved in something." When the *guerrilla* started to kill, it was because of suspicions, now they investigate. They cannot afford to make mistakes, and that gives us security. When the funerals started, in the tough times, not even the families could go. Now you go more easily to the

funerals even if the dead person was a thief or even a member of the *guerrilla,* because they know you are being seen there, they register us and if they investigate, and do not find anything, they realize that you are nobodies. (Madariaga 2006, 55)

This uncanny sense of the regularity of violence and the reliability of categorizations is questioned by others who stress the arbitrariness of the logic of violence and who claim that "following the rules does not guarantee staying alive" (Madariaga 2006, 55).

The ways in which fear becomes a way of locating oneself in a social space and the experience of life as a "colony of immediate powers" (Mbembe 2006, 306), a form of experiencing social regulation, are processes that deserve careful attention. In her study of Mayan widows of the political violence in Guatemala, Linda Green provides an account of violence and fear as part of people's everyday lives and as embedded in cultural conceptions. However, while this work focuses on the disruptive nature of fear and suffering, it does not explore the processes by which "unarmed civilians were configured as the enemy and treated as such" (Green 1999, 9). Such an exploration, which is a key aim of this essay, is not merely a contextualizing tool but rather a central element to understanding precisely *how* violence permeates everyday life and thereby shapes sociality. It also fosters a more nuanced view of the way in which people manage to navigate between their perceived senses of fear, trauma, and normality.

The dynamics of complex interaction between the armed actors and the civilians constitute a central component of the armed conflict in Colombia. Two problematic assumptions seem common to widespread understandings of these dynamics of violence. The first is that in order to turn another actor into an "enemy," it is necessary to dehumanize him, to withdraw a human connection to the target. The second is that situations of war always involve a starkly bipolar perception of reality as black or white, good or evil, of "them" or of "us," while during peacetime, perceptions of reality are more likely to permit shades of gray. Even though there may be a component of truth to these conceptions in particular instances, as generalizations, they each obscure two important processes inherent to the violence committed against noncombatants. As Kalyvas observes, "the observation that killers often dehumanize their victims sustains the perception that violence in civil wars is impersonal" (Kalyvas 2006, 21); but in Colombia, the selective character of violence entails the personalization of violence (Kalyvas 2006, 173). In fact, the violence requires information that is asymmetrically distributed among actors who share dense social spaces; so it is anything but impersonal. Second, and precisely because the violence *is* personalized in a shared social space, the indicators of "who is who" have a very fine-grained character. Indeed, many shades of "us" and "them" are possible, even within a limited space. The categories of "cooperants" and "informants" and "collaborators" rely on these semantic plasticities, and both produce and are reproduced by the often tragic consequences of such categorizations by conflicting armed actors.

The Role of the Civilians as Cooperants of the Armed Forces: Uribe Vélez and the Democratic Security Policy

The cornerstone of Alvaro Uribe's government since 2002, including after his reelection in 2006, is the Democratic Security Policy. This security plan has as its objectives the strengthening of the defense apparatus of the state, the recovery of territorial control from the *guerrilla* and paramilitaries, and the constitution of a network of cooperants among the citizens. One of the central premises of this policy is the idea that there is not an internal armed conflict in Colombia, but rather a terrorist threat. In the president's words:

> In Colombia there is only one conflict: the conflict between 44 million good citizens, who want their freedoms, who want to work, who want to study, and a band of renegades protected by the weaknesses of history, who appeal to terrorism . . . Due to these and other fundamental differences, I ask my fellow Colombians to no longer refer to them mistakenly as 'actors of the conflict'. (Uribe 2002a; all translations of Uribe are the author's)

The president has emphasized that citizens must take an active position against the armed groups as cooperants of the National Armed Forces or as their informants because, as he said in a meeting of international delegates in Cartagena, "in democratic societies there is no neutrality from citizens towards crime, there is no distinction between policemen and citizens" (Uribe, quoted in Semana 2005). The creation of the Cooperants Network, which is administered by the National Army, has been a clear step to turn these ideas into governmental practices. In a speech called "A Calling for the Soldiers in My People to Become Cooperants," Uribe defines the goals of this network in the following terms:

> The restoration of the public order is a task of the State . . . We need that all people cooperate with the Public Force. Let's accomplish the initial goal of organizing a million cooperants . . . Each soldier and each policeman will be a pedagogue to persuade the citizen in order to cooperate with the Public Force. (Uribe 2003)

One of the fundamental questions about the Cooperants Network is that of its consensual/voluntary or coerced/forced character, particularly with regard to the issue of remuneration for cooperation. The government oscillates between defining the act of informing as, on the one hand, a constitutional duty of citizens in solidarity with the state, for sporadic rewards, and on the other hand as something of which citizens must be "convinced" by the Public Force, who then makes regular payments to them.[4] In Uribe's words, again:

> There has been a profound discussion regarding the scope of the notion of solidarity in our Constitution. Some jurists state that, according to the Constitution, cooperation is voluntary. The Constitutional Court, in its latest jurisprudence about the regulations of the Democratic Security Policy, adopted this doctrine of voluntary cooperation. However, I am convinced of the opposite: in a Social State of Law, the principle of solidarity demands to see cooperation as mandatory. Even though I see it as a duty, in my government we want to put it into practice in a voluntary way. That is why we have asked the Police and the Army to construct citizen support through daily pedagogy . . . We do not want a single complaint about people being coerced to cooperate! (Uribe 2002b)

As for the issue of payments specifically, in an annual meeting with all the police commanders in Colombia, Uribe stated:

> As I was talking to the [army] commander in Bolívar, he said to me: "The problem is that people do not cooperate." Well, "insist, Colonel, insist." We need to insist every week and show that we are not going to fail with the reward each Monday so people can believe. There are two ways of offering a reward: one is occasional and the other is permanent. The occasional, generally is reactive, when something serious happens in order to find the delinquents, the government offers a reward. The permanent reward gives us more credibility because the state is not merely reacting, but taking the initiative . . . The quantity does not have to be too big; the important thing is its regularity: it should be serious, reliable and it should arrive every Monday. When people see that the flood of money is coming, they will start cooperating and collaborating. We want our citizens to know that the Public Force pays on Mondays . . . (Uribe 2002c)

We would do well to compare this "serious, reliable" payment scheme to previously cited statements by citizens regarding the "regulatory" role played by *guerrilla* and paramilitary groups in many places. But returning to Uribe's program, on the president's Web page, it is common to find news articles about the "rewards Mondays" with titles like "The Authorities Gave 36 Million in

Rewards." This particular article refers to money given to eighteen members of the Cooperants Network in the (regional) departments of Bolívar, Cesar, Atlántico, Caldas, and Guajira. One will also see references to "successful operations" that have taken place in different regions, thanks to the information given by the Cooperants Networks.[5]

A very problematic episode in March 2008 revealed some of the contradictions underlying this policy. The government decided to pay 2.5 million dollars to Pablo Montoya, a member of the FARC who killed Ivan Ríos, an important figure in the secretariat of this *guerrilla* organization. Montoya, alias Rojas, appeared in an army battalion with Ríos's severed right hand as proof that he had killed the *guerrilla* leader. Rojas argued that the pressure of the army and the lack of food had led him to this decision to betray his comrade. This episode generated a public debate regarding the legitimacy of the reward given by the government. José Gregorio Hernández, ex-president of the Supreme Court of Justice, declared that this episode implied, "the illegal establishment of the death penalty... From the ethical point of view, this measure is incomprehensible, because what is being paid is a crime and not information" (El Tiempo 2008). On the other hand, the minister of defense, Juan Manuel Santos, declared that not paying would have debilitated the information strategy framed in the Democratic Security Policy and the Cooperants Network (El Tiempo 2008). In the end, Montoya was not prosecuted and he received his reward.

The categories of cooperant, collaborator, and informant have become a central component of the Democratic Security Policy. And this fact reveals the state as yet another actor, which participates in the same scheme of categorization of the civil population as the nonstate (and thus, illegally) armed actors. The latter may then use the categorizations as a means to target persons working against their interests.

A common resource to understand Uribe's discourse is to see it as part of the post–September 11 rhetoric of the War on Terror. The amorphous character of terrorism as a source of threat is very functional in its political invocations in different contexts of conflict (Horsman 2008, 196). But even beyond this now obvious point, Uribe's policy also invokes the specific concrete local dynamics of the conflict by acknowledging the role of the civilian population's "know-hows" in their daily maneuvering among the different sides. Political scientist Ann Mason writes of this invocation,

> The integration of civilians into security initiatives risks promoting the privatization of security and justice, fostering military-paramilitary linkages; and the possibility that the *guerrillas* will retaliate against civilians who directly collabo-

rate with the army, or who are perceived as working in tandem with paramilitaries, is high. (Mason 2003, 401)

The idea of offering information to the government as an exchange for a regular economic benefit carries with it a very problematic notion of citizenship. And the lines between combatants and noncombatants, and between collaboration and everyday activity, become more and more imprecise in Colombia, even—and especially—from the standpoint of the state government.

Some Puzzles about the "Numbers of the Conflict"

Statistics about the armed conflict in Colombia, borrowing again some words from the Comaroffs, are "erected on an edifice of indeterminacies and impossibilities" (Comaroff and Comaroff 2006c, 218–19), and the parties in the conflict use these numbers to their own ends. One of the central problems in the general context of armed conflicts and situations with high levels of violence is the access to sources of information. Furthermore, even when information is obtained, there are problems of precision and reliability. However, preceding even these difficulties is the more fundamental problem of categorization.

A study by economists Jorge Restrepo and Michael Spagat invites analysts of conflict statistics to: "steer discussion away from definitional controversy and toward practical analysis" (Restrepo and Spagat 2004, 2). Their study proposes that most direct killings in the Colombian conflict are of civilians rather than combatants. More specifically, in their words: "The paramilitary claim that most of their victims are *guerrilla* supporters and, consequently, legitimate targets. However, in our methodology most of these victims are defined as civilians since they do not actively participate in the hostilities, do not wear insignia or uniforms and are not armed" (Restrepo and Spagat 2004, 4). Compare this statement with the crude terms with which Carlos Castaño, the former leader of the AUC, refers to paramilitary killings of *guerrilla* in Urabá: "In the region of Urabá it was worth it to kill some two hundred *guerrillas* dressed as civilians and a hundred in uniform. Go and see! This region is waking up from lethargy. Today there is employment, education, health and harmony among the employers and the employees" (Aranguren 2001, 225).

Restrepo and Spagat's methodological choices clearly illuminate important aspects of the situation of violence against civilians. However, these methods do not fully grasp the degrees of voluntary or forced involvement that mediate between civilians and combatants in some territories. In particular, the presumed sharpness of these two categories of civilian and combatant obscures how the figure of the cooperant or informant operates in these contexts. It also elides how the definition of armed action must encompass activities beyond the active participation in hostilities and the visibility of insignias. A closer understanding of the ways in which the illegal armed actors frame their actions is of great importance, not merely for analyzing rhetorics of violence and their ideologies, but also for a nuanced understanding of reported statistics. And we must not take these reports at face value but rather must ask, Who is counting what, and for what purpose?

Students of paramilitarism in Colombia have stated that the statistics of massacres have decreased in the past four years. But the dynamic that is emerging is much more complex, since the paramilitaries are assassinating their targets on a one-by-one basis, as a deliberate strategy of blending their actions with those of common delinquency (Rodríguez 2007). As for the *guerrilla,* their "war briefings" and "press releases" also deserve a closer look. In January 2006, the government's public briefing regarding a large-scale confrontation with the FARC reported that "455 members of the Public Force were killed and 1713 wounded" (FARC 2007); and the war briefing from the Oriental Bloc of the FARC from that same combat regarding the same confrontation gave the following numbers: that "the enemies killed were 1856 and 2345 wounded" (FARC 2007). There is no way to establish with any certainty the validity of any of these numbers. However, it is important to note that the considerable inflation from the side of the *guerrilla* likely refers to what they label generically as "the enemy" (which may include paramilitary operatives, Public Force soldiers, or civilian collaborators). It also acts as a declaration of military superiority and a morale booster for the *guerrilla*. Simultaneously, the FARC's press releases usually involve statements about the, "imaginary briefings from the Minister of War and the subaltern generals of the North American armed forces," which, according to the FARC, are attempts to obscure the actual growth of the *guerrilla* force (FARC 2007).

Two other controversies over numbers reveal the complexity of the politics of statistics in the Colombian conflict and their intersection with the categorizations of civilians by armed actors. The Consulting Office for Human Rights and Displacement (CODHES) and the Episcopal Conference of the Catholic Church state that the number of people in Colombia displaced by violence from 1985 to the present is more than 3.8 million. (This is the second largest number of displaced persons in the world, after Sudan.) By contrast, Social Action, the presidential agency for humanitarian help, estimates the actual number to be around 1.9 million. According to Marco Romero, president of CODHES, "it seems as if the government, before acknowledging the social and humanitarian crisis of displacement, tries to overlook it through statistics or administrative actions" (Universidad del Rosario 2006). Romero also claims that the official numbers lack rigor and the government only started with its database in 2000, whereas CODHES has had one since the 1980s. References to this dispute play a key role in many criticisms directed toward the legitimacy of Uribe's policies.

However, the disparities among these numbers are not only reflective of problems of validity, reliability, and political manipulation from the executive branch of the government. They also shape, and are shaped by, the ground realities of displaced persons receiving assistance from the state. Specifically, in situations and spaces in which the armed actors operate as regulatory forces (see Madariaga 2006) and where civilians' self-identification as victims may increase the probability of their becoming targets of violence, granting the availability of institutional resources for people to claim the assistance of the state is not enough. Moreover, displaced persons are compelled to prove their condition of innocence before the state offices, because their alleged involvement with the armed actors is at the heart of their victimization.

A second, and highly problematic episode, refers to the "false positives" of "enemies" killed by the military. Since 2006 there has been a generalized concern about the presentation to the public of successful military killings of *guerrilla* and paramilitary combatants that were, in fact, killings of civilian noncombatant populations. An investigation led by a human rights nongovernmental organization conducted between July 1, 2006, and June 30, 2007, revealed ninety cases of these montages by the army and police. And in January 2009, the Office of the Attorney General reported that it has investigated over 900 cases that occurred between 2007 and 2009. These episodes clearly put into question the legitimacy of the Public Force. They also support critiques of the presidential pressure on various offices to demonstrate the "successes" of the Democratic Security Policy (CINEP 2007). Another layer of this problem has been revealed by the resignation of the last two directors of the National Department of Statistics claiming that they were subject to pressure of the government to modify indicators.

As the Comaroffs argue, debates over the abuse of numbers end up, "affirming an underlying faith in their revelatory potential, intensifying the quest for ever more rigorous—uncorrupted—statistics" (Comaroff and Comaroff 2006c, 224). In the complex circumstances of conflict, such as in contemporary Colombia, it is particularly important to situate the promises of legibility mobilized by statistics and to critically relate these promises to the normative, political, and ideological frameworks that they invoke. If this situating and critiquing of number knowledges is not done, then statistics may become weapon of war or even a weapon of terror. They may become a means of harming civilians and combatants alike, through their inscription and classification of phenomena and people, and may contribute to the making visible of certain targets as well as to the rendering invisible of the politics of categorization.

Final Considerations

Following Michael Bhatia's account of the "politics of naming," naming fulfills two central functions: first, it recruits supporters by propagating a discourse of belonging and opposition; and, second, it justifies action through labeling (Bhatia 2008, 8).[6] Progressing beyond our capacity to question the "truthfulness" of the names, a central component to the analytical agenda of scholars of conflict and violence is to trace how these practices of naming are embedded in daily social life and how they come to acquire such functions in culturally and historically specific ways.

In this case, through the categorization scheme employed by all of the armed groups in the Colombian conflict, the line that divides civilians and combatants is an unstable one. And this instability serves to justify their violence as a way of bargaining with civilians and deterring them from supporting the opposing side(s). The government takes part in this bargaining for allegiance by trying to naturalize a distinction between, on the one hand, "the Colombian people" and the "citizens of good will" who are cooperants, informants, and collaborators and, on the other hand, the "terrorist threat" or simply the "violent" actors. The result is that the Uribe government and the nonstate armed actors together reproduce categorizations of civilians, which may serve to legitimize various violent actions in various times and places.

There is a problematic coexistence between the volatility of these forms of categorization and their formalization. On the one hand, it is possible to see how they are highly contingent on the fragile arrangements of threat, protection, and rewards through which both the nonstate armed actors and the state itself interact with the population in the zones where they aim to exercise control. But, on the other hand, these categorizations have been increasingly normalized in different instances of their usage: statistics, written reports of the armed actors about their "war actions," and the government's discourse to involve the civil population as cooperants of the armed forces.

In many regions in Colombia, violence and conflict inform the coordinates within and by which individuals locate themselves and create symbolic references to structure time and space. In this sense, a closer look at the Colombian case invites us to seek better analytical tools to understand the multiplicity of models of order and the ways in which they coexist and overlap. But the effort to understand these dynamics implies an intellectual and political tension for social scientists. There is undoubtedly a need to transcend the idea of conflict and violence as an anomalous state of society and to recognize their place in the everyday life of many people. But this need runs up against the problem of naturalizing distinct categories of actors who are, in fact, not so clearly distinguishable. The problems of categorization discussed here bring our attention to an important set of analytic and normative questions: What role do we social scientists give to what the armed actors proclaim about themselves and the nature of their targets? How do they—and how do we—approach the representations of "order" and "goodness" in the narratives and definitions of conflict actors? How do we assess the competing categorizations by and of the state and nonstate armed actors and their levels of specificity? And how do we understand and utilize the various types and levels of specificity, when the majority of global leaders agree that the state should have the monopoly on legitimate violence, as directed by a civil power? The shifting complexities of civilian categorization and participation in the multipolar Colombian armed conflict muddy a Blue in Green paradigm of security and order. The Colombian case has many layers and this is only an outline of some of them. However, understanding the logics by which the state and the nonstate armed actors categorize people and then deploy those categorizations to interested ends offers an illuminating entry point to addressing one of the most intractable realities of the situation in Colombia: the involvement of civilians in the conflict.

:: **NOTES** ::

1. Carlos Castaño, former leader of the AUC, describes this dynamic in the following terms: "Since we could not fight them [the *guerrilla*] where they were, we chose to neutralize the people who brought to their camps food, medicine, messages, liquor, prostitutes, and these types of things. And we realized that we could isolate them and that this strategy would give us very good results" (Bolivar 2006, 72).

2. It is important to stress that, since the 1980s, the presence of resources originating in drug traffic and illicit crops has transformed the logic of territorial expansion of these armed groups and is at the center of their territorial interests.

3. Urabá is a strategic territory that has been, historically, disputed among the paramilitary and different *guerrilla* groups, including FARC, ELN, and EPL (Ejercito Popular de Liberación, or Popular Liberation Army).

4. According to the National Army, the legal foundation of the Cooperants Network is article 95 in the National Constitution, which states, "All Colombians have the duty to act with conformity to the principle of social solidarity, answering with humanitarian actions before situations that endanger the life and health of people. In the same way, they must respect and support the democratic authorities legitimately constituted."

5. See, for example, http://www.presidencia.gov.co/prensa_new/sne/2003/abril/22/01222003
.htm. Even though there is an identity protection program, the government has instituted a celebration for the "day of the Cooperant" in which medals are given to exemplary citizens who have given information. While this may be intended to recognize and valorize cooperants, it also may increase the chances of their being targeted by nonstate armed actors.

6. Michael Bhatia was killed by a roadside bomb in Afghanistan on May 7, 2008, while working as part of a Human Terrain Team. See Gonzalez, this volume.

4

Seeing Red

Mao Fetishism, Pax Americana, and
the Moral Economy of War

:: JOHN D. KELLY ::

Introduction

Carl von Clausewitz is remembered for the aphorism that "war is politics by other means." This is not his exact wording. Clausewitz actually wrote about continuation of policy, sometimes, a continuation of political intercourse, always a continuation, by other means (Clausewitz 1989 [1832], 61, 87, 605, 610). Long before Weber defined the state as requiring a monopoly on legitimate coercion, Clausewitz sought to connect war to statecraft and to reconnect the means and ends of warfare to analysis of the means and ends of political and social and cultural relationships more generally. Weber's definition helps scholars realize that the connection of the state and violence was ineluctable. For Clausewitz, the point was to understand war. In the terms I will use, Clausewitz reframed profoundly the question of the moral economy of war, the cultural rules of war as a deliberate institution.

I will use "moral economy" to mean the moral compass intrinsic to an institution.[1] I refer not to transitions from traditionalism, or the good of something more generally, but to cultural inscription of moral expectations, moral roles, and duties and life chances built into mobile institutions considered as built environments. Thus one can speak of the moral economy of markets, of the state, of plantations, and, in this case, of war. What is the moral economy of war under Pax Americana? And what should it be?

I will argue here that many recent strategists and policy makers for the U.S. military have been profoundly confused about what should be the legitimate use of vast war powers. Full-spectrum dominance as a means to end the cold war has transformed into a nightmare haunting all other politics, for U.S. Americans and for others. The United States should stop searching for a nemesis suitable to its scale and start seeing real situations more clearly. In Iraq, yes, mistakes were made, but more than that, launching the Iraq War was a mistake, not a subtle mistake, but a gross one. I do not claim this last point as a particular insight. It does not require sophisticated anthropological analysis to see it. It was clear at the time to many thoughtful observers both inside the military and outside of it. So, politics happens. But we are also in a particular conjuncture in the relationship between global military politics and our discipline of anthropology.

With the Human Terrain Systems project; with the new Counterinsurgency Field Manual and its two million copies in circulation; and now with Defense Secretary Robert Gates's plan for a Minerva Consortium, the U.S. military has begun scripting a role for U.S. anthropologists in service to the U.S. military. With the Minerva project, Secretary Gates has announced Manhattan Project hopes for history to repeat itself (and one suspects he was not thinking of the opening of *The 18th Brumaire*[2]). These hopes for what Hugh Gusterson has called a "weaponized anthropology" come, I think, at a specific conjuncture at which the U.S. military is visibly failing on the ground. For all the efforts at criteria to specify failed states and to justify interventions on the basis of them (cf. Beckett, this volume), it is striking that no one has identified the U.S. military as the world's most conspicuous example of continuing failure at state making. The U.S. military has felt its repeated ineptitude at a particular point despite overwhelming competence elsewhere. In Beatrice Jauregui's terms, they get stuck, all too often, on the transition from Green to Blue.

The U.S. military is unprecedented in its firepower and generally effective as long as campaigns can be looked at through lenses that show the Green. But these days all the available missions, in some gray way—this is precisely where things are falling apart—turn out to have a major Blue component, a liberated population that actually needs law and order, a conquered population that someone has to admit to conquering. The U.S. military has determined, in a series of their own meetings and deep thinks over the last couple of years, with Iraq in particular on their minds, that they need anthropology to help them with this transition to Blue. The military hopes that science can replace government, specifically our science replace the conquered society's smashed government, drawing from custom the blueprints for order. This hope is clearly a nonstarter. The plan to ally with science as if that puts military judgments above politics has had a long and successful run in U.S. military history. But it is not enough to say that they definitely picked the wrong scientists this time. When specifically asked for advice, anthropology can and should answer—even though the answer is one that the military and the Republican administration may not want to hear. I think the answer lies in clarifying why the Green has so frequently failed to go Blue or enabled transition to Blue, to move from campaigns of liberation to successful civil and political societies governed by the laws of functioning democratic nation-states. This failure is a continuing and now an imperative problem for political anthropology.[3]

What "Seeing Red" Does to the Blue and the Green: Galula, Mao Fetishism, and Its Consequences

So what exactly is insurgency? How did we get from a "War on Terror" to a "long war" of "global counterinsurgency"?

Lieutenant Colonel John Nagl wrote the foreword to the University of Chicago Press edition of the *U.S. Army/Marine Corps Counterinsurgency Field Manual.* This joint counterinsurgency field manual is the first in decades for the U.S. military, officially replacing the army's 1986 *Counterguerrilla Operations* manual (FM 90-8) and the Marines' 1980 *Counterinsurgency Operations* (FM-82). The manual's prefaces and introductions reiterate, at least four times, a sad and shocking story of its genesis, the painful and costly gap in military planning for counterinsurgency since Vietnam. All see a brighter day ahead with the unity that the manual, process and product, can create, in what Philip Bobbitt, John Nagl, George W. Bush, and others have labeled the "long war" of counterinsurgency and/or counterterrorism. From Nagl's preface, "The story of how the army found itself less than ready to fight an insurgency goes back to the Army's unwillingness to internalize and build upon the lessons of Vietnam" (Nagl 2007, xiii). But by themselves the lessons of Vietnam are negative, a failure to take counterinsurgency seriously enough, Nagl argues (cf. Jacobsen, Hevia, and Caffrey, this volume). Where to turn if not to the American experiences in Vietnam and in Iraq for a workable model of insurgency? According to Nagl, they turned to David Galula. And to render my argument in short, Galula's answer is wonderfully useful, except in reality: to Galula, insurgencies are always Maoist-style revolutionary movements.

David Galula was a French military officer, raised in Casablanca, who retired from the French military as a lieutenant colonel after a career of fighting in "world war" in North Africa, Italy, and France and then in "irregular wars" in China, Greece, Indochina, and Algeria. In the early 1960s, he wrote his brief treatise *Counterinsurgency: Theory and Practice* while in residence at Harvard's Center for International Affairs. He died young in 1967. In 2006, his 1964 treatise was reprinted, the first volume in Praeger Security International's new series "PSI Classics of the Counterinsurgency Era," with a forward by Nagl. Lieutenant Colonel Nagl's career parallels Galula's. He served in both Iraq wars, coauthored the U.S. military's new counterinsurgency manual, and has himself retired and joined a Washington think tank to further pursue theory.

I think it significant that by this reckoning, the counterinsurgency era was the first round of decolonization, with China as its central theater. Vietnam as the final and tragic failure follows others in a string, including Galula's Algeria. Galula's tone is urgent, while Nagl's is more complex: urgent, but also elegiac, and frustrated. Nagl's Galula is the voice unheard, the lost genius, and the narrative resembles other famous lost cause stories.[4] But here the future is entailed. Nagl tells us that we must prepare. In the twenty-first century, many more soldiers than ever are destined to "follow Galula down the streets without joy" (Galula 2006 [1964], x).

To Galula, counterinsurgency is the asymmetric partner to insurgency. He is serious about this asymmetry. The French counterinsurgency forces in Indochina and Algeria were doomed because they never had enough troops to meet the 20:1 ratio that is commonly required for a counterforce to root out and destroy an insurgency. But counterinsurgency and insurgency are also inseparably connected, and the pair together are really "revolutionary war." Galula is aware that it is hazardous to try to develop laws of revolutionary war, since, as he reckons it, there have been few, "most of them since 1945" (Galula 2006 [1964], xiv; recall that he was writing in the 1960s.) But this does not stop Galula from treatise style: "A local revolutionary war is part of the global war against capitalism and imperialism. Hence, a military victory against the local enemy is in fact a victory against the global enemy and contributes to his ultimate defeat" (Galula 2006 [1964], 33).

Galula's conclusions are dour. Counterinsurgency is hard. But it is also vital, to defend capitalism and imperialism: behind local insurgency lies this global enemy and "his" global ambitions, a striking combination of transvaluation and personalization of this enemy. Thus the cold war lurks behind anti-imperial insurgency in the era of decolonization, and its theorist and paradigm is Mao. Mao's Chinese communists, in their doctrines and their acts, are seen to set the model for all other insurgencies. Theirs is thus the "orthodox pattern," with five stages, guerilla war no. 3, movement warfare no. 4, and so on. When the Algerian National Liberation Front (FLN) diverges, this is not evidence against the existence of a general pattern. No, it defines the alternative "shortcut pattern," with "blind terrorism" and "selective terrorism" starting much earlier, creating different strengths and vulnerabilities, all carefully diagrammed by Galula. There are other variables, for example, in geography and in type and level of outside support. But in all cases, it comes down to resolve. The fluid, patient, and charismatic insurgents always begin with a cause, "a well-grounded cause with which to attract supporters." Since it is "his sole asset at the beginning," it "must be a powerful one if the insurgent is to overcome his weaknesses" (Galula 2006 [1964], 8). The counterinsurgents can win, particularly if they gain skills with ideology and propaganda. But they need not rely on ideas. Ultimately, or rather, in the middle stages of war, things will get bad enough that the war of ideas is not the central theater of campaigning, and the counterinsurgents can win even if they do not have all the answers. We will call this Galula's amoral promise: "Which side gives the best protection, which side threatens the most, which one is likely to win, these are the criteria governing the population's stand" (Galula 2006 [1964], 8–9). In fact, the counterinsurgents benefit as the warfare heats up on many grounds. The better established is the fact of war, the more can be done legitimately, regardless of ordinary legal and moral strictures:

> Force, when it comes into play in a revolutionary war, has the singular virtue of clearing away many difficulties for the counterinsurgent, notably the matter of the issue. The moral fog dissipates sooner or later, the enemy stands out more conspicuously, repressive measures are easier to justify. . . . "
> The country's map reveals three sorts of areas:
> The "red" areas, where the insurgent effectively controls the population and carries out guerrilla warfare.
> The "pink" areas, in which he attempts to expand; there are some efforts at organizing the populations and some guerrilla activity.
> The "white" areas, not yet affected but nevertheless threatened; they are subjected to the insurgent's subversion but all seems quiet. (Galula 2006 [1964], 49–50)

Galula's eight-step tactical solution will destroy or expel the insurgent guerrillas area by area (mobile forces) and also, area by area, control and get to know the local population (static forces). Primacy must go to the territorial command, since securing local peace is the key. Eventually, a kind of democratic solution is envisioned by Galula, as the static forces, in order, destroy the insurgent political organization, hold local elections, test local leaders, manipulate logistics to support loyalists, and organize a national counterinsurgent political party. Victory is achieved *not* when the national counterinsurgent political party wins elections but when "spontaneous intelligence increases sharply." Then it is time for the final step, winning over or suppressing the last guerrillas.

Galula is cited as the most important counterinsurgency theorist not only for the technical details about how to defeat guerrillas but for the moral economy of counterinsurgency as a new type of war: a license to ignore, except tactically, the content of the insurgents' ideas while, at the same time, specifying that the insurgents are an enemy to eradicate because of their revolutionary project. The manual resurrects Galula's vision and largely ignores criticism of such doctrines that began in the same period, notably in historian Peter Paret's 1964 study *French Revolutionary Warfare from Indochina to Algeria: The Analysis of a Political and Military Doctrine*. Writing on the eve of U.S. escalation of its plan to resolve the successful decolonization of Indochina by replacing the reluctant French, Paret criticized the French counterinsurgency doctrine deployed in Algeria:

> It remained stunted, hamstrung by contradictions, advocating policies that were far in excess of the actual power at its disposal. But if the ideology was inadequate, its operational message was clear and unambiguous. The Army, it declared, was engaged in a permanent world-wide revolutionary conflict in which the differences between anticolonialism, anti-Western nationalism, and Communism were insignificant, and in which the traditional distinctions between war and peace had disappeared. . . . The insistence of the theorists and adherents of *guerre révolutionnaire* on a total politico-military effort, the rejection of compromise, pushed the Army more and more deeply into positions that were untenable politically as well as militarily. (Paret 1964, 29–30)

Notwithstanding the poignancy of Paret's 1964 confidence that the United States could do better, Paret saw the dynamics of the French debacle in Algeria far more clearly than Galula did. But Galula's value lies not in his critique of French imperial overreach. Galula's postcolonial quiescence with imperial, even totalitarian style in political planning has to be part of his appeal, among all French colonial military theorists, to Nagl. It is no accident that it is Galula and not, say, Paret, or Lyautey among French military theorists who has captured the U.S. military imagination.

There is a major irony here. In its 1943 version, the standard reader on the history of strategy, Princeton University Press's *Makers of Modern Strategy*, included a careful, laudatory article by Jean Gottman about colonial reformer Hubert Lyautey and the other pacification theorists. Lyautey's writings, and campaigns, set the strategies of French colonial armies and defined the French "colonial school" of warfare. Lyautey's doctrine was that generals should always be put in charge of the subsequent civil government under colonial conditions because "one conquers the city very differently if one is responsible to reopen the market the next day." Gottman detailed the successes of French colonial campaigns to pacify towns and then country, to isolate rebels and win over publics by military advances that were always also advances in trade and services, advances in civilization and social welfare. In Gottman's telling, the inevitable restiveness against successful colonization led to rebellions with their own connections to the outside world, less easily quelled, and eventually to the eclipse of the colonial school. The collapse is marked historically by the 1925 moment when World War I hero Philippe Pétain was sent in to relieve Lyautey after Lyautey had proved unable to end the Rif Rebellion in the Maghreb. Pétain used mustard gas to negotiate and heavy metal to blast the enemy to smithereens.

The 1986 new edition of *Makers of Modern Strategy* had, however, absorbed the important lesson that colonialism is immoral and wrong. Thus its new essay on Bugeaud, Galliéni, and Lyautey, while beginning with the observation that colonial military history remains one of the more neglected areas of military history, proceeds to doubt that there really was a French colonial school of military theory and practice or, at any rate, an effective one, since, after all, colonialism was contradiction ridden and wrong. To be fair, Douglas Porch in this essay makes many astute observations, notably that Lyautey's articles on "The Social Role of the Officer" and "The Colonial Role of the Army" and his—yes, quintessentially Lyautey's—famous concern about winning over "hearts and minds" "was more a public-relations exercise with the French people than a workable military formula in Morocco" (Porch 1986, 394). The same public-relations purpose might well explain much in the new counterinsurgency manual, but I think that General Petraeus et al. certainly act as if they take its doctrine seriously. Porch also shows that more force was used in Morocco than Lyautey would claim in his writings. But this should not distract us from the larger point: the U.S. military could learn more about strategy and tactics, when they cross the line from Green to Blue, from Lyautey's theories and practices about the army as "an organization on the march" than from Galula's cold war fantasy that has a Maoist political party lurking anywhere and everywhere, always really planning global revolution. But to learn from Lyautey the U.S. Army would have to admit that their enterprise resembled colonization. To be clear, I am not recommending colonization as a strategy, against counterinsurgency or otherwise. I am only saying that denial and fantasy have high costs. Seeing Red is enormously simplifying, when arriving in moral and political murk where the lines are not clear between friend and enemy, criminal and enemy, Green and Blue fields for the exercise of violence. Seeing Red, seeing a revolutionary enemy who must be blown to smithereens, is enormously simplifying, enabling, and self-deluding.

The ring of hell that the United States now sends its soldiers into, and carefully builds in a poverty-stricken overseas society in line with this manual's doctrines, can also be limned by what has been lost in the history of U.S. military manuals on counterinsurgency. Comparison with perhaps the most famous prior manual will have to suffice here: the 1940s *Small Wars Manual* of the United States Marine Corps. A measure of current counterinsurgency theory and practice, in other words, can lie not only in what is now added, for example, fifty pages of anthropology terms, but in what has been lost, notably, the penultimate chapter, chapter 14, about supervision of elections, and the final chapter, chapter 15, about withdrawal. The *Small Wars Manual* planned repeated more and less peaceful interventions principally into what it called "neighboring republics," and its commitment to republican and democratic political values was explicit. It has no discussion of when or how to delay or cancel an election or how to ensure that you have destroyed an enemy political party and selected the leaders for a new, allied party before holding a ballot. We might conclude from this, reflecting on Latin American history, that there was probably another manual, or more likely a different relationship between book and practice. But the final sentence of the first section of chapter 15 still reads like lost wisdom in this era of long-war planning: "Since eventual withdrawal is certain, it is a governing factor in troop assignment and field operations." And there is no sentence in the new *Counterinsurgency Manual* like the one ending 14-1-b of the 1940 *Small Wars Manual,* explaining the preference for peaceful election supervision to all other deployments of the Marines, because it responds to "the popular revulsion against armed interventions in the internal affairs of other countries, and supports the principles of self-determination and majority rule." The exigencies of self-determination are not discussed anywhere in the new manual.

The new manual did not simply inscribe Galula's doctrines. Nagl and others see differences as well as similarities between Galula's counterinsurgency era and the contemporary scene. But, in the hands of General Petraeus, David Kilcullen, John Nagl, and others, a long war of global counterinsurgency emerges as a more complex variant of Galula's global revolution against capitalism and imperialism. As Nagl sums it up in the foreword to the Galula reprint, we now live in an "age of competing and cooperating global transnational and regional insurgencies" (Galula 2006 [1964], x). This vision leads the new manual to put yet another duty onto the counterinsurgent military planner: "Counter-insurgents must be prepared to identify their opponents and their approach to insurgency" (U.S. Department of the Army 2007, 1–109). The procrustean bed must be reassembled for every circumstance. At one level, this means not to be John McCain, confusing al-Qaeda and the Shi'ite militias in Iraq. But there is another level, the one that enabled George Bush, after all, to fight al-Qaeda by invading Iraq.

The worst feature of Mao fetishism, the worst impact of seeing Red on the effort to transit from Green to Blue deployment of force in war-torn societies, is the lesson learned from Galula about how to win by reaching the middle of warfare. Under the right circumstances, Galula showed, you no longer needed to win the war of ideas, to have the better vision of a sustainable future and so on. When things were bad enough, you just had to be providing the most cred-ible security, the biggest threat to enemies, and the likelihood of victory (cf. Castaño, this volume). This cold pragmatism, morally "realist" in the sense so important in some branches of international relations theory, resolves indeed in practice the contradictions of theory, with a deliberate choice to save all the villages by destroying them.

General Petraeus had a partner in running a civilian military conference in February 2006 to finish the new counterinsurgency doctrine and manual. His partner was Sarah Sewall, director of the Carr Center for Human Rights Policy at Harvard University's Kennedy School of Government. Sewall's introduc-tion to the University of Chicago Press edition to the manual made explicit many of the most relevant principles here, the moral and political compass hidden in the manual's thin vocabulary of "host nation," as in the chapter on "Developing the Host-Nation Security Forces." How do we know which side to be on? How do we know whether an insurgency, say, for example, among people enslaved for over forty years by the Burmese military, merits recogni-tion as legitimate? We do not ask, by Sewall's doctrines. "America must align its ethical principles with the nation's strategic requirements," Sewall explains (U.S. Department of the Army 2007, xxii), especially when it comes to coun-terinsurgency. The "legitimacy of the host nation government is the north star" (U.S. Department of the Army 2007, xxxii), and "we need only consider insur-gents' eagerness to kill civilians" (U.S. Department of the Army 2007, xxxiv). Sewall talks of civilians and nations, but the real north star is always the state. The imperative is "sustaining the statist norm in the face of radical and violent revolutionaries" (U.S. Department of the Army 2007, xlii).

I do not agree with Sewall. Her argument for the moral foundation of the manual is summed up in another deliberately radical aphorism: "Counterin-surgency favors peace over justice" (U.S. Department of the Army 2007, xxxix).

Much can be said and has been said by Martha Kaplan and me in other venues about the bizarre persistence of the United States hope to make the democratic nation-state the end of history, the Truman Doctrine confidence repeated by the Wolfowitz crowd that democratic nations would spontaneously emerge when tyrants are toppled (see, for example, Kelly and Kaplan 2009, 2004). There is an astonishing pattern (documented, for example, by Stephen Kinzer in *Overthrow*) wherein (fourteen times at least in the last century) the U.S. military overthrows a foreign government without taking over power or even providing a permanent new government in its place. What is astonishing is not that the overthrows usually do not go well, do not lead to peace, justice, democracy, and prosperity, but rather that the United States keeps thinking that they will. I see in this manual an erosion of the underlying faith, epitomized by the Truman Doctrine, similar to what Bennett (forthcoming) finds in his reflections on the Iraq deployment in comparison with Sahlins's important observations about the destruction of conscience in Vietnam. I think Truman believed that underneath it all there was a freedom-loving Turkish nation in Turkey and a freedom-loving Greek nation in Greece, far more than Sewall, Petraeus, or even Wolfowitz believes in a nation in Iraq. President Bush's famous contempt for nation building was founded on such skepticism. But no alternative was sought, or even allowed, and the Bush administration ended up trying, ineptly, to nation-build for security reasons. Sewall does not want to try for justice but is willing to wield unprecedented military force simply to insist on peace. It is not working, to say the least.

After Clausewitz, we are led to see that war "must necessarily bear the character of policy and measure by its standards" (Clausewitz 1989 [1832], 610). The Green emanates from an organized Blue, and the originating state is responsible. After the United Nations Charter, the rules are much tougher, and cosmopolitan audiences watch carefully. To reframe a much borrowed trope from Benjamin Franklin, a dominant state that attempts to insist on peace without justice will certainly eventually produce a world without either.

Back to the Blue and the Green: Full-Spectrum Dominance without Hegemony

What, then, is to be done? Weber calls it Tolstoy's question, and I want to raise it. I think I owe you that after such a critique, starting with my own particular and strong reading of Weber. The problems here are not uniquely modern or uniquely American. The state, any state, is stuck with the problem that so many of them address with the divided solution of the Blue and the Green. Some problems come with, as Weber saw it, sustaining a declared monopoly on legitimate use of force. Most readings of this part of Weber have focused on authority in relationship to force, coercion, and its monopoly. But as I have detailed elsewhere, to Weber, this laden conception of the legitimate was actually the key to the whole definition. He could imagine rule by superior coercion without any legitimacy—yes, he lived before the era of full-spectrum dominance and this Iraq war, or one is tempted to say, full-spectrum dominance without hegemony. But he certainly saw expanding empires at work past and present and thought about them with clear sight. Weber could imagine rule by force alone, but in his writings on domination—or, as Talcott Parsons translated it during the cold war, on "imperative coordination"—Weber argued that outside of economic relations proper, authority without an articulated and accepted legitimacy was unlikely to last very long.

In other words, the problem that states are stuck with is claims of right among people who have been blocked from self-help by the state's asserted monopoly on coercion, on force, which necessarily entails a monopoly on vengeance and retribution, a monopoly on preemption, and even a monopoly on coerced restitution, imperative recompense. This is not a particularly novel problem, nor does it change when the state becomes a regulator of economic relationships, kinship, sexuality, and so on. In this sense (contra Foucault), power over life was a part of the state as long as power over death ever was. In this Weberian sense, the state emerges precisely when the conquerors who have established power over death via their control over coercion try also to establish power over life via forces and relations of communication, in the first instance in realms of ritual, language, and law: when they open a court in all senses. Weber's favorite example of domination without legitimacy is the way leading banks set the terms and flow of loans: if their position in capital markets is sufficiently dominant, let alone full spectrum, they need make no pretense (and generally do not) of any intention to attend to the needs, desires, and perspective of their clients. Nor does anyone in such a strictly economic relationship expect them to. What I would call the "moral economy" of their situation in the institution of lending enables them to act without such pretense, let alone any duty to sustain an actual mechanism to balance arrangements in light of such matters. The moral economy of the state is different.

Another way to reconsider this question is by way of alienation theory. On another of the less traveled roads in Weber, he reflects ironically on Marx's discussion of the alienation of labor at the advent of capitalism by locating a different and prior alienation, not of the producer from the means of production but of the warrior from the means of coercion. It was a much earlier moment in human history when the warrior no matter how skillful lost the ability to shape his own destiny, to self-help coercively, to coerce his way forward. Weber located the key moment when so-called feudalism emerged in Europe, when castles with moats and drawbridge and portcullis could send down laughter at the valiant man with his horse and sword, when even a legion of self-armed citizens were no match for a state, where the means of coercion required not merely knowledge and tools but large-scale destructive machineries, siege engines and castles, trebuchets and explosives, and so on. At that point, there are new conditions of possibility for a monopoly on violence—and ironically a new interest, in the pragmatic sense, in justice even among the powerful, for tactical reasons in the new zones of peace.

The problem that Beatrice Jauregui has identified as that of the Blue in the Green has vexed theorists of sovereignty and authority for a very long time. Rousseau finished the *Social Contract* by admitting that without a theory of diplomacy and interstate contestation his theory of justice in lawgiving was profoundly and hopelessly incomplete. Legal positivist John Austin determined the province of jurisprudence in his work *The Province of Jurisprudence Determined* by finding the reach of the sovereign in the extent to which police (the Blue, in our terms) enforced his will as law. The police then secured political society. In Rousseau's romantic anticipation of Foucault, or perhaps of the fascists, the Blue then is that which forces people to be free. But long before Rousseau, it was also clear as crystal that this honor, the establishment of secure society, also in another sense belonged, and problematically, to the effectiveness and moral character of the people in Green. Machiavelli underlined with irony and resolution the reality of the soldier's *virtù:* the soldier is a defender of civil society only by violating its moral strictures against violence. The soldier secures civil existence through actions that rendered the soldier problematic when viewed by fellow citizens. There is no doubt that this Machiavellian contradiction is still with us today—from the touchiness of officers about honor, to "Support the Troops" bumper stickers, and to other injunctions to find the wielders of violence on a different and higher moral plane.[5]

The moral economy of the state begins with its mode of managing its forces and relations of coercion. Its spaces, places, and situations are in these terms bounded and delineated on the lines between the Green and the Blue. The locations can proliferate and ramify. But the root contrast is clear and crucial: the Blue articulates closely with the other institutions of law and order, lawyers and courts, judges and parliaments. Whatever their liberality or lack thereof, these civil institutions are necessary for the police to orient their actions. The Blue maintains a space of law and order, a space in which the judge's power of habeas corpus can be proof of the sovereign's law's legitimacy, as well as its limit, a space that can lose its coherence, as when in Pakistan the lawyers riot, while a general in uniform rules. Even in a well-organized space of law and

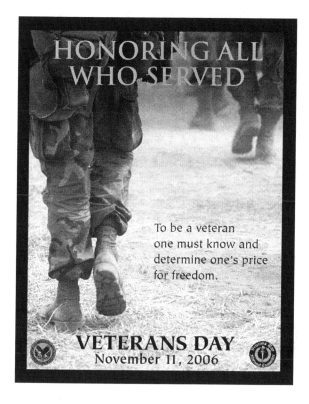

HONORING ALL WHO SERVED

To be a veteran one must know and determine one's price for freedom.

VETERANS DAY
November 11, 2006

order, relationships are not seamless. Weber writes about friction and opacity as limits to all state clarity in the exercise of its reasons, ways and means. Veena Das has illustrated this eloquently in her descriptions and reflections on the moments in which an Indian constable's word and deed, in its local moment, *is* the law.

But when is the Green the law? What kind of law, or justice, can be part of the moral economy of the Green? If the Blue space is the space of the state's law and order, where does the Green operate? Obviously, in the first instance, the Green operates outside the space of judges, law, and claims of civil rights violations, outside the civil sphere. The point can be clarified by way of one of the lowest moments, which is saying something, of the George W. Bush administration, the point at which it announced a military mission it titled "Infinite Justice." After al-Qaeda terrorists crashed planes and destroyed the World Trade Center and part of the Pentagon, killing thousands, the U.S. government decided to respond not to a criminal matter but to a military attack, to call in the U.S. Green and not a global Blue. The shock and awe of the nation and world were still the major factor for any public act; while Dan Rather could gain praise for asking, "Why do they hate us?" it was clear that it would take restraint for the 9/11 attacks to be labeled criminal. Short-term political rewards lay for the taking for any politician able to cobble some kind of repayment of shock and awe against a U.S. enemy. Nine days after 9/11, therefore, in an address to a joint session of Congress and to the American people, U.S. president George W. Bush announced his intention to attack American enemies. He said, "Tonight we are a country awakened to danger and called to defend freedom. Our grief has turned to anger, and anger to resolution. Whether we bring our enemies to justice, or bring justice to our enemies, justice will be done." How, exactly, did this president attach justice to the Green, to the attack on enemies? Flamboyantly. Until media criticism caused a shift, the U.S. military called their attack planning for the Afghanistan invasion "Operation Infinite Justice." Bush argued for policy from anger. And he called it justice. President Bush's triumphalist assertion that "justice will be done" was actually a mockery of ordinary language and belongs in the same set as "hasta la vista baby" and "what we have here is a failure to communicate." The moral economy of war is precisely not about justice. That is among the many reasons why war is not good. It is about gaining property, or security, often; revenge, very possibly. And as Hegel said, vengeance can be just. But the whole aphorism is, Vengeance can be just, but it is never justice. Justice is never infinite, thus the blindfolded goddess holds scales, to balance things.

At least since Hobbes, in the Western tradition, the possibility of justice has been located in the moral economy of the state, within peaceful civil institutions, the realm of the Blue form of legitimate violence. This in turn makes the reality and quality of its justice a reasonable measure of a state's virtue. Anthropology of acephalous societies has, at least since Mauss and Evans-Pritchard, radically challenged the Hobbesian equation that for justice it takes a state. But we should not take an invitation to try thereby to connect a reckless military to nonstate forms of morality and order. It cannot be done. The legitimacy of Green violence is grounded not in considerations of justice but only by either the necessity or the grandeur of the purpose.

Strategists for globalized counterinsurgency claim necessity for their strange brands of Green deployment, which have come to include what anyone else would ordinarily call conquest and occupation of foreign territories. Robert Pape has exhaustively documented that occupation of homelands tends to generate suicide bombing as a weapon of the weak and aggrieved among occupied people (Pape 2006). Within the moral economy of counterinsurgency, such things as suicide bombers become, in turn, more evidence of the need to walk Galula's streets without joy. Arno Mayer recently demonstrated that counterrevolutionary warfare planners routinely make their plans well in advance of actual revolutionaries, in anticipation of them. In the revolutions in both France and Russia, Mayer showed, the counterrevolutionary armies launched the actual violence, and yet, they garnered their legitimacy from the image of the revolutionaries as the threat and the instigators (Mayer 2002). Similarly, by fetishizing Mao, Galula seeing Red tried to legitimate endless colonial violence. And recent theorists of global counterinsurgency in the U.S. military fetishize Galula to justify their own interventions and portray themselves as heroic responders to global threat. They have forced complicated and volatile realities into the contours of their fantasy, with devastating results.

The new Obama administration has inherited a vast number of U.S. military deployments and literally has no choice but to reconsider them. For this reason and others, what the world really could use from anthropology now is not an explanation of the behavior and values of others that could guide U.S. soldiers in the field but a clearer explanation of what those U.S. soldiers and others are doing in the field. In classic Boasian mode, at last, we could use an account that shows us the shackles of our own assumptions, the lines and limits of our own political culture. Pax Americana is not another empire, Martha Kaplan and I have argued quite fiercely elsewhere (Kelly and Kaplan 2001a, 2001b, 2004, 2009; see also Kelly 2003 and 2006). Its successes in terms of peace and prosperity are not to be taken lightly. The logic and reality of Pax Americana has worked well by its first main criterion, "making the world safe" and keeping global peace, despite the stresses of the long cold war. Whereas between 1850 and 1900 over 20 million war deaths afflicted a world population below two billion, and between 1900 and 1950, over 60 million war deaths afflicted a world population yet to reach three billion, from 1950 to 2000, there were only around ten million war deaths for a world population that grew to well over five billion (Castells 1996, 458). Pax Americana is thus very real. But is it very just? Promises to deliver the means to future prosperity and justice metamorphose into quests for somewhere to pin blame for failed states. In the meantime the world has, after all, changed radically. The actual nation-states of the world mostly do not deliver prosperity and justice in due proportions. Nongovernmental organizations and diasporas change the basic terms of civil and political order. But none of these matters appear in the manual as anything more than obstacles and tangible factors to be managed by the counterinsurgents in quest for their mysterious global enemy. The death counts rise, partly in proportion to the threats that we feed and partly in the places we still cannot see. Pax Americana is at risk, and what it needs from us, I think, is, above all, clearer critiques of its ways, means, and limits.

: : **NOTES** : :

1. The most contemporary uses of the idea of "moral economy" stem from historian E. P. Thompson's 1971 article "The Moral Economy of the English Crowd in the Eighteenth Century." Thompson's usage has created an ambiguity. He sometimes seems to be discussing a social-evolutionary stage of economy and society and at other times, especially in his later discussions, the cultural and ideological aspects of all economic institutions. The first usage is the road I will not be taking. It depicts a moral economy as a virtuous and traditional understanding of human relationships as opposed to a modern , amoral, and more purely economic understanding. Thus, for another example of this view, Wikipedia's first definition of moral economy is "an economy that is based on goodness, fairness, and justice" (http://en.wikipedia.org/wiki/Moral_economy). I see many problems with this usage, including the once-upon-a-time idea that in the past people were fair, just, and good inside some kind of generalized traditionalism and the equally confused idea that at present there are no cultural values orienting economic and other institutions. My own definition of moral economy, stated in the text, is closer to the second sense discussed in the Wikipedia: "a name given in economics and anthropology to the interplay between cultural mores and economic activity." This Wikipedia discussion still maintains the connection between moral economy and traditionalisms whose mores limit profits. My own sense takes Thompson's anthropologically informed concept deeper into an economic anthropology, using one vocabulary for all economies and societies. It rejects absolutely the misleading conceptions of traditional versus modern societies. In my usage, to discuss the moral economy of any social institution is to discuss the meaningfully, culturally, morally inscribed roles intrinsic to it. One could speak of "the culture" of an institution, the culture of the stock market, the culture of counterinsurgency, and so on. But "culture" as a term has usually been deployed to discuss congeries of institutions with their own coherent interrelationships that are constitutive of a whole field of social relationships. To speak of the moral economy of an institution is thus to speak of its cultural content and dimensions, something like the chronotope of a discourse genre. In this usage, "economy" shades back into the Aristotelian sense, the division of labor and budgeting of a household, and emphasizes that the roles in the institution must work together in operation, just as "moral" implies not merely cultural but ethical, ends-oriented justifications available especially for the social roles thought central to the institution. The moral economy of war is Clausewitz's topic, and our own, and we are particularly interested in the contradictions within the moral economy of counterinsurgency.

2. Comparing Napoleon Bonaparte with his shallow and reckless nephew, Louis Napoleon, Marx observed, "Hegel remarks somewhere that all great world-historic facts and personages appear, so to speak, twice. He forgot to add: the first time as tragedy, the second time as farce" (Marx 1978 [1852], 594). The Manhattan Project marked the dawn of something that might or might not be a tragedy—I actually think its outcome remains to be determined . And the Minerva Project may yet mark the dusk of Pax Americana with intellectual farce. But let us hope for more than owls of Minerva, or even Angels of History. We need new routes out of tragedy.

3. Compare Ranajit Guha's original depiction of the central problematic of the "Subaltern Studies" school in South Asian history writing: the failure of the nation to come into its own (Guha 1982). I think the problems are not merely similar but also connected and that the political failures of the U.S. military make the contradictions of Pax Americana all the more conspicuous. Thus there is more than one reason to focus our political anthropology here, regardless the difficulties posed for ethnographic research.

4. "Lost cause" stories often provide fantasy wish fulfillments covering up major failures—see also Jacobsen, this volume. For another famous lost cause story, see Cohn and Silvio (2002), who argue that post–Civil War U.S. narratives of Dixie as heroic defense of chivalric traditions managed to win the peace in U.S. public and military memory after losing the Civil War. As Cohn and Silvio document, increasingly in twentieth-century public monuments and public memory, the U.S. Civil

War moved from a war over slavery to an unnecessary misunderstanding and a failed defense of regional autonomy and spirit.

5. A particularly disturbing example is the angry and obscure official U.S. Veterans Day poster for 2006 (Figure 4.1). It is strikingly different from all other such posters, which can be seen at the official Web site, http://www1.va.gov/opa/vetsday/gallery.asp. With boots on the ground in Iraq, and while the party in power was losing votes for promoting this unpopular war, the poster showed us the back of the boots of soldiers walking away, and declared that "To be a veteran one must know and determine one's price for freedom."

SECTION 2

ETHNOGRAPHIC EXPERIENCES OF AMERICAN POWER IN THE AGE OF THE WAR ON TERROR

:: JEREMY WALTON *and* SEAN T. MITCHELL ::

An observation, both real and surreal, both mundane and fantastic: the United States of America, omnipresent, ubiquitous yet curiously opaque, sometimes even stealthy. American military, American products, American media; desire for it, resentment of it, orientation to it, patronage from it. Across particularities of space and place, nation, language, and culture: USA. Yet this USA has hardly been uniform in its nature or effects, however global its horizons. The power that it marshals and represents has long been manifold. How might anthropologists locate American power within and across divergent contexts? This section explores the ways in which American power has been experienced, understood, imagined, and produced in the age of the War on Terror. Both the subject of critique and the object of aspiration, an apparently unipolar and definitely bellicose United States has become conspicuously central to political and social imaginaries worldwide. Of course, the mediations of these imaginaries are subject to local specificities of history, culture, and politics—the domain of ethnographic inquiry.

Together, these papers form a multifaceted inquiry into the modalities of American power outside of the hot theaters of U.S. troop deployment, Afghanistan and Iraq. In different ways, they consider how the images, discourses, and effects of global counterinsurgency or the "long war" have been deeply dependent on, and also generative of, the specific histories and contingencies of local situations. These papers consider sites, discourses, and anxieties from across hemispheres, from Brazil to the Palestinian territories, from Turkey to southern Uganda to the Los Angeles basin. Even those contributions that focus explicitly on the materialities and ideologies of the American military underscore the multiplicity and complexity—or, to use Mihir Pandya's phrase, borrowed from Ernst Bloch, the nonsynchronicity—of the productions and predilections of American power.

As a thematic ensemble, these five papers develop a loose narrative of the modalities of American power as both material production and ideological effect. In the first two essays, Sean T. Mitchell and Jeremy Walton examine localized discourses that articulate fantasies of American power in unexpected, instructive ways in contemporary Brazil and Turkey, respectively. Here we venture into the murky domain of conspiracy theory. As the familiar saying goes, "Just because I'm paranoid doesn't mean they're not out to get me." And just because some of the narratives discussed by these papers are implausible and paranoid—in fact, sometimes, nuttily wrong—does not mean that they are not on to something. In different ways, these papers set themselves to the difficult task of addressing the social importance of narratives that are false or unverifiable without taking the easy paths of either (1) merely demonstrating the functional coherence of these narratives or (2) merely debunking them, as neither of these two theoretical choices shed much light on the actual workings of power. The ethnography of fantasies of American power and their stunning boost in popularity offers a glimpse of a very real USA beyond the control of American authors.

Amahl Bishara and Liz Garland shift our attention to politically saturated contexts in which the very act of recognition or affiliation with the USA can be a matter of life and death. Through her vivid rendering of a single night of violence in the West Bank city of Nablus during the Second Intifada, Bishara interrogates the effects of both successful and unsuccessful laminations of American power upon physical objects and Palestinian subjects alike. In her equally riveting account, Liz Garland traces the disjunctures of her own experience as an American political subject, first in a moment of violence and dangerous hostility in southern Uganda following the Rwandan genocide, then as a witness, defined by presupposed commitments and complaints, within American courts. As Garland experienced and eloquently explains, the arrival of the War on Terror changed almost everything for the criminal and judicial proceedings involved. In effect, the murderous gang was recategorized from criminal to terrorist. If Mitchell and Walton focus our attention on imaginaries of American power and some of their oblique ideological and material referents, Bishara and Garland introduce us to the material invasiveness of American power and its complex effects in people's lives.

Finally, Mihir Pandya directs attention to the production of American power at its most material: the arms industry in Southern California. Here we are offered crucial ethnographic insight into the relationship between the material production of technologies of destruction and deterrence and the ideological production of American power within war- and peace-making institutions. As Pandya shows, temporality matters. The stealth bomber, a cold war idea, gained material form and the need for function in the age of the War on Terror. Weapons systems in development for years have to be geared to multiple imagined futures and institutional timelines and are not necessary adaptable to the contingencies of any one present.

On the whole, these authors share a concern for the dialectic of visibility and opacity, the play of display and disavowal in contemporary American power. The spectacularly visible and sometimes brutally tangible projection of U.S. power in the age of War on Terror has been complicated by fateful nonsynchronicities and by that power's (occasional) opacity and, sometimes, deliberate stealth.

5

Paranoid Styles of Nationalism after the Cold War

Notes from an Invasion of the Amazon

:: SEAN T. MITCHELL ::

Virtual World Wars

In the imaginations of its most paranoid U.S. proponents, the early twenty-first century's "global War on Terror" (GWOT)[1] is a fourth world war.[2] Yet, despite its many global effects, GWOT has not (thankfully) attained the world-encircling, world-threatening totality that the wars of the twentieth century brought to our planet. Nonetheless, while war in the early twenty-first century does not rage hot everywhere, it does impact politics and political imaginations everywhere. And, unlike in earlier periods of war, images, narratives, and anxieties about global war and its protagonists—particularly, the United States—circulate as they are produced and transformed instantly, globally, and nonhierarchically through the Internet. In this chapter, I examine the spread of the idea—today pervasive in Brazil and circulated through the Internet—that the United States plans a military takeover of the Amazon basin[3].

Since the start of GWOT, a long-standing Brazilian anxiety about an invasion of the Amazon has become widespread, migrating, in particular, from right-leaning groups in the military to left-leaning groups outside of it. This anxiety is partially the result of historical and social conditions, including the historical and contemporary projection of U.S. power itself and the enduring importance of the Amazon to Brazilian nationalisms.[4] But it is also the partially contingent result of the spread of Internet rumor. A series of virtual (and often fraudulent) maps, textbook pages, and other pieces of evidence of an imminent U.S. invasion of the Amazon have circulated widely in Brazil, picking up tokens of authenticity and becoming central to popular nationalisms. During nearly three years of ethnographic research into the conflicts around Brazil's fraught spaceport in Alcântara, on the eastern fringe of the Amazon forest,[5] I found that this virtual trail of evidence about a planned Amazon invasion shaped many people's understanding of the politics of the spaceport and of the nation[6]—even among people with no access to these documents or to the Internet but who had learned of them through word of mouth.

Finally, I suggest that ethnographers interested in shedding light on "order and violence in the current era," as this volume's introduction puts it, should be attentive to the social life of U.S. power worldwide. We should address its social and material effects, to be sure, but to understand the world of Pax Americana, we need also to produce fine-grained analyses of the historically and culturally mediated anxieties and fantasies that emerge in the face of U.S. power's danger, ubiquity, and opacity.

Invasions of the Amazon

In light of this discussion of ubiquity and opacity, consider an article from the June 2002 *Week in Review Section* of the Sunday *New York Times*. Reading it, one might forget that there is any power at all operating behind the scenes in international relations:

> Put reason aside, for a moment, and imagine this: American students are taught that the Amazon should be taken away from Brazil and made into an "international reserve" under United Nations administration. United States Army Special Forces are training in Florida to seize control of that zone once it is established. And, to accelerate the process, Harvard University advocates the immediate dismemberment of Brazil. All of this, of course, is pure imagination. The Brazilian Imagination. (Rohter 2002, 4)

Yet, the imaginaries that animate U.S.-Brazilian relations and Brazilian rumors of the foreign takeover of the Amazon are neither "pure" nor exclusively "Brazilian." They are informed by a complex history.

Accusations of foreign sabotage, espionage, piracy, and imperialism in the Amazon are not new. Taking up some 60 percent of Brazil's contemporary landmass and sparsely populated, the region and its people have never been under the confident control of metropolitan elites. In 1689, for example,

Samuel Fritz, a Jesuit born in Bohemia, was forbidden from returning to the Yurimagua village where he had set up a mission. He was suspected of espionage, and the Portuguese crown was concerned about its control over the upper Solimões. Finally, after eighteen months of waiting, the crown granted permission for Fritz's return to the forest, but only if accompanied by Portuguese troops who would see to the crown's territorial claims (Wright and Cunha 2000, 352; see also Hemming 1978, 437–8).

This fear of the vulnerability of the empire's Amazonian borders and of the alterity of its inhabitants motivated a series of eighteenth-century initiatives by the Portuguese crown to transform the region's inhabitants. The abolition of indigenous slavery in 1755,[7] the transformation of religious villages into towns with civil administration, and the encouragement of intermarriage between whites and Amerindians were attempts to secure and to create Portuguese subjects in the forest and thereby to help secure the borders against potential foreign invasion (Fausto 1999, 57).

The idea that Brazil must take measures to prevent foreigners from working with indigenous peoples in order to prevent the erosion of sovereignty in the Amazon resonates closely with concerns of many contemporary nationalists (see Faria 2007). Many of the documents that have circulated on the Internet, producing a storm of anxiety in Brazil about the Amazon's sovereignty, have their origin on a Web site entitled *"Brasil, ame-o ou deixe-o: Uma velha frase, uma nova necessidade"* [Brazil, Love It or Leave It: An Old Phrase, a New Necessity].[8] The site, which has not been updated since June 10, 2000, prior to the start of GWOT, is run principally by retired military officers from the *Clube Militar* ('Military Club') in Rio de Janeiro (Sedrez 2000a, 29). The many articles on the site are concerned primarily with a perceived foreign assault on Brazilian sovereignty through the internationalization and invasion of the Amazon (moved along by a supposedly antinational alliance between foreign nongovernmental organizations and Brazilian indigenous peoples); the foreign acquisition of Brazilian industrial firms (particularly in military industries); and the undermining of Brazil's armed forces.

One document on the Web site, cited often in contemporary allegations of U.S. designs on the Amazon, is a supposed map drawn up by naval captain Mathew Fawry in 1817.[9] Labeled "Most-Secret," the map is entitled, in the clumsy English that characterizes many of these documents, "desestabilization of the colony of Brazil"—an invented cognate of the Portuguese *desestabilização*. Although circulated as supposedly authentic, the map is actually from a 1994 novel, by Brazilian author Fernando G. Sampaio (*O Dia em que Napoleão Fugiu de Santa Helena* [The day that Napoleon escaped from St. Helena]), a speculative historical novel rich with international conspiracies, in which Napoleon escapes from exile in St. Helena to Brazil in a submarine built by Robert Fulton. To a native speaker of English, the map's fraudulent character is immediately obvious, with its frequent misspellings of English words—referring to "mape" rather than "map," for example, and picturing the "Soveiragny State of Amazon."

In spite of its recent origin as fiction, the map is widely circulated and cited as though it were a historical document, and it conveys a kind of conceptual map of nationalist anxieties about the Amazon. The map breaks up South America into a series of parcels, some marked "sovereign" and others, "colonies." Much of Spanish America is as one might see it on a contemporary map. Nonetheless, Ecuador finds its way to the east coast of South America in what is today Brazil's northeast; contemporary Bolivia bears its colonial name "Higher Peru," and, echoing contemporary accusations that the titling of indigenous land in the Amazon is part of an international plot to undermine Brazilian sovereignty (see, for example, Couto 1999), neither Chile nor Argentina is sovereign over South America's southern tip: instead the area is labeled "Indian Territory." The "Empire of Brazil" occupies only about half of contemporary Brazil's territory, in the south. The rest of the country is divided into the "Bahia (autonomous province);" the "Republic of Ecuador;" and a "Soveiragny State of Amazon," complete with a notorious sounding "border to be disputed" and another area of "possible french occupation" in the eastern Amazon. Two "U.S. naval Stations" are located near the Amazon's eastern fringe.

Critics, Brazilian and foreign, often focus on the clumsiness of the language; it makes the task of ridicule, the construction of "pure imagination," easier. Yet, although clearly fiction, the document is not the product of pure imagination; it reinterprets historical events. Matthew Fontaine Maury (not the aforementioned Mathew Fawry), a U.S. Navy lieutenant and superintendent of the U.S. Naval Observatory from 1844 to 1961, advocated the invasion of the Amazon. During a period of aggressive U.S. expansionism, when U.S. policy toward Latin America was shaped by Manifest Destiny and the Monroe Doctrine, Maury thought the Amazon could provide a solution to what he saw as the problems of the U.S. southern states. Concerned with the U.S. South's lack of industry and high proportion of African Americans, Maury thought that the colonization of the Amazon by southern whites with black slaves could help resolve both issues at once. In a document submitted to the U.S. Congress, Maury declared that the free navigation of the Amazon must be won "peaceably if we can—forcibly if we must" (Martin 1918, 151).

Maury provided an oceanographic rationale that the Amazon belonged to the United States—as though the very ocean currents conspired with his ambition. As Harrison (1955, 188) puts it:

> In the compilation of his charts Maury noticed that a log floating to sea from the Amazon River would be carried by the currents into the Caribbean ("this sea of ours"), past the mouth of the Mississippi, through the Florida Channel and into the Gulf Stream. The winds south from the United States through the Lesser Antilles to the mouth of the Amazon were generally favorable. Hence, Maury felt that the Amazon could be considered a natural extension of the Mississippi Valley. (Harrison, 1955, 188)

Some of Maury's writings about the Amazon were published in the *Correio Merantil* of Rio de Janeiro in 1853 (Martin 1918, 152), fomenting nationalist reactions similar to recent ones. Brazilian metropolitan elites at the time expressed both an anxiety about the distance of the Amazon from metropolitan control and a critique of arrogant U.S. power. Teixeira de Macedo, then Brazilian minister in Washington, warned:

> The Anglo-American is totally convinced that he should regenerate the whole world, give a new form of government to all human society, and rule by his influence all parts of the world, of which he holds today the centre, because of his position, which dominates the two big oceans, the Gulf of Mexico and the Antilles Sea . . . In his work, Lieutenant Maury claims and proves that communications between [Amazonian] Pará and New York are easier and shorter than between Pará and Rio de Janeiro, and consequently it is easier to rule the regions served by the Amazonas River from Washington than from the capital of the Empire of Brazil. (Cited in Sedrez 2000b)

Contemporary Brazilian nationalists often find similar imperialist goals behind ostensible U.S. humanitarian or environmentalist concerns in the Amazon. In 2000, one year before rumors about the takeover of the forest began to circulate extensively on the Internet, the military commander of the Amazon, Luis Gonzaga Lessa, argued that the defense of the Amazon rain forest might be used as an excuse for the invasion of Brazil. Lessa predicted that military intervention mobilized to protect the environment would be a "tendency of the next decade." Indeed, because humanitarian intervention has been central to post–cold war justifications of the U.S. deployment of military power, there is a prima facie plausibility to the idea that environmental intervention could be used as a similar justificatory strategy. Lessa and other critics of ostensibly environmentalist or humanitarian foreign projects in the Amazon see them as a front for other less benign interests. Lessa contends that the real foreign interest in the Amazon is the forest's possession of "one fifth of the planet's available water, one third of the tropical forests, and great subsoil wealth" (cited in Folha de São Paulo 1999).

I have shown, so far, that anxieties about U.S. designs on the Amazon are longstanding in Brazil and draw, in part, on a real history of imperial projection of U.S. power in the region. Far from being the products of "pure imagination"—to repeat the *New York Times'* evocative phrase—the conditions of plausibility for fears of a U.S. invasion are based on historical experience and have deep roots. Moreover, one can see how nationalists in the military (often on the political right) and antineoliberal leftists opposed to the domination of natural resources by foreign capital might come together around such ideas. This is particularly so in a post–cold war neoliberal context, in which, (1) the cold war convergence of ideology and interest between the United States and right-wing elements in Latin American militaries can no longer be taken for granted and (2) foreign political and economic interests have influenced and sometimes controlled important aspects of Latin American policy making (see Cervo 2000; Harvey 2005; Foresta 1992; Hunter 1997; Zaverucha 2005). However, before 2001, the idea that the Amazon was threatened by the U.S. military as certainly as it was threatened by U.S. capital was not yet broadly and credibly disseminated in left-wing circles. It took the combination of aggressive U.S. unilateralism during the early twenty-first century and a series of contingent events on the Internet to produce the convergence of many on Brazil's political left and right around similar fears of a U.S. invasion of the Amazon.

Here is how some of that contingency unfolded.

The Rumors Spread

An important step in the spread of the virtual collection of documents that provide the evidentiary basis of popular ideas about U.S. power in the Amazon was taken on May 11, 2000. Until then, the following text (hereafter referred to as the "Map Statement") lingered on the Brazil, Love It or Leave It Web site with little incident or distribution (cited in Almeida 2000a, 3):

> A fact that is, at minimum, surprising was revealed recently by Brazilians who observe the primary educational system in the US: in the world map that is in use in some important American schools, Brazil appears divided. In the map in question, Brazil would only exist south of the Amazonian region and the Pan-

tanal, and the rest appears as an "area of international control." In other schools, teachers have students perform an exercise in which they assist in the execution of an intervention, and if necessary, war, to take the Amazon from the "destroyers of nature (Brazilians)." This is only one piece of proof that the foreign idea of intervention in the Amazon has already evolved into the operative phase."[10]

On May 11, a professor in the Department of Ecology at Federal University of Rio de Janeiro sent this Map Statement to the widely read electronic journal *Ciência Hoje* ('Science Today'). She had received the message from a colleague, and, skeptical of its content, she later claimed, she was attempting to verify its truth. She clearly had no intention of spreading a hoax.[11] Nonetheless, the professor's message was published in the journal, lending it credibility and readership.

Later on May 11, Paulo Roberto de Almeida, minister-counsel at the Brazilian embassy in Washington, D.C., wrote to the journal in order to debunk the charges (Almeida 2000a, 4). The embassy, and Almeida in particular, continued to play a role in the electronic debates over the next few years, debunking the charges at every opportunity. Almeida also collected voluminous documents and correspondence related to the charges and made them available online.[12] It is worth noting that Almeida's attitudes toward the accusations changed over time. In his early e-mails in 2000, Almeida wrote as though he thought that the rumors might be true in some limited form; he was simply quick to discount their general political relevance. By pointing out the size, diversity, and noncentralized character of the U.S. educational system, he emphasized that any such maps could only exist as aberrations (Almeida 2000a, 4). In an e-mail to the editors of *Ciência Hoje,* Almeida advocated seeking out the isolated "geography idiots in the American schools," thereby undermining claims that American intentions on the Amazon were part of a consistent pattern. By October 10, 2000, however, Almeida was no longer arguing that the alleged maps were aberrations; he was arguing that they did not exist. To many respondents, and in the most explicit and aggravated terms, Almeida wrote, "THEY ARE NOT TRYING TO AMPUTATE OUR GEOGRAPHY . . . The maps DO NOT EXIST" (Almeida 2000b, 11; emphasis in the original).[13]

Shortly after the Map Statement was published in *Ciência Hoje,* the story began to pick up steam—in spite of Almeida's debunking. Senator Marina Silva of the Worker's Party, and from the Amazonian state of Acre, telephoned Michelle Zweede, of the University of Texas's Brazil Center, for help in investigating the accusations. Zweede e-mailed the Brazil, Love It or Leave It Web site in order to investigate but never received a response. A few days later, the allegations on the Brazil, Love it or Leave It site began to circulate on the Internet with one additional feature: they now appeared to be signed by Michelle Zweede and the Brazil Center of the University of Texas (Beck 2000, 73).

On May 17 or 18, 2000, the Brazil, Love it or Leave It site pulled the Map Statement from its Web site and published an apparent retraction (Beck 2000, 73). Entitled, *Retratação* ('retraction'), it stated in Portuguese that the authors of the site

> Were greatly gladdened to observe the discussions that had been generated, bringing back to life the topic "Amazonia," of such importance for all Brazilians.
>
> However, the following has been revealed: we did not cite the author of the accusation, or the source. It has now been a few months since we put up the page and when we set about to correct the problem, we were faced with the misfortune of observing the following: because of computer problems we can no longer find the source of the news (we lost the hard disk where it could have been found).
>
> We will do all that we can to rescue the source in order to fix the notice. After a great deal of research, it was not possible to locate the origin, or to find it on the internet, or with our collaborators. Despite there being a certain consensus in our team with respect to the author (the source), because we do not have the proof at our disposal, we have decided that it would be frivolous to maintain the denunciation on this page, and we are removing it. We hope only to do this temporarily, because we remain dedicated to clearing up the problem. (*Brasil, Ame-o ou Deixe-o* 2000)

Despite this partial retraction, which is hard not to read as an admission of fabrication, the Map Statement lived on. On May 23, Cesar Giobbi, the social columnist of the major daily, *Estado do São Paulo,* after receiving an apparent e-mail from Zweede—whom he considered a trustworthy source—published a small piece reproducing both the indignant tone and the content of the Map Statement (cited in Almeida 2000a). From this point on, allegations on the Internet about the internationalization of the Amazon in U.S. junior high school textbooks often came validated by the name of the *Estado de São Paulo,* even though the newspaper had promptly retracted the piece. Yet, despite the authority that the *Estado de São Paulo*'s name lent to the rumors, for a few months there was little additional public activity.

It was not until November 2001—as U.S. bombs fell in Afghanistan and, in speeches unavoidable on television and radio worldwide, U.S. president George W. Bush denounced "evildoers" and divided the world into the forces of good and the forces of evil—that the rumors about the possible Ameri-

Figure 5.1. Fabricated U.S. geography textbook seizes the Amazon.

can invasion of the Amazon, so long the concern of nationalist thinkers in the Brazilian military, resurfaced on the Internet and spread outside of military nationalist circles, including among many on the political left.

In mid-November, a purported page from a U.S. junior high school textbook, *Introduction to Geography,* appeared on the Internet and quickly began to circulate widely (Figure 5.1). The page shows a map entitled "The Former Int'l Reserve of Amazon Forest (Finraf)" accompanied by English text as clumsy as that used in the 1817 map. This map and accompanying text, supposed to be part of a North American government propaganda campaign to ready the American populace for the takeover of the Amazon, is explicitly insulting in its description of the seven nations possessing Amazonian territory. When discussions of this map take it seriously—and there are many such on the Internet and among varied political groups in Brazil—people tend to suggest economic reasons for the imminent Amazonian takeover, particularly the control of water and other natural resources.

The text accompanying the map, in English and couched in the universalist language of protecting a treasure for humanity, reads (misspellings and grammatical errors in the original):

3. 5. 5—THE FORMER INT'L RESERVE OF AMAZON FOREST

Since the middle 80's the most important rain forest of the world was passed to the responsibility of the United States and the United Nations. It is named as FINRAF (Former International Reserve of Amazon Forest), and its foundation was due to the fact the Amazon is located in South America, one of the poorest regions on earth and surrounded by irresponsible, cruel and aufrontary countries. It was part of eight different and strange countries, which are in the majority of cases, Kingdoms of violence, drug trade, illiteracy and a unintelligent and primitive people.

The creation of FINRAF were supported by all nations of G-23 and was really a special mission of our country and a gift of all the world, since the possession of these valuable lands to such primitive countries and people should condemn the lungs of the world to disappearance and full destroying in a few years.

We can consider that this area has the most biodiversity in the planet, with a vast number of species of all type of animals and vegetals. The value of this area is unable to calcule, but the planet can be cert that The United States won't let these Latin American counties explorate and destroy this real ownership of all humanity.

[A textbox beneath the map reads] We can see the location of the International Reserve. It took area of eight South America's countries: Brazil, Bolivia, Peru, Colombia, Venezuela, Guyana, Suriname and F. Guyana. Some of the poorest and miserable countries of the world.

Despite its origins among nationalist groups on the political right, the message and the map began to circulate among anti-imperialist and antineoliberal left-wing groups (Almeida 2001, 18), in particular, among a group of Brazilian academics. This dissemination of the materials sparked an intense e-mail debate between Paulo Roberto de Almeida and some of those scholars.

Under criticism, two scholars distanced themselves from the map that they had circulated, arguing that by forwarding it to listservs they were simply checking its veracity. In an inversion of the logic that Almeida used in May 2000 when he argued that any such map, if extant, must be an aberration, these two contended that the existence of that particular map was, in fact, less relevant than the general pattern of U.S. domination of the Amazon. "We all know that the Amazon is a strategic region (geopolitically and geoeconomically) that is being occupied and exploited by 'Technical Teams' from other countries, principally by the US. Researchers argue that Latin America, and principally the Amazonian region, is the 'fountain of life,' and because of this, there is international interest in exploiting and dominating it" (cited in Almeida 2001, 8).

In response to an inquiry from Almeida about the message containing the page from the geography textbook, one researcher who had been an early source for the message wrote,

> It was not I who originally sent the message, but if you want to know who the original source was, a suggestion: go to the CIA, the FBI, or the White House, now that you live in Washington, and ask them ... Those who believe that the US relations with the countries of Latin America are transparent are naïve and frivolous. As a Brazilian, I have to be alarmed at whatever news, even if it is a hoax, that refers to whatever attempt of the imperialist Yankees against the sovereignty of Latin Americans. (cited in Almeida 2001, 15)

Opacity, Conspiracy, and the Production of Reality

As these arguments developed they ceased to focus on the veracity of the evidence available; rather, the participants deployed evidence to elaborate coherent views of the world. By playing up its anomalous character, Almeida was able to make the map itself largely irrelevant to his arguments; by playing up the map's consistency with broader patterns, the academics who had circulated the map were able to do the same.

Paul Silverstein has pointed out that, "conspiracy theories rely on a particular narrative form that prioritizes internal consistency and coherence over perfect correspondence to some referential, observable truth" (Silverstein 2000, 3; 2002). But truth in world affairs is seldom easily observable. What are American military planners thinking about the Amazon's future? Those in Brazil who believe that the United States is set to take over the Amazon are generally quick to point out the many disjunctures between U.S. statements and actions in Latin America. Unless one accepts at face value the discussion of democracy, security, and economic integration that tend to show up in non-classified U.S. military statements about Latin America, it is extremely difficult to know what covert operations might be afoot. When power is opaque, it is not only the narrative form of conspiracy theories that prioritizes internal consistency over correspondence; correspondence becomes de facto impossible.

As the maps and related documents circulated on the Internet, with multiple versions landing again and again in mailboxes,[14] the story itself began to exceed the criterion of internal consistency by exceeding itself. It became an external piece of evidence through which correspondence could be assessed.

Consider another text that has circulated along with the supposed text-book page. It reads:

> All of us have heard it said that Americans want to transform the Amazon into a world park under the tutelage of the UN, and that American school books already cite the Amazon as being a global forest . . . Well, the didactic book, *Introduction to Geography,* by the author David Norman, a book amply used in American public schools, has come into our possession . . . Look at the attachment for proof of what is on page 76 of this book and see that the Americans already consider the Amazon an international and not Brazilian area. (cited in Shirts 2001)

As Matthew Shirts pointed out in December 2001, in the *Estado de São Paulo,* this e-mail begins with the assertion that the use of such textbooks in the United States is a piece of common knowledge ("all of us have heard it said"). But, as he puts it, "We have only heard this story in the earlier emails by the same group. The authors are inventing their own reality—via internet" (Shirts 2001). The more the story was circulated on the Internet, the more it came to seem like reality. It became, for the appropriately inclined, a part of reality, even if it had never had an existence independent of the Internet. And each new piece of evidence could be assessed in relation to that ostensibly external reality.

Of course, many of these narratives in Brazil betray as little knowledge of American politics as of English spelling or grammar. After all, who with knowledge of the Reagan administration's politics and enmity toward environmental constituencies in the United States would offer an environmentalist rationale for an imperial stance toward South America during the Reagan administration? But that is not the point. In the mid-1980s, when the sinister FINRAF was created, the military regime that had ruled Brazil since it came to power in a coup d'etat secretly supported by the United States was giving up power; U.S. intervention and counterinsurgency in Central America were at their height; and environmentalists were beginning to push on a large scale for the international protection of the Amazon,[15] long held by many Brazilian nationalists to be the key to Brazilian development and sovereignty. And, at the start of the GWOT, when these messages about a U.S. invasion of the Amazon found their way into many popular nationalisms in Brazil, the United States government was declaring a planetary project of "Full Spectrum Dominance," in the name of its own paranoid and self-referential fantasy, in which the U.S. "responsibility to history . . . [was to] rid the world of evil" (U.S. National Security Council 2002, 5; see also Kelly and Masco, this volume). U.S. power is a real specter in all these facts, but in that power's ubiquity and opacity, its nuances are lost and do not even matter much; they are harnessed to, and partially generative of, local political concerns.

During the period of GWOT, as many of the chapters in this volume attest, U.S. military power achieved new levels of projection, opacity, and paranoia, while simultaneously the tools of media production were democratized worldwide. It should come as no surprise then that U.S. power should be harnessed to so many different political concerns and generative of so many "paranoid style[s]" of politics, to use Hofstadter's (1965) still fine phrase. And in the years that I conducted ethnographic research on the conflicts surrounding Brazil's satellite base on the edge of the Amazon (2004–2006), the maps, testimonies, and book pages that had been circulated on the Internet alleging an imminent U.S. invasion had become important elements in local nationalisms, moving swiftly from the political right to the political left and taking on their own complex political life (for further elaboration of this, see Mitchell 2008, 178–230).

Conclusion: The Ethnography of Pax Americana's Imaginaries

To explain the convergence of significant segments of Brazil's left around some of the concerns of its political right, this chapter has looked to the broader sociopolitical context of those concerns: the opaque but violently omnipresent character of U.S. power in the region and the world, a source of anxiety that traverses political divisions in the age of GWOT; a long history of metropolitan concern with the sovereignty of the Amazon in Brazil; the spread of global environmentalist networks and discourses that seem to call for the internationalization of the Amazon; and a common enmity toward neoliberal politics among the nationalist right and antineoliberal left. But I also trace lines of contingency that have made this popular convergence of left- and right-wing nationalisms around the Amazon possible: in particular, a series of frauds and accidents spread through the Internet in the early years of the twenty-first century.

Contemporary Brazilian nationalisms and ideas about the Amazon are rooted in Brazilian history, but they have also been shaped by contingent events in the age of GWOT. Those ideas, as I have shown, are often paranoid in their style and sometimes false in their claims, but the referent of their paranoia—and a necessary condition of that paranoia's widespread plausibility—is the worldwide projection of U.S. military power that, in the age of GWOT (as in that of the cold war) is itself wildly paranoid.

Recently, Lutz and others have called for ethnographers to investigate the "topography of U.S. power" worldwide (Lutz 2006, 593, 2002; see also Gill

2004; Kelly 2002). This goal is crucial. The contours of that topography are imagined as much as they are material, and those imaginaries shape the political and cultural contexts that ethnographers research. To understand the complex social life of the United States' omnipresent, opaque, and tenuous unipolarity, we need ethnographically and historically nuanced analyses of its effects in determinate social contexts—effects that are material, social, and, sometimes, fantastical.

:: **NOTES** ::

I thank William P. Mitchell, John D. Kelly, Jeremy Walton, Beatrice Jauregui, Greg Beckett, Daphna Mitchell Manuela Carneiro de Cunha, Dain Borges, Jean Comaroff, and Joseph Masco for suggestions on this paper or one of its earlier manifestations. This research was made possible by funding from a Fulbright-Hays Doctoral Dissertation Research Abroad Grant and a National Science Foundation Doctoral Dissertation Improvement Grant, and I worked on different versions of this paper while a fellow at the Center for the Study of Race, Politics, and Culture at the University of Chicago and at the Kellogg Institute at the University of Notre Dame.

1. In keeping with common government usage during the George W. Bush administration, I use the acronym GWOT (Global War on Terror), to refer to the wars that groups in that administration sometimes also referred to as the "global struggle against violent extremism" and the "long war."

2. In this apocalyptic vision, the cold war was the world's third world war and the Iraq War, "the second scene, so to speak, of the first act of a five-act play" (Podhoretz 2004, 18).

3. This chapter is not about U.S. power in Latin America as such but about some of the imaginaries that it has helped generate in the age of GWOT. Nonetheless, it is worth bearing in mind that, as Grandin (2004, 2006) has shown, Latin America was a twentieth-century "workshop" for the U.S. strategies of military and political intervention in the Middle East, which, as this book goes to print, have so far marked the twenty-first century. A list of just a few key overt and covert U.S. military incursions into Latin America in the twentieth and twenty-first centuries must include the Mexican and Spanish-American wars; a century of often massively violent occupations and coups in Central America, the Caribbean, and South America (in Guatemala in 1954, Brazil in 1964, Chile on September 11, 1973, Grenada in 1983, Panama in 1989, Haiti in 1994, and Venezuela in 2002, to name a few); and the George W. Bush administration's deepening militarization of counterinsurgency warfare supported by Plan Colombia, inaugurated ostensibly as U.S. support not for counterinsurgency but for counternarcotics operations. This list could, of course, go on extensively. What matters for this chapter is that U.S. military projection, in its frequent duplicity, opacity, and paranoia, is an intense matter of concern across the political spectrum and across national borders—especially and enduringly in Latin America.

4. On the importance of the idea of national territory to Brazilian nationalisms, see Burns (1995), Carvalho (1998), Garfield (2004), and Holanda (2000 [1959]); for recent analyses of the importance of the Amazon within military nationalisms, see Castro (2006), Lourenção (2007), Marques (2007), Martins Filho and Zirker (2000), and Martins Filho (2005); and for recent anthropological studies that examine national and international imaginaries of Amazonia, see Nugent (2007), Raffles (2002), and Slater (2003).

5. The spaceport, the Alcântara Launch Center, is the hub of Brazil's space program and a site of conflict over land, race, inequality, sovereignty, and development in Brazil (see Mitchell 2008).

6. I argue elsewhere that nationalist discourses about the spaceport and its relation to the Amazon tend to cluster into two broad groups (Mitchell 2008). The first I term "developmentalist nationalism." Developmentalist nationalists imagine a state-driven industrial push to create a powerful Brazil, both industrially and militarily. Bearing as it does important symmetries with the left-leaning developmentalism that gained prominence in Latin America during the Great Depression (Sikkink 1991, xii–xiii), one might expect developmentalist nationalism to have a broad base on the left. However, in contemporary Brazil, this form of developmentalist nationalism tends to be concentrated in the military, often on the political right (see Peixoto 2003). As Miller (2006, 205; see also Goebel 2007) points out (identifying Hobsbawm 1995), scholars, particularly on the left, have often underestimated the importance of conservative nationalisms in Latin America. The second, which I call "territorial nationalism," is focused on the defense of national sovereignty, especially in the Amazon. Although developmentalist nationalism today has a very limited constituency on the political left, territorial nationalism has gained wide popular support, particularly on the left.

7. The year 1755 is usually cited as marking the definitive abolition of indigenous slavery, but it is worth noting that, as Cunha points out, it had been abolished (ineffectually) on previous occasions and legal provisions persisted for the continuation of some legal indigenous slavery even into the nineteenth century (Cunha 1993). All slavery was abolished in Brazil only in 1888, making Brazil the last country in the Western Hemisphere to abolish slavery.

8. http://brasil.iwarp.com.

9. http://brasil.iwarp.com/mapa1.htm.

10. This and all other translations from the Portuguese are my own. Except when I specify otherwise, all of the correspondence about the Amazon in the following pages took place in Portuguese.

11. If she is to be made a heroine or villain in the story, she is certainly an unintentional one.

12. The material is available at http://www.pralmeida.org/04Temas/07Amazonia/00IntrDossAmaz2003.html. I rely on the documents on Almeida's Web site extensively here, but because he is a partisan source, I have done my best to verify the veracity of the documents that I have used.

13. Almeida's use of capital letters responded directly to an earlier message with the capitalized heading, "ATTENTION PROFESSORS!!! THEY ARE TRYING TO 'AMPUTATE' OUR GEOGRAPHY."

14. I have received multiple versions from Brazilian friends and colleagues since 2001, continue to receive them today, and have often heard about these maps from rural Brazilians who do not have access to the Internet.

15. Accusations of foreign intentions on the Amazon often cite statements by such diverse world leaders as Francois Mitterrand, Helmut Kohl, Mikhail Gorbachev, and Al Gore that advocate some sort of international sovereignty over the Amazon (see, for example, Oliveira 2001). George W. Bush is now often accused of having suggested during the 2000 U.S. presidential debates that the debt of Third World nations might be forgiven if they relinquish sovereignty over their tropical forests. Indeed, during the debate of October 11, 2000, Bush did suggest that poor and indebted countries might "trade debt for valuable rain forest lands" (Commission on Presidential Debates 2000). He was probably referring to the idea of debt-for-nature swaps, whereby debt is forgiven in agreement for promises of environmental conservation. Because of nationalist concerns and Brazil's relative economic strength, debt-for-nature swaps have been repeatedly rejected in Brazil.

6

Hungry Wolves, Inclement Storms

Commodified Fantasies of American Imperial Power in Contemporary Turkey

:: JEREMY WALTON ::

Donald Rumsfeld felt the hairs all over his body begin to tremble. He felt like he was listening to a description of sacred, holy matters. He didn't understand why he felt this way, exactly, but it was as though a secret emotion deep within his genetic memory had been awakened. This concealed emotion suggested that the city belonged uniquely to him. The word "Istanbul" was more important than anything else. Rumsfeld recalled the symbols of the Roman Empire that appear on the official insignia of the United States government, and felt a natural affinity for the city.

Uçar and Turna (2004, 26)[1]

This passage, taken from near the beginning of the Turkish novel *Metal Fırtına* (Metal Storm), presents a curious fiction: Donald Rumsfeld, who at the time of publication was still the secretary of defense of Turkey's longtime North Atlantic Treaty Organization (NATO) ally, the United States, is introduced as an ambitious boogie man and consummate enemy of Turks. The secretary of defense (2001–2006)—regarded worldwide as a primary neoimperial force within the George W. Bush administration—also makes a notable appearance on the packaging for another recent Turkish media phenomenon, the 2006 film *Kurtlar Vadisi: Irak* (Valley of the Wolves: Iraq), which serves as a fascinating companion piece to *Metal Storm*. While Rumsfeld is not a character in the film itself, he, the "real" Rumsfeld, is quoted on the inside cover of the DVD:

"The film is a work of imagination, it has no basis in reality." Just below Rumsfeld's cautionary disavowal, we are treated to Secretary of State Condoleezza Rice's supposed response to the film as well: "We need to win the hearts and minds of Muslims." Rumsfeld's and Rice's concern is, perhaps, comprehensible; *Valley of the Wolves'* greatest star is its barbaric antagonist, the American military. An early scene depicts the indiscriminate slaughter of men, women, and children alike at a wedding in northern Iraq by an American army squadron. Later, the audience is guided through a prurient rehashing of the infamies of Abu Ghraib, featuring an actress resembling Lynndie England and teetering pyramids of naked prisoners. Nonetheless, it remains curious that the film's makers chose to appropriate Rumsfeld's and Rice's anxieties over the film as an argument and advertisement for the film itself; through their inclusion, the purchaser of the DVD is encouraged not only to consume and to enjoy the film as a viewer but to participate in a political event as a Turk and a Muslim.

What are the horizons of the politics that these media commodities inhabit and enact? What are we to make of Rumsfeld and Rice as fetishes of American power?[2] Above all, why is this fetishistic presentation of American power so popular, so marketable, so pleasurable? On the basis of a fine-toothed reading of *Metal Storm, Valley of the Wolves,* and several other recent Turkish media events, this essay argues for an interrogation of globalized contemporary American power beyond its institutional loci and domestic discourses. It probes the logics of a "vernacular conception of power" (Comaroff and Comaroff 2003, 294) that finds its voice in the troubled registers of fantasy and conspiracy. Ultimately, I argue that these commodified fantasies of American domination and dominion articulate a nostalgia for an obvious, black-and-white geopolitical topography of power. In this longing for explicit, objective relations of power, they are evocatively symptomatic of the far less certain geopolitical era they inhabit.[3]

From a marketing and sales perspective, *Metal Storm* and *Valley of the Wolves: Iraq* constitute the most important Turkish print media and cinematic events of the nascent millennium. *Metal Storm* was greeted with astronomical popularity upon its first pressing in 2004 and has gone on to break multiple sales records for domestically published fiction. Its two authors, Orkun Uçar and Burak Turna, have each written and published a number of different sequels, thus guaranteeing the continuation of the brand franchise. *Valley of the Wolves,* for its part, spun off from a wildly popular television melodrama and was the most highly anticipated Turkish cinematic debut of the summer of 2006. The most effective coup of the advertising campaign leading up to its premiere was the private advance screening provided to select members of the government, including Prime Minister Recep Tayyip Erdoğan; both state-run and private television and newspaper outlets reported the general enthusiasm of the luminaries with their own reverent enthusiasm. All told, the film grossed over twenty-five million dollars domestically, an unheard of sum for a Turkish production. And, although *Valley of the Wolves: Iraq* did not make much of a splash across the Atlantic, it succeeded in packing theaters in Germany and other European nations that have large Turkish immigrant populations, at least until many distributors withdrew it from circulation following protests by a variety of Jewish organizations and Members of Parliament from across the political spectrum.

In addition to their immense popularity, *Metal Storm* and *Valley of the Wolves: Iraq* share a crucial thematic ground, which is, indeed, constitutive of their popularity. They are each commodified fantasies of an imperialist American power that is simultaneously bloodthirsty, irresistible, bombastic, ignorant, and, above all, imminent. What type of public do these fantasies presuppose and call into being? How does this public intersect with and interpret contemporary Turkish nationalism? Finally, if the object of these fantasies is, in fact, imperialist American power, what is the imagined nature of this imperialism in relation to hegemonic regimes of power and publicness within Turkey itself?

At the close of "The Work of Art in the Age of Mechanical Reproduction," Walter Benjamin famously identified the mode of aesthetic consumption that is characteristic of fascism: "(Humankind's) self-alienation has reached such a degree that it can experience its own destruction as an aesthetic pleasure of the first order (Benjamin 1968, 242)." Benjamin's meditations seem particularly prescient in the contemporary American moment, when (as has been so frequently noted) life regularly imitates art and it is often difficult to distinguish between Jerry Bruckheimer productions and al-Qaeda depredations. The aesthetics of self-annihilation—whether coded as news or entertainment—enjoy immense popularity in contemporary America and lend credence to those who decry the postmodern empire's political and cultural dispensation as neofascist (e.g., Wolf 2007). Nevertheless, Hollywood and CNN do not maintain a hegemony over the experience of one's own destruction as aesthetic pleasure—however much they may provide the aesthetic templates for such fantasies in other corners of the globe. Since September 11, 2001, and, more pertinently, since the beginning of the Iraq War, narratives of the threat that the United States poses to Turkey have become hot commodities. In the most extreme and successful examples, Turkey is faced with invasion, occupation, and ultimate evisceration.

The dramatic action of the novel *Metal Storm* primarily involves the bombing of Ankara and Istanbul by the American armed forces, although the detonation of a nuclear device in Washington, D.C., provides a moment of redemption and a fulcrum for the novel's plot. One crucial aspect of *Metal Storm*'s genius—and a reason for its phenomenal popularity—is its flagrant willingness to subject even the most sacred sites of the Turkish state and nation to American violence. The bombardment of Anıt Kabir, Mustafa Kemal Ataturk's mausoleum in Ankara and the exemplary site of the ritual production of Turkish secular nationalism, provides one of the most titillating moments of national self-annihilation in *Metal Storm*.

> People seemed to have lost consciousness entirely. Some ran around haphazardly, some were crying, some stared at the rubble with empty eyes, without a clue as to what to do . . . people of all ages were climbing the hill on which Ataturk's tomb used to be, running forward into the debris. Although there were a few policemen and army officers in the area, there was nothing they could do to stem the oncoming tide of people—no one was in any condition to listen to orders. They shared but a single goal, to recover Mustafa Kemal's body from the wreckage and convey it to safety. (Uçar and Turna 2004, 155)

In comparison with *Metal Storm*, *Valley of the Wolves: Iraq* maintains a rather sedate register of violence; it opts for a brand of gritty realism over explosive sensationalism. The film begins with a depiction of an actual incident that occurred between American and Turkish troops on July 4, 2003, in the town of Sulaymaniyah in Iraqi Kurdistan. The "Hood Event," as it is known in Turkey, occurred when a battalion of American soldiers arrested a group of Turkish special forces, who were ostensibly conducting a secret mission against the Kurdistan Worker's Party (PKK) separatists based in northern Iraq. After being captured, the Turkish soldiers were paraded with hoods covering their heads and detained by American army forces for some sixty hours; they were only released after intense diplomatic wrangling by Ankara. While the Hood Event only generated a few minor media ripples in the United States, Western Europe, and elsewhere, both the Turkish press and representatives from the military and government issued vehement condemnations of the affair; it marked one of a series of diplomatic nadirs between the United States and Turkey related to the Iraq War, and the status of Iraqi Kurdistan in particular. (Not coincidentally, the plot of *Metal Storm* also has its ignition point in northern Iraq.) The opening sequence of *Valley of the Wolves* intersplices a reenactment of the Hood Event with footage of a Turkish military officer sitting behind a desk in Ankara who narrates the events in a letter to a friend and fellow officer. He finishes the text of his letter with the confession that he can no longer endure the shame of the incident, seals and addresses the envelope to his friend, and extends his hand toward a waiting pistol. In fact, one of the Turkish officers involved in the Hood Event did commit suicide several months following the incident. *Valley of the Wolves* derives its dramatic impetus and narrative arc from the fictional quest to avenge the death of the humiliated Turkish officer. For our purposes here, however, we can restrict ourselves to the portrayal of the officer's suicide itself. Does the self-afflicted gun wound of the officer in *Valley of the Wolves*, who is himself the synecdoche of a shamed Turkish military, partake in the same semiotic and politic logics as the destruction of Ataturk's tomb in *Metal Storm*? What is the nature of the public that is both presupposed and broadcast here? Better yet, how do these wounds to the mass public body enact and articulate a certain corporeal and ideological coherence?

In his trenchant reworking of Habermas's theory of the public sphere, Michael Warner directs attention to the transcendent, universalizing logic of contemporary publicness—the fact that participation and incorporation within the mass subject of publicness demand abstraction from all individual particularities (Warner 1992, 377). Warner's second key intervention is to note the embodied, affective dimensions of contemporary publicness, in opposition to the sublime, tepid principle of critical rationality that Habermas originally adduced in defining the bourgeois public sphere (Warner 1992, 392ff). Finally, Warner emphasizes the performative function of publicness. A public does not exist in serene coherence prior to acts of publicity themselves; rather, publics come into being through interpellation, through acts of address themselves (Warner 2002, 67). By combining these three crucial observations—the abstractive, affective, and performative dimensions of publicity—we can arrive at a more nuanced understanding of *Metal Storm* and *Valley of the Wolves: Iraq*. Both the novel and the film performatively address a Turkish national public, which achieves a certain ironic coherence through the violence done to its own mass body. In these moments of articulation, this hypothetical national public achieves embodiment by its audience. In so doing, this public occludes and incorporates a congeries of particularities—religious, linguistic, and ethnic, among others—that would otherwise disrupt its consistency.

One of the most remarkable political gestures of *Valley of the Wolves* is its inclusion of spoken Kurdish—a language that was only recognized by the Turkish state in 2002—and, more generally, its fraternal presentation of Turks and Kurds, equal victims of predatory American interlopers. From the perspective of the national mass public, *Metal Storm* contains a similar dramatic (re)constitution of the national body as multi- or postethnic. Civan, a Kurdish-American F-18 pilot, is sent on a mission to bomb Anıt Kabir, Ataturk's tomb (this scene occurs prior to the actual destruction of the tomb, described earlier). As he approaches his target, he recalls his childhood in Diyarbakir, the largest city in Turkish Kurdistan, prior to the first Gulf War, and his father's promise that he would one day return to his homeland, a promise that has now been ironically realized. At the last moment, he changes his mind, abandons his mission, and chooses to use his jet, kamikaze fashion, as a weapon against his own aircraft carrier, the USS *George Bush* (Uçar and Turna 2004, 142ff). Above all, the creative, occlusive logic of publicness is in question here: particular, problematic differences (in both cases, Kurdish identity) are incorporated within the abstract horizons of a de-ethnicized Turkish national public. This is, in a sense, a postmodern rendition of Benedict Anderson's famous argument concerning nationalism, in which communities are not so much imagined as viscerally embodied, often by means of violence (Anderson 1991 [1983]).

This interpellation of the Turkish national public that *Metal Storm* and *Valley of the Wolves* each endeavor to perform, however, only provides a partial sketch of the politics of fantasy and fantasy of politics that these media texts marshal. In order to complete this sketch, we must address the specific fantasies that undergird this national public. As I suggested above, the horizon of Turkish nationality within which all problematic differences and divergences are subsumed coherently is, in a crucial sense, a fantasy.[4] As Slavoj Zizek has noted, "the stake of social-ideological fantasy is to construct a vision of a society . . . which is not split by an antagonistic division, a society in which the relation between its parts is organic, complementary" (1989, 126). In respect to Turkey in particular, Yael Navaro-Yashin has admirably deployed Zizek's observations in order to argue that cynicism is an ineluctable feature of contemporary fantasies of the Turkish State (Navaro-Yashin 2002, 160 ff). I would add that this cynical fantasy of the state is complemented by a radically uncynical fantasy of the nation. This uncynical fantasy of the nation is a crucial object and project of both *Metal Storm* and *Valley of the Wolves: Iraq*.

As fantasies, state and nation are porous, unstable categories; while a pragmatic cynicism may separate the fantasy of the state from that of the nation in one context, a unitary fantasy of the nation-state, in which each term collapses into the other, is also possible. *Metal Storm* and *Valley of the Wolves: Iraq* both articulate a fantasy of the collapsible nation-state by means of a fantasy of American imperialist power. Here we return to the importance of Donald Rumsfeld's covetous desire for Istanbul and the American military's barbarisms in northern Iraq. In its distilled form, this fantasy envisions a ravenous, pernicious American imperialism that is supported by the brutal technological sophistication and sadistic indifference of the American military. This imperialism is an imminent threat to Turkish national sovereignty; as in Iraq so too, perhaps, in Turkey.

It is almost needless to point out that this fantasy of American military imperialism contradicts the diplomatic realities of the Turkish-American relationship. Recent tiffs over the increasing incidence of American arms among the PKK in northern Iraq and the U.S. congressional proposal to recognize the Armenian genocide notwithstanding, Turkey and the United States were close allies at the height of *Metal Storm* and *Valley of the Wolves'* popularity and remain so as this book goes to press. The Incirlik Air Force Base outside of the southeastern Turkish city of Adana is a key headquarters for the United States military in the Mediterranean and has played a vital strategic role in the current Iraq War. Moreover, the United States has been a staunch advocate of Turkish European Union membership, and the Turkish and American militaries regularly share intelligence and technology. How then are we to understand commodified fantasies of American imperialism such as *Metal Storm* and *Valley of the Wolves,* which fly in the face of diplomatic realities and the fact that the Turkish military, state, and government are complicit in certain instantiations of American military might?

Briefly, I propose that there is a specific narrative, epistemic mode that is characteristic of these fantasies of American imperialism and its imminent threat to Turkish sovereignty: conspiracy. A recent article in one of Turkey's most popular weekly tabloid magazines, *Aktuel,* vividly underscores the salience of conspiratorial hypotheses as both a mode of understanding and a valuable media commodity. I picked up the issue of *Aktuel* in question during a brief visit to Istanbul for a wedding in February 2008, after spotting its headline from afar: "Even Öcalan is a member of Ergenekon, and his service is ongoing!" (Yalnız 2008). Since late January 2008, the Turkish media had been in a fervor over a police raid of an apartment in the Istanbul neighborhood of Ümraniye that contained a massive stockpile of weapons allegedly belonging to one Veli Küçük, a former brigadier general in the Turkish army, associate of the infamous nationalist lawyer Kerim Kerinçsiz, and leader of a shadowy ultranationalist/fascist militant organization known as Ergenekon. This police raid lifted the veil on the activities of Ergenekon, at least partially: the organization was immediately implicated in attacks on several journalists from the newspaper *Cumhuriyet* ('Republic'), the assassination of the Turkish-Armenian journalist Hrant Dink in January 2007 (whom, in fact, Kerim Kerinçsiz had earlier sued for "insulting Turkishness" under the much-maligned Turkish Law 301), and, possibly, the fatal attack on the Turkish Council of State (*Danıştay*) in Ankara in May 2006.[5] More generally, Ergenekon, with its reputed skein of close relationships with the Turkish armed forces and National Intelligence Service (*Milli İstihbarat Teşkilatı, MİT*) was taken to be the illicit branch of a broad nationalist operation aimed at antagonizing Turkish

Kurds and other "enemies of the nation" in order to justify and legitimate a
variety of military and police incursions, such as the Turkish military offensive
against the PKK in northern Iraq in early 2008.[6]

Without entering fully into the stultifyingly Byzantine history that pre-
cedes the existence of Ergenekon itself—much of which involves NATO's Gla-
dio operation during the 1950s and 1960s and the covert funding of counter
guerrilla nationalist groups in Turkey during the civil violence between left-
wing and right-wing groups in the seventies—a few fundamental points can
be drawn from the *Aktuel* cover story. The reportage focuses on an interview
with a former chief of police intelligence, Bülent Orakoğlu, who claims that
Abdullah Öcalan, the imprisoned leader of the PKK, is in cahoots with the
ultranationalist, anti-Kurdish members of Ergenekon. The article deflects the
initial political absurdity of this claim by alluding to the traditional, spectral
antihero of Turkish conspiracy theories: the "deep state" (*derin devlet*), which,
regardless of the apparent maneuvers and goals of politicians, state bureaucrats,
and military figures, is the ultimate, hidden base of military-political power in
Turkey and the cause of all superficial events.[7] Crucially, according to the article, the deep state, along with its avatar Ergenekon (and, in this case, Abdullah
Öcalan as well), is merely a tool for an international political plot ultimately
attuned to the NATO and Central Intelligence Agency (CIA) agenda known
as the "Greater Middle East Project" (*Büyük Ortadoğu Projesi*). It is only by
virtue of this ultimate geopolitical conspiracy, determined by an American
military dispensation, that the statement "Öcalan is a member of Ergenekon"
achieves a logic: all local actors, regardless of whether they happen to be ultranationalist "gray wolves" (*bozkurtlar*) or separatist Kurdish militants, are
ultimately pawns in a much broader American game of geopolitical chess. Furthermore, this appeal to the machinations of NATO and the CIA undergirds
a single conspiratorial narrative of disparate Turkish political crises, including the Susurluk scandal, the postmodern coup of February 28, 1997, and the
murder of Hrant Dink, among others (Yalnız 2008, 24–27). Although it may
appear *as if* disparate political motivations and actors are responsible for these
different events, the logic of conspiracy demands that they are all epiphenomenal to the ultimate plot, which is open to constant speculation but never full
comprehension.

Hypotheses of conspiracy also constitute an ineluctable mode of vernacular knowledge production in contemporary Turkey (Silverstein 2002, 646).
Throughout my fieldwork, I was confronted with catchall, conspiratorial explanations for the contemporary topography of global power, and American
influence in particular. September 11, 2001, was, predictably, a frequent object
of speculation, and anti-Semitic fantasies of secret Jewish cabals were com-

monplace in discussions of both Turkish and American economic and political affairs. Crucially, however, the vernacular quality of conspiracy in Turkey is inseparable from its mass mediation.[8] As a media commodity, conspiracy militates against the distinction between news and entertainment. While the article from *Aktuel* discussed above counts as news, a similar conspiracy of American power is a clear aspect of the entertainment provided by the *Valley of the Wolves: Iraq* and *Metal Storm*. In one non sequitur scene in the middle of *Valley of the Wolves,* a Jewish-American doctor, played by graying American actor Gary Busey, is depicted in an anonymous medical facility (presumably somewhere in Abu Ghraib) as he harvest organs from deceased prisoners. The organs are placed in small ice chests, labeled according to their destinations: New York, London, Tel Aviv. Here the scandal of Abu Ghraib is repackaged as entertainment in order to serve as a piece in the puzzle of a conspiracy that is only alluded to. *Metal Storm* ups the conspiracy ante even further: at different points in the novel, Armenian and Greek territorial aspirations, international support for a Kurdish nation-state, evangelical Protestantism, an American energy corporation's desire to control Turkish supplies of boron, and old-fashioned racism are each adduced as the real reasons behind the American attack.

Conspiracy is crucial to mediating and reconciling the tension between a cynical fantasy of the Turkish state and a deeply uncynical fantasy of the Turkish nation. Through the fantasy of conspiracy theory, the cynical awareness of state corruption (Navaro-Yashin 2002) is subsumed within the presumed threat to the sovereignty of the nation. In other words, *Metal Storm, Valley of the Wolves: Iraq,* and *Aktuel* each articulate a coherent national public that is both the object and creation of conspiratorial intervention from the outside. This is the fantasy of conspiracy, and its political consequences should not be underestimated. Indeed, even as I write, I idly keep one eye on the Turkey-Germany Eurocup semifinal match being played in Basel, Switzerland, and am struck by the similar ideological, identitarian horizons of the passionate Euro-Turk hooligans and texts such as *Metal Storm* and *Valley of the Wolves.* Conspiracy, like fandom, imagines a coherent corporate body—a nation, its team—threatened from without, whether by shadowy global cabals or strapping young, foreign men on a pitch.

Unlike football, however, conspiracy is more than a means of performing neo-Durkheimian collectivity. As an epistemic and narrative mode, conspiracy theory exceeds nations, states, and their oft-muddled internal politics. The commodified conspiracies that are so prominent in the contemporary Turkish media and market are also symptomatic of globalized regimes of military and political power, however obliquely.[9] Rummy's sneer and Condi's paternalistic caution are important. As a conclusion to this essay, I would like to meditate briefly on the relationship between conspiracy theories and the modalities of power that they take as their object.

In the era of a post-9/11, globalized Pax Americana (Kelly 2003), multiple ideologies and interpretations of American power compete for precedence. From different vantages, American power, in military, civilian, and cultural-economic forms (and, one might add, as institutionalized by such international bodies as the United Nations and World Bank) exists simultaneously in different modalities: neocolonial and imperialist, regulatory and peace-keeping, paradoxically hegemonic and liberatory. While adjudicating among these conjugations of American power is beyond the scope of a paper such as this, I nonetheless argue that commodified conspiracy theories such as those of *Metal Storm* and *Valley of the Wolves* demand serious attention as a means of comprehending, contextualizing, reinscribing, and contesting contemporary American power. Such attention does not take the claims of conspiracy theories at face value, but it also resists dismissing them as mere mad ravings or militant rants.

In closing, I would like to propose an understanding of conspiracy theory as an imperial epistemology, in Hardt and Negri's sense of the term "imperial" (2000). In this understanding, conspiracy would represent a nostalgia on the part of imperial subjects for modern, imperialist regimes of power, power that is not yet deterritorialized, not yet disperse. And indeed *Metal Storm, Valley of the Wolves,* and the more recent reportage on the crepuscular Ergenekon organization each suggest such a nostalgia for located, objective power, a power that can be accurately identified as American. On the other hand, they also evince a potential for commodification and practices of consumption that extend beyond a simple focus on biopower, empire, and their multitudes. After all, biopower also produces open wounds; imperialism can serve as a means to postmodern empire; and the multitude persists in consuming fantasies of and for itself. Pace Hardt and Negri, contemporary global power is too multitudinous, too diverse, and too fragmented to be identified as merely territorial or deterritorialized, merely military or economic or cultural, merely imperialist or imperial. Accordingly, fantasies of the geopolitical modulate among its many poles, rendering power coherent and comprehensible in contextually specific ways. Conspiracy theories, like those I have explored in this paper, are a vivid, often highly profitable genre of such renderings.

By the end of *Metal Storm,* Donald Rumsfeld has assumed the throne of the American presidency, but his dreams of Istanbul have been thwarted. The rapacious American military ultimately overextends itself, and Turkey is saved, no small thanks to a helping hand from Vladimir Putin. The reader closes the cover of cheap paperback, but the fantasy and its public do not dissipate immediately or thoroughly. Geopolitical realities may reassert themselves on the cover of the next newspaper that the reader purchases: American imperialism is not, after all, an imminent threat to Turkish sovereignty. But this reality does not contradict the fantasy, the imagination: the United States looms dangerous and inclement, nonetheless.[10] And it is in this indeterminant space between geopolitical realities and commodified fantasies that contemporary American power achieves some of its most vexatious and unexpected iterations.

:: **NOTES** ::

1. All translations from Turkish texts are my own. I would like to thank Paul Silverstein, Yael Navaro-Yashin, Bea Jauregui, Sean T. Mitchell, and John Kelly in particular for their precise reading and suggestive, incisive comments.

2. I invoke the category of the fetish, in both its Marxian (1977) and anthropological sense, to indicate a sign that simultaneously embodies, articulates, and yet also exceeds a thorough understanding of the structures of power that it represents.

3. I should note that, in a certain respect, the scope of my analysis is necessarily limited by the fact that I did not have the opportunity to conduct thorough research on the readership and audiences of these media texts. Therefore, I rely on a sort of textual ethnography, a method by which I imagine myself recruited to the role of ideal reader or audience member myself.

4. Implicitly, all publics, in their performative mode, involve a fantasy of coherence, although a thorough discussion of the nuances involved in synthesizing the theory of contemporary publics with that of fantasy is beyond my limited scope here.

5. Further evidence of a connection between Ergenekon and Alparslan Arslan, the gunman in the attack on the Council of State, was presented in a Turkish court as recently as July 2008.

6. As this volume goes to press, the Turkish media is aflame with further arrests of Ergenekon suspects, who are claimed to have plotted a coup against the ruling Justice and Development Party (*Adalet ve Kalkınma Partisi*) of Prime Minister Recep Tayyip Erdoğan and President Abdullah Gül, a "post-Islamist" party that advocates European Union membership and toleration of public expressions of Islamic piety, such as the wearing of the headscarf by women in Turkish universities. See Mustafa Çoşkun (2008).

7. See also, in this regard, Nobel Laureate Orhan Pamuk's novel *Snow* (2004), which amounts to a prolonged meditation on and fantasy of the secretive, conspiratorial relationships among Turkish politicians, intelligence officers, military and paramilitary groups, and Islamists, among others.

8. And, I might add, from the strategic silences and tacit approval of the Turkish state. The relationship between official state discourse and conspiracy, both in Turkey and across contexts, is one that demands more careful scholarly scrutiny.

9. And, certainly, conspiracy theory is by no means a uniquely Turkish phenomenon. For a recent anthropological overview of variations of conspiracy theorizing in different national contexts, see the collection *Transparency and Conspiracy. Ethnographies of Suspicion in the New World Order* (West and Sanders 2003).

10. For a meditation in the American press on this dynamic of conspiracy with specific reference to *Metal Storm*, see Schleifer (2005).

7

Rwandan Rebels and U.S. Federal Prosecutors

American Power, Violence, and the Pursuit of Justice in the Age of the War on Terror

:: ELIZABETH GARLAND ::

In 1999, the headquarters of a national park in southwestern Uganda was attacked by an armed force of more than one hundred Rwandan Hutu rebels, who abducted and subsequently murdered a Ugandan park warden and eight Western tourists, including two U.S. citizens. I was conducting fieldwork in the park at the time of the raid and survived the incident by luck, when the rebels failed to search the part of the campsite where I was hiding. While an attack on tourists in central Africa may seem far removed from the anti-Islamist conflicts at the center of the War on Terror rhetoric, the ensuing international efforts to identify and punish the perpetrators of the raid provide a telling glimpse into the operation of U.S. power under the Bush administration, the ways American power is apprehended and engaged by the United States' foreign collaborators in the antiterrorism crusade, and the violent processes that are sometimes spawned as a result. At a personal level, the incident and its aftermaths have also served, for me, as a particularly visceral instantiation of the ironies and moral compromises inherent in the vision of justice promulgated by the United States in the course of the War on Terror.

My own experience of the raid on the park in Uganda was profoundly mediated by my status as an American citizen. While I was hiding in my tent that morning, frantically wondering if the rebels would discover me, one of the many contingency plans I hatched in the event that they did was to show them my U.S. passport, in the incoherent hope that they might think twice before harming a citizen of such a powerful nation. As it turns out, such a move on my part would have been the gravest of mistakes, for as we later learned from notes left on the bodies of the victims, the rebels were specifically targeting American and other "Anglophone" tourists, in order to protest U.S. and British support for the current, Tutsi-dominated governmental regime in Rwanda. In spite of the dangers of being a U.S. citizen that morning, however, I was quite grateful for my American status later that afternoon, when the U.S. ambassador to Uganda sent a chartered airplane to evacuate me and two other American survivors from the park. The other Western survivors of the raid were permitted to fly out with us on the same flight, but it was clear to us all—and to the village full of terrified Ugandans we left behind—that our capacity to be whisked to safety derived from the power, wealth, and largesse of the American government.

Just days later, U.S. officials launched a formal investigation into the incident, which, based on the rebels' stated intent to harm Americans, they labeled an act of international terrorism. My first experience of this investigation came when I was debriefed by security officials and Federal Bureau of Investigations (FBI) agents at the U.S. embassy in Kampala. I remember being shocked by the officials' near total ignorance of security issues in the southwestern part of the country, which shares borders with both Rwanda and the Democratic Republic of Congo. The officers seemed completely unaware that the region was regularly plagued by the presence of Interahamwe rebels (remnant groups of Hutu extremists who had fled into Congo in the wake of the 1994 Rwandan genocide) or that these groups were a constant source of anxiety to the rural population. More fundamentally, the U.S. investigators seemed not to know even the most basic information about the Rwandan genocide itself—for example, that extremist Hutus had committed the killings and that Tutsis and moderate Hutus had been the victims, or that hundreds of thousands of Hutus had fled the country for fear of reprisals when the conflict ended and the current Tutsi regime assumed power. To me it seemed ludicrous that people with so little knowledge of the political or historical context in which the raid had taken place would be able to shed light on what had happened. At the time I wrote off their investigation as little more than a public relations stunt.

My impression in this regard only solidified over the course of the next year, as, in my capacity as an official victim of the attack, I received occasional updates from the FBI agents assigned to the case, describing what to me seemed like a remarkably bungling, inappropriate approach to the entire matter. In one letter, for example, agents reassured me that they had been working tirelessly in their effort to identify the individuals who committed the murders and the masterminds that instructed the rebel forces to carry out this savage, brutal, and vicious act. Enclosed was a sample poster from the State Department's Rewards for Justice program, depicting a briefcase full of bundles of fifty-dollar bills (no kidding) and offering up to five million dollars in reward money to Ugandans or Rwandans who came forward with useful information about the case. To me, the radically individualistic language of a quest to catch the "murderers" and "masterminds" clashed strongly with my own more systemic, historically grounded understanding of the rebel attack as one incident in an ongoing regional conflict in which many thousands of people have blood on their hands. I did not relish the thought that, simply because two Americans had now been killed, the Bush administration intended to superimpose its own notions of acontextual, individual guilt and innocence on the culturally specific processes of punishment and reconciliation already underway in the region. Moreover, as an ethnographer, and as an American who often visits Africa, I was dismayed by the crass wielding of American economic power in the rewards campaign as a technique for relating to and gathering information from African people. It also seemed like a singularly bad idea to encourage people in the region to imagine Americans carrying around suitcases full of money as part of an effort to deter crime against tourists.

If I was unimpressed with the U.S. investigation of the incident, however, the same could not be said of my Ugandan friends and informants from the rural villages around the park, many of whom were interviewed by the FBI in the wake of the incident. They reported, excitedly, that they had been brought to Kampala by special car, put up in a "posh residential house" in a wealthy suburb near the embassy, and interrogated extensively by both Ugandan police officers and American agents. Although they were conscious that the investigators were trying to determine whether they had been collaborators with the rebels in the attack, and hence were under suspicion, they were also clearly titillated to find themselves participating in a high-level international criminal investigation. One man e-mailed me at the time to say that the FBI had promised that he could come to the States to testify at the trial, if the "bad guys" were eventually apprehended, and that he had always dreamed of coming to America one day.

Things fell silent for several years after this, until March 2003, when I got a phone call out of the blue one evening from the lead FBI agent saying that they had caught the perpetrators! They had in U.S. custody, she said, both of the killers of the American victims and one additional man who had been a leader in the raid; the men had been extradited from Rwanda earlier that day. Given that more than a hundred rebels had participated in the attack, the thought that the FBI had somehow netted the exact men responsible for the American deaths was highly surprising, and I got off the phone feeling flummoxed and skeptical—certainly not flooded with the relief the FBI agent seemed to have anticipated.

My skepticism intensified the following day, when the Department of Justice issued a press release announcing the indictment of the three men, proclaiming the arrests as a victory in the War on Terror. "This indictment should serve as a warning," said then assistant attorney general Michael Chertoff. "Those who commit acts of terror against Americans will be hunted, captured, and brought to justice." The timing of this announcement—March 2003—seemed anything but coincidental. The Bush administration was at the time in the thick of its campaign to circumvent United Nations (UN) opposition to its planned invasion of Iraq and frequently mentioned the Rwandan genocide as an example of the danger of relying on the UN as the arbiter of international law. Paul Kagame, president of Rwanda, made a state visit to Washington the week the indictment was announced and was received with fanfare as an important ally of the United States; in the course of that visit, he announced Rwanda would join the administration's Coalition of the Willing—one of only five African nations to do so. In this context, Rwanda's decision to allow the captured rebels to be extradited to the United States, in violation of its own statutory provision prohibiting rendition of Rwandan citizens to other countries for prosecution, can be understood as part of a series of exchanges between the two nations, in which the governments of both countries sought to capitalize politically on the alignment of Hutu rebels with the forces of terrorism more generally. I was distressed, though not surprised, to learn soon after that Attorney General Ashcroft intended to seek the death penalty against the three men. Upon their arrival in the United States, they were transferred to the ADX Florence "supermax" prison in Colorado, where they were held in solitary confinement as terrorism suspects for the next three and a half years as they awaited trial.

The long delay of trial in this case was due largely to the difficulty of building an adequate defense for the defendants, given both the challenges of conducting discovery in multiple foreign countries and languages and the complexities of establishing mitigation factors for the sentencing phase in a federal death penalty trial. As lawyers wrangled over technical issues relating to the discovery process, details gradually seeped out about the manner of the men's arrests and the nature of the prosecution's case against them. All three men had been captured in Rwanda in 2001, as part of a crackdown on Hutus suspected of participating in the antigovernment rebel groups operating out of Congo in the years since the genocide. They had been identified as participants in the raid on the Ugandan tourist park while in a detention camp with other prisoners, and then eventually turned over to federal agents at the U.S. embassy in Rwanda. The United States' entire case against the men, it seemed, rested on confessions they had made to FBI agents while in Rwandan custody at the detention camp. I heard from a colleague, who knew one of the translators working on the case, that the men alleged they had been tortured while in Rwanda, and the defense eventually filed a motion to suppress the confessions based on this claim. In the fall of 2006, in an extraordinary 150-page ruling, a Clinton-appointed federal judge granted the defense's motion, confirming the allegations of torture and ordering the confessions suppressed.

Lasting five weeks, with testimony from nineteen witnesses and a transcript 3,913 pages long, the suppression hearing was a minitrial in itself, during the course of which the judge had to reconcile the radically different versions of events presented by the defendants, who claimed to have been tortured into confessing while in Rwandan custody, and by the U.S. prosecutors, who claimed no abuse of any kind had taken place and that the confessions were completely voluntary. The judge's ruling on the facts presented during this hearing provides a vivid image of the process by which U.S. FBI and State Department officials collaborated with their Rwandan counterparts to extract information from terrorism suspects by means of torture. The hearing is thus an important source of insight into the dynamics of U.S. involvement in torture and into the role of extraordinary rendition in the War on Terror more generally. While this is not the context to go into a detailed discussion of this material, a couple of highlights may be observed:

First, at no time does it seem that U.S. officials explicitly asked that violence be used to extract information from the suspects, or that they consciously sought to violate and/or circumvent due process in the handling of the defendants. What they did do, however, was request assistance from the Rwandan regime in locating suspects who had participated in the raid on the Ugandan park, after Rwandan forces captured more than 2,000 Hutu rebels in security operations in 2001. There is no evidence that Rwanda was even investigating the Ugandan raid prior to this request from the Americans—it had, after all, not taken place on Rwandan soil or involved Rwandan victims. Once the Americans expressed interest, however, the operation assumed top priority for the Rwandan security forces, instantly bypassing the vast backlog of genocide-related crimes slowly making their way through the Rwandan justice system. The midlevel Rwandan officials involved in the case clearly believed themselves to be carrying out the wishes of both the American officials and those at the highest levels of the Rwandan government. They saw it as their job to extract confessions from the suspects and to do so in ways that would satisfy the Americans' desire to convict the killers of the two American victims and hence claim U.S. jurisdiction over the case.

Second, the U.S. officials relied upon an extremely narrow reading of their responsibility to afford the suspects due process, often citing respect for Rwandan sovereignty to justify their systematic blindness to the treatment the men were receiving. While the defendants were advised of their Miranda rights on every occasion that the federal agents interviewed them, they were done so in the presence of the very Rwandan officials charged with detaining them (including, on many occasions, the one said to be their principal torturer) and sent back to Rwandan custody every evening after the interviews were completed. The U.S. officials never interviewed the men outside the presence of the Rwandans. They did not visit the holding facilities in which they were kept and never inspected their bodies to determine whether they had been abused. Most chillingly, they did not question why the men frequently returned after a long day of questioning to offer evidence further incriminating themselves the following morning. They seemed never to think about what could be happening to the suspects during the night while they were back at the detention camp, in Rwandan custody.

It was a tremendous blow to the prosecution team, then, when the judge ordered the confessions suppressed as involuntary. Lacking any other evidence, the Justice Department was forced to drop its case altogether—a highly unusual occurrence, given the high profile and expense of the investigation and the fact that the defendants had already been detained in U.S. custody for such a long period of time.

As my narration of these events suggests, for me the political and legal issues surrounding the three men's extradition to the United States have largely swamped the question of what they did or did not do on the morning of the raid on the park in 1999. In spite of the terrible things they are accused of having done, and might have done to me, watching the U.S. government marshal its considerable might against them did not leave me feeling avenged or protected, but rather vaguely alienated from my country's system of justice and discouraged about the prospects for the rule of law, both in Central Africa and in the United States. On the other hand, the last word in this case in many ways belonged not to the zealous antiterrorism crusaders of the Bush administration Justice Department, but to the cooler headed, meticulous process of evidentiary review on which our national legal system is founded. I have taken comfort that in this instance, at least, the system worked as it was meant to, even if that fact is a sad, displaced sort of justice to achieve.

Time has not stood still in the years since this case was thrown out, of course, and new layers of irony have continued to be piled atop the earlier ones in this story. In the weeks following the case's dismissal, the three men were transferred to an Immigration and Customs Enforcement (ICE) detention center administered by the Department of Homeland Security in Virginia, where they remain to this day. Facing deportation back to Rwanda, and fearing further torture there, all three have petitioned for political asylum in the United States, the very country they were originally charged with terrorizing. Against the idealistic vision of the United States suggested by the possibility of asylum, however, lie the ongoing realities of the new political order forged in the crucible of the War on Terror. Unwanted by either Rwanda or the United States, and no longer afforded the free legal counsel they were entitled to while facing federal charges, the men have been unsuccessful at getting their asylum claims heard by immigration officials. Their petitions—and their lives—now languish in the same, off-the-radar, apparently permanent, legal limbo faced by thousands of other ICE detainees.

Weapons, Passports, and News

Palestinian Perceptions of U.S. Power
as a Mediator of War

:: AMAHL BISHARA ::

An American visitor to the West Bank is likely to be audience to the maxim that Palestinians are critical of the United States government but fond of the American people. One may hear a statement of this kind in taxi cab conversations or read it in post-9/11 political analysis (cf. Mansour 2005, 158). While this adage fits in a tidy sentence, Americans visiting the West Bank will find its implications to be far reaching. Palestinians' welcoming stance toward Americans is often elaborated in the form of carefully prepared meals or round after round of generously sweetened tea and coffee. At the same time, Americans may meet with voluminous expositions on how the U.S. position as the preeminent Middle East peace negotiator is belied by disproportionate U.S. political, military, and economic support for Israel.

Yet Palestinians' views of the United States and its power are more rooted in concrete experiences than these popular policy analyses suggest. I will show this by analyzing Palestinian practical assessments of American passports, weapons, and media during an Israeli incursion into the West Bank city of Nablus and in its aftermath. Especially during the hot moments of the second Intifada, the Palestinian uprising against Israeli occupation that began in September 2000, manifestations of U.S. power have been available for Palestinians to see and hear: the gold flash of an eagle emblem on the navy passport of an American passing smoothly through an Israeli checkpoint, the boom of a U.S.-made warplane streaking across the sky. During the Intifada, Palestinians have also sought to make use of their own connections to the United States as they manage conflict with Israeli authorities.

The role of passports and weapons as objectifications of U.S. power that can mediate between Palestinians and Israeli authorities warrant attention in part because of the particular circumstances of the second Intifada. During this time, Israel expanded a system of checkpoints and other forms of closure that have isolated Palestinians from each other, Israelis, and much of the rest of the world.[1] While some forms of Israeli counterinsurgency involve close contact with individuals or a presence inside Palestinian cities, in general Israel has used weapons and strategies that maintain a distance between Palestinians and the Israeli army. In these circumstances, some of the most pivotal kinds of contact have occurred indirectly, by way of objects. That many of these objects were associated with the United States is a reflection of the robust role the United States has played in the Israeli-Palestinian conflict, the international arms trade, and Palestinians' emigration patterns, as well as in widespread Palestinian mappings of the concentrations of global power.

Palestinians sometimes do come into contact with American journalists or humanitarian workers. For a variety of reasons, the second Intifada has seen a growing presence of Western nongovernmental organizations, activists, and journalists in the West Bank and Gaza Strip (Bishara 2008; Hanafi and Tabar 2005; Seitz 2003). Their presence generates the kind of contact Anna Tsing describes as "friction." Tsing's concept of friction encourages analysis of how people with different interests, resources, beliefs, and skills can collaborate. Even when it may not seem that these global connections have come to fruition, Tsing encourages scholars to analyze "the unexpected and unstable aspects of global interaction" (Tsing 2005, 3) that may lead to transformations in power relations. Although the structures of power I describe in the northern West Bank city of Nablus are quite durable, Palestinians can sometimes mobilize objects of U.S. provenance or well-worn transnational circuits of media for their benefit.

The View from Nablus

Nablus is a nearly 2,000-year-old city in the northern West Bank with a rich and well-documented history of regional and international trade in such items as soap and olive oil (Doumani 1992). It is home to one of the largest Palestinian universities, Al-Najah University, and to the Palestinian stock market.

However, for long periods during the Intifada, it was the most inaccessible city in the West Bank. Its 134,000 residents live between two mountains, with the downtown deep in the valley and neighborhoods built on steep inclines (PASSIA 2008, 335). An Israeli checkpoint at each end of the valley and restricted roads virtually all around controlled access to the city.[2] Nablus was the only city in the West Bank to which I was repeatedly (although inconsistently) refused entry by Israeli soldiers during my fieldwork from 2003 to 2005. For internationals wishing to visit Nablus without special press or other institutional credentials, as for local Palestinians whose identity cards did not specify Nablus as a place of residency, access was often a question of negotiating with soldiers or finding an illicit route of entry. The mountains were a formidable barrier to passage by foot; donkeys and off-road vehicles were among the improvised means of traversing the difficult terrain.

Although Nablus residents inhabited a narrow space, they cultivated embodied means of situating themselves in more expansive geographies. On cool summer evenings, I would sit with Nablus residents on their porches overlooking the valley, and they would comment on the bustle of a wedding procession down the street and then moments later on the lights of Israeli factories farther off to the west. Many Palestinians had worked in these factories before the Israeli closure of the West Bank tightened. One night, as we pondered the view, my host told me that from her aunt's house up higher on the mountain they could even see the distant shimmer of sunset on the Mediterranean Sea. Its beaches have been emphatically off limits to the vast majority of Palestinians since 2000. When, overlooking the valley, I exclaimed that it seemed we were really high up already, my companion, a recent college graduate with a usually buoyant air, told me with a weary shrug of her shoulders that if I turned around and looked up, I would see how immense the mountains really were.

Deploying U.S. Weapons against U.S. Passports in Nablus

Looking not only oriented Nablus residents with regards to their geographic location; sometimes it allowed them to locate themselves in global political networks. Attending to the particulars of the landscape as a "lively actor" (Tsing 2005, 29) reveals that people often gain the perspectives and traction that lay bare the structures of power through the specificities of terrain. During some nights of the second Intifada, Nablus residents watched Israeli forces bomb their city from the sky. On these nights, it was not just Israeli power that was on display. Palestinians knew that many of the most menacing of the weapons used against them during the second Intifada were U.S. made: F-16 aircrafts, Apache helicopters, Hellfire missiles, and armored Caterpillar D-9 bulldozers (Abrahams 2004). These are much more destructive weapons than were used in the first Intifada, which started in 1987. I often heard Palestinians tell heroic stories of artfully dodging bullets and throwing stones during either of the two Intifadas. From everyday asides, I knew that they tolerated much of the Israeli army's arsenal with an exhausted irritation, as when an old Israeli-made Merkava tank settled loudly outside one's house in the middle of the night during an arrest raid. Yet Palestinians described the palpable horror of hearing a low-flying helicopter roar overhead and even glimpsing its gun's red laser viewfinder on a nearby surface; they described the stunning crash of a missile falling a few cars ahead of their own as they drove through town. These new American weapons were distinctly frightening.[3]

It was not only the big weapons of the second Intifada that Palestinians knew to be from the United States; it was also many of the smaller ones. Palestinians were aware that the M-16 rifles that Israeli soldiers brandished were U.S. made. They were more powerful than the Soviet-designed Kalashnikovs, or AK-47s, that Palestinian Authority security forces were permitted to carry. Tear gas canisters were stamped "Federal Laboratories, Saltsburg, Pennsylvania" (Fisk 2001). In the wake of protests, children gathered spent canisters, and if they could not sound out the long words, if they did not know where exactly Pennsylvania was, they knew enough to associate the long strings of roman letters with the United States.

The use of warplanes and missiles drastically changed the kinds of contact that occurred between Palestinians and Israelis during the second Intifada. An iconic tactic of Israeli counterinsurgency during the first Intifada was the breaking of protesting youths' bones, which temporarily prohibited them from throwing stones (Kifner 1988). This tactic required intimate contact between Israeli soldiers and Palestinian youth. Its effects were serious, but they were also limited. During the second Intifada, extrajudicial killings of Palestinian militants carried out by missiles or helicopter gunfire put noncombatants at tremendous risk, severely escalating the possibility of violence in Palestinian cities and contributing to the bloody and spectacular aesthetics of the second Intifada (Allen 2008). The technology of airpower obviously facilitates the goal of halting insurgency quite differently than do army batons.[4]

July 6, 2004, was one of those nights when much of Nablus was kept awake by the air war, as Israeli planes targeted two militants and an apartment building that they were said to have entered. If, as Allen Feldman writes, "the perception of history is irrevocably tied to the history of sensory perception" (Feldman 1994, 407), this was an acutely corporeal history in the making. I was not there that night, but in a visit to Nablus three months later while doing research about Israel's policy of extrajudicial killings, I interviewed several people: the widow of one of the victims, a doctor who lived on the top floor of the targeted building, a health worker who arrived on the scene as the attack was ending, a Nablus public relations official, the city's unofficial medical examiner, and three other people who heard and saw the night's events unfold from their homes.

As an anthropologist primarily studying journalism, I was undertaking this research in part in order to understand how people related to Western journalists. Because I was based in Jerusalem, I did not have many close contacts in the city, and my position there simulated that of foreign journalists. During these days of research, I found that the story of that night had become notorious in Nablus. While many had first-hand memories of watching the attack, they also knew details about the evening that they could not have witnessed but must have read about or heard. As they told me their stories, I realized that they were striving to expand this community of knowledge to and through me.

The geography of the city itself sharpened Nablus residents' perceptions of the events. Those on the southern mountain had a clear view of who was being hit on the northern mountain. Those on the northern mountain saw the planes as they spit out missiles above their city; they saw the missiles glide into range. And then they listened for the proximity of the impacts. That night, which apparently began as an Israeli attempt to either arrest or assassinate a leader from the leftist Popular Front for the Liberation of Palestine (PFLP), five people were killed in Nablus: an Israeli officer, two PFLP members, and two Palestinian noncombatants.

One man, a university professor who was on the southern mountain, chronicled the beginning of the incident in terms of the sounds of the weapons. He said that the character of a sound signaled the type of weapon that had made it, and from this, he could identify who was likely bearing the weapon. He said the clash started with the sound of a small explosion; he surmised this was a Palestinian pipe bomb. Immediately, he heard the dry, clear bursts of Israeli gunfire and the less distinct booms that he attributed to Palestinians' Kalashnikov rifles. This, he told me, is probably when the Israeli officer, Captain Moran Vardi, who was twenty-five, was hit.[5] Soon after, the Israeli air fire began. The professor's voice shook with fury as he articulated the names of the planes he heard and saw: Apache helicopters, F-16s.

After the conflict had erupted, wanted men from the camp had evidently taken refuge around the apartment building, so it had become a target. Inside, Khaled Salah, a professor of electrical engineering at Al-Najah University, huddled on the floor with his wife, Salam, their daughter, Diana, age twenty-three, and two of their sons, Muhammad, sixteen, and Ali, eleven. For hours, they read the Qur'an and watched the red glow of the bullet tracers that stuck in their walls slowly fade. Missiles hit the bedroom and the kitchen. Later, his wife told me that the air had smelled of perfume from broken bottles, that in the moments of silence between the gunfire, they could hear water dripping from pierced tanks on the roof. The family made desperate calls to the U.S. consulate pleading for intervention, because Diana was a U.S. citizen.

After several hours of fire, the city fell quiet, and people on both sides of the mountain heard the soldiers call out over loudspeakers in Arabic for the residents of the house to come downstairs. Khaled Salah tried to open the door to their apartment, but he found it jammed. According to his daughter, Diana, he went to the window and called down to the soldiers in English, "We can't open the door. The door is damaged. I am a peaceful man. We all are peaceful people. I have children. My daughter has an American citizenship. I have an American green card, I have no weapons. Only my children are here. Come and open the door. I can't open it."[6] She said he continued in Arabic: "Help . . . help . . . somebody come and open the door."

Passports are not only brought out or brought up when requested by an authority; they can also be actively deployed (Caplan and Torpey 2001). Certainly, in locations of violence, passports and other documents of identification have powers that exceed the licensing or restricting of movement (Gordillo 2006; Longman 2001). But in this case as in a handful of others (Chu 2008), it is the carrying of a foreign—and specifically a U.S.—passport that seemed to be imbued with protective qualities.

Under what local epistemologies of state, documentation, and warfare might a U.S. passport—or more tenuously, a permanent resident card—act as a shield against one of the world's strongest armies? Did Khaled Salah imagine that the soldier would believe it to be some kind of "friendly fire" for an Israeli soldier to shoot at a Palestinian-American family with weapons made in the United States? I doubt it. Nor was Khaled Salah invoking a legal privilege accorded by these documents. Pleas made with foreign passports, especially the use of foreign passports to pass through checkpoints, were common and occasionally effective during the second Intifada (Kelly 2006). But, legally, holding a foreign passport did not change the status of a resident, as it was the local status of a person—whether she was on a tourist visa, held an Israeli or Palestinian passport, or held an Israeli residency card—that determined one's status.[7]

Rather, I imagine that Khaled Salah attempted to use the U.S. passport, first, to intimate his status within Palestinian society and thereby assert his innocence and, second, to suggest that killing him would cause public relations problems for Israel. The first line of this argument, that Palestinians who were U.S. citizens or residents were much less likely to be militants than the general population, worked on the patchwork logic of a few widely held assumptions. U.S. passport holders and U.S. permanent residents were generally people who had some financial resources to travel and educational or familial connections through which documents could be obtained over time. Such a person of privilege, this logic suggested, would not be involved in militant operations. As Khaled Salah himself said, "I am a peaceful man," a characterization repeated by his wife when I interviewed her later. Moreover, if one had obtained U.S. documents recently, they quite literally served as a kind of certification of being "clean," because it is known that the United States does not give residency cards or passports to anyone with significant infractions in an Israeli security file. This was an argument about the divisions among different kinds of Palestinians that insinuated that the U.S. passport holder was a "good" Palestinian (Mamdani 2004).

The second line of argument, that killing a Palestinian American would create a negative public image of Israel, was also plausible but hardly ironclad. Rachel Corrie, the blond U.S. citizen who was crushed by a Caterpillar D-9 bulldozer in Gaza on March 16, 2003, as she tried to prevent the Israeli military from destroying a Palestinian family's house, was well-known and held in high esteem in the Palestinian territories. But most Palestinians would have had no way of ascertaining the extent to which her death had gained notoriety in the United States. The Israeli soldiers on duty that night in Nablus might or might not have known that the driver of the bulldozer in Gaza had never been prosecuted.

Indeed, one difficulty in tracing out the logics of either of these arguments—that is, about local status or international public relations—is that Palestinians' perceptions of their validity might differ from Israeli soldiers' perceptions of them. But it is precisely the lack of a direct conversation on these and other issues that characterized such incidents and rendered objects like the passport so critical. The tenuousness of the logics in play is one (and not the only) reason that, as Khaled Salah called out into the night, it would have been utterly unclear how and on what basis the soldiers would respond. In this standoff between a person wielding a U.S. passport as a shield and an arsenal that included U.S. weapons, the power remained in the hands of Israeli soldiers, who controlled the weapons and whose discretion it was to recognize or ignore the U.S. passport.

On this night, chance was not in Salah's favor. The soldiers did not respond to his calls for help. Instead, a few minutes later, Israeli soldiers fired up at the apartment, killing him immediately and critically injuring his sixteen-year-old son, Muhammad. Salam and Diana Salah implored that an ambulance be summoned, but the Israeli soldiers dispatched only a neighbor to help open the jammed door. Salah's wife and daughter were forced to come downstairs with the rest of their neighbors.

By the time the building was evacuated, one of the two PFLP militants had already been killed during the ambush, while a second, Yamin Faraj, the commander of the military wing of the PFLP in Nablus, had survived injured. A doctor who lived on the top floor of the building recounted to me that the soldiers searched and bound all of the men of the building as they waited on the street. A short while later, he recalled, one of the handcuffed men was unbound and forced to drag Faraj from his hiding place. Then, he said, the Israeli soldiers shot Faraj in the head.[8] An ambulance was permitted access to the building only hours after the shooting, and by then Muhammad Salah was dead.[9]

Making News of Calamity

If the passport and residency card failed to provide the Salah family with protection from being fired at, would they provide the family any kind of recognition in the wake of tragedy? If the passport failed as a shield, might it later serve as a permit for representation, or at least for being represented? The incursion was covered by outlets including the Associated Press, the Agence France-Presse (AFP), the BBC, *Ha'aretz,* the *Washington Post,* and the *New York Times.* I surmise that one reason this night of violence received the coverage that it did was because of Khaled Salah's identity, mentioned in most of these reports. The aspects of his identity that warranted remark were his status as a professor, his family's U.S. residency cards and passports, and the fact that he had earned his Ph.D. at the University of California. That an Israeli officer had been killed also made headlines. In these international media, the extrajudicial killing of a militant was recorded only by the AFP.

Some of the articles that noted the Salahs' status were nevertheless framed in a language of just-the-facts detachment that would not likely generate readers' empathy.[10] For example, the *Washington Post* noted both Salah's education and his immigration status in ways that almost defied a (nonimmigrant) reader to recognize any qualities or experiences he might share with Salah:

> A statement by the university said that Salah earned his doctorate in electrical engineering from the University of California at Davis in 1985. A spokesman for the U.S. Consulate in Jerusalem said that Salah's wife said in a conversation

Tuesday with consulate staff that he had a green card to work in the United States. (J. Anderson 2004)

Both the *New York Times* and the *Washington Post* articles cited Palestinian sources—the Salah family and medical workers—in sequence with the Israeli military spokesperson (J. Anderson 2004; Myre 2004), a common technique that can create the impression of balance and objectivity while refraining to offer an evaluation of the facts at hand (Mindich 1998). None of the articles mentioned that some of the weapons used in the attack were made in the United States. Perhaps this is because passports are meant to confer an identity upon their holders, while the provenance of an object seems less important once it has been sold. Perhaps it is because people are recognized as actors and victims—and thus news subjects—in a way that objects are not. And perhaps it is because the use of U.S. weapons in such conflicts is matter-of-fact and no longer newsworthy.

Two articles that were written based on reporting in Nablus were authored by Ali Daraghmeh, a Palestinian reporter for the Associated Press who lives in Nablus (Daraghmeh 2004), and Gideon Levy, an Israeli journalist working for the Israeli newspaper *Ha'aretz* who is known for his incisive coverage of Israeli occupation (Levy 2004). They too focused on the professor with ties to the United States rather than on the militants. The *Ha'aretz* article, published weeks after the attack, was the longest. It provided a chronicle of the night of the attack and extended quotes from Salam Salah. Levy's article circulated on the Web far beyond the *Ha'aretz* English Web site, both in repostings and as a source for further articles in outlets as diverse as the New England–based *Jewish Journal* (Arnold 2004) and Ramallah-On-Line (Fraser 2004a). My own initial article, based on the research I describe here, analyzed the impact of assassinations and targeted killings on Nablus (Bishara 2005).

Each of these longer features articulated a distinct political position, but their authors all built upon a face-to-face interview with Diana or Salam Salah or reinterpreted such an encounter after reading another source. Certain sensations recounted by Salam Salah, like the scent of broken perfume bottles, caught the attention of more than one author (Bishara 2005; Levy 2004). Certain sentiments passed through layers of mediation. When I interviewed Salam Salah, she recounted the hours of siege in detail; from her words, I imagined that as much as they were terrified in those moments, she treasured them as the last time her family sat close together. Levy's article captured this same sentiment: "They lay on the floor, folded into one another, five members of a family like one body" (Levy 2004). This passage was reframed in a poem by activist and playwright Genevieve Cora Fraser. It begins,

Entwined as a ball
Of thread the family
Clung and enveloped
One another in love
In terror in their last
Moments together (Fraser 2004b)

Fraser wrote the poem without meeting the Salah family, apparently drawing on other available media. Yet it contained remnants of Salam Salah's narrative. This poem then itself created a cycle of more contact and mediation. The
Salah family read Fraser's poem online and invited her to visit. Fraser wrote
again about the family's tragedy after she had met Salam, Diana, and Ali and
asked for public support for the family's request of a U.S. inquiry into Khaled
and Muhammad's deaths (Fraser 2005).

When I met Salam Salah, she remained despondent, and it was hard to tell
whether media coverage was any real consolation. But her willingness to meet
poets, journalists, and anthropologists suggests that coverage meant something to her. During our meeting, she showed me some of the few family pho-
tos that had not been destroyed during the attack. They portrayed a family trip
to Colorado, her late son's birthday party, her husband shoveling snow. She
was angry at the U.S. role in the operation—not because of the weapons' place
of manufacture, but because the consulate had done nothing while they were
under fire. But still, she told me that her eldest son, Amr, was in Massachusetts,
studying to be an electrical engineer, like his father, and organizing the effort
to demand a U.S. investigation into the attack.

Conclusions

While U.S. officials assert that the United States is the prime negotiator of
peace, during the second Intifada, Palestinians have known objectifications
of U.S. power to be mediators of war. These objects have been the means by
which Palestinians and Israeli soldiers interact during a period when the possibilities for direct connection have been highly attenuated. In the West Bank,
U.S. power is not abstract: Palestinians sense U.S. power and make sense of it
in political analysis. This U.S. presence is evident for Palestinians, who viscerally know weapons by their sounds and appearances and who are intellectually
aware that Israel acquires these weapons with U.S. military aid. Yet, in U.S.
news media accounts of specific incidents of violence, the history of weapons
is generally not recognized as playing an active role in conflict.

Palestinians do not only discern U.S. power, they act upon and with it. A

U.S. passport can be a makeshift shield in a moment of peril. Given the limited resources at their disposal, Palestinians may feel that wielding their little piece of U.S. power is a worthwhile maneuver, even as they know there are no guarantees for success. After a crisis, a U.S. passport may be a kind of permit to representation of an event in Western news. In processes that are collaborative but not egalitarian, foreign journalists and researchers and Palestinian doctors, bureaucrats, militants, journalists, and others remediate and reframe incidents of violence. With vivid language, Palestinians may introduce their interviewers to the corporeal dimensions of living under siege, and they often remark to Americans that the weapons they faced were made in the United States of America. These moments of contact do not forestall violence. They do not even grant Palestinians permission to narrate their own stories (Said 1984), but at least they make space for Palestinians' statements to be read alongside those of the Israeli military spokesperson. Clearly, these developments happen within social and political hierarchies, but they also can be shaped by the distinct details of particular local stories: looming, rocky mountains and broken perfume bottles. They are fueled by the "grip of worldly encounter" (Tsing 2005, 1) that can give substance and meaning to universalist aspirations to justice. This is the generative unpredictability of friction about which Tsing writes. Although these media may not effect change, they can be "a hair in the flour [that] ruins the legitimacy of power" (Tsing 2005, 206). Whether horrifying or empowering, U.S. power is a palpable part of the Palestinian-Israeli conflict, as it is in many conflicts around the world. Under these circumstances, U.S. neutrality or invisibility is inconceivable. We can instead look to people in places like Nablus to learn about the far-reaching contours of American power and the multiple ways in which it is deployed.

:: **NOTES** ::

Acknowledgements: I am grateful to Beatrice Jauregui, John Kelly, Sean Mitchell, and Jeremy Walton for organizing the conference on Anthropology and Counterinsurgency and editing this volume. This paper benefited from discussion at the conference and from readings of various drafts by Lori Allen, Nidal Al-Azraq, Summerson Carr, and Julie Chu.

1. As of April 2008, the United Nations identified 608 obstacles within the West Bank alone, an area slightly smaller than the state of Delaware. This does not count the barriers to entering Israel itself. Gaza has been even more drastically isolated (United Nations 2008).

2. A map by the Israeli human rights organization B'Tselem, "The Forbidden Roads Regime," elucidates prohibitions on Palestinian use of roads in the West Bank (B'Tselem 2004).

3. Each year since 1985, the United States has given Israel an average of $3 billion, much of which has been military aid. At $2.4 billion in fiscal year 2008, military aid from the United States represents 20 percent of Israel's total defense budget. Of this amount, 75 percent must be used to buy U.S. defense equipment (Sharp 2008, 3–4). Israel's use of Apache helicopters, F-16 planes, and M-16 rifles against Palestinians during the second Intifada has been documented elsewhere (cf. Human Rights Watch 2002, 2005).

4. *The Journal of Palestine Studies* found that in the first five years of the Intifada, 322 people were killed as targets of Israeli assassination attempts, while 240 bystanders were killed in assassinations or assassination attempts (Esposito 2006, 196).

5. A statement by the Israeli military spokesperson seems to confirm this account (J. Anderson 2004).

6. This quote is taken from the transcript of a press conference at Al-Najah University. A related quote can be found in "Death in a Cemetery" (Levy 2004), and Salam Salah gave me a similar account when I interviewed her.

7. Moreover, carrying a U.S. passport with a tourist visa did not itself guarantee free movement, as evinced by the difficulties I faced entering Nablus with my U.S. passport.

8. An eyewitness cited in an AFP report also confirmed that an execution took place (Saada 2004). Also, doctor Sameer Abu Za'rur, who had been serving as the city's volunteer medical examiner during the Intifada, went on the record when I interviewed him about Faraj's death: "I know there are rumors that he was shot point blank. I can't say anything about those rumors. But I can tell you that above his eyebrows, there was nothing."

9. In contrast, the Israeli army's statement about the incident suggested that their deaths were an unfortunate collateral effect of the operation: "Dr. Salah and his son Mohammed were apparently killed by IDF gunfire, but there was no intention to do them harm" (quoted in Levy 2004). This statement points to one aspect of another famous conceptualization of "friction" in warfare, Carl von Clausewitz's observation that circumstances of war must be expected to be unpredictable (Clausewitz 1989 [1832], 66). One political scientist suggests that within a theory of just war, friction should prohibit certain tactics like missile attack and air strikes simply because too much can go wrong when they are used (Smith 1994).

10. For more on the history and effects of detachment as a journalistic value, see McChesney (2004) and Mindich (1998).

The Cold War Present

The Logic of Defense Time

:: MIHIR PANDYA ::

The American state's expanded focus on national defense after World War II remains largely unaccounted for in public memory. During the cold war, U.S. military spending averaged nearly 300 billion dollars annually (Center for Defense Information 1996). Most of these monies were funnelled to academic, governmental, and industrial networks that supported military-sponsored research and production. While there are significant studies about how the cold war shaped commercial (Cohen 2003), familial (May 1988), and political (Schrecker 1998) life, and insights into how the nuclear imaginary found purchase in the American psyche (Boyer 1985; Gusterson 1996; Masco 2006), the scale and consequence of the larger material architectures of national defense and their traces in American culture remain undervalued.[1] An anthropological analysis of these postwar defense networks helps reveal the cultural and institutional legacies of this formative system.

In the defense economy, diverse populations, government departments, corporate cultures, large-scale projects, strategic orientations, and funding structures move in complex syncopation. This disjointedness is reinforced by corporate and government concerns over security and proprietary knowledge. The resulting segmented production environments operate according to differing internal timelines. In terms of military-industrial production, parallel, segregated, yet contingent processes of design, manufacture, and deployment emerge, creating multiple, overlapping cultures of time. Ernst Bloch wrote: "Not all people exist in the same Now. They do so only externally, by virtue of the fact that they may all be seen today. But that does not mean that they are living at the same time with others" (Bloch [1932]1977: 22). Distinct communities may coexist in the same space, he suggests, but each can abide by the logic of a different age. Bloch labels this temporal depth in the present "nonsynchronicity." His insights about the varied structures of time within seemingly unitary economic forms help explain the achievements and the failures of defense networks that matured in the postwar period.

In this essay, I use the life of the F-117 Stealth airplane to illustrate the contingencies at play in military industrial production. The F-117 was the first airplane manufactured for combat to use Stealth technology. The term "Stealth" refers to a series of design and materials innovations that allows planes to fly with significantly reduced radar signatures.[2] This airplane's design life began in the early 1970s, and its major operational life was bracketed by the first and second gulf wars. I trace the conditions that led to the initial development of Stealth technology. I then explore the design and manufacturing history of the F-117 in order to illustrate how and why nonsynchronicity sediment in military industrial production. Lastly, I examine the operational life of this airplane in Iraq to show how nonsynchronous features within the defense economy shape the conceptual and material horizons that frame American military policy and help define its application. The life of the F-117 suggests that interpreting recent moments of American military experimentation like the War on Terror requires stepping back and examining one of the forces that structures that circulation, namely, the defense economy.

The Origins of the Stealth Project

In order to understand the production of Stealth, it is important to place its evolution within the history of the postwar joint venture between the military and industry.[3] As a commodity, an airplane is defined by its complexity and its price. Most commercial and military aircraft today have thousands of parts and cost millions of dollars to build. The industrial supply chain required to make them necessitates a depth of economic capacity that few countries possess. For example, in the commercial sector only two companies worldwide— Boeing and Airbus[4]—currently bid for the largest commercial contracts. The market that supports this industry is also singular. Governments are the usual clients for both commercial and military aircraft because only they have the institutional and financial structures to support large-scale, long-range, complex, and expensive production processes. Governmental needs define this industry's strengths and vulnerabilities. As a result, aerospace is acutely sensitive to cycles of governmental spending, political mood, and changing regulatory environments (Pattillo 1998). The current twenty-first-century capacities and limitations of military airplane manufacturing evolved through the large ruptures and institutional formations created by war, turning aircraft production into a nationalist commercial endeavor and making its uses international. In this global history, we can situate the contexts for Stealth's production and track how Stealth in turn shaped the military industrial inheritances of the present.

Integrated air defense had become the international norm by the early 1970s. These systems showcased new radar-guided surface-to-air missiles, which most combat aircraft could no longer outrun. The uneven bombing campaigns of the Vietnam War made these limitations a concern for the U.S. Air Force.[5] These lessons were reinforced by proxy through the heavy losses of the American-supplied Israeli Air Force in the 1973 Arab Israeli War.[6] Over time, the ripple effects of these losses propelled a shift in thinking about American airpower. As a senior consultant to the air force in this period described it, "fighting plane for plane . . . had become too expensive" in both life and treasure.[7]

The development of Stealth was part of a strategic shift in the mid-1970s. Overall, military planners moved to offset the costs associated with heavy losses of both materials and men with technological capability. These wartime lessons were coupled with a growing (then) present-day anxiety. William Perry, the Undersecretary for Research and Engineering in the Department of Defense at the time, would later recall that the Soviet Union and the Warsaw Pact warehoused "about three times as many tanks, artillery [pieces], and armored personnel carriers as we had, and we thought that they had a serious intent to use them, to send a blitzkrieg down through the Fulda Gap [a region of low elevations between the former East and West Germany]" (Air Force 1997). The resultant "offset strategy," as it was called, had three initiatives: Stealth; guided missile systems; and revamped command, control, and communications equipment. The Defense Advanced Research Projects Agency (DARPA) in the Department of Defense had begun work on early formulations of an airplane with a minimal radar signature. But it was soon decided that the project needed to be outsourced to private sector companies who were better equipped to develop these airplanes.

Several companies were invited to a competition to bid for the Stealth contract.[8] In a symptomatic oversight that revealed the potential costs of security-related segmentation within the military bureaucracy, the Lockheed Corporation of California, as it was then called, was not among those initially invited to submit a proposal. At first glance, this omission made sense, because most military planners thought that Lockheed's last experience in combat aircraft had been during the Korean War. Unbeknownst to the air force, Lockheed had a secret history. Since World War II, Lockheed had built highly classified reconnaissance aircraft for the Central Intelligence Agency (CIA). These planes included the U2 spy plane, the SR-71 surveillance plane, and flocks of other low-observable aircraft (planes or drones designed to have a small radar presence). Working on the functional requirements for reconnaissance meant that Lockheed had acquired some practical knowledge in masking airframes (the exterior shell of a plane) and had conducted other in-depth radar-related research. Due to the classified nature of their work, and institutional partitions within the defense community, knowledge about Lockheed's capabilities remained secret.

Lockheed entered the competition via the combined effects of two circulatory agents in the defense economy: rumor and prestige. One story recounts how an in-house Soviet weapons expert attending a conference in Dayton, Ohio, at Wright Patterson Air Force Base, heard from a colleague in Tactical Air Command about the new endeavor (Rich and Janos 1994, 23). Another version describes how a high-level engineer at Lockheed learned of the competition while probing contacts in the Pentagon for potential business (Aronstein and Piccirillo 1997, 15). No matter which story is true, rumors of the secret competition circulated, and someone at Lockheed learned that a variety of companies had been invited to build a Stealth test plane.

After Lockheed found out about the competition and tried to intervene, they ran into another barrier. They first needed permission from the CIA to share their radar-reduction test results from previous projects in order to make their case to join the competition. Lockheed attempted to smooth the path by sending their request to the CIA through their most esteemed associate, Kelly Johnson. Mr. Johnson was the famed former head of Lockheed's Skunk Works, which was and remains the premier design shop within Lockheed. He was well regarded within the agency, and he personally made the case. It worked. At the last minute, doors were opened, test results were shared, and Lockheed was allowed to join the competition (Rich and Janos 1994). The first round was won by Lockheed's Skunk Works.

The origins of the F-117 outline a part of the military economy composed of strategic concerns (in this case, compensating for Soviet numerical advantages), companies (Lockheed and others), competitions, and government bureaucracies (DARPA, the CIA, the Air Force, the Pentagon). These actors operated with seemingly necessary but unwieldy structures of secrecy. Barriers of segregation (for example, the near exclusion of Lockheed from the Stealth

competition) made for uneven flows of information. Systems of secrecy re-
inscribed rumor, prestige, charisma, trust, and affiliation—intimate interper-
sonal forms of social regulation. These cultural traits of defense production
did not dissipate when Stealth moved to the design and manufacturing phase.
They only changed forms to include other populations, sites, and landscapes.

Design and Manufacturing Timelines

The arrival of Stealth was preceded by a series of technological reorientations.
From the 1940s to the 1970s, the center of balance in the airplane business
shifted from a focus on the airframe to its interior. Enabled by the development of integrated circuits, airborne digital computers infiltrated military
aircraft. The availability of high-speed memory made digital avionics systems
capable of real-time mission software—time-sensitive computations that expanded processes like "fly by wire," where the pilot was not directly flying the
plane, in the mechanical sense, but rather his commands were being translated
digitally to the aircraft. Stealth appeared at the tail end of this industry-wide
shift from a focus on the airframe to the digital reimagining of instrumenta-
tion. The Stealth project reset the proposition. It used new calculative technologies that reconstituted the insides of the airplane to transform the exterior of
the aircraft in order to mask its presence.

In the mid-1970s, mathematicians at the Skunk Works came to the conclusion that detectable radar signatures could be minimized by discarding the
classical rounded look of an airplane. They figured out that a new craft could
be made up of the smallest possible number of properly oriented flat panels.
This led them to precisely calculate the radar cross section (RCS), the foot-
print of a plane on radar, by adding smaller flat panels into a whole, with the
aide of rapidly evolving digital technology (Aronstein and Piccirillo 1997, 16).
The Skunk Works team produced Echo 1, an RCS prediction program. However, as testing continued, it became apparent that the Echo 1 program did
not account for how electric currents behaved at the edge of surfaces, like the
triangular flat panels with which engineers had hoped to cover the airframe.

In a telling irony, the solution to this software problem came from the Soviet Union. In 1962, a graduate student named Pyotr Ufimtsev, who would
later become the chief scientist at the Moscow Institute of Radio Engineering, published an unclassified technical paper called *Method of Edge Waves
in Physical Theory of Diffraction*. This paper was translated by the Air Force
System's Command's Foreign Technology Division in 1971 (Crickmore 2003,
8). In his essay, Ufimtsev drew on the work of nineteenth-century mathema-
tician James Clerk Maxwell, which showed that electricity, magnetism, and

light are all manifestations of the electromagnetic field. Ufimtsev modi-
fied Maxwell's work to address the way certain geometric configurations—
including edges—reflected electromagnetic radiation. Mathematicians at the
Skunk Works incorporated Ufimtsev's calculations into the Echo 1 program.
While some more sober accounts suggest that both very good fortune and innovation led to the Skunk Works computational breakthroughs (Aronstein and
Piccirillo 1997, 16), the story of the Ufimtsev intervention is often repeated.
It couples serendipity with the heroic efforts of individuals and enlivens what
to the outside world may seem like less than glamorous labor. What remains
unsaid in these renditions is the discomforting reality that Soviet knowledge
powered American innovation at a tense time in their mutual history.[9]

The calculations generated by the Echo 1 program were used to make a
thirty-eight-foot wooden model of an angular, arrowhead-shaped plane. The
model was transported from Burbank, California, to the radar test range at
White Sands, New Mexico. Over the course of one month, Lockheed and
Northrop (the other finalist, also testing its model) competed to see whose
entry could consistently deliver the lowest RCS results. Lockheed won, and
its victory led to a contract for a test plane called Have Blue in April 1976. The
successful tests also propelled the air force to begin putting together the weapons requirements and other preliminary studies for the projected production
aircraft, which would be called the F-117.[10]

A systematized negotiation process commenced between the procurement staff in the air force and the prime contractor, Lockheed, for the F-117.
Through this process, specific design decisions were made about who would
do what, for how much, and when. Meanwhile, in Nevada, the test aircraft
Have Blue continued flying, and a separate team from Lockheed and the air
force compiled information about its design and use. In November 1978, the
final go-ahead was given for the production of the F-117, and a system program
office was set up in Dayton, Ohio, at Wright Patterson Air Force Base. The
actual production of the F-117 began in Burbank, California, in 1979 and continued there until the early 1980s.[11] The F-117 was then flight tested largely out
of public view at Nellis Air Force Base in Tonopah, Nevada. This process of
testing and redesigning the aircraft took the better part of a decade.

Anecdotally, it seems that labor problems were a factor throughout the
building of the F-117 and, later, the B2. For example, during the initial phases
of production for Have Blue, the shop floor workers at Lockheed went on
strike. Engineers came down and set up residence in the hangars and put the
first planes together themselves.[12] The boom in aerospace production in the
Los Angeles basin during the making of the B2—it was, after all, the period of
Star Wars and the other giants of the 1980s—and the rigid security require-

ments of the project limited the available labor pool. These problems reflect themselves in coded commentaries of the manufacturing process: "Tens of thousands of newly hired people had to be vetted for security and tested for drug use. The vetting system was swamped, and many employees spent weeks in limbo, on the payroll but unable to work"[13] (Sweetman 1999, 65). Not only were there varied projects underway related to Stealth, all following their own timeline—the Have Blue project, the F-117 planning, initial planning for a new Stealth bomber, and different contactors and subcontractors for each project—but Stealth was only a part of the larger defense economy operating at full speed in places like Southern California.

The F-117 served both as plane and as possibility. It showed that Stealth technology worked and spurred a desire within the air force and other armed forces to morph Stealth's abilities to new ends. Its flaws (the F-117's limited weapons capabilities, its lack of maneuverability in the air, and its stringent maintenance and deployment requirements) as much as its potential to travel without being seen fostered new projects. Stealth technology was immediately applied to a virtually invisible reconnaissance plane and a stealthy long-range bomber that could carry nuclear payloads. The first never made it to production, and the latter is the much-maligned B2 bomber, a fractured icon of technological sophistication and gross expense.

This manufacturing history is often revealed in technical accounts as a coherently orchestrated evolution of Stealth technology and commodities. However, my research suggests that these were somewhat disarticulated processes. Even in the well-run F-117 program, there were many segregated, parallel, and yet contingent operations occurring at the same time in California, Nevada, and Ohio. These separate but interdependent processes moved according to their own internal technical demands, institutional cultures, and management philosophies. One result of these nonsynchronous processes was that the way time worked varied in different design, manufacturing, and testing environments.[14]

In the public sphere, the military-industrial complex, as it is labeled, is something to which we almost automatically assign a conspiratorial rationality. This economy sustains a sense of coherence through procedures of secrecy and segmentation. These security requirements, like other contingencies in production, sometimes extend and sometimes shorten the lives of the processes they are created to protect. Stepping outside of these logics and examining the temporal dimensions of the defense business suggests that as a system its coherence is less than absolute; yet its influence shapes the everyday experience of many actors, even though the shapes of its inheritances are not necessarily those predicted.

The Uses of the F-117

When the F-117 flew in the first Gulf War, twenty-five years had passed since its inception. In the meantime, a major incentive that powered its creation—the Soviet Union—had itself disappeared. When finally deployed at the start of the first Gulf War, the F-117 was successful in military terms: thousands of missions were flown and targets destroyed, without a single plane being shot down. Stealth lives on through its progeny—missiles, ships, and satellites, among other weapons and systems—and, most directly, in new generations of combat aircraft. Stealth also lives on through the legacies of its use. Some of the popular accounts of the F-117's performance during the first Gulf War suggest that this plane helped military planners reconceptualize the city as a battlefield. From January 17 through February 28, 1991, the F-117 was deployed as the vanguard of the air campaign during the first Gulf War. Over forty F-117s flew 1,270 sorties. They dropped 2,087 bombs, and, according to the military, 1,669 bombs hit their targets (Aronstein and Piccirillo 1997, 154). General Buster Glossen, who commanded the 14th Air Division and was director of campaign plans for U.S. Central Command Air Forces, noted, "The single most important accomplishment of the F-117 during the Gulf War, however, was that it saved thousands and thousands of lives. Very close behind is the fact that it revolutionized the way we're going to fight wars in the future, and the way people think about wars" (Crickmore 2003, 68).

To what degree this is true can certainly be debated, especially considering the reevaluation of the category of "the casualty," both civilian and soldier, that happened in the American imagination in the wake of Vietnam. But it is possible that the successes of the F-117 in Baghdad in the early 1990s fostered the perception that relevant government sites could be targeted without risking exorbitant civilian losses. The fragmenting of this city into zones of legitimacy and illegitimacy for the purposes of distanced warfare is partially related to the F-117's use after the close of the cold war. When American troops entered Baghdad on the ground and attempted to establish order in the early days of the second Gulf War, they discovered a shattered city. One could argue that the city never recovered from the bombing campaigns of the early 1990s owing to a variety of factors, including the deep corruption and negligence of the ruling party and the devastating effects of a decade of international sanctions. This narrative mildly discounts the effectiveness of the F-117. The degree of destruction that the F-117's nightly raids wrought on Iraqi lives and infrastructure is not currently known but could help account for the extended ruins discovered thirteen years later.

As the geographies of Baghdad show, the use of a cold war instrument in a post–cold war context has very specific, and at times unintentional, material consequences. Pentagon planners who hoped to restart Baghdad immediately in the wake of invasion discovered a broken infrastructure incapable of being instantly reincarnated. In this case, the physical and social ruins the F-117 helped create in Baghdad during the first Gulf War later defined the battle spaces of the second Gulf War. Both of these conflicts left their long lasting and unintended scars on civilian and military institutions, landscapes, and populations. As this case study shows, in order to diagnose America's current capacities at home and abroad, we must account for one past in particular— the inheritances of the cold war—conceptually *and* materially.

The Cold War Present

The long life of the F-117[15] illustrates the variety of institutions, communities, and processes involved in one segment of the larger American defense economy. The complexity and scale of building the F-117 bred segmentation. Segmentation in turn generated varied temporalities within the communities and processes of design, manufacturing, testing, and use. These networks also developed separate and discrete cultures of time because they operated under strict security regulations to protect corporate and governmental proprietary knowledge. As a result, there were nonsynchronous features to the ways in which American power took on material form during the cold war.

While disarticulation is a feature of most complex manufacturing processes and a feature of many bureaucracies, this segment of the economy, I would argue, is distinct. In this case, the lengthy lives of military commodities point to the effect of disarticulation on the axis of time along with space. As the use of the F-117 in Baghdad during the first Gulf War intimates, the inheritances of the past live in the present. In terms of the newer manifestations of American power, such as the currently circulating War on Terror, it is important to recall that the instruments of this "war"—from equipment to strategy—are at least partially structured by techniques and technologies designed for past contingencies. That misalignment needs to be accounted for because the cold war lives on through its conceptual and material legacies.

:: **NOTES** ::

1. Understanding the causes of this pervasive cultural forgetting requires accounting for layers of historical contingencies, from evolving differences between civilian and military governance, to

the changing culture of military service. But these silences are also produced, in part, by the military economy. Their internal structures of classification and secrecy hide production processes from public scrutiny. As a result, the military engineering of American civil society remains shrouded by intent and over time by habit.

2. A radar beam is an electromagnetic field, and the amount of energy reflected back from the target determines the visibility of the aircraft (Rich and Janos 1994, 20). Since World War II, airplane designers sought to minimize a plane's radar presence through a variety of changes in speed, flying altitudes, agility, electronic countermeasures, and eventually combinations of all of the above (Crickmore 2003, 5).

3. While academic institutions played decisive roles in the evolution of military production (Leslie 1993)—especially through advancements in computational and nuclear technology—the core logic of the airplane exists in the institutional relationships of the military industrial apparatus.

4. Boeing is a publicly traded American company, and Airbus is a European aerospace consortium with major manufacturing sites in France, Germany, Spain, and the United Kingdom. While there are other nations—for example, Canada and Brazil—involved with airplane production as manufacturers and subcontractors for smaller commercial aircraft, Boeing and Airbus are at present the only players in the biggest commercial markets.

5. The United States lost 2,251 combat aircraft during the Vietnam War; 1,737 of those losses were linked to "hostile action," and 514 aircraft were lost because of mechanical failure or pilot error (Schlight 1996, 103).

6. The Israeli Air Force lost over one hundred of the most advanced American-designed combat aircraft in a little over two weeks (Aronstein and Piccirillo 1997, 11).

7. GM, personal interview, September 10, 2007.

8. These companies were Northrop, McDonnell Douglas, General Dynamics, Fairchild, and Grumman (Aronstein and Piccirillo 1997, 14).

9. The timeline and causes of the collapse of the Soviet Union are contested in this community. For some, Stealth technology helped bring down the Soviet Union. According to these participants, Stealth did so by both its technological capacities—to fly unseen until it was upon its target, thereby nullifying the opposition's numerical advantage—and its financial grandiosity—which caused the Soviet Union's eventual financial failure from its efforts to catch up with or counteract Stealth. This later category of expense was an especially entangled web in the next major Stealth project, the B2 bomber, which followed the F-117 in the 1980s and early 1990s.

10. With the pragmatic capabilities as yet unknown for Stealth technology, some of the requirements were differently imagined by the Air Command and the engineering staff. This became a particularly acute issue in the design and construction of the B2 bomber, which followed on the heels of the F-117. As one engineer who worked on the B2 told me, high-level decision makers in the military bureaucracy wanted everything including "a goddamn pony," but they lacked, according to members of this civilian subbranch of the air force, an appropriate sense of the possible. MB, personal interview, February 10, 2008.

11. These early Stealth airplanes—the F-117 and the B2—were some of the last major aerospace projects assembled in Southern California. Most Stealth planes were built in the Los Angeles basin, in Burbank, El Segundo, and Pico Rivera; later work was also done in Palmdale, California. Prototypes were tested in places like the Tejon Ranch just above Malibu, in Hellendale, and in other locations in the Antelope Valley. The finished F-117s were tested and readjusted for years in Tonopah, Nevada, the self-proclaimed "Home of Stealth." After these projects, aerospace manufacturing largely left Los Angeles. But the industry remains in the region as a new incarnation, more focused on design and research rather than manufacturing.

12. JD, personal interview, January 2, 2008.

13. The effects of these processes have been theorized by Hugh Gusterson (1996) in the context of the secrecy procedures in the national laboratory system. In his study of engineers at the Lawrence Livermore Laboratory, Gusterson traces the spatial logic of secrecy at work—badges, secured zones, classification, investigation—and follows its social after-effects home.

14. A similar pattern repeats in the history of procurement for the Stealth project. Stealth was funded surreptitiously and existed financially only in generic black budgets that limited congressional oversight. These financial barriers, on one hand, allowed for the relatively unfettered evolution of the F-117, according the Lockheed engineers. But it would be precisely these same limits on oversight, on the other hand, that would be one of the fatal complications in the life of the B2 program, when Congress focused on the B2 as an exemplar of wasteful spending.

15. The F-117 retired in a series of well-publicized but private events in the spring of 2008.

SECTION 3

COUNTERINSURGENCY, PAST AND PRESENT
Precedents to the Manual

:: JEREMY WALTON *and* BEATRICE JAUREGUI ::

U p to this point, our collection has adopted a panoramic perspective on questions of political anthropology, counterinsurgency, and American power. The first section, through
ethnographic inquiries into the culturally and historically specific
articulations of the "Blue in Green" paradigm of civil-ized security,
has spoken from the anthropology of state and military power to set
a context for further discussion of counterinsurgency and its alleged
exigencies. Departing from the same fundamental inspiration, to set
an important context, the second ensemble of papers has marshaled
and coordinated ethnographic insight on a different object: divergent experiences and conceptions of American power from across
the globe. In this, our third and middle section, our conversation
again shifts thematic gears in order to trace another important context: the colonial and postcolonial history of counterinsurgency,
with an eye toward the practices and ideologies that continue to sustain it. While some of the volume's earlier contributions—notably
John Kelly's analysis of the striking influence of David Galula's understanding of Maoist insurgency on the *Counterinsurgency Field
Manual No. 3-24*—have already raised the specter of this history,
the four papers composing this section address it directly.

Our treatment of the roots of counterinsurgency begins with
Dustin Wax's consideration of nearly a century in the history of the
relationship between the discipline of anthropology, and more or

less explicit counterinsurgency campaigns of the U.S. government. Wax traces the recruitment of anthropology to an agenda of American hegemony back to the early twentieth century, when U.S. policy makers debated the merits of cultural assimilation and regional marginalization of Native American populations. He then proceeds from reservations directly to internment camps, where many of the same anthropologists who worked with the Bureau of Indian Affairs became "community analysts" with the War Relocation Authority, which oversaw the incarceration of more than 100,000 Japanese-Americans during World War II. With his incisive analysis of the "warping effect" on anthropological work of its production in service to the U.S. government generally—and during World War II, in service to the militarized security state specifically—Wax anticipates the arguments against the Human Terrain Systems (HTS) Program that both Roberto Gonzalez and David Price will make in the fourth section of the book.

James Hevia's contribution adds another chapter to the history of counterinsurgency, beginning with a focus on military officer and theorist Charles Callwell's development of the protoinsurgency concept of the "small war" within the context of the British Empire during the nineteenth century. Crucially, Hevia draws a direct link between (1) European colonial projects of globally spreading "civilization" by means of military, economic, and cultural subordination and (2) counterinsurgency as it developed in the period following World War II, during which the U.S. military industrial complex rose to global dominance. Following this, Kurt Jacobsen provides a critical reading of the U.S. attempts to "pacify" Vietnamese populations during the Vietnam War and of recent revisionist histories of these attempts as strategically and tactically right-minded, even if ultimately unsuccessful. Provocatively and compellingly, Jacobsen frames his critique as a neopsychoanalytic interpretation of War on Terror counterinsurgency programs as compulsive repetitions of habits and aspirations molded in the crucible of the Mekong Delta.

Finally, Joseph Masco discusses the integration of historical imagination and actual deployment of counterinsurgency to theorize the production and structural logic of political vengeance (a.k.a., revolutionary war, a.k.a., terrorism) or "blowback." Reading together (1) the U.S. military's screening of *The Battle of Algiers* (1966) for troops preparing to fight insurgents in Iraq following the 2003 invasion and occupation, and (2) the plot of *The Spook Who Sat by the Door*—a 1973 "Cold War race fantasy" film depicting an insurgency by African Americans in Chicago—Masco considers the disturbing effects of U.S. projections of its military might on domestic politics. He ultimately concludes that counterinsurgency (as counterterror), as a new U.S.-propagated paradigm of planetary power, is the very apotheosis of terror itself.

Each of these four papers maintains a distinct historical and theoretical focus, but they are united by their concern for the politics and practices of counterinsurgency past, present, and future. Wax raises historically conscious objections to the changing relationship between anthropology and counterinsurgency that the next section of the book, "The U.S. Military and U.S. Anthropology," will debate in more detail. Similarly, Hevia and Jacobsen each shed critical light on the prehistory of the counterinsurgency manual itself and thus provide a backdrop for understanding the "cultural turn" in U.S. counterinsurgency doctrine, which Hugh Gusterson will identify and analyze in the final section of the book. Masco deftly connects history, memory, action, and anticipation and shows how cinematic imaginaries may not only envision real developments but also help shape them by informing and accelerating anxieties, especially those of counterinsurgency itself. Through their complementary historical vantages, all of the papers in this section provoke reflection upon how not just modes of warfare but modes of consciousness and conscience regarding warfare can be both created and destroyed in contexts of counterinsurgency—whether the modes in question are those of social scientists, policy makers, soldiers, citizens, or, in some cases, all of the above. More than an historical segue, then, this section forms the thematic center and bridge of our book, linking the ethnographic purview of our earlier discussions to the ethical and political debates yet to come.

10

The Uses of Anthropology in the Insurgent Age

:: DUSTIN M. WAX ::

The *Counterinsurgency Field Manual No. 3-24* defines insurgency as "an organized movement aimed at the overthrow of a constituted government through the use of subversion and armed conflict" (U.S. Department of the Army 2006, 1-1). Counterinsurgency, it goes on, consists of all "military, paramilitary, political, economic, psychological, and civic actions taken by a government to defeat insurgency." Counterinsurgency then is a concerted effort at the state level to defend and maintain the status quo from subversive action. In its current incarnation in programs like the U.S. Army's Human Terrain System (HTS), counterinsurgency is embedded in military and paramilitary action. But there is nothing in the definition above that restricts our understanding of counterinsurgency solely to its military expressions. Of far greater concern, in fact, are the, "economic, psychological, and civic actions" encompassed in that definition.

Viewed in the broad terms suggested by the U.S. Army's definition, counterinsurgency appears as a foundational element in the development of anthropology as a discipline. Adequate knowledge and understanding of the conquered Other has been central to the Enlightenment ideal of benevolent rule and has been seen as the key to resolving and, better yet, preventing the development of dissent into revolt.

Take, for example, Thomas Jefferson's prescient instructions to

Captain Meriwether Lewis on the eve of the departure of the Lewis and Clark expedition:

> The commerce which may be carried on with the people inhabiting the line you will pursue, renders a knowledge of those people important. . . . And, considering the interest which every nation has in extending & strengthening the authority of reason & justice among the people around them, it will be useful to acquire what knowledge you can of the state of morality, religion, & information among them; as it may better enable those who endeavor to civilize & instruct them, to adapt their measure to the existing notions & practices of those on whom they are to operate. (Jefferson 1803)

Jefferson's instructions highlight the importance of adequate information about "them" in establishing the fledgling government's authority—and, inter alia, anticipate the likelihood of resistance and armed revolt.

By the mid-nineteenth century, these types of concerns would be formally institutionalized within the Department of Interior, culminating with the establishment of the Bureau of Ethnology in 1879 (later the Bureau of American Ethnology). If we are looking for precursors to HTS's embedded social scientists, we need look no further than the Bureau of Ethnology anthropology of the second half of the nineteenth century. Franklin Hamilton Cushing and Matilda Coxe Stevenson arrived at Zuni Pueblo with a military escort, in the company of Stevenson's husband, Colonel James Stevenson of the U.S. Geological Survey. This military backing served Cushing well; by his account, the proposal to throw him bodily off the Mesa was discouraged only because of the fear that "'Wa-sin-to-na [Washington, in other words, that is, the U.S. government] might visit [Cushing's] death on the whole [Zuni] nation" (Cushing 1967, 16).

James Mooney, another Bureau ethnologist, also blurred the line between anthropologist and military advisor, spending twenty-two months in the field, mostly with the support of the War Department, studying the spread of the Ghost Dance through the Plains tribes. When not in the field interviewing Indians, Mooney enjoyed thorough access to the officers and soldiers fighting the Indians in the West as well as unfettered access to the files of both the Indian Bureau and the War Department. The result, *The Ghost-Dance Religion and the Sioux Outbreak of 1890* (published as *The Ghost-Dance Religion and Wounded Knee;* Mooney 1973), is exemplary history, but it is suffused throughout with evidence of Mooney's unreflexive acceptance of the military's mission. His bleak introduction describes the "doom that now seems rapidly closing in on" the Indian peoples (661); and there are statements peppered throughout the work justifying that doom in the name of progress. For instance, Mooney writes of Sitting Bull: "[H]e represented the past. His influence was incompatible with progress, and his death marks an era in the civilization of the Sioux" (861). It is clear that he supports the military agents of the Indians' demise and the U.S. government whose hegemony they defend. With regard to the fact that Wounded Knee quickly devolved into a bloodbath, he writes that this was "no reflection on the humanity of the officer in charge" (870).

This uncritical acceptance of the status quo as the baseline against which cultural difference is measured is one of the main dangers of anthropology's alliance with counterinsurgency. And it is a theme running through anthropology's history. For example, Evans-Pritchard's *The Nuer* (1940) completely ignores the colonial situation, which Evans-Pritchard accepts uncritically, even as troops surround the village in which he's working. Despite his recognition that the Nuer had recently been forced into submission by the Sudanese government (his employer), Evans-Pritchard fails to include either the Sudanese government or the British colonial empire in his description of the Nuer political system—which, he says with no apparent irony, "includes all the peoples with whom they come in contact" (5). Evans-Pritchard's almost willful erasure of the colonial context from his description of the Nuer (see, for example, Rosaldo 1986 and Hutchinson 1996) stands as a strong example of how allegiance to a particular political order can shape the ethnographer's observations and how s/he makes sense of those observations.

The same story has been repeated whenever anthropologists have turned their attention to producing ethnographic and theoretical knowledge that would be "of use" to governments. This is well documented in the British colonial context by, for example, Stephen Feuchtwang (1973) and in the American context by George Stocking (1992, 178–211). Despite the good intentions of most of the anthropologists involved, their efforts to secure a piece of the funding pie led to the advancement of a certain model of functionalist anthropology whose very premise was the maintenance of the social order as defined by Western colonial and imperial powers.

The working assumption of those who advocate closer relations between anthropology and military and intelligence agencies seems to be that this history does not matter—that in fact the long history of anthropological service to power should be taken as an endorsement of renewed and continued service (e.g., McFate 2005a; cf. Wax 2008). The reality, however, is that the view of human reality produced by that history is not only partial but distorted, telling us at least as much about our own assumptions and implicit alignment with the status quo—even among some of the most radical anthropologists—as they do about our subjects.

In what follows, I examine a small slice of anthropology's history, the period when the model of government anthropology that would become dominant in the years after World War II was first being developed. The two big applied anthropology programs of the 1930s and early 1940s—the Applied Anthropology Unit under the Indian New Deal and the community analyst program under the War Relocation Authority—demonstrate well the ways that anthropology can be compromised in the service of goals not its own, especially when, as anthropologists have tended to do, we lose sight of the power imbalances inherent in the social context that makes our work possible. As such, these programs exemplify many of the hazards that anthropologists have so far failed to adequately address in working under conditions in which their goals, methods, and access are determined by outside political actors, rather than scientific exigency, or the needs of the peoples with whom anthropologists work.

In the end, I could have picked almost any time period, and practically any anthropological exercise with even the most tenuous relation to the state, to demonstrate the "warping effect" in action. At its very core, the demands of anthropology as a scientific discipline are fundamentally incompatible with the demands of counterinsurgency in the broad sense suggested by the U.S. Army field manual. I will close this essay, then, with what I feel are five key incompatibilities that cannot be resolved without doing irreparable damage to anthropology.

From Workers' Revolt to Alien Internment

Much of the language around social disorder and unrest has been framed using bodily metaphors of health and illness. It is not surprising then that problem-based research has often taken an explicitly therapeutic approach to its subjects, asking "how might health be restored to the ailing society?" This approach is seen clearly in the industrial anthropology of Lloyd Warner and his students in the early 1930s. This research was shaped by the rising functionalist approach to human behavior and was explicitly "therapeutic." The smoothly running factory or corporation under study was represented as a functioning community, and any deviation from this state—labor unrest, loss of productivity, miscommunication between management and workforce—was understood as a sign of illness. Thus, the industrial anthropologist's goal was to understand the basis of the problem and recommend remedies (Baba 1998).

The work by Warner and his students set the tone for applied research over the next couple decades and also provided much of the core personnel. In addition to Warner, men like Conrad Arensburg, Elliot Chappel, Burleigh Gardner, Frederick Richardson, Donald Sayles, and William Foote Whyte would put their mark on applied anthropology, bringing the methodological and theoretical approach of industrial anthropology into two of the largest and most influential applied anthropology projects of the next decade: the Applied Anthropology Unit (AAU) at the Bureau of Indian Affairs (BIA), and the War Relocation Authority's (WRA's) efforts in the administration of the wartime Japanese-American internment camps.

The New Deal for Indians (and Anthropologists)

The passing of the Indian Reorganization Act (IRA) in 1934, and the anthropological programs that were authorized under it, marked a watershed moment in the relationship between anthropology and the U.S. government. The AAU of the BIA and the Soil Conservation Service (SCS) under the Department of Agriculture—along with the BIA's later Indian Education, Personality and Administration Research Project—employed unprecedented numbers of anthropologists. However, the "Indian New Deal" was far from an unqualified success for anthropology. On the contrary, the administrators of the Indian New Deal—including the anthropology-friendly Commissioner of Indian Affairs John Collier—frequently clashed with the anthropologists over matters of methodology, policy and its implementation, and ultimately the practicality and desirability of the IRA's goals themselves (Kelly 1980, 1984; McNickle 1979; Steward 1969; Stocking 1992).

Collier's plan called for "a halt to the division of Indian reservations into individually owned plots of land . . . , the formation of tribal governments with written constitutions guaranteeing Indians freedom from government interference, the guarantee of federal loans to Indian groups which formed tribal governments, and the purchase of additional land for these incorporated tribes and bands" (Kelly 1980, 6–7).

This plan was grounded in an antiassimilationist stance that occasionally bordered on the absurd. Collier was convinced of a semi- or quasi-spiritual Indian "essence," which he felt had been dissipated by a half-century and more of explicitly assimilationist Indian policy. He imagined his policy as offering to the Indian the possibility to "return" to that "authentic" Indianness, as imagined through the lens of Boasian salvage ethnography (Steward 1969).

From the beginning, the AAU anthropologists were challenged by limitations imposed on them by a BIA bureaucracy that was amenable to neither the anthropologists' input nor the needs of adequate research. Julian Steward, who worked with the AAU for a year, notes that while the anthropologists could reasonably have expected their work to have informed policy, instead they found themselves constrained by a policy that had already been set, expected solely to implement Collier's plan, not to contribute to it (Steward 1969). Further, the anthropologists found their model of long-term, in-depth fieldwork to be at odds with the fiscal structure of federal government bodies. The projects were allocated funds not for the length of the project but for the fiscal year, to be reviewed for the following year's budget. Since any funds not used by the end of the fiscal year would revert to Congress, which tended to see nonexpenditure as a sign to reduce appropriations, there was a great deal of pressure not so much to achieve results but to spend the budget in a timely fashion (Kelly 1980).

Most importantly, however, in the failure of the Indian New Deal anthropology projects, was the degree to which both Collier and the anthropologists of the AAU underestimated the state of Indian cultures in the 1930s. Convinced that assimilation was harmful to Indians, Collier imagined a return to a utopian precontact state. He saw the changes that had occurred under American and colonial rule as signs of the failure of Indian culture to maintain its ideal state in the face of conquest—a kind of nonfatalist twist on Mooney's views a half-century earlier. While, contrary to Collier, the BIA bureaucrats were convinced that rapid assimilation was the best thing for the Indians, like Collier, they saw the Indians' continued resistance to assimilation policies as (also) a failure within the Indian communities. Both parties expected the anthropologists of the AAU and SCS to identify these failures and to propose methods for their solution. When their experiences in the field failed to conform to the expectations of either faction in the bureau, the anthropologists were accused, by both sides, of deliberately obstructing the efforts of the BIA. For instance, when Julian Steward's efforts to convince the BIA to redraw the territorial units they had imposed on the Great Basin region to bring them more in line with the traditional regions occupied by the Great Basin societies, he was regarded as sabotaging the program. When he later told Collier that young men in Idaho were boasting of stealing the admission fees taken for the Sun Dance, Collier declared that no Indian would do such a thing to their own community and again accused Steward of undermining the program's goals (Steward 1969, 33).

Left unrecorded in all this back-and-forth about assimilation were the specific ways that Indian cultures were selectively integrating and rejecting the cultural norms of the greater American society and steadfastly refusing to either assimilate or return to an imagined lost pure state. Thus, anthropologists were caught in the middle of intra-agency differences about what the future of American Indians should be. They became stuck trying to solve social problems that were more an artifact of functionalist theory than of direct observation and were unable to pursue lines of investigation that were raised by their field experience. And the anthropologists involved in the AAU were largely unsuccessful in fulfilling the program's main goal: to craft tribal constitutions that would appropriately reflect Indian groups' actual beliefs and practices. As the program faced termination for its failure to produce results, most AAU researchers found themselves involved in the rather less scientifically rewarding project of helping to convince their research subjects to adopt "one-size-fits-all" constitutions drafted by BIA lawyers. Ultimately, although the scientific results were not impressive, the AAU and SCS did produce something significant, namely, networks of experienced government anthropologists who became the core of researchers called upon to assist in the war effort after the bombing of Pearl Harbor.

From Reservation to Internment Camp:
The War Relocation Authority

Three months after the December 1941 attack on Pearl Harbor, the U.S. government ordered the removal from the West Coast of all Japanese immigrants and Americans of Japanese descent and created the WRA to supervise their relocation. The internment of Japanese-Americans was highly controversial from the start, and the establishment of the WRA was intended to minimize what many felt was a grievous but "necessary" human rights violation. As part of this effort, twenty-one anthropologists and sociologists were employed as "community analysts" over the next several years to help administer the camps and to promote a policy of "reintegration" into "normal American life" (Spicer 1979, 220). Some of these anthropologists—including John Provinse, Solon Kimball, Robert Redfield, Conrad Arensberg, John Embree, Edward Spicer, and Morris Opler—had been involved as researchers or consultants in Indian New Deal programs. All of them, however, fell victim to the same mistakes that had led to the rather less than spectacular results of the Indian New Deal (Spicer 1979; Starn 1986; Suzuki 1980, 1981, 1986).

Like the industrial anthropologists and IRA ethnographers of the 1930s, the WRA community analysts adopted the assumption that the artificially created and military-supervised internment camps were functioning communities and that any problems that arose in the camps could be understood within the context of those communities. As resistance to both the internment and the secondary goal of relocation grew among the internees, the community analysts focused increasingly on the behavior and psychology of the "disloyals" or "pro-Japans," that is, people who had, in the assimilation model that informed the camps' policy, failed to adequately assimilate to American culture. Very little of the community analysts' writing considers the possibility that, like Evans-Pritchard's Nuer, the internees had little reason to trust the intentions or policies of the people in whose charge they had been put (Suzuki 1981). Just like the industrial anthropologists who saw labor unrest as a deviation from the ideally functioning community of the factory or corporation rather than as an organic response to the exploitive situation inherent to the workplace, the community analysts for the most part saw resistance as a problem to be solved rather than as a reasonable, even healthy, response to internment.

This perspective was embedded in the reasons that the social scientists were hired in the first place. Autumn 1942 saw a series of riots and strikes at several camps, climaxing with military intervention at Manzanar. It was clear that the administrators of the camps, many drawn from the Indian Service or the military, were ill prepared to deal with a culture that many of them thought of as completely alien if not actively threatening. It was felt that anthropologists could provide the administration with the knowledge of Japanese culture and personality that would enable the smooth running of the camps. This goal of stability and order automatically put a premium on information about the factors that obstructed the administrator's goals.

One of the main social problems investigated by the community analysts was the resistance of internees to the relocation program. Although the WRA had initially intended the camps to house the Japanese and Japanese-American evacuees for the duration of the war, they soon shifted the focus of their policy from detainment to relocation in communities scattered across the Midwest and eastern United States. The community analysts were called upon to recommend ways to ease the transition of the evacuees into their new communities, as well as to help the administrators understand the resistance to relocation that was hindering their efforts. Despite widespread resentment among the internees over their treatment at the hands of the government—especially considering that many of the internees were U.S. citizens—and their awareness of growing anti-Japanese racism as the war intensified, the community analysts saw the unwillingness to relocate as primarily due to "personal insecurity" (Embree 1944, 287) caused by maladjustment to camp life. Others blamed resistance on the inadequate communication of the WRA's goals to internees, the development of pro- and anti-American factions, and the structure of the "Japanese psyche" (see, for example, Weston LaBarre's analysis, based on forty-four days residency in the camps, of the Japanese as "compulsive neurotics"; in Suzuki 1980, 33). The few anthropologists who might have been able (or willing) to see the internees' resistance as a product of the structure of the camps itself, rather than as a deviation from that structure, were either overwhelmed by conflict with the administration or were prevented from making their objections known owing to a restriction on wartime publishing (Opler 1987).

The relative paucity of publications based on the community analysts' fieldwork, and the tendency of such work as was published to focus on policy issues rather than ethnographic description or theory building, is symptomatic of the ways the needs of the WRA and the limitations of their functionalist framework constrained these anthropologists working in the internment camps (Suzuki 1981, 1986). Work of a traditionally ethnographic nature, such as Morris Opler's documentation of pre–World War II Japanese-American culture and Marvin Opler's descriptions of religious and leisure activities in the camps, was devalued and actively discouraged. Indeed, Morris Opler was almost fired for his "old-fashioned ethnographic nature" (Suzuki 1981, 42). Where the community analysts' work was most valuable was not in advancing an understanding of Japanese or Japanese-American culture, nor in furthering the study of institutionalization in general, but in providing the administration of the camps with reassurance that they were doing the best they could, given the circumstances, and in creating a positive image of the camps' administration for outside consumption. While many within the WRA rejected the racist premises inherent in the internment itself, the work of the community analysts allowed them to see the execution of the internment as essentially fair and democratic—in Robert Redfield's words, "strikingly American" (in Starn 1986, 708).

Reconsidering Applied Anthropology

The role of adjutant policy makers extracted a high cost in terms of disciplinary autonomy. In both the BIA and WRA projects, neither research goals or methodologies nor even conclusions were wholly determined by the researchers themselves. When Julian Steward— whose job it was, in part, to predict the outcomes of particular policies—pointed out factors that could contribute to negative outcomes for the AAU, he was chastised. When Marvin Opler strenuously objected to the administering of loyalty oaths to the internees and to the segregation of those who refused to sign, predicting "low morale, anger, frustration, and despair" (Suzuki 1981, 33), his report was virtually ignored. The very language in which anthropologists could report their findings was closely regulated and highly euphemistic: "registration" instead of loyalty oath, "stop order" instead of permanent incarceration in the camp, "community" instead of camp, "internees" instead of evacuee or prisoner, and so on (Suzuki 1981). Community analysts were instructed to use this language in their dealings with their subjects as well, to avoid distressing the internees.

For all their training, anthropologists in these types of programs have not worked as anthropologists—in many cases, they have not been *allowed* to. The rare exceptions—such as Opler, who pursued topics that they felt were interesting anthropologically regardless of their immediate utility—were marginalized, even threatened, and their work fell on deaf ears. Work that did not conform to the diagnosis already made by policy makers—or worse, challenged that diagnosis—was eliminated from consideration in the very programs that anthropologists had been hired to assist; and, as much as possible, those anthropologists were prevented from following those lines of research.

As Montgomery McFate has made clear in her letter responding to *Newsweek*'s critical look at the Human Terrain program (in Weinberger 2008a), it is not for our specific knowledge or theoretical orientation that anthropologists are valued for counterinsurgency—it is for our methodologies, our ability to extract from informants information that may be useful in their own subjugation. We see this in Warner's industrial research, in Collier's Indian New Deal, and in the WRA's community analyst program: anthropologists are valued only inasmuch as they contribute information that makes the *application* of policy (and not the *creation* of policy) run smoothly. Indeed, because anthropologists were distantly removed from policy making, findings that challenged the appropriateness of the decided-upon course were almost always ignored or seen as efforts to undermine the programs.

Conclusion: Five Incompatibilities

In the end, anthropological research in all its glorious messiness is essentially incompatible with counterinsurgency—that is, with efforts to consolidate and maintain the status quo in the face of popular dissent. Historically, anthropologists who have accepted the devil's bargain of "helping" to reconcile the subjugated to their subjugation have either done bad anthropology to the satisfaction of their superiors or have done good anthropology that was ignored and often resulted in their marginalization and even removal from the field.

On the other hand, as the relationship between anthropology and the military in the U.S. dwindled in the late 1960s and early 1970s, anthropology woke up as if from a slumber. The interpretivist/symbolic approach of Geertz and Turner put human meaning front and center in the discipline. From other quarters came a rebirth of political economy and explicitly Marxist approaches to social behavior. Feminist anthropologists highlighted the significance of women's experiences to a functioning society. In the wake of anthropology's long struggle to be useful to power, we saw the emergence of new and complex understandings of gender and race—and later ethnicity, sexuality, and identity. A new focus on intersubjectivity led to a heightened awareness of power relations in the field, leading to a reconsideration of the terms of consent and rapport. Postcolonial approaches spelled out the ways in which anthropology had been shaped by its relation to power and the questions and erasures this relationship had created in our understanding of humankind. Free of military constraints, anthropology developed an understanding of transnational flows of goods, money, people, and ideas; finally moved past the obsession with assimilation to discover nuanced interplays between cultures even in the face of massive power imbalances; and was able to find dignity and even strength in tiny assertions of power and self in Andean mines, Chinese silk factories, and Yemeni wedding parties (Nash 1993, Rofel 1999, and Caton 1990, respectively).

This was possible, I would argue, not in spite of the withdrawal of military funding in the wake of Vietnam-era fiascos like the Thailand Affair and Project Camelot, but precisely *because* of the military's removal from the field. In effect, this removal freed anthropologists to pursue interests whose immediate application was uncertain at best.

In the end, I argue that the needs of anthropology are fundamentally incompatible with the needs of counterinsurgency and that the inevitable tension produced by attempts to unite them strongly limits anthropology's potential. Here then are five ways in which anthropology suffers in a military context. This list is intended to be neither exhaustive nor exclusive—nor, ultimately, is it limited solely to anthropology's relationship with the military.

1. Coercion versus Rapport

Thus far, the debate over the ethical standing of anthropological research being carried out under the auspices of the military has centered on the issue of "informed consent" (see, for example, David Price and Montgomery McFate's appearance on the Diane Rehm Show on October 10, 2007, http://wamu .org/programs/dr/07/10/10.php; q.v. Price 2007). Regardless of whether ethical standards are met or not (and in the case of HTS and similar research, that is very debatable), good anthropology is made of something rather more than a bureaucratic attention to the letter of a code of ethics or institutional review board standards. Good anthropology depends on the establishment of *rapport* between an anthropologist and her or his subjects. It may be possible that a person can give informed consent in its most literal sense to an anthropologist or other social scientist embedded in a military unit, armed or accompanied by armed personnel, and clearly identified as a member of the occupying force. But it is unlikely that something approaching willing, meaningful exchange can occur under such conditions.

No matter how skilled the ethnographer, the situation itself is coercive; as a member of an occupying power, no matter how tangentially, the anthropologist's relationship with her or his subjects cannot help but be strained. This is inherent in the veiled threat behind practically every public pronouncement supporters of HTS and counterinsurgency work in general have made—that if the anthropologist cannot minimize conflict, more people will die.

2. Political Ends versus Anthropological Ends

Anthropology has, at least since Boas, depended on its holistic approach as a guide to adequate field research. Anthropologists depend on their ability to follow the seemingly irrelevant and trivial in order to put together the big picture. In an end-focused environment like counterinsurgency, however, this ability is not guaranteed, not least because of the threat of violence. The standard against which counterinsurgency must be judged is the particular needs of military hegemony.

This was exactly the case in the Japanese relocation camps, where good research was marginalized and discouraged because it failed to advance the goals of maintaining order in the camps and distributing the Japanese-American population across the Midwest, while informing on disloyals and assisting in the pacification of resistance were encouraged and became the norm. Not only is this hardly conducive to rapport building, it is unfair to those research subjects who participate in good faith and who may have their own expectations about the benefits of cooperating with the anthropologist. Under these conditions, anthropologists cannot adequately respond to people's real concerns.

Likewise, the success or failure—and thus the continued existence—of counterinsurgency programs is determined not by the quality of anthropological research it produces but by the achievement of goals that have nothing to do with anthropological practice or theory. I can think of no adequate compensation for the loss of control over the means, aims, and duration of research necessary to perform adequate research.

3. Application versus Theory

The practical assessment and goals of counterinsurgency work put a premium on practical information. So, for example, in a *Newsweek* article, HTS anthropologist Marcus Griffin points out how he has learned to read signs of material well-being or deprivation in things like how well-stocked community groceries are (Ephron and Spring 2008). Ostensibly the poorly fed are more likely to take an unkind view of the occupying forces, so this is useful information for a counterinsurgency unit to gain. As the name "Human Terrain" suggests, this is meant to be value-free mapmaking, questioning what features are in the "terrain" and how do we get around, over, or through them.

What concerns me here is the apparent vacating of theory altogether, leaving anthropology as merely a set of investigative practices. Montgomery McFate makes this very clear in a letter to *Wired Magazine*'s "Danger Room" regarding the *Newsweek* article mentioned above: " . . . [S]ocial scientists are trained to apply their knowledge of analytical frameworks and research methodologies across different locales, based on the premise that the dynamics of human behavior exhibit certain universal features. . . . [W]hat social scientists bring to the table is a way of looking at the social world, studying it, and analyzing it in a way that is distinct from the way the military approaches these issues" (in Weinberger 2008a; emphasis added).

This is anthropology reduced to a methodology, stripped clean of local knowledge, local meaning, and local language—as well as of theoretical orientation and area background. It is anthropology as travel guide, little more than a list of phrases and practices for the visiting occupier to use with the locals. And it is anthropology as triage—a quick inventorying of symptoms, off-the-cuff diagnosis, and hopefully an immediate prescription: "Get more food down here STAT!" Implicit in this model, however, is a particular image of what a healthy, noninsurgent society *should* look like. Dissent, armed revolt, and insurgency are seen as symptoms of a sick society, and the army sees itself as seeking and providing the cure. Left unthought of in the therapeutic view is the idea that, given the situation, maybe insurgency, disorder, and unrest are the healthiest responses, maybe even the *only* healthy responses. As scientists, we are trained to consider a range of possibilities, including that what appears abnormal to an outside observer may in fact be perfectly functional. In the counterinsurgency model, normalcy/health is only that condition which most closely meets the interests of the occupier.

4. Secrecy versus Openness

Secrecy is a problem in anthropological research in two senses. In the first, it is a lack of information provided to research collaborators and subjects in the field with which meaningful consent can be formed. The second is perhaps more troubling, from a disciplinary standpoint—the trapping of anthropological knowledge behind national security firewalls. Any body that seeks to artificially limit the circulation of anthropological research hinders the development of the field—and encourages bad anthropology. We are familiar enough with the ease with which anthropologists can mistake, misinterpret, and just plain miss the reality around them in the field. Because human behavior is so complex, the only even partial corrective for the mistakes and biases that necessarily inhabit our work is and has been the response to and appraisal of our work by our peers.

The ability to openly publish and respond to published work is not just a way to score "brownie points" toward tenure, it is essential to the quality of our work. Anthropology has progressed largely through a process of comparison, integration, and criticism. Work that is necessarily secret does not engage in this disciplinary conversation—which means it is not and cannot be properly evaluated as anthropology. It can only ever be evaluated as policy—to little effect, historically.

5. External versus Local

Finally, counterinsurgency must always be directed toward a set of goals that originate outside the community being studied. We have seen, in generations of applied and development anthropology, including the examples I have discussed above, that although most such goals can be maintained so long as there is external direction, they are ultimately unsustainable—and often directly harmful (Escobar 1995). Although they have yet to be adequately worked out in practice, the ideals of action research—developing goals and the means of attaining those goals in cooperation with local populations—are far more in tune with anthropology's humanistic and humanizing ideals. But an approach that relies on eliciting local goals and directing action toward them is unlikely to find support in an insurgent context in which those goals are, for many, the end of subjugation.

Conclusion

I have tried to keep my comments here as general as possible, because my opposition to anthropologists doing counterinsurgency research is not limited to the specific failures of the misguided and apparently failing HTS program currently in practice. This is why I decided to open with the U.S. Army's definition of counterinsurgency. This definition allows for the kind of slippage between nominal counterinsurgency, military/intelligence activity of other sorts, colonial domination, and in fact all forms of hegemonic control that I have taken as my subject.

Contra the insistence of some critics, this is ultimately not a merely partisan complaint, and it is certainly not only about opposition to the "long war" we find ourselves in. This is about a fundamental incompatibility between the aims and practices of occupying powers, however broadly imagined, and the aims and practices of anthropology. It is, in the end, a moral evaluation; but it is a practical one as well, inasmuch as the moral enables the practice of anthropology among humanity.

11

Small Wars and Counterinsurgency

:: JAMES L. HEVIA ::

In the annotated bibliography of the *U.S. Army/Marine Corps Counterinsurgency Field Manual* the first entry is *Small Wars: Their Principles and Practices* (FM3-24), by Charles E. Callwell. The edition cited is a 1996 University of Nebraska reprint of the third edition, which was originally published in 1906, ten years after the first edition appeared. The annotation reads, "A British major general who fought in Afghanistan and the Boer War provides lessons learned that remain applicable today" (391).

In an article that appeared in *Harper's* in February 2007, the reference to Callwell's *Small Wars* in FM3-24 led Edward Luttwak to wonder whether counterinsurgency was evolving backward. This may have been a bit harsh on Luttwak's part, considering that for all practical purposes, once the acronyms, flow and organization charts, and Power Point slides are stripped away, counterinsurgency seems hardly to have evolved in any particular direction at all. But as tempting as it may be, I actually do not want to get bogged down in the question of progress, retrogression, or stagnation. Rather, I want to do some comparison between small wars and counterinsurgency with a focus on military intelligence and culture.

Callwell and Small Wars

Charles Callwell was a member of a technomilitary elite that emerged in Great Britain in the second half of the nineteenth century. These professional military men were the products of training programs that had been substantially modified in the 1860s and 1870s as a result of a series of parliament-directed reforms. Collectively, the group constituted a new kind of imperial masculinity, one that was based less on battlefield prowess and élan and more on mental dexterity and technical acumen. Callwell graduated from a two-year program at the Royal Military Academy in 1877, was commissioned in the Royal Field Artillery, and completed an advanced training course for new officers at Woolwich. The training programs placed a heavy emphasis on mathematics (especially calculus and mechanics), drawing, techniques of field reconnaissance, and the drafting of formal reports.

Upon completion of these programs, Callwell was sent to India and South Africa, where he participated in the second Afghan War and the first Boer War, respectively. After returning to Britain in 1884, he completed the two-year staff college program at Camberley. Throughout his early career he published regularly in military journals, including that of the Royal United Service Institution, from which he won a gold medal for an essay on lessons learned from colonial campaigns since 1865. This essay was the modest beginning of what would become *Small Wars* a decade later.

In the following year, 1887, Callwell, like many officers who had completed similar training, was assigned to the Intelligence Branch of the Quartermaster General's Department in the War Office, the unit responsible for logistics in the British army. Engineers and artillery officers were the prime recruits of the intelligence branch. In this position, he carried out several reconnaissance missions in the Austria-Hungarian and Ottoman empires and in French colonies in North Africa. In 1893, he turned to the writing of *Small Wars,* using the classified records of campaigns that were stored in the Intelligence Branch archives.

Before turning to Callwell's book, I would like to make a few observations about what his career helps to clarify, in terms of a relationship among technocracy, intelligence, and what is now called asymmetrical warfare. The first thing to be noted is the link between logistics and intelligence. Intelligence, as perceived by the British, was essentially information about physical terrain that would allow for the effective mobilization and application of military force. In order to gather such information, certain skills were required, all of which involved the use of specialized technologies and various techniques for organizing, storing, recovering, and reassembling materials for use in military deployments. The assemblages that resulted took standardized forms: route books, which detailed expeditious ways of getting from here to there; military reports, which might be understood as tactical intelligence for the preparation of the battlefield; and, lastly, campaign records. These genres of writing and record keeping were all under the purview of the intelligence branches in London, and in colonial India, in the late nineteenth and the early part of the twentieth century, where they were not only assembled but frequently updated. As such, the intelligence branches constituted the site at which campaigns were planned, deployments of men and material were organized, and institutional memory was stored. Callwell drew on this archive to write *Small Wars.*

Structurally, *Small Wars* is a complex book on a number of levels and may be read more than one way. For example, it is perhaps the most comprehensive record ever assembled in one source of resistance by subjugated populations to Euro-American imperial expansion in the second half of the nineteenth century. And yet, it is hardly ever read that way, or as what it also is—a world history from a technomilitary point of view. Instead, it seems mostly to have been read as a guidebook for dealing with low-intensity warfare in the border regions of empire or as an explication of tactics for dealing with opposition to foreign occupation of territory. It is perhaps as a tactical guide that it appeals to the assemblers of the new *U.S. Army/Marine Corps Counterinsurgency Field Manual* (2007). But it also has appeal because Callwell devoted substantial space to tactics of mountain warfare, warfare in Afghanistan, and ways to deal with "fanatics." He is also quite good at reorganizing the massive empirical material on British military campaigns in Africa and Central, South, Southeast, and East Asia into overarching categories into which events are filed as examples or cases. Such cases include causes of insurgency, objectives, intelligence, hill versus bush warfare, supply, and so on. This emphasis on classification and categorization makes the book both a history and a science of a specialized type of warfare.

Throughout Callwell's book there are absolutely no questions raised about the justification for this kind of warfare. There is a simple distinction made between civilization and barbarism, which provides the former all the justification necessary to discipline the latter. So, for example, when dealing with the category of fanatics, Callwell explains that because their tactics are aggressive and designed to deliver shock, regular forces have no choice but to "conform to the savage method of battle" (1996 [1906], 31). On this logic, torture and the destruction of villages and crops could be encouraged and justified.

The evocation of the fanatic is one place in which the ethnologic emerges in Callwell's text; for the fanatic is associated with particular racial types that make up a subgroup of the uncivilized or savage. More common, however, ethnology is located under intelligence. In the section of the book that deals with intelligence, Callwell draws a sharp contrast between intelligence gathered about European powers and that gathered about places in which small wars occur. In the case of Europe, information about military capabilities, topography and communications lines, and military resources are readily accessible, sometimes through firsthand observations and other times through the statistics generated by civilized nation-states. This is not the case in the "uncivilized" world. Not only is there little knowledge of terrain and military resources, but the fighting qualities of the enemy can only be "imperfectly gauged" (Callwell 1996 [1906], 43). Moreover, it is difficult to gather concrete information from the locals. This is because Orientals and savages—that is, people of color to be found in theaters of war—have only the vaguest ideas of time, numbers, and distances, even when they try to tell the truth (1996 [1906], 50). However, British experience in Africa and India showed Callwell that an efficient and well-organized field intelligence apparatus could overcome the problem, essentially through aggressive on-site reconnaissance.

But while the natives might be incapable of producing accurate information, the irregular forces of the enemy had a number of advantages over the modern army. They had a strategic advantage because of their low level of organization, which allowed for greater mobility and speed of movement. They also had certain tactical advantages because they were operating on familiar ground and could rely on the indigenous noncombatants as a primary source of information about the movement of the occupying forces (cf. Castaño, this volume). The locals might not understand modern weapon or tactics, but being "closer to nature," they were far more observant than Europeans. "By a kind of instinct," Callwell tells us, "they interpret military portents even when totally deficient of courage or fighting capacity" (1996 [1906], 54). Moreover, they were able, in a most mysterious fashion, to communicate their reading of portents over great distances and at high speed.

These characteristics of the indigenous—strategic advantage, mobility, light weight operations, and mysterious means of communication—would become foundational for all future studies of low-intensity conflicts and guerrilla warfare and would become the objects against which the superior brainpower of the techno elite would be pitted.

How then to deal with this seemingly organic yet invisible network and to pacify or suppress the resistance? Callwell makes a number of suggestions.

First, regarding the indigenous information system, he suggests overloading it with fictitious information. Second, the indigenous strategic advantage can be offset by actively gathering knowledge of the physical terrain of the the-ater of war—the natural and built environment. Less important, apparently, is knowledge of the strength, organization, and fighting qualities of the enemy. As such, small wars, Callwell asserts, are thus more properly thought of as wars against nature (1996 [1906], 44). Third, although the natives might be savage or uncivilized, they still had material things. As a general strategy of punish-ment and suppression, the object was to figure out what they prize and take it away from them (1996 [1906], 40, 145–46). Here we see not only a justi-fication for plunder, but the rationale for the punitive expedition. Moreover, if such punishments are not carried out, the natives will hold the European forces in contempt. "The uncivilized races," Callwell tells us, "attribute leni-ency to timidity" (1996 [1906], 148).[1]

But, how to know what the natives prize? This is where ethnology finds its place in intelligence—it functions to determine the values of the uncivilized or the savage. In India and other parts of the British Empire, political and mili-tary intelligence units were responsible for determining such values. They not only collected information about other peoples from all available sources but cultivated native informants, usually in the form of the native scouts or resi-dent agents, who provided such information.

In sum, success in small wars was predicated on the assembly of accurate information about the physical characteristics of the theater of war, knowl-edge that could then be applied instrumentally to suppress resistance. Knowl-edge of the natives was only important insofar as it could provide clear objects against which to direct punishments. It was through punishment that the na-tive learned to fear and respect the invader, which would presumably pacify them for a reasonable period of time.

Postwar Counterinsurgency

After World War II, it was quite difficult to advocate openly the punishment regime outlined by Callwell. Some of the earlier order did not, of course, disappear—it just became covert. In Malaya, Vietnam, and Algeria, the Brit-ish and French addressed insurgency as essentially an information problem and used native informants and torture to break up resistance cells (see, for example, the film *The Battle of Algiers;* for an analysis of how this film may have been read by U.S. counterinsurgency strategists, see Masco, this volume). But once decolonization occurred and the problem of the new nations was described as one of development, other elements entered the picture.

American social sciences did yeomen work during the 1950s and 1960s to help the Pentagon, Central Intelligence Agency (CIA), and State Department develop programs to deal with the problem of "Communist subversion" in the new nations. As Christopher Simpson has documented in *Science of Coercion* (1994), the link between the academy and the cold war state included things like Operation Camelot, the U.S. Army School of the Americas, and the symbiotic relation between something called the Special Operations Research Office and American University social scientists. Out of this cooperation, new strategies of counterinsurgency emerged, including psyops, or psychological warfare, which took Callwell a step further. Now it was not only a matter of sorting out what the indigenous people valued but also what they feared and loathed.[2] It was also important to determine what elements in the indigenous cultural and social structure might serve as obstacles to modernization and develop strategies for dealing with them. The social sciences provided ways of getting at these things.

I want to talk a bit about Iraq and Afghanistan, but I want to get there via what was called a low-intensity conflict, in this case, the one in Vietnam. Here my concern is with a program that was made operational in 1968, which combined the small war emphasis on the physical terrain with what is now being called in Iraq and Afghanistan the human terrain. The program in question was dubbed "Civil Operations and Revolutionary Development Support" or CORDS. One of the key authors of CORDS was John Paul Vann. Similar to many nineteenth- and twentieth-century British intelligence personnel, Vann began his military career in logistics. In the late 1950s he completed an M.B.A. and Ph.D. in public administration at Syracuse and the course at the Army Command and General Staff College at Fort Leavenworth before arriving in Vietnam in the early 1960s. Disillusioned by the ineptness and corruption of the Diem regime, and by the decentralization of U.S. counterinsurgency efforts, Vann resigned his commission 1963.

Convinced that the fundamental problem in Vietnam was one of structural order and lines of communication—in other words, a management and administration problem—Vann returned in 1965 as an official of the U.S. Agency for International Development or USAID. In this position, he argued that development, psychological operations, and counterinsurgency had to be brought under a uniform chain of command and implemented in such a way that outcomes could be assessed. This was the logic of CORDS. The program linked intelligence and rural development projects and centralized the various agencies such as USAID, the CIA, and United States Information Service under one civilian director, who reported directly to the U.S. military commander in Vietnam. CORDS became one leg of a strategy, the other part of which was the Phoenix program, which was designed to eliminate the Vietcong command structure essentially through assassination and incarceration (Sheehan 1988, 730–32). But perhaps what is most important is that in the CORDS format, counterinsurgency comes out as systems building, organizational efficiency, and information management, with a dose of behavioral science thrown in. It is a rational integrated structure, the implementation of which has built into it the means for assessment.[3]

Why have I taken this detour through CORDS? In part because I wanted to provide an example of the link between intelligence and culture in what was then being called low-intensity warfare. But it is also because in the spring of 2006, articles about CORDS and its virtues began turning up in Army magazines such *Military Review,* a publication out of the U.S. Army Combined Arms Center at Fort Leavenworth, whose commander was Lieutenant General David H. Petraeus, himself the holder of an M.A. in public administration and a Ph.D. in international relations and a theorist of asymmetrical warfare.[4] CORDS was revisited, it would seem, because it provided, according to the authors of these articles, a model of a successful counterinsurgency program, one that coordinated intelligence, development, and a civic action program— coordination that was presumably absent in Iraq and Afghanistan.

The Petraeus-inspired *U.S. Army/Marine Corps Counterinsurgency Field Manual* is, therefore, an acknowledgement of the strategic and tactical shortcomings of US operations in those two countries. And like the British military before it, the U.S. military has not only identified culture as a problem, but located it in the intelligence section of the operation. In this section of the manual, the main emphasis appears to be on both the physical characteristics of the theater of battle and the human elements in the theater— how to sort them out, identify their features and characteristics, and assess them. The result is a comprehensive insurgency analysis that is the input to designing counterinsurgency operations—sort of like assessing the market and making up the business plan. Table 3.9 of the *U.S. Army/Marine Corps Counterinsurgency Field Manual,* shown below as Table 11.1, provides the basic template for information collection and analysis that will lead to a plan.

If the tasks are read from top to bottom as most to least important, "culture" appears after the identification of insurgents strategies, motivations, and grievances but before a subsequent set of determinations. Presumably, cultural knowledge—or perhaps more properly, the processes by which cultural knowledge is gathered—has use value for the various determinations that need to be made in order to formulate a counterinsurgency plan. At the very least,

Table 11.1 Comprehensive insurgency analysis tasks

- Identify insurgent strategic, operational, and tactical goals, objectives, and imperatives.
- Identify motivations, fears, concerns, and perceptions that shape the actions of insurgents and their supporters.
- Identify grievances, fears, and concerns that the insurgents exploit.
- Determine how culture, interests, and history inform insurgent and host-nation decision making.
- Understand links among political, religious, tribal, criminal, and other social networks.
- Determine how social networks, key leaders, and groups interact with insurgent networks.
- Determine the structure and function of insurgent organizations.
- Identify key insurgent activities and leaders.
- Understand popular and insurgent perceptions of the host-nation, insurgency, and counterinsurgents—and how these affect the insurgency.

---

this would transform culture into strategic or tactical knowledge for planning purposes.

What are we to make of the movement in counterinsurgency theory from small wars, to low-intensity conflicts, to asymmetrical wars? Is it just terminology? I think what we see in all of this is a shift from the world as seen by the engineer or artillery officer to the world as seen by military officers with M.B.A.s, M.P.A.s, and Ph.D.s in public administration and systems-theory-heavy international relations. The logics used by both may be understood as "instrumental reason," but the targets are quite different. As understood by Charles Callwell, small wars gave primacy to the physical terrain. Asymmetrical wars, as conceived by the "Petraeus generation" (Dehghanpisheh and Thomas 2008) attend to the necessity of knowing the human terrain. The former wishes to teach a lesson that will not be forgotten, while leaving the natives essentially as they are. The latter wants to transform the natives into new kinds of subjects. One sees no nations, just savage and uncivilized land. The other sees a nation ripe to be built. Both arrive uninvited, but one comes and goes quickly, while the other seems never to know when to leave. What they share, however, is perhaps more significant. The counterinsurgency strategies of both yesterday's small wars and today's asymmetrical wars understand the indigenous as a problem requiring the use of force or persuasion in order to alter behavior. As such, their roots are in the Euro-American colonial encounter with Africa, Asia, Latin America, and the Pacific in the nineteenth century. Human Terrain Systems are simply one of the most recent euphemisms the forces of occupation use in these particular histories of violence.

:: NOTES ::

1. These assertions were commonplace among British colonial army officers. See Nevill 1999 [1912], where "the Zulu, the Turcoman, the Arab, and the American Indian" are all said to understand that "vengeance is the prerogative of might, forbearance the corollary of weakness" (374).

2. See, for example, Richard Drinnon's discussion of the psychological warfare operations of Edward Lansdale in the Philippines (1980, 393–94).

3. According to David Passage, a member of a CORDS team, participants received an intensive six-week training program on the cultures, civilizations, and economies of Vietnam and other countries in Southeast Asia. CORDS teams were then deployed at the village level to advise Vietnamese counterparts on implementation of programs. Passage's description of the CORDS training program appeared in the *Foreign Service Journal* in November 2007 and was essentially a critique of what he saw as the rather slipshod approach of the Bush administration's Provincial Reconstruction Teams that had been deployed in Iraq (Passage 2007, 13–16).

4. See Coffey (2006) and Andrade and Willbanks (2006, 9–23). There are also numerous articles in the 2006 run of *Military Affairs* dealing with counterinsurgency and ethnography.

12

Repetition Compulsion?

Counterinsurgency Bravado in Iraq and Vietnam

:: KURT JACOBSEN ::

"Repetition compulsion," in layman's terms, is the performing of an action again and again in order to gain release from an earlier trauma by somehow "getting it right" this time. The small abiding tragedy here is that sufferers rarely achieve this mastery but instead get caught within a harmful behavioral loop they cannot understand or escape (see Freud 1960 [1920]; Bibring 1943, 486). Like all psychoanalytic concepts, the term is derived from, and properly situated in, the domain of the experience of individuals not of collectivities or institutions. Sliding over this individual/collective threshold has spawned many a dubious, not to say idiotic, proposition. Still, with all due methodological caveats, there are social phenomena that exhibit all the earmarks of repetition compulsion, even if they are played out by major institutions in the international arena. At all times one must be acutely aware of the alternative or overlapping "rational" sources of action. Yet international politics is, at best, only partly a rational enterprise to which psychoanalytically oriented observers therefore may have something illuminating to contribute. One case I nominate is the resurrection of counterinsurgency practices.

The *Counterinsurgency Field Manual No. 3-24* benignly defines pacification as "the process by which the government assert[s] its influence and control in an area beset by insurgents" and which includes "local security efforts, programs to distribute food and medical supplies, and lasting reforms (like land redistribution)" (U.S. Department of the Army 2006, 73). Yet pacification in Vietnam, for an egregious example, was responsible for the killing and maiming of untold numbers of noncombatants as well as armed fighters who at times seem only to have gotten in the way—and, incidentally, it was unsuccessful. Judging from upbeat references sprinkled throughout the manual, its authors vehemently disagree. Civil Operations and Revolutionary Development Support (CORDS), a coordinating committee of U.S. agencies formed in 1967 to stamp out the southern resistance, is credited with "considerable success" (U.S. Department of the Army 2006, 73). For many Vietnam-era beholders, however, the term "pacification" and its synonym "counterinsurgency" are just stale euphemisms for military suppression of popular resistance movements during interventions abroad. This strategy was rehabilitated within the Bush administration—and this time, chagrined authorities were determined to get it right.

According to the *Oxford English Dictionary*, "pacification" denotes "the condition of being pacified, appeasement, conciliation" (*Compact Edition of the Oxford English Dictionary* [OED] 1971, 2049–50). One example given is an "ordinance or decree enacted by a prince or state to put an end to strife or discontent" (OED 1971, 2049–50). The verb "to pacify" means "to allay the anger, excitement, or agitation (of a person); to calm; quiet; to appease." More ominously, its meaning also includes "to reduce to peaceful submission," as when Hobbes writes, "Counts . . . were left to govern and defend places conquered and pacified." Who today fails to recognize the rueful Tacitus quotation about unstinting Roman retributive techniques: "they make a desert and call it peace" (Tacitus 1894, 35);[1] or perhaps, as Harry G. Summers reminds those with family bibles at hand, the fate of the Midanites in the Book of Numbers?[2]

The strategy of pacification has been around as long as the nasty services it justifies have appealed to ambitious occupiers. Counterinsurgency operations may be defined as the employment of military resources for purposes other than conventional warfare (Brush 1994, fn.8). You do not pacify criminal gangs or bands of malcontents; you pacify entire populations. In its revived form the counterinsurgency doctrine is supposed to be a sagacious mix of enticement and coercion, a finely discriminatory wielding of carrot and stick, rather like a sepia-colored scene of a grim nineteenth-century schoolmaster confronting a mischievous pupil who needs taming. The "patient," plunging into "remakes" of earlier situational psychic mayhem, imagines, if s/he has a glimmer of awareness, that s/he is equipped this time to surmount old painful barriers—such as, for American elites, "kicking the Vietnam syndrome."

A purely public relations–motivated image of counterinsurgency is encouraged by those who see it as a solution to an Iraqi population that, however internally divided, overwhelmingly wants the foreign schoolmasters out. One can hardly blame the U.S. military for its bemoaned neglect of counterinsurgency, if such shrewd scholars as Walter Laqueur deduced, just after Saigon fell, that given the completion of decolonization, potent insurgencies were a thing of the past (Laqueur 1976, 409). But any rusty tool in a governing elite's coercion kit of course will be discovered anew when events require it.

The reputed "neglect" of counterinsurgency is much exaggerated too, as even a cursory scan of the manual shows. In fact, counterinsurgency, almost from the moment that the last American helicopter fled Saigon, has been reinterpreted—compensatingly, shrinks might say—as a proud parade of heartening successes.

According to proponents, modern counterinsurgency techniques, given enough "learning and adopting" to local milieus, can suppress armed opposition anywhere, if properly applied. So begins the internalized siren song of repetition compulsion. Whether one ought to attempt to do such a thing is a question that just never seems to come up. This is task-oriented, "ours not to reason why" scholarship. In the manual, one beholds a brief for deployment of a ravenous "learning organization" that, curiously, is forbidden to learn certain things or to reach unwelcome conclusions. The bedrock credo is expressed in the solemn invocation of an Algerian war veteran's belief that "[i]f the individual member of the organization were of the same mind, if every organization worked to a standard pattern, the problem would be solved" (U.S. Army Department of the 2006, xix).

As early as 2004, as it became clear that the "mission" was not "accomplished" in Iraq, billions of dollars were already slated for covert operations. One does not need a military genius to tell you that such operations would target not only Iraqi "rebels" and "foreign fighters" (as the Pentagon calls them), but also any nationalist opponent of the U.S. occupation, including hitherto nonviolent ones. The conundrum is, "How do you eliminate the extremists without alienating the population?" (U.S. Army Department of the 2006, 27). Readers are urged to let the trained military men and women, manual in one hand and Armalite in the other, sort them out.

Why, an analyst might ask the anxious state on his capacious couch, must you relive old painful memories? One very good answer, of course, is "because we covet their oil"; but this cannot be said aloud. For many, reviving a pre-Vietnam sense of the United States' unchecked military grandiosity is a bonus too.

Counterinsurgency in Vietnam was replete with a civic action dimension aiming at what is called "nation building" today. The best-known example was the Phoenix program, designed to "neutralize" the leadership of the South Vietnamese resistance. The optimistic take on the failures of this strategy is that the U.S. Marines (or Central Intelligence Agency [CIA] or U.S. Army Special Forces, in different versions) had acquired a hefty stock of fine-grained counterinsurgency wisdom over decades of operations (especially in Central America) but (oops) forgot to apply it.[3] The animating faith is that violent techniques must work, regardless of local context or overarching superpower goal or annoying barriers imposed by the local political coalition. For all the manual's pretensions to address local sensitivities, it is about nothing but the use of power, applied with the most, if not the best, intelligence available.

The ultimate aim is to create an indigenous security force that carries out counterinsurgency tactics without the need of intense external supervision. Local recruits have often been drawn from exile groups who had long-nursed grudges to settle; but U.S. forces have not been bashful about also working with former members of Saddam Hussein's secret police. Up until his bum's rush exit, Secretary of Defense Donald Rumsfeld gave secret commando units a free hand globally to strike at suspected terrorists, even though authorities admit that poor intelligence often results in the wrong victims being fingered. "The local people do not mind, or they won't if handled with a firm but supportive hand"—this is the prime lesson a group of self-labelled "revisionists" have drawn from Vietnam.

It is an old, inescapably gory story. The squaring of brute force with idealist objectives is what makes, in Sahlins's phrase, a "hardheaded surrealist" of anyone charged with the task (Sahlins 2000 [1966], 238). Iconic images of Yank soldiers burning Vietnamese villages hark back to atrocities inflicted in the Philippines over 1898–1901; and one may gallop further back to the spectacle of the U.S. cavalry sweeping the North American continent clean of obstructive natives (for further discussion of "counterinsurgency" against Native Americans, see Wax, this volume). Pacification requires a sophisticated domestic propaganda apparatus because states depend on their power to define the sticky situations they wade into. No one knows how well this power works better than children who grew up playing war games in the postwar John Wayne movie era. Those innately "backward" natives had their merits—too bad they got in the way of manifest destiny.

Go far enough West and you wind up in the East, across the Pacific, where the exploits become a bit harder to explain away to a populace taught to loathe imperialism—at least, the epicene European kind (see Drinnon 1997). In South East Asia, U.S. authorities failed to make their definitions, or their dominance, stick. In the first few years of insurgency after the Iraq invasion, it was deemed the height of sophistication for critics to dismiss Vietnam analogies (not to mention the oil motive) as strident, puerile, and overdrawn. But by the end of 2005 even housebroken pundits were not so sure the analogies did not hold in some important ways. Bush's aides largely subscribed to the fanciful story that "pacification in Vietnam worked, so why not try it again?" Sometimes material circumstances—not intrapsychic impulses—force patients into repetition, although the reasons why they got into those circumstances bears examination, both in terms of material interests in play and the psychic mechanisms accompanying and easing their pursuit.

Freud, after the outbreak of World War I, remarked that psychoanalysis inferred that

> [T]he primitive, savage and evil impulses of mankind have not vanished in any of its individual members, but persists, although in a repressed state, in the unconscious [and] It has further taught us that our intellect is . . . a plaything and tool of our instincts and affects. If you will observe what is happening in this war—the cruelties and injustices for which the most civilized nations are responsible, *the different way in which they judge their own lies and wrong-doings and those of their enemies and the general lack of insight which prevails*—you will have to admit that psycho-analysis has been right in both these theses. (Freud 1915, emphasis added)

Rehabilitating Vietnam Strategy

The revisionists' case hinges on their "ironic" view that counterinsurgency succeeded at the moment the American withdrawal got underway (see, for example, Butterfield 1983; Manning 1989; Lewy 1980; Summers 1982; Hosmer, Kellner, and Jenkins 1986; Thompson and Frizzell 1977; Colby 1989). "We" (the United States) won, but foolishly bugged out. Here is a thoroughly modern wrinkle on the odious "stab in the back" stories that accompany every loss by a great power. The implication is that military strategy and performance was sound and merely required more time for necessary fine-tuning to kick in. This widespread interpretation of the American loss in Vietnam got great play in powerful circles. The ruptured assumption is that there really was a smart surgical way to win the war without annihilating the bulk of the population, going nuclear, or expanding the conflict into China.

Take Mark Moyar's account of the Phoenix program, a volume laced together with jaw-dropping implausibilities, contradictions, and tendentious arguments (Moyar 1997; for contrary view see Valentine 1990). The study is, to say the least, unfailingly provocative. Mass murder can become "an effective counterinsurgency tool," even if you murder uninvolved people. The locals will

understand if overeager authorities rub out the wrong person every now and
then, if it is all for a good cause (Moyar 1997, 300).[4] The fact that such a silly
book can be regarded as "balanced" in academic circles is a distressing sign. In
2006 Cambridge published his follow-up screed, *Triumph Forsaken,* which
contended that Diem was a "very wise leader," that strategic hamlets worked
just dandily, that the domino theory was valid, and that Vietnam was "a wise
war fought under foolish conditions" (Moyar 2006, xiv, xx, 283, 416).

In Vietnam torture was used, Moyar admits; but, you see, the cruel South
Vietnamese always "were the despair of America for killing every suspect
turned up" (2007, 375). One must not fret about frequently fatal torture techniques, because they were used "almost always against hard-core Communist
cadres and soldiers rather than civilians of uncertain loyalties" (Moyar 1997,
375). How on earth does Moyar know? He then implies that Americans today,
as supposedly then, are mere squeamish bystanders while Iraqis torture other
Iraqis. It is all the fault of "those foreigners." Denial and projection are "walking point" here and everywhere else in this subgenre.

The Phoenix program was hatched to help attain a gruesome "crossover
point," where dead and wounded exceeded the National Liberation Front's
(NLF) ability to replenish itself. During Nixon's first two and a half years,
the State Department reported that the CIA program murdered or abducted
more than 35,000 Vietnamese civilians. Ex-operatives testify that orders were
given to kill South Vietnamese army and even U.S. personnel who were considered, on almost anybody's say-so, security risks.[5] Due process was absent.
Phoenix was not remotely calculated to court hearts and minds—except insofar as "black teams" sneaked out, dressed in enemy gear, with ensuing assassinations blamed on the NLF (Toohey and Pinwell 1989, 87–88). Moyar
also says that in the "overwhelming majority of cases the people whom Allied
forces killed were found with weapons or incriminating documents in their
possession" (Moyar 1997, 389). So, most of the 385,000 snuffed-out civilians
carried weapons. On the other hand, the Ninth Infantry Division operating
in the Mekong Delta over the first half of 1969 reported an "official body
count of 11,000 with only 748 captured weapons" (Young 1991, 222–23). One
searches in vain in the manual for the word "massacre" and a discussion of its
necessary place in overall strategy.

Another zealous rehabilitator of pacification is Zalin Grant, whose book
Facing the Phoenix, the publisher's blurb tells us, is based on shrewd reckon-
ings of a South Vietnamese spy, whose plan to defeat communists by community action "was perverted by the CIA." According to the Web site NameBase,
Grant believes that certain players had a good handle on how to neutralize

the enemy through local political action and enlightened aid programs. Just as they were making significant progress, however, they were defeated by "corruption in Saigon and by big-bang, big-bucks conventional-warfare mongers like William Westmoreland" (Grant 1991).[6] So, if only "we" had disposed of the regime "we" were defending, and the U.S. military authorities that were defending it, "we" would have won.

Call a psychiatrist.

This reverie constitutes logical thinking in high circles. Lewis Sorley too argues that "accelerated pacification" from November 1968 onward was deliriously successful (Sorley 1999, 14). Sorley estimates 465,000 South Vietnamese civilians were killed and, startlingly, that "many of them [were] assassinated by Viet Cong terrorists or felled by the enemy's indiscriminate shelling and rocketing of cities" (Sorley 1999, 383)—a level of firepower tantamount to American/South Vietnam (SVN) levels. Sorley, oddly, waters down his case consistently by drawing attention to the April 1968 "mini-Tet," the August/September "third offensive," and subsequent NLF-spurred actions, who seem highly aggressive for an extinct organization. This accords with a CIA analyst who, after the January-February 1968 Tet offensive, "also noted that although the enemy had suffered heavy losses, their forces appeared to be regrouping and could mount further large-scale action in a matter of weeks" (Allen 2001, 265). The enemy is always on the run, and we always are just about to rout them from their positions. Just one more push. It is repetition compulsion, which is not, as I mentioned in cases of collectivities, unrelated to pursuit of material goals.

Another study attests that Americans, through land-to-the-tiller reforms, won over Vietnamese villagers by 1970. The revisionists' image of the Vietnamese is something straight out of an imperial era *Boys' Own* magazine. The "impressionable villagers" were "attracted by military presence and strength" and the "use of highly destructive weaponry in the villages" resulted in a weakening of communists and an increase of support for Americans (Moyar 1997, 394). This strange behavior occurs because, you know, a well-known feature of warfare is that the victims rally to their oppressors, like Stockholm syndrome writ large. The peasant is depicted as primitive, apolitical, and childish but just rational enough to be amenable to the observer's means of analysis and persuasion. A can-do spirit doubtless has its place in the military; but in scholarship, as well as in intelligence analysis, it is an unfailing source of distortion. Bush's White House established an Office of Special Plans to create just such distortions in data in order to mislead Congress and the public. Employees in government agencies have little choice, other than whistle-blowing; but why do scholars succumb to imposed official views?

For one thing, there is remunerative work for skilled people willing to tell hard-line bosses what they want to hear. An American Psychological Association member, who prodded the organization to sanction members who assist interrogations, concludes that the leadership was reluctant to do so for fear of losing funding (Summers 2007). A managerial mentality comes insidiously into play among for-hire scholars, who accept as their own the edicts of policy elites. One international relations axiom, for example, is that where resistance arises, more than proportionate force must be deployed. And force must be seen to work, even if it really does not.

Here is the sublime conformist mind-set attributed by Noam Chomsky to the New Mandarins of the Vietnam era: devout, cold-blooded, hard-nosed, numerical, and officious (Chomsky 1968). They were then, and are today, ready to convert "a pleasing hypothesis into a fact"—which, as Arendt reminds us, is a highly fecund source of official lies (Arendt 1972, 42). For example, in the face of revelations of murder and intimidation by authorities in Vietnam, the rote response was that "they" (the NLF/North Vietnamese Army) did it too. This response ignores, or denies outright, that "they" did not do these things at a level anywhere near the U.S. scale and that they did not do it to Americans who contrived to stay in Little Rock or Texas. Lately, these studies have become grist for the mill of rational choice analyses, a direct heir to 1960s era systems analysis, so beloved by Secretary of Defense Robert McNamara. The soft issue of social justice (because it is not measurable) cannot arise within the conceptual boundaries of rational choice theory, and therefore it does not matter (see, in this vein, Kalyvas and Kocher 2003).

The case for counterinsurgency relies on dodgy data, such as the U.S. Hamlet Evaluation Study, conducted by government agents in 1970–71 (Elliot 2003). The fact that these evaluations rely on agencies connected to counterinsurgency—and that information was extracted under duress—generally does not register at all or is acknowledged briefly and then never mentioned again. Hence, in the twenty-first century one can draw on the sort of evidence that led to the belief that "every quantitative measure we have indicates that we are winning this war," as McNamara once blathered. As Lapham writes, McNamara was " . . . caught up in a dream of power that substituted the databases of a preferred fiction for the texts of common fact. . . . What was real was the image of war that appeared on the flowcharts and computer screens. What was not real was the presence of pain, suffering, mutilation, and death" (Lapham 1997, 30).

McNamara since has done some penance; however, fresh and unchastened McNamara mentalities proliferate (cf. Morris 2003; Jacobsen 2004).

Hearts and Hectares

A key myth resuscitated by Vietnam revisionism is that the land-to-the-tiller program reaped hearts and minds in vast numbers. This verdict ignores three things: first, by then great swathes of SVN were under NLF control; second, in these areas land already had been redistributed; and third, the Thieu reforms were neither very redistributive nor popular. In the 1950s, 80 percent of peasants in the Mekong Delta were tenants; but only 1 percent of the people owned 44 percent of rice land in SVN overall. By 1960, the NLF had redistributed 77 percent of arable land in the My Tho province that David Elliot studied. Diem's "reforms" actually restored to landlords the land previously redistributed by the Viet Minh before partition (Selden 1969, 36). The land-to-the-tiller program featured a Stolypin-like emphasis on creating a class of affluent peasants. The sanctioned distribution of uncultivated land in insecure areas (full of unexploded ordnance and trigger-happy patrols) required capital if the land was to be put to use, for which only usurious loans were available (Long 1971, 50). In any case, the politics of the ballyhooed "pacified areas," after 1968, also often were based on "nod and wink" arrangements. "What the Pentagon describes as 'secure areas' in Vietnam," Kolko noted, "is often a staging and economic base as secure and vital to the NLF as its explicitly identified liberated zones" (Kolko 1971, 42).

On the eve of the Tet offensive, U.S. monitors claimed that U.S. and Government of the Republic of Vietnam (GVN) forces controlled 67 percent of South Vietnam (Kolko 1971, 42). The reports that pacification enthusiasts relied upon were equivocal at best. Moyar mentions flaws riddling the Hamlet Evaluation Study but nonetheless says it "did track a positive trend" (Moyar 1997, 258–9). Yet Elliot found that the Mekong Delta area was "strongly pro-VC [Viet Cong]" in 1969–70, well after Tet supposedly killed off most insurgents. Elliot noted that few locals "defected from the war effort" (Hunt 2003, 600). Studies by Eric Bergerud, James Trullinger, Jeffrey Race, and David Hunt and Jayne Werner likewise testify that the districts they studied overwhelmingly favored the NLF when the U.S. ground troop escalation began, and popular support remained high through all the bloody ups and downs throughout the war (Bergerud 1993; Trullinger 1980; Race 1972; Hunt and Werner 1993; Long 1973). The NLF surely was hit hard during and after Tet (Young 1991, 224–5). Still, CORDS director Robert Komer admitted that, even if his claim of decimating the NLF was true, "we were never able to translate this into positive and active rural support for the government of Vietnam" (Thompson and Frizzel 1977, 108).

What then was supposed to have changed such that revisionists see the villagers favoring US/GVN forces? The customary case made is that, after many fits and starts, the peasants transformed into market-oriented individualists—as Irish peasants had in the early twentieth century (see Lyons 1971). Yet those land reform specialists not linked to the southern authorities found "a class-oriented program" at work and that "no amount of wishful or ideological thinking could turn Diem, Kah, Ky or Thieu into champions of the laboring poor" (Brigham and Murray 1994, 117). The evidence indicates that middle peasants actually were more likely to yield NLF recruits, since they had the resources and the ability to participate. There was no steady erosion of communist or community ties on the part of these better-off peasants (Schulzinger 1997, 201).

Imputed gains of pacification were illusory or temporary. Underlying grievances were never meant to be addressed. And they still have not been addressed, given their treatment in the manual—"perceived injustices" are cited as though they are ruses (U.S. Army Department of the 2006, 99–100). A self-serving census-taking attitude also meant that opinions were taken at face value. Long points out that, for people under a repressive regime, the questions, "Do you believe the people should be masters?" and "Do you believe in democracy?" were understood as more resonant of the NLF than of Saigon but were coded to favor the latter. So far as southern insurgents were concerned, as a U.S. general acknowledged, "when NLF casualties got too high . . . they just backed off and waited" (Schulzinger 1997, 200). The NLF held the initiative at all times. The *Pentagon Papers* disclose that a post-Tet system analysis study finding that while "we have raised the price to NVN [North Vietnam] of aggression and support of the VC, it shows no lack of capability or will to match each new US escalation. Our strategy of attrition has not worked" (Gravel 1971, 557).

After Tet

Tet itself was as much a popular uprising as anything else. One tireless cliché is that Tet was a political victory but a military defeat. But this sententious comment is an ultimately unimportant distinction. The insurgents sustained heavy losses, but it led to little wavering of popular support for them.[7] The U.S. high command's appraisal was that the insurgents regained the countryside as U.S. and SVN troops shifted into the cities. The cities, for that matter, were none too secure (see Gravel 1971, 556; Hunt 1995, 136–8). Further, the statistics do not weigh NLF losses against prisoners freed from all the cities and jail, who replenished the ranks (Franklin 2000, 95). Despite "accelerated pacification" afterward, it remained possible for the NLF and NVA to launch equally devastating but not so highly publicized offensives after Tet. Generals Westmoreland and Wheeler both privately acknowledged that Tet was no victory (Buzzanco 1996, 96).

The manual claims that by 1970, 93 percent of rural SVN—from which there had been a massive forced migration—resided in "relatively secure villages" and that the insurgency had been "uprooted" (U.S. Army Department of the 2006, 75). Yet Hunt found that "US/GVN sweeps and mass killings seem to have pushed fence-sitters over the edge" (Hunt 2003, 606), so that many young people volunteered for the NLF. Blaufarb argues that the crime of Phoenix was "ineffectiveness, indiscriminateness, and, in some areas at least, the violation of the local norms to the extent that it appeared to the villagers to be a threat to them in the peaceful performance of their daily business" (Blaufarb 1977, 276). His view is that the American analysts involved "erred in not appreciating the extent to which the pathology of Vietnamese society would distort an apparently sound concept" (Blaufarb 1977, 276). How could they do otherwise? It was this pathology that the troops were defending.

The objective in My Tho province always was "to destroy rather than 'pacify' the rural communities" (Hunt 2003, 609). The bombing, pillaging, refugee flight, the GVN and NLF drafts, cadres killed, and cumulative hardships mounted. Even so, the six villages of one official Hamlet Evaluation Study remained "nearly completely controlled by the revolution as much in January 1968 as a year before." There is no reason to believe things changed drastically afterward. This anomalous result, for some analysts, can be comprehended only in the terms of a game of gang warfare in which rivals are treated as symmetrical and as equally illegitimate. This simply "must" be the way insurgents behave, because the model demands it (cf. Kelly, this volume). There is no space for the notions of nationalism or solidarity or sacrifice, but only for self-regarding mafias who compel obedience. This depiction cannot explain why the NLF was far more successful than the US/GVN, despite taking unbelievable punishment. For if strict rational choice were the NLF's operating code, they would have been wiped out in quick order.

Carrot and stick, at the first sign of sustained resistance, became all stick. A CIA official told a journalist, "We're going to beat the communists at their own game, use their methods, cut off their cocks, cut up their women and children, if that's what it takes, until we break the communist hold over these people . . . *We can stand it*" (Welsh 1968, 293). Disembedded press members had seen the Strategic Hamlet Programme disintegrate before their very eyes, despite "happy talk" reports to the contrary (Prochnau 1995, 419). But the tradition of "doctoring" reports goes back at least as far as the British Royal Air Force portrayals of its use of phosphorous bombs, chemicals, and gas upon recalcitrant villagers in the Middle East in the 1920s, stretching up through the Nixon administration's secret bombing of Cambodia and Laos, and finally reaching the initial denials of use of phosphorous bombs in Iraq today. As Henry Cabot Lodge told Secretary of Defense McNamara, "If you think these people are going to tell you or say in front of [General] Harkin what they really think unless it is what Harkin thinks, you just don't know the army" (Prochnau 1995, 438).[8] Some things never change and do not require repetition compulsion to explain why.

Over 1970–72 government agencies were divided in their appraisals of pacification, depending largely on whether or not they understood the Vietnamese conception of protracted war (Tang 1985, 86–87). The vaunted gains in control of the countryside through accelerated pacification were always questionable. A Military Assistance Command Vietnam estimate said VC strength fell from 189,000 to 120,000 in the three years after Tet. Yet, even if one took their reckoning as gospel, the result was that the VC adapted tactics so that small-unit actions accelerated from 1,374 in 1968 to 2,400 by 1972 (Hunt 2003, 253). Better than brigade actions, certainly, but hardly proof of victory around the corner. Even if "victory" somehow had beckoned, Chalmers Johnson attested later that "Many senior analysts were passionately opposed to President Johnson and Richard Nixon's policies, and after the Pentagon Papers had been made public many of the analysts were quietly exultant that their pessimistic estimates of whether the US could win the war were now in than official part of the public record" (Johnson 1997, 36). And in spite of all the work to revise the history of pacification, it is clear, as Senator John Murtha's controversial speeches indicated, that the Pentagon too was also pessimistic—or at least divided—about its prospects. Even without leaks of *Pentagon Papers* proportions, rationales for the Iraq intervention have unravelled. The best anyone can come up with is that U.S. forces now must tamp down the cyclonic forces they triggered by invading Iraq. One sign of madness is the belief that only one's will power or actions matter, not those of the other folks involved. It does serve to keep twinges of conscience (or accountability) at bay, so perhaps madness is not quite the word for what is going on here.

Conclusion

In Iraq, the psychic mechanisms in play are secondary to the material interests pursued by the neocon (and post-Rumsfeld) visionaries who "make reality"; but they are nonetheless important in sustaining their grandiosity. Could the Iraqi occupation, under any imaginable circumstances, have succeeded? The quaint delusion is widespread that Bush might have avoided an intractable insurgency if only he had made a shrewder move here or there. Maybe if the army had been kept intact, things would have worked out. Maybe if the Saddam loyalists had been kept behind their desks, things would have worked out. Maybe if the United States had amassed a military force twice its size (as many military commanders urged) before invading, things would have worked. Maybe if honest contractors had gotten electricity and water running again, things would have worked out. Maybe if the U.S. rulers would not privatize everything in sight to sell it off to cronies, things would work out.

So goes the mournful litany—with verses added daily. Presumably, if all the conditions above were met, Iraqis would sit perfectly still while the West siphoned away their resources.[9] The Coalition Provisional Authority long ago established a "parallel government structure of Commissioners and Inspectors-General . . . who, elections notwithstanding, will control Iraq's chief ministries . . . ." and apparently despite President Barack Obama's plans for a phased withdrawal (Perusek 2005, 23). But one might concede that it all might have worked out if a U.S. government of a radically different character had invaded—except that such a government might have read intelligence data honestly and therefore opted not to invade. Finally, in its view that a good leader should pull off a bad mission, the manual reads as though it were ghostwritten by Graham Greene's (1955) fictional Quiet American, Alden Pyle, and is not one iota the wiser for the intervening half century of sobering experience (assuming, of course, Pyle had not been killed off in the novel). What would Freud, or Machiavelli, have made of that?

:: **NOTES** ::

1. Tacitus was quoting, perhaps apocryphally, a Caledonian chieftain, Calgacus.

2. Harry G. Summers puts Vietnamese civilian casualties at 365,000 (which is small compared with 2.5 million Korean War civilian casualties). See Summers (2007, xii).

3. Larry Cable posits that the lessons the marines learned from interventions in the Caribbean "were not properly institutionalized and diffused" (Cable 1986, 96).

4. Moyar goes on to say, "Allied uses of violence in the subsequent eras were aimed primarily at Communist soldiers inside the hamlets, rather than at the hamlet residents. The villagers appreciated this factor and attached considerable importance to it" (Moyar 1997, 300).

5. I interviewed a former U.S. Army Intelligence officer in Vietnam who listened to Phoenix program radio traffic ordering the killing of several South Vietnamese soldiers who supported the wrong (non-NLF) southern faction (Jacobsen 2001, 4182–83).

6. http://www.namebase.org/sources/UB.html.

7. In subsequent actions, "Communist forces had clearly demonstrated that they had not been destroyed during the earlier Tet fighting" (Willbanks 2007, 82).

8. George Allen, CIA and defense analyst, also says, "Two plus two always makes four. But first someone has to decide that two is actually two" (Prochnau 1995, 438).

9. The British military's conceit that they possessed a magic formula for conducting a "decent" occupation of the Middle East finally crumbled under scrutiny too (see Fisk 2005).

13

Counterinsurgency, *The Spook,* and Blowback

:: JOSEPH MASCO ::

On August 27, 2003, U.S. special operations officers at the Pentagon—then confronting an amplifying insurgency in post–U.S. invasion Iraq—organized a screening of the classic 1966 Gillo Pontecorvo film, *The Battle of Algiers.* As *Washington Post* reporter David Ignatius (2003) saw it, the screening marked a "hopeful sign that the military is thinking creatively and unconventionally about Iraq," noting that a Pentagon advertising flyer for the event had asked provocatively:

> How to win a battle against terrorism and lose the war of ideas . . . Children shoot soldiers at point blank range. Women plant bombs in cafes. Soon the entire Arab population builds to a mad fervor. Sound familiar? The French have a plan. It succeeds tactically, but fails strategically. To understand why, come to a rare showing of the film.

Sound familiar? Looking back on the summer of 2003, this is a striking moment of self-reflexivity among U.S. war planners. *The Battle of Algiers* offers a textbook study of both insurgency and counterinsurgency. The film documents not only the various forms of armed resistance to French power but also the counterterror strategy, media manipulation, and torture practices that enabled the French to "win" the battle. Thus, what was presented to U.S.

special operations theorists as a study in tactics and countertactics—terror and counterterror—in the decolonization struggle over Algeria was also a pointed lesson about the political limits of counterrevolution. After all, to "succeed tactically but fail strategically" is hardly an endorsement of the French approach. And yet, in the years to follow, the U.S. military reproduced the full range of counterinsurgency techniques documented in Pontecorvo's film—contributing to what is now the second longest war in U.S. history (following the counterinsurgency campaign in Vietnam). Indeed, the film screening was followed not by a fundamental revision in the U.S. global project known as the War on Terror but rather by a profound reinvestment in the conceptual power of counterinsurgency.

Filmed with a beautifully grainy black and white cinematography, in a documentary or newsreel style, *The Battle of Algiers* articulates an astonishingly clear vision of the uses of terror—by both revolutionaries and the state. Cast largely with nonactors (including a few participants in the actual battle of Algiers), the film ultimately presents many of the techniques recently adopted by al-Qaeda and the broader insurgencies in Iraq and Afghanistan. The revolutionary National Liberation Front (FLN) party organizes itself in cell structures and instructs its members not to talk for twenty-four hours if caught by the French military to allow comrades to escape; its supporters do not wear uniforms but frequently use the veil as both disguise and cover for smuggling weapons. The escalating campaign of street attacks on French military personnel (by men, women, and children) leads to attacks on civilians, including a bombing campaign involving multiple, simultaneous strikes as well as suicide attacks. In response, the French military moves to identify and decapitate the terrorist cell structure via assassination, raids on homes, and ultimately the destruction of whole neighborhoods (not unlike the U.S. effort to pacify the Iraqi city of Fallujah in 2004). The French also embrace a full spectrum of torture techniques—stress positions, the use of electricity, and (what Americans now call) water boarding. Colonial Mathieu, the leader of the French forces, when questioned about these techniques by the media states that the word "torture" is never used—it is simply interrogation designed to break the subject's resistance within the twenty-four-hour window in which information might stop a bombing (thus presenting a version of the "ticking time bomb" scenario often evoked since 2001 in the United States to justify torture).[1] By the end of the film, the French forces have killed or captured the known FLN members but have also fomented a national revolutionary movement that within a few years will force the French to abandon Algeria. Thus, the tactics of counterinsurgency win a reprieve for French interests but ultimately produce a more massive countermovement among the general Algerian population. Pontecorvo's film may be positioned by U.S. military personnel today as a careful study of the techniques of terror and counterterror; however, it presents an even more powerful argument about the structural contradiction of the colonial project and the political power of decolonization.

Theorists of counterinsurgency have consistently recognized that success depends on perception management—"victory" is as much grounded in public sentiment as in military action. David Galula, for example, states categorically that the "basic mechanism of counterinsurgency warfare" is to "build (or rebuild) a political machine from the population upward" (Galula 2006 [1964], 95). Thus, it is as much about constructing a positive view of external governance as eliminating insurgents. Counterinsurgency involves both the destruction and construction of a public; indeed, it is ultimately a fight over the annihilation and production of a nation. Peter Paret, like Galula, a theorist of the Algerian insurgency, underscores the French effort to psychologically reprogram Algerian revolutionaries to be colonial subjects:

> The first step in the process was to "disintegrate the individual." The internee was isolated, his fears and guilt feelings were exploited by his monitor, he was made to feel ashamed of his past and induced to acknowledge his errors. The period of brainwashing (*lavage de crane*) was followed by a period of reconstruction or brainfilling (*bourrage de crane*). Lectures and discussion presented the internee with the Army's views on history, current affairs, and the future of North Africa. In the final stage, the individual was brought into a disciplined group of converted fellow prisoners, which acted as an unfriendly collective superego toward recalcitrant inmates and which participated in the psychological campaign against the FLN beyond the barbed wire by writing propaganda letters to relatives and issuing manifestos. (Paret 1964, 64)

To disintegrate the individual. The recent French defeat in Indochina provided a specific motivation for this project of remaking the colonial subject in Algeria, as well as for its brutality. However, the effects of counterinsurgency are totalizing: as Paret notes, it is a characteristic of counterrevolution that it transforms revolutionary and counterrevolutionary alike (in terms of both national and moral identities). This raises important questions today not only about how to translate the almost exclusively colonial context of counterinsurgency theory into the current American global project but also about the long-term effects of the War on Terror on U.S. national culture.

The Battle of Algiers, from this point of view, raises the vital, but underanalyzed, issue of the temporality of counterinsurgency—for what does it really mean to say that a counterinsurgency campaign can be successful? What

are the secondary effects of such targeted violence now, and into a deep future? And finally, what are the domestic costs of counterterror as U.S. national
policy? For U.S. officials did not take the lesson of the film to be the impos-
sibility of delivering democracy to Iraq via invasion and counterinsurgency.
Rather they seem to have accepted the value of torture, media manipulation,
and covert action in extending American power throughout the region. Indeed, the recent failures of U.S. operations in the region have been positioned
within U.S. security debates as a failure of expertise or knowledge rather than
as an illustration of a lack of popular support for the U.S. military presence
in Iraq or for the fundamental ideological weakness of the War on Terror as a
concept.

Thus, as the failure to achieve stability in both Afghanistan and Iraq has
become more obvious, one key move of U.S. military planners has been to assume that more expertise will solve the problem of counterrevolution, which
as now resulted in the widely publicized "cultural turn" at the Pentagon (see
Gusterson, this volume). These efforts include deploying social scientists on
the front lines in Human Terrain Teams, as well as recruiting academics to help
on key military problems via targeted funding.[2] This effort to finally "get it
right" has also produced the first new *U.S. Army/Marine Corps Counterinsurgency Field Manual* in a generation, updating the lessons learned from Korea
and Vietnam as well as from the covert campaigns in Central America during
the 1980s for use in the current wars in Afghanistan and Iraq (see Nagl 2005;
see also Jacobsen, this volume). However, the record of previous U.S. counterinsurgency engagements, like the screening of Pontecorvo's film, presents
a continuing lost opportunity to recognize the limits of military action designed to produce or destroy a new national consciousness or to acknowledge
the long-term global effects of deploying U.S. military power in this manner.
As a result, counterinsurgency theory today says much more about the fantasy
of U.S. military power and official desires to realize U.S. hegemony than it does
about expert knowledge of politics on the ground.

This remains a vital problem because the George W. Bush administration's
inauguration of a Global War on Terror in 2001 committed the United States
to nothing less than a planetary program of counterinsurgency. President Bush
declared war not simply on the perpetrators of the attacks on Washington and
New York in 2001 but on terror itself, promising to cleanse the world of both
the act and the emotion via an elimination of al-Qaeda and related networks.
The radical nature of this concept of war is hard to overstate. It was, and is,
(1) an overt assertion of American global hegemony, as the Bush administration declared a right to wage preventative and preemptive war against any state
and to deploy military forces covertly into any nation-state in pursuit of ter-

ror; (2) a de facto declaration of a permanent state of war (for when can terror ever be finally and absolutely purged from individual minds or collective experience?); (3) a deployment of terror to create a state of emergency that allows suspension of international and domestic law—constituting a rather fundamental revision of the social contract within the United States and a direct challenge to the idea of international law; and (4) a radical experiment in U.S. military power, linking new technologies of direct and covert action within a novel concept of global war. This War on Terror was imagined from the start as a multigenerational project that would link foreign and domestic policy under a new kind of permanent war footing. In this regard, "terror" has been deployed in a revolutionary way within the United States, enabling an official break with collective expectations of governmental process, legality, and the limits on both militarization and violence. Declaring a War on Terror, in short, has reconstituted the United States as a counterterror state, a transformation that fundamentally changes the citizen-state relationship as well as the U.S. position within the international order.

Secretary of Defense Donald Rumsfeld's dream of a "revolution in military affairs" was constituted before 2001; but, after the attacks, this project was fused with the War on Terror concept to create a new global laboratory for war (for example, see Rumsfeld 2002). His commitment to a smaller military armed with high technology, a reliance on expeditionary forces, and a broad spectrum of covert actions was ultimately designed not just to pursue al-Qaeda into Afghanistan and then topple Saddam Hussein's government in Iraq. It also was meant to send a signal to world leaders. The invasions of Afghanistan in 2001 and Iraq in 2003 were designed to demonstrate overwhelming American military power and the will to use it and thereby communicate to all political leaders not aligned with U.S. interests that after the fall of Saddam Hussein's regime "you could be next." Thus, the invasion of Iraq (politically justified by a fabricated linkage of Saddam Hussein to al-Qaeda leader Osama Bin Laden and by exaggerated fears of nuclear, biological, and chemical weapons attacks on the United States) provided a global theater for demonstrating U.S. power. Indeed, each stage of the invasion—from the shock-and-awe bombing campaign to the quick military "victory" and occupation of Iraq through the current counterinsurgency operations—was not only massively violent but also a theatrical effort to both establish and make visible the United States as the sole global military superpower.

In doing so, the Bush administration mobilized the cold war model of global engagement for a new century by replacing deterrence with counterterror as the central motivating logic. The achievement of the early cold war was the establishment of a mode of governing that was extraordinarily stable, which produced a cold war consensus that linked policy makers, military leaders, journalists, and academics to an unprecedented degree through anticommunist militarization. After the September 2001 attacks, the Bush administration sought to articulate a state structure that could orchestrate American domestic and foreign policy on a similar scale, while locking into place a more aggressive military-industrial agenda for the twenty-first century. Many of the domestic logics and cultural assumptions of the cold war state have been simply reworked to enable a War on Terror. The mobilization of U.S. citizens through nuclear fear, the protection of U.S. policy through expanding state secrecy, and the reliance on covert action are all techniques developed in the United States during the cold war to produce militarized consent on state-articulated terms. To a large extent, the Bush administration's media strategy for the War on Terror has been reliant on the cultural tropes of the cold war—in particular the idea of an imminent nuclear threat—to enable a global counterinsurgency campaign. The "terrorist armed with a WMD [weapon of mass destruction]" has been the linking image between past and future, suturing together the collective understandings about global threat developed during the cold war but redirecting them against a global al-Qaeda conspiracy. But if the tools for mobilizing the American public as a nation under imminent threat are grounded in cold war logics, the waging of preventative war in Iraq represents a profound new stage in U.S. militarism.

So what kind of "national security" is the United States pursuing in the twenty-first century? And how does it differ from its cold war predecessor? It is easy to find a precise vision of U.S. power in its military policy. In a U.S. Joint Chiefs of Staff report on the status and future orientation of the combined U.S. military, known as *Joint Vision 2020,* U.S. military leaders asserted their goal as "full-spectrum dominance," defined as the ability to

> defeat any adversary and control any situation across the full range of military operations. . . . US forces are able to conduct prompt, sustained, and synchronized operations with combinations of forces tailored to specific situations and with access to and freedom to operate in all domains—space, sea, land, air, and information." (U.S. Joint Chiefs of Staff 2000, 6)

The freedom to operate in all domains. As part of this mission, the United States is now spending more money on defense than the rest of the world combined—close to a trillion dollars a year.[3] Much of this amount is black budgeted, meaning there is no possibility for either government accountants or the public to discover how it is being spent.[4] The United States is also the world's largest arms dealer (Grimmett 2007, 4). As of 2008, the United States

maintains more that 761 military bases in 132 countries as well as a triad of
bombers, submarines, and missiles that can obliterate any city on the planet
in thirty minutes or less.[5] The militarization of space and cyberspace has also
proceeded through incremental expansions in U.S. missile defense and satellite systems. Concurrently, the Bush administration has systematically resisted
international institutions, treaties, and logics that could infringe on the idea
of full-spectrum dominance across military, political, and economic domains.
To this end, President Bush has relied on the emergency powers granted to the
Commander-in-Chief to an unprecedented degree, avoiding the usual legisla-
tive process in the United States by evoking imminent threat as a basic matter of course and thus rather fundamentally changing the American political
process.

   To get at how nuanced and imaginative this view of American power is,
consider how the Project for a New American Century, the conservative think
tank that provided much of the geopolitical vision and military policy for the
George W. Bush administration, imagines the foot soldier of the near future:

> Future soldiers may operate in encapsulated, climate-controlled, powered fight-
> ing suits, laced with sensors, and boasting chameleon-like "active" camouflage.
> "Skin-patch" pharmaceuticals help regulate fears, focus concentration and
> enhance endurance and strength. A display mounted on the soldier's helmet
> permits a comprehensive view of the battlefield—in effect to look around cor-
> ners and over hills—and allows the soldier to access the entire combat informa-
> tion and intelligence system while filtering incoming data to prevent overload.
> Individual weapons are more lethal, and a soldier's ability to call for highly
> precise and reliable indirect fires—not only from Army systems but those of
> other services—allows each individual to have great influence over huge spaces.
> Under the "Land Warrior" program some Army experts envision a "squad" of
> seven soldiers able to dominate an area the size of the Gettysburg battlefield,
> where in 1863, some 165,000 men fought. (Project for a New American Cen-
> tury 2000, 62)

Future soldiers. This science fiction seeks to enable the kind of quantum leap in
military power that the cold war state was able to produce with some regularity in nuclear technologies; it also assumes a permanent revolution in military
affairs and an unending war posture. Arguing explicitly that the project of cold
war containment should be replaced with a new global Pax Americana in the
twenty-first century (cf. Kelly, this volume), the writers of this 2000 report
were already calling for a massive expansion of the security state as well as for
immediate military action in Iraq well before the 2001 terrorist attacks on

the United States.[6] The War on Terror provided a new overarching logic—as well as a new marketing strategy—for this idea of total dominance, an idea of American power promulgated largely by politicians and advisors without any first-hand military experience. In this vision, a handful of future supersoldiers, linked to the combined U.S. military forces on land, sea, air, space, and cyber-space, could call in nuclear strikes, direct space-based weaponry, and through near instant global engagement maintain a terrifying technological edge over all potential adversaries. The dream image of the supersoldier here is an index of the Bush administration's dream for American superpowerness, which extends across the full spectrum of military, economic, and political affairs.[7] This is the long-standing fantasy of the *uber*-soldier, who embodies the full strength of the U.S. military on the front line as global counterinsurgent. The military rebranding of the War on Terror as the Global War on Terror or GWOT was designed precisely to underscore the totalizing reach of the conflict and with it, of American power. In light of the failure to stabilize Afghanistan and Iraq, the GWOT recently has been downgraded in military discourse to simply the "Long War"—a telling conceptual reduction in the definition of the war from a named enemy to simply one of temporal duration.[8]

Nevertheless, the global infrastructure of U.S. counterterror has been partially exposed in recent years: in addition to a retaliatory war in Afghanistan and a "preventative" war in Iraq, the Bush administration has pursued a "rendition" program of kidnapping, one that does not recognize state borders or international law. The U.S. Central Intelligence Agency (CIA) and other U.S. agencies have established a global gulag stretching from Guantanamo Bay, Cuba, to sites in Eastern Europe, Thailand, and the Middle East to hold these detainees and others picked up on the global battlefield (see Mayer 2007). These prisons, as well as the concepts of the "detainee" and "torture" that support them, have been defined via Bush appointees in the Justice Department to be outside of international law and U.S. law or even subject to the humanitarian review of the International Red Cross. Thus, rather than re-indoctrinate prisoners on the French Algerian model of counterinsurgency, the Bush administration has sought a system for permanent imprisonment for subjects who are not protected by the Geneva Convention or endowed with habeas corpus rights. The War on Terror was thus designed to be a pure statement of U.S. hegemonic power—with individuals taken at will on and off the battlefield and installed in sites that were not subject to legal review, where prisoners could be interrogated with techniques known for generations to be torture.

Domestically, the Bush administration has set up a system outside of the law for wiretapping and electronic surveillance, in addition to expanding the uses of state secrecy to foreclose legal challenges and to protect even the most basic rationales for counterterror policy. President Bush has also declared the right to designate citizens as "enemy combatants" and thereby revoke U.S. citizenship—and with it, the right to contest one's imprisonment. Over the past two years, the U.S. Supreme Court has challenged a number of these propositions, creating a state of limbo in the United States between the national security rulings of the judicial branch, the national security legislation passed by Congress, and the actions of an executive branch that has evoked state of emergency war powers to trump such legal and congressional review. Thus, the ambiguity at the international level over the terms of the War on Terror has been matched by the ambiguity at the domestic level over the power of the executive branch and the status of basic civil liberties under the U.S. counterterror project. It is important to recognize the Bush administration as a truly revolutionary political project, for the declaration of a global counterterrorism project has fundamentally changed the terms of American democracy at home and abroad.

Former National Security Advisor Zbigniew Brzezinski has argued that the fundamental problem with U.S. foreign policy in Iraq is that "America is acting like a colonial power in Iraq. But the age of colonialism is over. Waging a colonial war in the post-colonial age is self-defeating" (Brzezinski 2007). Thus, Brzezinski reiterates the ultimate lesson posed by *The Battle of Algiers,* namely, that counterinsurgency is simply violence when it is not supported by a widely shared indigenous political worldview and in this case by an ethical and legal commitment to democratic process, human rights, and legality. David Kilcullen, a key theorist of the Iraq counterinsurgency and a contributor to the new *U.S. Army/Marine Corps Counterinsurgency Field Manual,* has been more blunt, stating in 2008, "The biggest stupid idea was to invade Iraq in the first place" (Ackerman 2008). However, for Kilcullen, the problem remains one ultimately of expertise, reportedly leading him to write a second manual, "Counterinsurgency: A Guide for Policy-Makers," for elected officials. Thus, while there seems to be a rather remarkable failure rate in U.S. counterinsurgency campaigns there remains a deep and abiding commitment to the idea of counterinsurgency. Put more directly, the view of "freedom and democracy" that the Bush administration has promulgated through a War on Terror has not only failed to be achieved in Afghanistan and Iraq, it has—through torture, media manipulation, financial corruption, and an overwhelming reliance on military force—substantially undermined the conceptual power of U.S. claims on those terms for a global audience. The resulting global resistance to the United States is not simply a problem of U.S. military expertise or of not understanding regional cultures; it is an inevitable reaction to pursuing U.S. national interests through a global counterterror campaign. Counterinsurgency is, *at best,* a short-term military technique to buy time for a political process to generate mass support; it is not and cannot be a long-term system of planetary rule. The global reaction to the U.S. War on Terror is increasingly less likely to depend on the exceptional power of the U.S. military and more likely to turn on the antidemocratic and often illegal actions taken in the name of counterterror. The effort to fuse counterterror with the rhetoric of democracy is not only oxymoronic, it massively undermines any U.S. claim to moral authority (which counterinsurgency theory posits as the necessary foundation of any successful nation-building project). Moreover, the day-to-day practices of contemporary U.S. counterterror—kidnapping, torture, secret prisons, rejection of the Geneva Convention and habeas corpus rights, black propaganda, and preventative war—all produce profound global effects, regardless of the fantasy of American power supporting them. The War on Terror thus needs to be assessed not only for its lack of internal coherence as U.S. policy but also for the global reactions to such violent concepts and actions now and into a deep future.

In this regard, a striking omission from U.S. counterinsurgency theory is a discussion of what the CIA calls "blowback" (see Johnson 2000). Blowback commonly refers to foreign retaliation for U.S. covert actions. However, the concept has a secondary aspect of equal importance to the first: because covert actions are invisible to U.S. domestic audiences, U.S. citizens have no way of understanding the rationale or history behind such retaliatory acts. Thus, what is in local terms a reaction to U.S.-sponsored violence becomes for U.S. citizens literally unrecognizable. This has a perverse effect that is amplified by the War on Terror concept. Since U.S. citizens have no insight into the terms of U.S. covert warfare around the world, retaliatory acts against U.S. interests appear to the American public be without cause or context and thus irrational. Since the premise of the War on Terror is that the terrorist is an irrational and violent being dedicated to destroying the United States, blowback empowers yet another level of American fantasy, namely, that the United States is not a global military actor until provoked by irrational violence, terrorist acts, or imminent threat. Thus, the War on Terror as a form of domestic U.S. strategy promotes a self-fulfilling prophecy of global chaos, which works to justify both extraordinary military expenditures at home and global military engagements abroad. Thus, the Bush administration's argument for an aggressive counterinsurgency campaign in Iraq—captured by the slogan "we need to fight them there, so we don't have to fight them here"—is wrong on two scores, because (1) the terrorist "them" in this formulation is in reality a vast set of interests responding to a vast array of global conditions rather than a singular political subject and (2) war always comes home in some fashion.[9] In addition to creating new generations around the world willing to fight the United States through terrorist acts and exposing U.S. personnel to the types of U.S. tactics supporting the war on terror—kidnapping, torture, preemptive strikes—counterterror always has a domestic counterpart to the geopolitical.

In this regard, the Pentagon might also have screened for its counterinsurgency theorists back in the summer of 2003 another classic film devoted to counterinsurgency and decolonization: *The Spook Who Sat by the Door* (1973, directed by Ivan Dixon).[10] Based on the novel of the same name by Sam Greenlee (1969), *The Spook* tells the fictional story of the first African American CIA agent, Dan Freeman (played by Lawrence Cook), who, after spending five years learning tradecraft in Langley, returns to Chicago to mobilize gang members in a national insurgency of black liberation. The film is both a brutal critique of cold war militarism and a race fantasy, as the white/black divide in the United States is presented as both intractable and in a state of unacknowledged war. The decision to integrate the CIA, for example, is driven by the crass political calculus of a congressional reelection campaign, not by a commitment to racial equality. After the first class of one hundred African Americans is reduced to just one viable candidate, Freeman is welcomed into the "finest intelligence and espionage agency in the world" as the "best of your race." Assigned to a new position as "Reproduction Section Chief," Freeman spends the next five years running the photocopy machine in the basement of the CIA and serving as the token African American CIA agent to be displayed for visiting officials. Unknown to his superiors, however, Freeman's ingratiating manner is in fact a strategy designed to unlock the secrets of insurgency and espionage training. In addition to becoming an expert in martial arts, guns, explosives, and espionage techniques, Freeman spends his nights studying in the CIA library and reads the classified materials he is asked to photocopy during the day, thus gaining an insider's view into U.S. cold war policy and CIA counterinsurgency tactics. On leaving the CIA, Freeman moves to Chicago to assume a cover identity as a ghetto social worker. But his true mission, as he tells the clueless head of the CIA, is "to teach my people some of what I learned here," by which he means not white supremacy but rather the techniques of terror and armed resistance.

Freeman then organizes the African American gangs on the South Side of Chicago, telling them, "if you really want to mess with whitey, I can show you how," before recommending that they look into the histories of "Algeria, Kenya, Korea and 'Nam" for examples of what he has in mind. Presented as a filmic mirror image of his CIA training, Freemen then teaches former gang members firearms, explosives, and hit-and-run military techniques while or-

ganizing them into cells with a military command and control structure. He
also uses white prejudice as a weapon, stating that "a black man with a broom is
invisible in this country." To prove his point, he assigns one of his subordinates
disguised as a janitor to rob the mayor's office while the mayor is sitting in it.
As his insurgency takes off, Freemen also correctly judges that the leadership
of the CIA and Federal Bureau of Investigations (FBI) will blame the Soviet
Union for the violence in Chicago rather than acknowledge any indigenous
military expertise coming out of the ghetto.

Freeman transforms Chicago gang members into soldiers of a new revolutionary army and prepares them for a national campaign. Telling his cell that
"what we have now is a colony and what we want to create is a new nation," he
recruits gang members in major American cities to the cause. He also targets
African American soldiers coming back from Vietnam, approaches prisons as
indoctrination centers, and imagines turning African American workers in
police departments, businesses, and city jobs into double agents. After a police shooting starts a riot in the Chicago ghetto, the Black Freedom Fighters
begin formal guerrilla operations, shooting police, then fighting the National
Guard, and eventually waging war against the Army's Eighty-Second Airborne
Division. As the violence escalates, the head of the CIA first contemplates establishing concentration camps for the black residents of Chicago but then
realizes that the city is too dependent on African American labor to do so
and therefore launches a "decapitation" project to get the leadership of the
insurgency. The South Side of Chicago thus becomes the site of a terror and
counterterror campaign, mirroring many of the logics also documented in *The
Battle of Algiers*.

Freeman articulates the geopolitics of the film when a lieutenant asks if the
freedom fighters can win:

> *Freeman*: In guerrilla warfare winning is not losing. When you sleep on the
> floor you can't fall out of bed.
> *Lieutenant*: Then what are we trying to do, man?
> *Freeman*: Fight whitey to a standstill. Force him to make a choice between the
> two things he seems to dig most of all. There is no way the United States can
> police the world and keep us on our ass too—unless we cooperate. When we
> revolt, we reduce it to a simple choice: whitey finds out he can't make either.
> *Lieutenant*: What about the other brothers and sisters on the street?
> *Freeman*: Their choice is when we start. If they don't follow our program and
> turn us in to the cops, we lose in a week. But if they support us, then its hit
> and run, harass and hound, and we can paralyze this country.

We can paralyze this country. Seeking to "turn the American Dream into a nightmare," Freeman uses the terror tactics he learned in the CIA—including sabotage, assassination, and radio propaganda—to promote black liberation. His guerilla war brings down the full weight of the U.S. military on Chicago but also ignites a revolutionary movement that sweeps across the country ghetto by ghetto, leaving the United States in the last frame of the film in a full state of national emergency.

The Spook Who Sat by the Door explores an essentialized race fantasy within the structure of terror and counterterror. Not unlike the Bush administration's framing of the War on Terror as a "with us or against us" global realignment, *The Spook* engages revolutionary violence through a set of binary racial oppositions within the United States. It doing so, however, it powerfully acknowledges the domestic costs of cold war covert actions by playing out the logic of revolutionary violence at home. It also anticipates the revelations of the Church and Pike commissions on domestic CIA and FBI activities made public three years after the release of the film. These commissions documented the surveillance and harassment of civil rights leaders over several decades of the cold war.[11] Thus, the film plays out a version of what the CIA and FBI actually feared: that the civil rights movement within the United States could embrace revolutionary violence and promote an Algeria-like uprising within the United States. It is important to remember the lessons learned about the security state at this cold war moment, namely, that U.S. covert actions were never limited only to foreign territories but also (1) included the infiltration, surveillance, and subversion of domestic groups including the anti-Vietnam War movement, the Black Panthers, and the American Indian Movement; and (2) sought to undermine the political power of civil rights leaders from Malcolm X to Martin Luther King (see Cunningham 2004). As a result of these post-Watergate revelations, new laws were written to limit the domestic scope of U.S. intelligence agencies. These new domestic security laws were either eliminated by the passage of the U.S. Patriot Act a few weeks after the 2001 attacks or, in the case of domestic wiretapping laws, simply ignored by the Bush administration in the name of counterterror. Thus, among the first acts of the new counterterrorist state in the fall of 2001 was to return to covert actions within the United States and to position all citizens as potential terrorists. Thus, if the message of *The Battle of Algiers* concerns the limits of counterinsurgency when confronted with the political power of decolonization, *The Spook* reminds us of the domestic side of global militarism and the multigenerational consequences of legitimizing the techniques of terror as simply another form of politics.

The Bush administration's declaration of a War on Terror in 2001 installed terror as the operating logic of the security state. This logic has two immediate effects: (1) it eliminates the (always somewhat illusionary) distinction between the foreign and the domestic by constituting the entire globe as a battlefield, and (2) it requires the production of terror in the name of ending it. Importantly, counterterror is not the elimination of terror but rather the apotheosis of it; this fact is visible in the U.S. tactics of preventative war, rendition, torture, and extralegal imprisonment. By constituting the terrorist threat as a singular global problem, the Bush administration sought to open a literally unrestricted field for planetary military action and to establish the terms of a new kind of American global hegemony. Instead, it has undermined the very concepts it has used to justify a War on Terror—national security, democracy, human rights, and individual freedom. It has also set the terms for generations of blowback against U.S. interests around the world and rather fundamentally altered the terms of the social contract within the United States. Unbuilding the War on Terror thus requires a vision even more revolutionary than the neoconservative project that launched it because it must confront the very idea of American power and consider a postnational form of security. In addition to disavowing covert action abroad, the immediate challenge of a postcounterterror state is to recognize and constitute a nonmilitarized form of politics. Indeed, after five decades of a nuclear "balance of terror" and eight years of a War on Terror, it might well be that the most difficult and necessary project of all is to think past terror and counterterror and pursue a radically demilitarized United States.

:: NOTES ::

1. For the history and critical analysis of the "ticking time bomb" scenario, see Luban (2005) and the Association for the Prevention of Torture (2007).

2. For a military overview of the Human Terrain Team concept, see http://www.army.mil/professionalwriting/volumes/volume4/december_2006/12_06_2.html. For a military overview of the Minerva Project, see http://minerva.dtic.mil/overview.html; and for a critical analysis of the program, see http://www.ssrc.org/essays/minerva/.

3. For a discussion and breakdown of U.S. military spending, see Higgs (2007), and for a ranking of world military spending, see http://www.globalsecurity.org/military/world/spending.htm.

4. For analysis of the $34 billion in military research and development black budgets, see Center for Strategic and Budgetary Assessments (2008). To this formal military estimate, one must add the "black" budgets located in the intelligence agencies, the Department of Homeland Security, and the Department of Energy (which includes the nuclear weapons laboratories) for which there is no current public accounting.

5. See Chalmers Johnson (2000, 2004, 2008).

6. For example, founding members of the project who later joined the Bush administration include Dick Cheney (vice president), Donald Rumsfeld (secretary of defense), Paul Wolfowitz (deputy secretary of defense), and Scooter Libby (vice president Cheney's chief of staff); see http://www.newamericancentury.org/statementofprinciples.htm.

7. For example, the Air Force Space Command stated in 2005 that the U.S. military is committed to a "global strike" force capable of nuclear and nonnuclear strikes on any target in the world "executed within compressed timelines (from seconds to days) . . . exerting persistent effects at potentially great distances from the continental United States"; see Kristensen (2006) for a detailed discussion of the global strike program.

8. For example, see White and Scott Tyson (2006). For a history of the concept and its media deployment, see Center for Media and Democracy, "The Long War" at http://www.sourcewatch.org/index.php?title=The_Long_War.

9. For example, in a speech to the Ohio Highway Patrol on June 9, 2005, President Bush stated,

This is a long war, and we have a comprehensive strategy to win it. We're taking the fight to the terrorists abroad, so we don't have to face them here at home. We're denying our enemies sanctuary, by making it clear that America will not tolerate regimes that harbor or support terrorists. We're stopping the terrorists from achieving the ideological victories they seek by spreading hope and freedom and reform across the broader Middle East. By advancing the cause of liberty, we'll lay the foundations for peace for generations to come.

For a full transcript, see http://www.whitehouse.gov/news/releases/2005/06/20050609-2.html.

10. I would like to thank Ryan Holland for alerting me to this film and also for his trenchant analysis of the relationship between policing, militarism, and gang life in Chicago from the cold war through the War on Terror (Holland 2004).

11. The fourteen-volume published report of the Church Committee is available at http://www.aarclibrary.org/publib/church/reports/contents.htm. See also the National Security Archive for various declassification projects on cold war activities, including the "CIA's Family Jewels" report—a long delayed history of illegal activities by the CIA created during the Church Committee hearings in 1975 but only made available to the public in 2007: http://www.gwu.edu/~nsarchiv/NSAEBB/NSAEBB222/index.htm.

SECTION 4

THE U.S. MILITARY AND U.S. ANTHROPOLOGY

:: SEAN T. MITCHELL *and* JOHN D. KELLY ::

S hould anthropologists conduct research in war zones for the use of the U.S. military? Should anthropologists play other roles within the U.S. military? Can anthropologists justify a collective refusal to take part? The recent cultural turn in the U.S. military has raised these questions acutely for U.S. anthropologists. The essays in this section offer unambiguous, although differing, answers to these core ethical, political, and practical questions. These questions are new, but they resonate with longstanding disciplinary dilemmas. The mission of anthropology is again at stake.

American anthropology struggled to redefine itself in the early 1970s, amid prolonged and gruesome counterinsurgent war in Vietnam and, in the wake of decolonization, the worldwide proliferation of new political movements, both inside and outside of the new nation-states that had transformed the political context of anthropological research. Many American anthropologists at this time called for an anthropological research that was politically "relevant" (see Hymes 1999 [1972]; Stocking 2001, 278–9; see also Asad 1973). These calls for relevance presaged the attention given to politics and power in their many forms by the anthropology of the following decades. But although American anthropologists of this time sought relevance for their studies of politics in what was called during the cold war, the "third world," national politics in the United States remained principally concerned with the first and second worlds, locked in their epochal struggle for domination of each other and for the future of the third.

For all the obvious insanity of a struggle that littered the world with nuclear weapons destined to outlast any possible sociopolitical conditions for their domestication, the first and second worlds were understood in U.S. institutions of governance and war-making to be essentially rational and modern, while the third world was understood to be ruled by culture, irrationality, and tradition. As Carl Pletsch shows in a seminal 1981 essay, the division of labor in the American social sciences of the cold war era was organized by these orienting categories: rational and modern versus cultural and traditional (first and second versus third) and free versus ideological (first versus second). Because they were rational and thus predictable, the first and second worlds could be studied by nomothetic social sciences: political science, economics, and sociology. Idiographic anthropology would have to be content with description, not prediction, and with the third world, not the first or second that so dominated the policy agendas of U.S. policy makers. As Michel-Rolph Trouillot later suggested, for this reason, anthropologists of the period found themselves trapped in a familiar "savage slot" that had previously been filled by anthropologists of the colonial era. And, although many American anthropologists in the latter decades of the twentieth century sought political relevance for their work and produced work of enormous political insight, American anthropology did not, for the most part, achieve the kinds of relevance to broader politics that it sought.

In the twenty-first century, a new kind of relevance has come knocking on American anthropology's door. Montgomery McFate, the high-profile proponent of an anthropologized counterinsurgency, made the case for anthropology's relevance in a 2005 essay entitled "The Military Utility of Understanding Adversary Culture":

> Although the United States armed and trained for 50 years to defeat a Cold War adversary, Soviet tanks will never roll through the Fulda Gap. The foe the United States faces today—and is likely to face for years to come—is non-Western in orientation, transnational in scope, non-hierarchical in structure, and clandestine in approach; and it operates outside of the context of the nation-state. Neither al Qaeda nor insurgents in Iraq are fighting a Clausewitzian war, where armed conflict is a rational extension of politics by other means. These adversaries neither think nor act like nation-states. Rather, their form of warfare, organizational structure, and motivations are determined by the society and the culture from which they come. (McFate 2005b)

In McFate's assessment, the societies and cultures of traditional anthropological inquiry, conceived during the cold war principally as objects of global military struggle, have here become the source of global war's subjects, the new nemesis. The logical conclusion of this understanding of "the foe the United States faces today" and "their form of warfare" is that the U.S. military must call upon anthropologists for their interpretation (still with reason only on the side of the West). This has all occurred in precisely the terms that one might have predicted in 1981, with the help of Pletsch's essay, had one known that the ideology of the cold war would be followed by the ideology of the long war against parts of the third world itself. In the imaginaries that orient U.S. military deployments, the hyper-rationally sinister and atheist communist bureaucrats of yesterday have been replaced today by irrationally violent and freedom-hating fanatics. And in a reinscription of the cold war division of intellectual labor, the ostensible human science of the irrational and unpredictable, anthropology, is called in the United States to more prominent and pressing duty than it ever was during the cold war.

This volume embraces divergent viewpoints, with which we the editors, ourselves not always of one mind, sometimes disagree. And it is precisely through this diversity of perspective that we intend to demonstrate the limits of keeping anthropology mired in the savage slot. Many policy makers still seem to believe that anthropology's only role in informing military theory and practice should be that of translator of the ostensible irrationalities of the human terrain that populates U.S. military theaters. Whether this role is appropriate is one of the questions hotly debated in this section. However, such translation is certainly not the only kind of role anthropology can and should play.

The utilitarian conceptions of rationality and tradition underlying cold war divisions of intellectual labor were grounded in a modernization theory blind to many of its own assumptions: the policies of cold war Washington and Moscow were shaped by culture as much as the practices of insurgents in contemporary Fallujah and Tora Bora. Indeed, this very division of intellectual labor ignores a century of anthropological research that has shown all rationality to be mediated by culture—not merely the rationalities of the United States' military adversaries. This volume pursues the culturally mediated rationalities of global counterinsurgency, order, and violence in the world of Pax Americana; this section pursues the relations of anthropologists with the U.S. military.

The papers in the previous section, section 3, discussed the historical foundations of counterinsurgency theory and practice. The worldview orienting counterinsurgency, and the use and misuse of anthropology in counterinsurgency, are discussed in essays throughout the volume. But the essays in this section do not limit their focus to discussion of underlying intellectual and political issues. Rather, they directly address the contemporary dilemma for U.S. anthropology as a discipline. Each writer is a professional anthropologist, with a strong view about what, now, is to be done by American anthropologists in response to the U.S. military's call for anthropological participation. The discussion here is serious, and often heated.

This section includes the only paper in the volume that was not part of the April 2008 conference, or the American Anthropological Association panels that led to this conference. In order to gain greater insight into the Human Terrain System (HTS) as it now exists, we asked a Human Terrain Team anthropologist, Marcus Griffin, to read the conference papers and contribute his own account and defense of the program. Rather than directly engage the debates that inform the other three papers in this section, Griffin provides a detailed description of the HTS program as he has experienced it in Iraq, presenting his own view of its moral purpose in his discussion of his operational activities. Griffin's essay, the last to be written for the volume, is now the first in this section and provides an empirical point of departure.

Roberto Gonzalez and David Price have been important public voices in the efforts to organize professional dissent against anthropological participation in the U.S. military's counterinsurgency operations. Their papers here offer thorough critiques of anthropological engagement in HTS as well as arguments for the importance and power of an anthropology that is independent from involvement with military agencies. Kerry Fosher continues her articulate public defense of anthropologists working within U.S. military institutions, focusing on the differences made by anthropological voices, from the teaching academies to the battlefields themselves. Fosher's essay is an argument for pluralism in anthropological engagement. Fosher argues for a big tent approach that extends institutional ethics codes to guide military ethnographers, while Price and Gonzalez document the actual consequences when anthropologists serve military purposes. All engage difficult questions about the ethics of professional practice.

In our April 2008 conference, these papers and the papers of the next section were mixed together in a two-session discussion of "Counterinsurgency and the Study of Culture." We hope that readers will find it more helpful to divide these papers into two sets: this group that orients directly to the issue of whether, and how, professional anthropologists should participate in the U.S. military and a second group that reopens ethnographic discussion of the construction and destruction of conscience in U.S. military deployments. In our conference, we put the papers under one rubric to ensure that discussion of the most practical and political of questions was mindful of its most immediate ethnographic context. For this volume, we invite readers to consider all the papers together but also want to serve readers seeking conclusions about the practical implications. Where anthropologists should draw the lines concerning protection of and service to their profession, protection of and service to their country, and protection of and service to their informants are not the only questions demanding better answers in the present moment. More generally, the authors in this volume seek many kinds of positive contributions that political anthropology can make. But the lines need to be drawn, and these papers address key questions directly.

14

An Anthropologist among the Soldiers
Notes from the Field

:: MARCUS B. GRIFFIN ::

Much is written about the Human Terrain System (HTS), but none of it seems particularly informed by what Human Terrain Teams (HTTs) actually do in Iraq and Afghanistan. After reading an article about the militarization of anthropology in *Anthropology Today* in the summer of 2007, I wrote the editor with the suggestion that I could provide a "notes from the field" essay sometime in the spring of 2008. That offer was politely declined on the grounds that the editorial board could not ensure that the information I wrote about was collected in an ethical manner. I shelved writing formally about the work until such time as I felt I had done enough of it to have something say (I kept a blog for six months, but this was really just to stay in touch with my students). At the time of this writing, I have worked with three different units for a total of thirteen months in Iraq, in addition to five months of training at Fort Leavenworth, Kansas. What follows is a sampling of what I tried to accomplish in those months and how the work came to be. My intention for this essay is to encourage informed discussion of the use of social science in stability operations by illustrating how I used it.

Taking the concept of operations (CONOP) and putting it into practice within a Brigade Combat Team (BCT) that has little experience with an HTT is no small task. Figuring out how to work within the BCT in addition to learning exactly what a BCT is as a war fighting organization and how it functions consumed much of my time initially. What follows is a description of how I tried to operationalize the CONOP for the two BCTs I served during my deployment. I am currently serving a Marine division as I write this (I Marine Expeditionary Force Forward) but will reserve lessons learned from this unit for a different essay.

Human Terrain System Mission and Capabilities

The HTS provides Brigade and Regimental Combat Team Commanders and their staffs with dedicated, embedded, and area-specific research to reduce or prevent threats while deployed. Understanding local cultural, political, social, and economic factors is crucial to successful counterinsurgency (COIN) operations conducted in stability and reconstruction operations environments. The ability of commanders to make operational decisions based on relevant social and cultural information will enable them to increase indigenous support of the elected government while reducing indigenous support to insurgents. Sounds good. "Game on," as they say. But how?

I deployed to northwest Baghdad in August 2007 with three other personnel on my team: an E-6 research manager, an O1 human terrain analyst, and a retired E-8 civilian team leader. Shortly after arriving, the team leader assumed the duties of a research manager, while team leadership functions shifted to me. The O1 returned to the United States for personal reasons. As a team of three and me doing double duty as the team leader and social scientist, we tried to figure out how to serve the BCT. With the assistance of staff officers who went out of their way to help us integrate, we came up with a series of reporting requirements. Every Thursday evening a weekly report was due to the task force to which we were assigned. Every Saturday morning a report was due to the BCT commander providing an overview of the past seven days and a projection of activities for the next seven days. Each month a report was due again to the BCT commander covering the last thirty days and projecting the next thirty days pending his guidance. In addition to these reports, regular analytical reports on specific activities or events as they happened were submitted. I also got together with the task force commander (who was also the BCT's deputy commanding officer) once a week for coffee or dinner to discuss casually what needed to be done. Finally, we participated in the weekly schedule of task force meetings and provided briefing materials for each. We had the reporting schema worked out, but what to report on was now the trick. By paying attention to the information needs of the unit, I was able to get the team on track and doing the work.

The general guidance the BCT commander gave us was to "figure out Shia politics." There were Shia militia and political parties fighting each other, not Sunni antagonists, and the infiltration of Iraqi security forces by these militias was compromising the ability of the government to provide security to its people. I thought long and hard about "figure out Shia politics" and decided that one way to get at it would be to study the cultural basis for leadership and followership. A second and related effort was to study the social bonds created and maintained through reciprocity.

At the small Forward Operating Base (FOB) I worked on, I had access to a great number of Iraqis. I was not interested in probability sampling at this point, and felt that haphazardly meeting and talking with whomever I could was sufficient. Naturally, I looked into the demographics of the people I spoke with, but that was not my initial interest. There were sixty or more local national interpreters working on the FOB and two dozen Iraqi vendors catering to the service needs of soldiers: selling pirated DVDs and cheap electronics from China, cutting hair, repairing uniforms and tailoring clothes, and selling tourist-trap knickknacks. I started the long process of making myself known among these men. The interpreters knew English of course, and most of the vendors spoke a smattering of English. I was fortunate enough to be provided an interpreter by the task force, and he quickly became my assistant and provided me with needed credibility among the veteran interpreters. Together we sat with people in their shops or outside offices and talked about how men lead men, and I listened to stories of how people did things for each other, sharing food, favors, and consideration. Sometimes I was told parables taught in grade school. From these discussions I tried to get a feel for underlying expectations regarding social control, obligation, and its roots in the Qur'an.

This worked well with the first BCT that we members of the HTT served, but that first BCT redeployed three months after we got there. The reporting procedure we had developed fell apart, and we started all over from scratch. Every organization has its own way of doing things, and the task force went away as did most of the interpreters. After a month of uncertainty, we ended up with largely individual efforts among the three of us HTT members with me working at the BCT headquarters at Camp Liberty by myself and apart from the others. Fieldwork is never what you hope it is going to be, so I simply adapted to the new situation and with the help of several staff officers, I struggled to find ways to contribute on my own until I had a coherent team once again with additional personnel located with me at headquarters. This crucible helped me to think through what can be done and what should be done and how. What follows are several undertakings that eventually led me to finally answering for myself with confidence the nagging question of: "What is it that you do here?" We

1. Provide descriptions and analyses of civil considerations (community profiles and studies) for each *hayy* (neighborhood), district, and area of operations (AO).
2. Maintain an understanding of local leadership, how they interact with each other, and what their interests and concerns are.
3. Provide specialized assistance to BCT and battalion (BN) projects to facilitate completion, efficiency, and social impact.
4. Provide guidance to soldiers regarding how to collect human terrain information to improve their Intelligence Preparation of the Battlefield and reporting efforts.
5. Respond to requests for information from BCT and BN.

The Work Itself

Because the military divides up physical terrain into AO that are assigned to specific units from high headquarters run by general officers all the way down to individual platoons led by first lieutenants, I had to figure out a way to depict the human terrain in some useful fashion. The challenge was to come up with a means of describing and analyzing human terrain in a way that was meaningful to me as an anthropologist yet also meaningful to soldiers. Otherwise the insight would never be used and I might as well go home. There was no mistaking that army subcultures and dialects had to be learned and mastered if I was to be understood or even given the time of day.

Prior to relocating from an FOB to the BCT headquarters on Camp Liberty, one of my research managers found a hardcopy of the COIN manual *FM 3-24* for me. I had read through it while in training at Fort Leavenworth, but it was not particularly meaningful to me at the time. While in the midst of daily operations in Baghdad, however, I discovered a potential means of creating the human terrain depiction I wanted. I was not satisfied with it, but it was a good starting point. I have recently expanded it, but the new version is untested and outside the scope of this essay.

According to the COIN manual, human terrain is called "civil considerations" and is characterized with the acronym, ASCOPE. This stands for areas, structures, capabilities, organizations, people, and events and is broken down as follows. I and others on my team, not to mention many soldiers throughout the BCT, sought out the content for each category:

ASCOPE

Areas
Key civilian areas are localities or aspects of the terrain within an AO that have significance to the local populace.

1. Indicators
2. Areas defined by political boundaries such as districts, municipalities, and provinces
3. Areas of high economic value such as industrial centers and farming regions
4. Centers of government and politics
5. Culturally important areas
6. Social, ethnic, tribal, political, religious, criminal, or other important enclaves
7. Trade routes and smuggling routes
8. Possible sites for temporary settlement of dislocated civilians or other civil functions

Structures
Civilian and military: focus on location, functions, and capabilities to support operations

1. Headquarters and bases for security forces
2. Police stations, courthouses, and jails
3. Communications and media infrastructure
   a. Radio towers
   b. Television stations
   c. Cellular towers
   d. Newspaper offices
   e. Printing presses
4. Roads and bridges
5. Ports of entry
6. Dams
7. Electrical power stations and substations
8. Refineries and other sources of fuel
9. Potable water sources
10. Sewage systems
11. Clinics and hospitals
12. Schools and universities
13. Places of religious worship

Capabilities

These capabilities are to save, sustain, and enhance the life of the citizenry.

1. Public administration
2. Public safety—security forces
3. Emergency services—fire and ambulance
4. Public health—clinics and hospitals
5. Food
6. Water
7. Sanitation

Organizations

1. Religious organizations
2. Political parties
3. Patriotic or service organizations
4. Labor unions
5. Criminal organizations
6. Community organizations
7. Multinational corporations
8. International governmental organizations (that is, the United Nations' World Food Programme)—consider activities, capabilities, limitations
9. Nongovernmental organizations (that is, Red Crescent)—consider activities, capabilities, limitations

People

People in this category are limited to nonmilitary

1. Population support overlay
2. Religion, race, and ethnicity overlay
3. Perception assessment matrix

Events

1. National and religious holidays
2. Agricultural crop, livestock, and market cycles
3. Elections
4. Civil disturbances
5. Celebrations
6. Disasters (natural and manmade)

To populate the categories in ASCOPE, I went out to Joint Security Stations (JSSs) and stayed several days at a time going on foot patrols with platoons into the surrounding community, talking with local residents, visiting schools and markets, and discussing what I saw with the soldiers. JSSs and Combat Outposts (COPs) were one of General Petraeus's strategies for getting soldiers among the population to protect the population from sectarian violence and militia abuse. When company commanders initially asked what I wanted to do, all I had to do was refer to ASCOPE and they had something operationally familiar to reference my otherwise odd willingness and interest in going on patrols. This familiarity was sufficiently persuasive such that one company commander would completely redo his patrol schedule whenever I came around. One of my research managers also went on patrols in another district, and the company commander of that area quickly saw the value of the effort and tasked his unit with continuing the effort in the physical absence of HTT. We could see the progress company commanders achieved and we could provide input from afar because we all had access to an intranet mapping program called TIGR, a program I encouraged commanders to use as a means of recording ASCOPE data as well as visually showing patterns in that data. Because of the inherently operational nature of this effort and the mapping system the ASCOPE depiction relied upon, the results are classified secret to ensure enemy combatants cannot exploit patterns of movement and analysis in order to ambush and kill soldiers. Unfortunately sharing examples of ASCOPE work here could potentially get people hurt or killed, whether American or Iraqi. Nonetheless, creating community profiles through ASCOPE to inform stability operations was an enduring effort of my team.

The Outdoor Classroom: Walking the Walk

Being out at JSSs allowed me to try other ways of providing input at the tactical level (among the population) beyond fostering ASCOPE profiles. The most obvious was to explain what I was seeing and what it meant to me as we walked the streets. Because I had some experience with archaeology and my father, also an anthropologist, had made sure I was exposed to each of anthropology's subdisciplines, I looked for material indicators of community well-being that could be used as talking points for platoon leaders and others on patrol. This would help patrolling soldiers ask different types of questions from the usual ones, e.g., how many hours of electricity residents were getting, what items were missing from their food ration that month, and whether or not they got their cooking fuel ration and, if so, how much of it was pilfered from the canister.

What to look for can be subtle or it can be obvious. A rundown and poorly maintained house is an obvious sign of joblessness and little confidence in the future or indicates the occupant is a squatter displaced owing to threats of sectarian violence. Subtle indicators require greater observation skills and an attitude that always questions why something is the way it appears. The process is not that different from looking for crush wire or oddly placed concrete blocks on the street indicating a hidden roadside bomb. A person just has to be continuously observant and constantly asking, "Why is that like that? What is the meaning of this?"

One day I was walking the streets with a platoon in the district of Ghazaliya. The company commander was along with me, as he usually was whenever I walked the streets in his AO, so we had a platoon-plus-sized security element, about twenty-six men. We were stopping at random houses along the street and talking with residents about employment, asking if they were seeing strangers coming around, and encouraging them to call either the security station or the local police. I would ask questions about early childhood illness or underemployment or marriage prospects, depending on the age and gender of folks I encountered. Car bombs had been a problem lately so the soldiers always asked about abandoned or unfamiliar vehicles in empty lots or parked on side streets. At one particular house while the company commander was asking these questions, I walked around the side yard with another soldier simply to see what I could see. I was trying to use what I knew of contemporary archaeology and often looked at material culture to tell me something about the family's situation. I usually looked at the surface scatter of trash piles in empty lots, although I had to be careful of that practice because improvised explosive devices (IEDs) are sometimes hidden in trash.

In this person's side yard, however, I gravitated toward the cylindrical, concrete, rubbish-burning container. The ashes were simply that: ashes with a bit of burnt plastic mixed in. On top of the container, however, was a metal sheet that had a darkened smudge in a circular pattern. I puzzled over what was causing the discoloration, roughly the size of a medium-sized pizza. Then it dawned on me. I recalled a patrol the previous day, one where the platoon was investigating abandoned homes for weapons caches. A woman had sent a child running after us in our humvees with several round pieces of freshly made flat bread called *khubz*. Sitting behind the driver, I watched her through thick bulletproof glass as she cooked over a cylindrical concrete oven, laying the pieces of dough on the hot metal sheet and then flipping them over. Standing in the side yard, I realized that it was not an outdoor oven, it was a trash incinerator. And that is why, as I remarked over the vehicle radio headset that previous day, the bread had an odd tang to it. I make bread, and there was something wrong with that bread. We ate it anyway, but now I knew what was wrong with the bread. The off flavor was due to burning trash contaminants. In an urban environment with little wood for cooking fires and sporadic fuel for gas ovens, people here were using trash to cook over! I explained all of this to the soldier I was with, which then led to new sets of questions regarding cooking bread over trash fires and prevalence of illness. The soldiers now had a means of discerning how pervasive cooking fuel shortages were; they could look for signs of recent use of trash incinerators to cook bread eaten daily. This observation of material culture and its surrounding context also seemed to lead to a greater appreciation by soldiers for how challenging daily life was behind the boring statistic previously collected about cooking fuel. This also got some of the soldiers working in Civil Military Operations thinking about what kinds of alternative fuels might be introduced in the worst neighborhoods.

Another "outdoor classroom" activity was going to the local open market and looking carefully at what was sold, its quality, availability, and origin. Again, instead of simply looking at people in a market selling things, we started with questioning why food was the way it was, which led to other insights and an increase in rapport between soldiers and community members. For example, at some times tomatoes would be of high quality with few if any bruises and cucumbers were firm with no wrinkled ends and no mold. At other times and places, these same staple vegetables would be in rough shape, have black spots and rotten sections, and be available in rather small quantities. Talking to vendors about these differences led to an insight regarding illegal militia or gang-led checkpoints extorting money from transporters. Other causes were parts of the city being off limits to Sunni vendors owing to a sudden risk in the area in which wholesale distribution points existed. Other factors were specific road conditions and traffic delays. Choke points in the distribution chain became clearer and suggested further investigation by either coalition forces or Iraqi security forces. The ability to notice changes in food availability and ask pointed questions seemed to indicate to vendors and community members that these particular soldiers actually cared about how things were going in their community. After all, these soldiers from the JSSs and COPs were a part of the community. Based on several trips to markets and a bit of research into food distribution and quality, I came up with the following guide to assist soldiers in assessing community well-being and using that assessment to develop talking points when engaging local residents. The guide was not meant to be definitive but to get soldiers started and allow them to adapt and improvise once they got going. The outdoor classroom, the mentoring that resulted from seeing their surroundings in an anthropological light, was meant to teach them to fish, and then we were to step back and simply let them fish. Our soldiers are quite intelligent, despite stereotypes to the contrary, and I wanted to leave room for their creativity and insight to flourish in implementing the guide. The following is what I ended up with and gave to the BCT commander, who then passed it on to the rest of the organization with his guidance to use the indicators to improve reporting on markets by subordinate units.

Indicators of Well-Being: Measuring the Economics Line of Effort (LOE), Human Terrain System, 2/101 Airborne Division (Air Assault), April 2008

Purpose

This guide is meant to help company commanders, platoon leaders, and squad leaders systematically track population well-being in their specific AO. These indicators may be used to assist in satisfying Division (DIV), BCT, and BN assessment reporting requirements regarding the economics (LOE). There are many other indicators possible than those listed here, and users should feel free to add or subtract according to their needs but should keep the following in mind:

- Using a large number of indicators runs the risk of becoming too time-consuming to be of utility at the tactical level.
- All of the indicators may be used as talking points during population engagements.
- The indicators are not foolproof and are prone to error. However, by combining observation of the indicators with conversations about them in regard to well-being of families will minimize error and maximize insight.

Problem

Patrols and the organizations to which they provide information are in need of valid indicators of economic well-being for local societies not accurately represented by polling data or national/regional economic statistics. Indicators of supply-chain economics fill this need and serve as the basis for talking points with the local community in order to explore reasons for fluctuations in well-being. Keeping track of the availability, quality, quantity, and pricing of several items listed below will enable a company commander or platoon leader to know (1) the baseline well-being of the specific local community surrounding the market and (2) changes in that well-being over time.

Fragile and Quickly Perishable Foods

The following items need speed of delivery, refrigeration, and/or electricity to maintain quality and minimize loss (Table 14.1).

Table 14.1 Quality Measures

Item	Poor	Fair	Good
Cucumbers	Wrinkled ends; portions soft to thumb press; may be fat and yellowing/overripe	Firm but color not vibrant	Firm to hard, sap residue may exist on one end, strong or glossy green color
Tomatoes	Black spots/portions rotted, deformed to crushed flesh, skin may be wrinkled	Soft flesh, dull color, only slight stem rot if at all	Firm flesh, strong tomato smell, vibrant red coloring, no black spots and stem is greenish
Bananas	Green and hard or yellow with many brown spots, flesh is very soft to mushy	Yellow with few brown spots, skin easily pushed in with thumb	Yellow skin with no brown spots, firm and not easily damaged by thumb
Fish	Strong unpleasant odor, eyes are cloudy, scales may be dry	Flesh is firm but may be dry or sticky, eyes are dull, smell has no particular odor	Clear and glossy eyes, flesh is firm, scales are wet with protective slime. Smells of fresh or salt water. Excellent fish will still be alive (usually carp and catfish)
Eggs	Shell is thin and almost translucent when held to light, some eggs in tray cracked	Shell is firm, egg floats in bowl of water	Shell is firm, egg sinks in bowl of water, shell may be brown, rich to taste when eaten after boiling
Bread	Stale, brittle	Soft to stiff, no strong aroma	Soft, pliable, with rich aroma
Dairy	Nonexistent	Shelf-stable dairy products	Fresh milk and cheese

Better quality items tend to cost more, but the purchase of an item may not always be in keeping with its higher quality (that is, buying soft tomatoes for cooking instead of firm tomatoes for eating raw).

Living Area

These indicators shed light on long-term economic condition and feelings about future well-being (Table 14.2).

Table 14.2 Living Area Quality Measures

	Stressed	Not stressed	Doing well
Housing	Disrepair	Actively being renovated or repaired	Good condition with glass or stained glass windows
Front yard	Neglected	Has grass and small trees	Roses, ornamental shrubbery, healthy citrus and date trees
Rugs	Threadbare, thin, or nonexistent	Imported, machine loomed, synthetic materials	Made locally, handwoven, natural fiber thread and vegetable dyes

The basic premise underlying these measures is that people will not invest significant money in their living area if losing it is too great a risk. In assessing aspects of a family's living area, attitudes about quality of products need to be carefully considered in order to not be influenced by American values and standards.

Meat: Fish, Lamb, Chicken, Goat, Beef

Observe the availability, abundance, price and quality of meats. Query the three most common quantities in kilos a person tends to purchase at one time. Observe people that purchase organ meat and fat versus leg, loin, or neck and speak with them.

Luxury/Preferred Foods

Observe availability, quality, quantity, origin and pricing of the following items:

Honey (instead of sugar or date syrup)
Saffron and diverse herbs and spices (instead of salt or common herbs)
Iraqi rice (instead of American or Asian rice)
Soda pop abundant (instead of water)
Imported juice (instead of water)

These items satisfy wants rather than needs and indicate that economic stress is not an issue.

Electronics

Observe latest stereo equipment/iPods/ flat panel screens and pricing. Are there satellite dishes on rooftops? Consumer electronics are a good measure of disposable income and exposure to global popular culture. However, people may hide their electronics and other displays of wealth out of fear that they will be confiscated or other people will demand more of them.

Cosmopolitan Goods

Observe the availability of beer, perfume and cosmetics, fashion clothes, leather shoes, and cosmetics. The presence or absence of these items indicates tolerance for moderate political and religious views as well as participation in a global/cosmopolitan lifestyle characterized by consumption of imported commodities.

Origin, Availability, Quantity, and Quality of Stock

Observe whether stock comes from any of the following areas:

China
Saudi Arabia/Syria/Jordan/Turkey
Europe
United States
Korea/Taiwan
India

The origin of goods available for purchase indicates the degree to which the local community is tied into trade networks out of the country or region. Network disruption is usually felt as a loss and provides talking points to explore local grievances, expectations, and aspirations.

Other Kinds of Work in Brief

There were other kinds of work that I engaged in when not out in the streets with soldiers. Because I primarily worked at the BCT headquarters, I attended a great many meetings and when appropriate contributed to them. Occasionally someone on the staff would want to know something about a given topic and ask me to provide a brief report. Other times I would notice a need for better understanding of the sociocultural context of current events and put

together a short report on my own and send that to the commander. Most of
the time I listened more than I spoke and then spoke not so much in a meeting
as with the appropriate officer who might benefit from my take on things. That
way he could use the insight in a manner he saw best for his staff or bring it to
the attention of the commander in his own reporting.

Early in 2008, the BCT was thinking of sweeping through a troublesome
neighborhood given that it was a stronghold for criminal gangs that had splin-
tered off from a sectarian militia. IED cells were using that neighborhood as a
safe haven and exporting their violence into another district, blowing up Iraqi
police and army commanders, local advisory councilmen and women, and
U.S. Army personnel as they drove past the hidden roadside bombs. While
there was rent extortion taking place in that neighborhood, word on the street
was that local residents did not want U.S. forces coming through or even driving around on patrols because that stirred up even further trouble. Many new
residents had been brought in from the underprivileged neighborhoods of
Sadr City by militias, and they were loyal to those militias rather than to the
existing government. They had little to do with long-standing residents as well.
The BCT staff got together to discuss the feasibility of clearing the neighborhood of criminal elements and extremists. I participated in those meetings,
and while I do not recall everything I may have contributed to the planning, I
do recall reinforcing the commander's interpreter's argument that the timing
for the mission was really bad owing to a cultural consideration.

We were approaching *Eid Al Adha,* or the Feast of the Sacrifice, and not
long after that *Ashura. Ashura* is particularly important symbolically to Shia
Muslims (at least those in our parts of Baghdad). During this time, people
recall the martyrdom of Hussein and his betrayal by the Caliph. So *Ashura*
highlights a desire for retribution for wrongs committed and liberation from
oppression and encourages getting in touch with the suffering of Hussein as
emblematic of what it means to be Shia in the face of Sunni domination. I
put together a short brief on *Ashura* and *Eid Al Adha* and passed that on to
the staff. I could imagine the second- and third-order effects of clearing this
neighborhood during *Ashura* would be impassioned rejection of U.S. forces
presence, particularly by newly migrated and disenfranchised Shia residents
living in the nice homes of Sunni families either displaced or killed for being
Sunni. If anything, the clearing operation needed to wait until after *Ashura.*
Otherwise many people would likely get hurt and killed in the effort to bring
the neighborhood under government control. In the end, the operation did
not take place, but I think it had more to do with logistics and the point of
view of the BN commander who was responsible for the neighborhood than
anything I had to say in a few meetings and a couple of brief culture reports.

BCT staff exist solely to provide information for the commander to base his decisions on and then to carry out his orders. Attributing reduction in violence to one staff element, such as myself, is next to impossible in this case or any other case in which I was involved. But what is important is that the commander had the information at hand to make his decision and that he was provided needed sociocultural information among other types of information to make his decision. There are people likely alive and uninjured today that otherwise would not be had the commander made a different decision based, perhaps, on less information.

Conclusion

The work I have done to use the anthropological perspective is not glamorous or heroic. The work is simply based on basic modes of inquiry with an effort to remain open to the insight each of anthropology's subdisciplines may provide. I illustrated three of the five objectives I came up with in an effort to make operational the mission capabilities briefing given to commanders and policy makers at the start of my tour of duty in 2007. The HTS program continues to grow and develop an ability to deliver on its core competence: providing social and cultural information to commanders conducting stability operations in their AO. The program was required to expand very quickly, and as with any rapid growth there are attendant growing pains. These will be worked out in time. I hope that this essay will encourage readers to help find solutions to the conflict in Iraq (and elsewhere), rather than treating HTS as some kind of whipping child for their anxiety about U.S. forces being in Iraq and U.S. foreign policy in general. Iraq is a truly wonderful place with wonderful people so deserving of freedom and a chance at prosperity. In my experience, the U.S. Army's HTS is directly helping to resolve conflict and create a space for prosperity and freedom to take hold in Iraq.

15

Indirect Rule and Embedded Anthropology

Practical, Theoretical, and Ethical Concerns

:: ROBERTO J. GONZÁLEZ ::

Between July 2005 and August 2006, the U.S. Army assembled the Human Terrain System program (HTS), which embeds five-person Human Terrain Teams or HTTs with combat brigades in Iraq and Afghanistan. Teams include uniformed social scientists, some of whom are armed (González 2009). Although HTS is a relatively small (and dramatic) means by which anthropologists are articulating with the military, its rapid growth and high profile have raised many practical, theoretical, and ethical questions.[1]

The commercial media have often portrayed HTS as a lifesaving program thanks to an orchestrated Pentagon public relations campaign led by Laurie Adler, a former employee of the Lincoln Group, a powerful Washington public relations firm (e.g., Rohde 2007; Peterson 2007; White and Graham 2005). Yet the way in which HTS has been packaged—as part of a "gentler" counterinsurgency—is unsupported by evidence. Despite claims that the program has reduced U.S. "kinetic operations" (military attacks) in Afghanistan by 60 percent, Pentagon officials have not provided the data upon which such claims are based, and there has been no independent confirmation of such assertions. Indeed, there is no verifiable evidence that HTTs have saved a single life—American, Afghan, Iraqi, or otherwise. Yet since its creation, three HTS team members have lost their lives, and one HTT has unleashed lethal force in Afghanistan.[2]

According to former HTT member Zenia Helbig, a group that gave a positive assessment of HTS included evaluators with a vested interest in it, and
according to a current employee, a forthcoming evaluation of Iraqi teams was
also conducted by interested parties (Helbig 2007a). It appears that HTS is
designed to rally public support for an unpopular military occupation and
simultaneously to collect new intelligence.

As the Pentagon launched HTS, some military personnel described it as "A
CORDS for the 21st Century," in reference to Civil Operations Revolutionary
Development Support, a Vietnam War–era counterinsurgency effort (Kipp
et al. 2006; see also Jacobsen and Hevia, this volume). CORDS generated the
infamous Phoenix program, in which South Vietnamese and U.S. agents used
intelligence to help target some 26,000 people for assassination, mostly civilians (Valentine 1990). This history provides a critical reference point for understanding the potential uses of HTS.

Others are also calling for a revamped Phoenix program, while ignoring its
associated war crimes. Australian political scientist David Kilcullen, former
advisor to General David Petraeus, recommends that U.S. forces initiate a
"global 'Phoenix Program'" against "Islamist insurgency." He argues that "the
unfairly maligned (but highly effective) Vietnam-era Phoenix program . . . was
largely a civilian aid and development program, supported by targeted military pacification operations and intelligence activity to disrupt the Viet Cong
Infrastructure" (Kilcullen 2004).

With a $190 million budget, HTS is among the largest social science
projects in history.[3] It deserves scrutiny, since its supporters have discussed aspects of the program that do not square with military journals, job announcements, and journalists' accounts. For example, some maintain that data is open
and unclassified, yet James Greer (HTS's deputy director) has reportedly said,
"When a brigade plans and executes its operations, that planning and execution is, from an operational-security standpoint, classified . . . Your ability to
talk about it, or write an article about it, is restricted" (Glenn 2007). Doubts
about the program's ethical propriety motivated the American Anthropological Association's Executive Board to formally express disapproval of HTS in
November 2007.

"Human Terrain": From Concept to System

In an article that has become a definitive statement on HTS, human terrain
is defined as "the social, ethnographic, cultural, economic, and political elements of the people among whom a force is operating" (Kipp et al. 2006,
9). It is often contrasted with geophysical terrain—a familiar concept for

officers trained for conventional warfare against Soviets—and implies that "population-centric" wars are the future (Kilcullen 2007).

Human terrain's roots stretch back forty years, when it appeared in a U.S. House Un-American Activities Committee (HUAC) report about the threat of Black Panthers and other militants (U.S. HUAC 1967). Human terrain was linked to population control at a time when U.S. government agencies were undertaking domestic counterinsurgency:

> Traditional guerrilla warfare . . . [is] carried out by irregular forces, which just about always dispose of inferior weapons and logistical support in general, but which possess the ability to seize and retain the initiative through a superior control of the human terrain. This control may be the result of sheer nation-wide support for the guerrillas against a colonial or other occupying power of foreign origin; it may be the result of the ability of the guerrillas to inflict reprisals upon the population; and it can be because the guerrillas promise more. (U.S. HUAC 1967, 62)

Contemporary human terrain studies emerged in 2000, when retired U.S. Army Lieutenant Colonel Ralph Peters (2000, 4, 12) argued that it is the "human architecture" of a city, its "human terrain . . . the people, armed and dangerous, watching for exploitable opportunities, or begging to be protected, who will determine the success or failure of the intervention . . . the center of gravity in urban operations is never a presidential palace or a television studio or a bridge . . . It is always human." Before long, military personnel, Central Intelligence Agency (CIA) operatives, think tanks, and neoconservative pundits had adopted human terrain.

It is worth considering "human terrain" in linguistic terms. The Sapir-Whorf hypothesis (which postulates that language influences the thought—and consequently actions—of its users) suggests that the phrase will have objectifying and dehumanizing effects. Consider the words of Lieutenant Colonel Edward Villacres (2007), who leads an HTT in Iraq: the objective is to "help brigade leadership understand the human dimension of the environment that they are working in, just like a map analyst would try to help them understand the bridges, the rivers, and things like that." This verbal juxtaposition portrays people as geographic space to be conquered. More serious is how the term vividly illustrates Orwell's notion (1961 [1946], 366) of "political language . . . designed to make lies sound truthful and murder respectable."

How was "human terrain" systematized? By 2006, some military leaders were complaining about mismanagement of the wars as casualties mounted, Iraqi insurgents attacked, and Taliban fighters regrouped. Some began seeking "gentler" counterinsurgency tactics, according to an uncritical account by U.S. Army War College anthropologist Shiela Miyoshi Jager (2007, v): "the post-Rumsfeld Pentagon has advocated a 'gentler' approach, emphasizing cultural knowledge and ethnographic intelligence . . . This 'cultural turn' within DoD [Department of Defense] highlights efforts to understand adversary societies and to recruit 'practitioners' of culture, notably anthropologists, to help in the war effort in both Iraq and Afghanistan."

Early advocates included Major General Robert Scales (2004, 4–5), who told the House Armed Services Committee that the British "created a habit of 'seconding' bright officers to various corners of the world so as to immerse them in the cultures of the Empire . . . At the heart of a cultural-centric approach to future war would be a cadre of global scouts . . . They should attend graduate schools in disciplines necessary to understand human behavior and cultural anthropology." Alongside Scales's ringing endorsement of imperialist strategy, the political groundwork was set for cultural-centric warfare.

He would not need to wait long. In 2005, Montgomery McFate and Andrea Jackson published a pilot proposal for a Pentagon Office of Operational Cultural Knowledge focused on human terrain and consisting of social scientists with "strong connections to the services and combatant commands" (McFate and Jackson 2005, 20). Soon after, Jacob Kipp (2006, 8) and colleagues from the army's Foreign Military Studies Office outlined the HTS to "understand the people among whom our forces operate as well as the cultural characteristics and propensities of the enemies we now fight."

By early 2007, BAE Systems began posting HTS job announcements. (BAE Systems and other military contract firms were awarded the Pentagon's HTS contract.) Zenia Helbig reported that BAE staff (responsible for training) were inept and more concerned with maximizing profits than meeting program objectives: they hired unqualified instructors, did not discuss ethics, and recruited social scientists ignorant of Middle Eastern languages and societies. Helbig's claims (echoed by current HTS employees) describe a pattern of waste and war profiteering characteristic of a privatized Pentagon.

By February 2007, the first HTT arrived in Afghanistan. Others deployed to Iraq in summer 2007. Proponents insist that HTTs are giving commanders an understanding of local culture—a dubious claim, since none of the Ph.D. anthropologists in HTTs have regional experience (Helbig 2007b). However, HTTs were designed to collect local data on political leadership, kinship groups, economic systems, and agricultural production (see Figure 15.1). According to Kipp and colleagues, this will be sent to a database accessible by other U.S. government agencies, including presumably the CIA. Furthermore, "databases will eventually be turned over to the new governments of Iraq and

Figure 15.1 Human terrain team members attached to the 4th Brigade Combat Team, 82nd Airborne Division, speak with local children near the village of Nani, Afghanistan, May 2007. Photo courtesy of U.S. Department of Defense.

Afghanistan to enable them to more fully exercise sovereignty" (Kipp et al. 2006, 14).

According to the same authors, HTTs will create an "ethnographic and sociocultural database of the area of operations that can provide the commander data maps showing specific ethnographic or cultural features" (Kipp et al. 2006, 13). HTTs use specialized software "to gather, store, manipulate, and provide cultural data from hundreds of categories" (Kipp et al. 2006, 13). According to the Department of Defense's (DOD) budget justification, the goal is "to collect data on human terrain, create, store, and disseminate information from this data, and use the resulting information as an element of combat power" (U.S. Office of the Secretary of Defense 2007, 18).

HTS supporters have equivocated when asked whether a database might be used for targeting. In an interview, one stated, "The intent . . . is not to identify who the bad actors are out there. The military has an entire intelligence apparatus geared and designed to provide that information to them. That is not the information that they need from social scientists." Yet the DOD's 2008 Global War on Terror Amendment includes HTTs in precisely this category (military intelligence), alongside counterintelligence teams (U.S. Department of Defense 2007, 18).

In sum, HTS may perform various functions. Images of a "gentler" counterinsurgency could serve as propaganda for those opposing military operations in Iraq and Afghanistan: propaganda offering the wonderful compromise of a war that makes us feel good about ourselves. From a different perspective, HTTs could feed information into a database accessible to the CIA, Iraqi interior ministry, or Afghan army for designing propaganda, targeting suspects, or applying other forms of hard power. Policy changes, shifting alliances, personal vendettas, or mistaken identity could easily transform innocent Iraqis or Afghans into future targets.

Anthropology and Indirect Rule

What if we take HTS proponents' claims at face value? Let us suppose that HTTs are providing expertise about local societies for commanders—nothing more. The program would still raise thorny ethical, theoretical, and practical problems.

In terms of ethics, HTS gives priority to military requirements: combat and counterinsurgency support, intelligence collection, and tasks euphemistically called "Phase Four" or "stability operations." Aspects of HTS appear to violate anthropological ethics, particularly researchers' "primary ethical obligations . . . to the people with whom they work" and the need "to ensure that their research does not harm the safety, dignity, or privacy of the people with whom they work" (American Anthropological Association 1998). Furthermore, knowledge about local political hierarchies, kinship structures, and social networks could facilitate a kind of indirect rule, as could coopting regional headmen.

The idea that HTTs should promote these processes, as HTS supporters argue, is reminiscent of the attitude of C. K. Meek, a British anthropologist charged with helping colonial administrators fine-tune a system of indirect rule among Nigerian Igbo following the Women's Riots of 1929. He was aware that government officials thought anthropology should serve as "the handmaiden to administration" (Meek 1937, xv). Meek's peers probably considered him a reformer, since he advocated indirect (not direct) rule. Yet his work denied the possibility of Igbo self-determination. Underlying it was the paternalistic notion that Igbo were unable to enter the modern world without British protection.

Aspects of Meek's work bore some resemblance to earlier efforts undertaken in the Middle East. For example, T. E. Lawrence and Gertrude Bell helped establish a de facto system of British colonial rule in Mesopotamia after World War I. Although the roles they played differed in some respects from that of Meek, they were guided by similar assumptions: an enthusiasm for applying the tools of cultural familiarity for more effective control, the unquestioned assumption that European powers were exceptionally able at managing native peoples, a fundamental belief in the correctness of imperialism, a willingness to accept the limited number of policy options acceptable to the British elite, and a lack of attention to the aspirations of large numbers of native people for genuine self-rule.

Lawrence—immortalized as "Lawrence of Arabia" by the U.S. media—is best known for helping to coordinate the so-called Arab revolt against the Ottoman Turks beginning in 1916. When World War I erupted, Lawrence (who had previously done archaeology work in Syria) was eager to lend his geographic and cultural expertise to the war effort. He was assigned to the British army in Cairo and began providing weapons and money to Arab fighters led by Prince Feisal. Using guerrilla tactics such as dynamiting the vital Hejaz Railway, Lawrence's Arab allies disrupted Turkish supply lines throughout the Middle East. They eventually helped British troops take Jerusalem and Damascus, and by 1918, the British occupied all of modern-day Iraq.

Feisal's fighters cooperated with the British after many assurances that they would be rewarded with political autonomy (see Figure 15.2). For years, Lawrence had been seeking to convince British government officials that a peculiar form of Arab "independence" would be beneficial. In a 1916 intelligence report, he noted that the Arab revolt against the Turks was

Figure 15.2 T. E. Lawrence (*middle row, second from right*) and Prince Feisal (*center*) at a 1921 conference in Cairo. Photograph courtesy of the U.S. Library of Congress.

beneficial to us, because it marches with our immediate aims, the break up of the Islamic "bloc" and the defeat and disruption of the Ottoman Empire, and because *the states [Sharif Hussein] would set up to succeed the Turks would be . . . harmless to ourselves . . .* The Arabs are even less stable than the Turks. *If properly handled they would remain in a state of political mosaic, a tissue of small jealous principalities incapable of cohesion.* (quoted in Dreyfuss 2005, 41)

Lawrence was not alone in advocating for Arab-led states. Writer and archaeologist Gertrude Bell, who had gained respect among British commanders for her analyses of intelligence about Arab groups, also supported Iraqi independence—of an odd sort. Bell attempted to persuade British officials to create a system of indirect rule by employing Iraqi administrators.

Even so, she doubted that Shia clergy were up to the task, since they were "sitting in an atmosphere which reeks of antiquity and is so thick with the dust of ages that you can't see through it—nor can they" (quoted in Buchan 2003). She feared the prospect of Shia leaders in a majority Shi'ite region. In 1920 she wrote, "The object of every government here has always been to keep the Shia divines from taking charge of public affairs" (quoted in Howell 2006). Perhaps it is for this reason that she once wrote, "Mesopotamia is not a civilized state" (quoted in Buchan 2003).

The proposals offered by Lawrence and Bell did not convince British government officials to grant Arabs even nominal autonomy after the League of Nations awarded Britain a mandate over Mesopotamia in 1920. Many Sunni and Shia understandably viewed the mandate as a form of colonialism since the British immediately imposed direct rule under the leadership of High Commissioner Sir Percy Cox. They eventually rose up against their British masters, killing hundreds of occupying troops in the insurgency. The government resorted to aerial bombing and killed nearly 10,000 Iraqis.

By 1921, Winston Churchill (then secretary of state for the colonies) consulted with Lawrence and Bell. They were finally vindicated: to save costs, the British established a combination of direct and indirect rule based on the model of colonial India. The British installed Feisal as the colony's ruling monarch, effectively creating a puppet regime.

After Feisal was installed as king, Bell and Cox administered divide-and-rule policies that survived beyond the twentieth century. After 1932, when Iraq gained nominal independence, British commanders were still allowed to maintain military bases there. (The country was already important to the British because of its vast oil resources.) The Iraqi monarchy lasted as a British client regime with little change until 1958.

A lesson to be learned from the work of Lawrence and Bell is that in the end, it is unlikely that a social scientist will influence decision makers pursuing imperial imperatives. Lawrence gained the trust of thousands of Arabs, lived among them for more than five years, spoke their language, and led them in battle. He (and others) promised them autonomy after the war, but in the end the Arabs were betrayed: British politicians extended direct (and later indirect) rule.

Another lesson to take is that the social scientists' perspective is not necessarily opposed to that of colonial officials. Although Meek, Lawrence, and Bell might have been considered "liberal" in the 1920s—since they advocated indirect rather than direct rule—many would argue that the end result was not substantively different. Even after King Feisal assumed power, British advisers still made key decisions, thousands of British troops were based in the region for decades, and the British-owned Iraqi Petroleum Company was granted concessions over Iraqi oil. Like Meek, both Lawrence and Bell maintained a paternalistic view that took for granted the necessity of European intervention in the affairs of people deemed less civilized than the West.

There are differences between these early-twentieth-century anthropologists and those assisting U.S.-led occupations today: some colonial anthropologists were "reluctant imperialists" (James 1973) attempting to extricate themselves from colonial funding sources—not peddle their services to them. By contrast today, some are unfazed by anthropology's colonial roots. For example, an HTT anthropologist recently blogged, "Is the use of the anthropological perspective by the military promoting imperialism? Who can really say? Is anthropology antithetical to imperialism? Not if you look at the discipline's origins in colonialism in the late 1800s." In other words: HTS may promote neocolonialism ("Who can really say?"), but since the discipline is rooted in colonialism, that's OK (Griffin 2007).

Beyond Neocolonial Anthropology: Social Responsibility and Social Science

It is revealing that an HTS architect cowrote a key chapter of the army's new counterinsurgency manual *FM 3-24* (U.S. Army 2006). It provides a starting point for understanding the intellectual underpinnings of HTS.

FM 3-24 resembles a handbook for colonial rule—although "imperialism" and "empire" are taboo words. The authors approvingly draw historical examples from British, French, and Japanese colonial counterinsurgency campaigns in Malaya, Vietnam, Algeria, and China. Theoretically speaking, it is vintage structural-functionalism. Absent is the notion of culture as a product of historical processes—never mind that for a half-century anthropologists have stressed that global forces have profoundly shaped societies. Instead, the authors reify culture and treat it as internally coherent, bounded, one-dimensional. In Orientalist fashion, their work reproduces a colonial "us" representing a colonized "them," ignoring the practical conditions of embedded anthropology.

Apart from *FM 3-24*, an HTS architect contributed to a four-hundred-page report commissioned by the Pentagon. The report, *Iraq Tribal Study: Al Anbar Governorate* (Todd et al. 2006) outlines a strategy for "influencing the three target tribes" through (essentially) bribes: "Iraq's tribal values are ripe for exploitation. According to an old Iraqi saying, 'You cannot buy a tribe, but you can certainly rent one' . . . Shaikhs have responded well to financial incentives," note the authors (Todd et al. 2006, 7A-12).

Iraq Tribal Study reportedly influenced discussions at the U.S. Army Command and General Staff College while Petraeus was director, before his current Iraq assignment (Pincus 2007). It frankly discusses the benefits of renting tribes. For example, the authors review Ottoman rule and the British Mandate for clues on adapting imperial techniques to the twenty-first century. One section, "Engaging the Shaikhs: British Successes, Failures, and Lessons," states:

> Convincing the shaikhs that the British were the dominant force . . . had a powerful effect . . . Subsidies and land grants bought loyalty . . . Controlling water (irrigation canals), the economic lifelines of the shaikhs' constituencies, was a powerful lever as well. It may be useful to examine the tribal landscape for modern parallels to the irrigation canals of the Mandate period. Development funds immediately come to mind, but there are certainly others. The key lies in putting into the shaikh's hands the ability to improve their peoples' livelihoods, and thereby the shaikh's own status. (Todd et al. 2006, 5–23)

In the next paragraph, the authors describe how the British handled recalcitrant sheiks:

> the British were successful in their use of force against the tribes . . . Punitive assaults, both by infantry column and with air strikes, on the villages of shaikhs judged uncooperative brought about short-term cooperation and long-term enmity. Enabled largely by airpower, the British were able to stay in Iraq—with minimal resources—through its independence in 1932 and beyond. (Todd et al. 2006, 5–23)

Such passages appear designed to incorporate British tactics to U.S.-occupied Iraq. The authors of *FM 3-24* and *Iraqi Tribal Study* imply that a culturally informed occupation—with native leaders coopted by coalition forces, policing carried out by a culturally sensitive occupying army, copious funds doled out to tribesmen, and so on—will result in a lighter neocolonial touch, with less "collateral damage" and a lower price tag. The question of whether military occupation is appropriate is not addressed, nor is the legitimacy of insurgents' grievances explored.

This is not just an academic question. The *Iraqi Tribal Study* appears to have informed Petraeus's Iraq strategy, specifically support for the Anbar Awakening, which has paid out $767 million (and another $450 million soon to follow) to mostly Sunni groups as a reward for resisting al-Qaeda (Dehghanpisheh and Thomas 2008). But "balancing competing interest groups" (to use David Kilcullen's 2007 euphemistic phrase) will likely aggravate the civil war between and among Sunni and Shia groups (Rosen 2008). Seen from this perspective, it seems less like global counterinsurgency and more like a high-stakes divide-and-conquer strategy (see Figure 15.3). In the meantime,

Figure 15.3 Tribal engagement or indirect rule? A member of the Albu Issa "tribe" with U.S. Marine Corps Major General John Allen in Fallujah, Iraq, January 2008. During the meeting, U.S. officials gave a Mameluke Sword to al-Anbar's sheiks to thank them for their partnership. The sheiks have received generous payouts from the U.S. military since 2006. Photograph courtesy of U.S. Department of Defense.

Newsweek reports that "Petraeus says he instructs his young officers, 'Go watch "The Sopranos" in order to understand the power dynamics at work in Iraq'" (Dehghanpisheh and Thomas 2008).

Discussions about HTS might benefit from reframing the issue. In addition to debating the ethics of embedded anthropology, or the theoretical and practical concerns of global counterinsurgency, we might ask, To what extent is our discipline is being compromised, as anthropologists are recruited in support of an invasion and occupation that has led to one million Iraqi deaths? We might also ask, What is the social responsibility of social scientists?

It may also useful to look to the past for enlightenment. As the British colonial anthropologists were hard at work in the 1920s and 1930s, Jomo Kenyatta, a Kikuyu man from British East Africa, arrived in London and began attending seminars conducted by Bronislaw Malinowski. Kenyatta (1938) was profoundly influenced by anthropology, and wrote a moving ethnography of Kikuyu life in which he developed a sharp critique of colonialism:

> In the present work I have . . . kept under very considerable restraint the sense of political grievances which no progressive African can fail to experience . . . I know that there are many scientists and general readers who will be disinterestedly glad of the opportunity of hearing the Africans' point of view, and to all such I am glad to be of service. At the same time, I am well aware that I could not do justice to the subject without offending those "professional friends of the African" who are prepared to maintain their friendship for eternity as a sacred duty, provided only that the African will continue to play the part of an ignorant savage so that they can monopolise the office of interpreting his mind and speaking for him. To such people, an African who writes a study of this kind is encroaching on their preserves. He is a rabbit turned poacher. (1938, xii–xiii)

Kenyatta then did something that neither Meek, nor Lawrence, nor Bell were able to do—to envision a future beyond colonialism:

> But the African is not blind. He can recognize these pretenders to philanthropy, and in various parts of the continent he is waking up to the realisation that a running river cannot be dammed for ever without breaking its bounds. His power of expression has been hampered, but it is breaking through, and will very soon sweep away the patronage and repression which surround him. (Kenyatta 1938, xii–xiii)

Kenyatta became an ardent activist, nationalist leader, and revolutionary and was imprisoned for the better part of a decade for his political activities.

His ethnography examined the painful consequences of British colonialism from the perspective of the Kikuyu and inspired thousands of Africans, Europeans, and others to oppose the imperial imperative. He founded the Pan-African Federation with Kwame Nkrumah in 1946, an organization dedicated to promoting independence for African nations. He would become the first prime minister and president of an independent Kenya in the 1960s.

His work demonstrates how the anthropologist need not play the role of a servant to the most powerful in society. There are other options, other choices. Social science can just as effectively lead the way to a more democratic future. It is capable of challenging power just as easily as serving it.

It is worth remembering Senator William Fulbright, who in 1967 delivered these words on the Senate floor:

> Among the most baneful effects of the government-university contract system the most damaging and corrupting are the neglect of the university's most important purpose ... [T]hose in the social sciences ought to be acting as responsible and independent critics of their government's policies ... When the university turns away from its central purpose and makes itself and appendage to the government, concerning itself with techniques rather than purposes, with expedients rather than ideals ... it betrays a public trust.

Perhaps the time has come to reorient our work more directly toward the general public, toward the "responsible and independent" critique suggested by Senator Fulbright at a moment with many parallels to the present. While it may be appealing to imagine that our ethnographies will influence policy makers, politicians, and Pentagon brass, there are other means of creating alternatives to human terrain and the "clash of civilizations," and there are other audiences anxious to read, hear, and see what we have to say.

Anthropology holds great promise for those seeking a more just world, but it is most likely to succeed when we maintain an independent role (outside of the military and its contract firms) and when we communicate widely, publicly, and persistently. Marshall Sahlins's (1966) idea of the "destruction of conscience" in Vietnam was first published not in an academic peer-reviewed journal, nor much less in a book-length ethnography, but in the pages of *Dissent* magazine. The teach-in was effective not because it brought policy makers and think tanks onto America's college campuses but because it brought ordinary people concerned about their country and its role in the world. In the end it is by sharing what we have learned with the general public that we might spark lasting progressive change in democratic societies.

: : NOTES : :

1. The number of anthropologists working for the DOD or its contract firms far exceeds those working in HTS or other counterinsurgency programs. Anthropologists are employed in a wide range of military tasks including officer education, organizational studies, and program evaluation, to name a few.

2. In May 2008, political science Ph.D. student Michael Bhatia was killed in a roadside bomb attack in Afghanistan. Approximately one month later, political science Ph.D. student Nicole Suveges was killed in a bomb attack in Iraq. In November 2008, HTT social scientist Paula Loyd reportedly suffered second- and third-degree burns over 60 percent of her body after she was doused with a flammable substance and set on fire by Abdul Salam, an Afghan man whom she was interviewing. Another member of her team, Dan Ayala, allegedly executed the man minutes after the incident occurred and now faces murder charges (Schogol 2008). In early 2009, Paula Loyd died from her injuries.

3. Between fiscal years 2006 and 2008, HTS had a budget of $190 million.

16

Soft Power, Hard Power, and the Anthropological "Leveraging" of Cultural "Assets"

Distilling the Politics and Ethics of Anthropological Counterinsurgency[1]

:: DAVID H. PRICE ::

The Pentagon occupation of the academic mind may last much longer than its occupation of Iraq, and may require an intellectual insurgency in response.

Tom Hayden, *Nation*, July 14, 2007

Introduction

In the fall of 2007, after some publicity following the Network of Concerned Anthropologists' circulation of our "Pledge of Non-participation in Counterinsurgency," I heard from several acquaintances working for military and intelligence organizations. Among the reactions to my participation in drafting and supporting this pledge were views ranging from disappointment to expressions of desires to sign that were complicated by anticipated negative workplace repercussions. The most illuminating response came from one military-employed anthropologist who simply asked, given the wide range of activities that comprise counterinsurgency, how could anyone sign on to such a blanket condemnation?

I found this response to be insightful because, while there are no doubt many anthropologists who express blanket opposition to counterinsurgency because they envision it necessarily entails the sort of starkly ethically problematic, even armed, counterinsurgency work associated with the Vietnam War's Phoenix program, there is much more to counterinsurgency—the full range of which might, at first blush, strike many as not inherently raising political or ethical concerns.

News of uniformed Human Terrain anthropologists embedded with armed troops easily sets off most anthropologists' alarm bells, but I would like to complicate such visions of counterinsurgency by adding much more mundane (and acceptable to many) forms of counterinsurgency to the mix—while maintaining that these forms of counterinsurgency remain ethically and politically problematic.

As the military strives to shift to less violent manipulations of the environments and peoples in Iraq, Afghanistan, and elsewhere, anthropologists risk confusing military coercion of occupied peoples with acts of "humanitarianism." The problem is that insurmountable ethical problems arise when anthropologists aid the manipulation of occupied people (see Jorgensen and Wolf 1970). There are only differences in degree, rather than in kind, between the waging of armed counterinsurgency campaigns and using culture to coax occupied people into submission by selectively restoring desperately needed infrastructure and human rights. The problem with counterinsurgency is not that it allows the military to wear different cultural skins; the problem is that it finds anthropologists using biopower and basic infrastructure as bargaining chips to force occupied cultures to surrender (Foucault 1978; Niva 2008).

In this paper, I begin by making a few conceptual distinctions, highlight some key counterinsurgency claims made by the military, and use this frame to briefly review four historical instances (three from World War II and one from the cold war) to illustrate embedded problems with using anthropology in counterinsurgency. But most importantly, I use this history to argue that the ethical and political issues of counterinsurgency have dogged anthropology in consistent and enduring ways that can direct us in the present.

Lansdale and Soft and Hard Counterinsurgency

To get at these distinctions, let me begin with a brief consideration of the range of counterinsurgency activities undertaken by that grandfather of modern counterinsurgency, Edward Lansdale. While Lansdale is most often recalled for his dashing militarized counterinsurgency campaigns, like so many other cold warriors, he realized that effective counterinsurgency was a multifront campaign combining elements of (what political scientist, Joseph Nye would later call) soft power and hard power.

Nye coined the phrase "hard power" to describe situations in which force or threats of force are used to get one's way; while "soft power" signifies the ability to get "others to want the outcomes that you want—[it] co-opts people rather than coerces them" (Nye 2005, 5).[2] I borrow from Nye to try and differentiate between what can be called hard and soft counterinsurgency, with "hard counterinsurgency" being defined as kinetic or armed counterinsurgency campaigns and "soft counterinsurgency" being the not necessarily manifest elements of armed campaigns that are designed to win the hearts and minds (and sometimes debts) of local populations as part of a cooptive effort to curry favor, influence policy, decrease dissent, and increase complacency.[3]

In his memoir, *In the Midst of Wars* (1972), Edward Lansdale famously described his development of counterinsurgency methods in the Central Intelligence Agency's (CIA) covert war against Huk rebels seeking to overthrow Philippines president Magsaysay. Lansdale's passages describing his harnessing of local superstitions are among the most quoted passages by those examining the roots of modern counterinsurgency. One passage recounts how he freighted off Huk insurgents by exploiting local beliefs in vampires after capturing an insurgent, killing him, and draining blood out of the corpse by two neck wounds and then leaving the body to be found by other Huk (see Lansdale 1972, 72–73). Similarly, Lansdale bragged about using battlefield counterinsurgency techniques like the "eye of God" where loudspeakers mounted on aircraft identified and described insurgents on the battlefield, creating distrust within the enemy ranks as well as creating an impression of panopticism (Lansdale 1972, 73–74). He used Vietnamese soothsayers to publish an almanac laced with dire predictions for Vietnamese living in communist-controlled areas (Lansdale 1972, 226–27).[4]

Lansdale was not alone or the first to use cultural knowledge of superstitions as a modern battle weapon. A decade earlier, Gregory Bateson ran Burmese psyop campaigns that similarly tried to harness local superstitions. On one of his missions to Burma, Bateson learned of a local belief that the color yellow symbolically foretold the end of a period of foreign occupation (see MacDonald 1947, 144). Bateson recommended that the Office of Strategic Services "drop yellow dye into the Irrawaddy River and [then] spread rumors that when the Irrawaddy runs yellow, Japan will be kicked out. He won permission . . . but the dye, which turns yellow in ocean salt water, just sank in the fresh water" (Fitch 1999, 100). I like this story for several reasons, not the least of which is the familiar and honest failure of such a harebrained exploit.

But Lansdale's sales-pitchy accounts of similar stunts were seldom complicated by such mundane realism, and he became famous through bragging about aggressive and flashy forms of "hard," armed, counterinsurgency operations exemplified by the Huk vampire or eye of God examples. But Lansdale is less remembered for practicing more soft forms of counterinsurgency. His memoir also describes how the Philippines economic system created such hopeless levels of debt for peasant farmers that Huk communist rebels made inroads with farmers by exploiting these inequities. Lansdale recognized that

> ... a tenant farmer was barely able to pay the interest on borrowed money, much less make an appreciable dent in the principal he owed. And this condition went on for years, [until] that farmer was ripe for revolt against the system that had put him in such a fix. I felt that some relief might be possible through the liberalizing of rural credit. Magsaysay had strong feelings on the subject and started to press for the creation of an enlightened government-sponsored system of rural credit, while I worked on the shorter-range problem of getting some immediate relief. (Lansdale 1972, 76)

Lansdale understood that a society with unmet basic economic, health, sanitation, and other infrastructural needs would breed insurgents, and he advocated for a range of development operations as soft counterinsurgency tactics.

Note that Lansdale did not want to fix the system that "had put [the peasant] in such a fix"; Lansdale was working to protect and sustain the system. What Lansdale bought with such a microloan program was short-term stability and temporary loyalties, not long-term solutions: short-term stability was its own goal.

There are good reasons to question whether the forms of hard counterinsurgency that Lansdale liked to brag about ever worked the way he claimed (then or now), but I would stress that soft counterinsurgency (while expensive and complicated) has a better record of results—although these programs are not always recognized as counterinsurgency.

Current U.S. Army and Marine Corps definitions of counterinsurgency clarify that it need not be directly associated with military efforts to subdue groups vying for power and legitimacy. *FM 3-24* identifies six forms of counterinsurgency: political, economic, military, paramilitary, psychological, and civic actions (*FM 3-24* chapter 1, line 22–25). I do not know, but I imagine if American anthropologists articulated their opposition to specific forms of counterinsurgency, some opponents would express decreasing levels of opposition if these forms were arranged in order descending from those with the highest likelihood of kinetic engagement to those with the least. Thus, objections would decrease with anthropology's contributions to the following forms of counterinsurgency:

- military
- paramilitary
- psychological

- civic action
- political
- economic

More opposition would be associated with anthropologists' contributions to *military* hard counterinsurgency programs than to, say, *economic* soft counterinsurgency programs. I understand this stance, but even setting aside the political issues, given the inherent ethical problems in using anthropology for manipulation and given linked motives of manipulation, I find it shortsighted.

Colonel Schweitzer's Clear Vision

To illustrate my concerns for both hard and soft counterinsurgency, before turning to historical examples, let us consider two recent examples of the military's textual expressions of its interest in anthropology.

In October 2007, after I read army colonel Martin Schweitzer's claim in the *New York Times* that Human Terrain anthropologists were responsible for his unit's 60 percent reduction in combat operations, I filed a Freedom of Information Act request for army records substantiating this extraordinary claim (Rohde 2007, A1).

In February 2008, the army notified me that no such records exist, but as a courtesy, Colonel Schweitzer sent me a lengthy personal reply from Afghanistan arguing that the claims in the *Times* were correct, writing:

The overall attacks by insurgents in . . . Afghanistan decreased dramatically over the last eight months. The Human Terrain Team helped us tailor our operations to focus on the family unit, the village and the districts—not the enemy, thereby shifting the brigade's operational focus from combat/kinetic operations to counter-insurgency operations. The fact is the continual removal of insurgents (kinetic operations) has only allowed us to achieve transitory success in the past five years. Simply stated, the enemy is no longer the Center of Gravity; the people of Afghanistan are, . . . and our metrics of progress are now measured in how much access the people have to their government. For example, "what percent of the population have access to schools . . . ; infant mortality rates; medical access . . . [and] agricultural development . . . " to name a few. We no longer measure progress by how many enemy have been removed . . .

. . . . The HTT's ability to operationalize the Pashtunwalli Code has been instrumental in helping the Coalition and Afghan Security Forces apply a counterinsurgency methodology, which focuses on the people. The fact is the actual percentage of reduced kinetic activity is far greater than the "60 percent" that I stated. *Ultimately, success will require us to change the environment and to do that will require a continued deliberate focus on the culture and population of Afghanistan.* There are no better-qualified professionals to provide this advice than the anthropologists . . . advising this command . . . (Schweitzer to DP February 11, 2008, emphasis added)

There are a number of points in Schweitzer's letter on which I could elaborate, but what is relevant for this discussion is his focus on the soft counterinsurgency tactics used to "change the environment" through domination.

When Colonel Schweitzer's statement is combined with a recently leaked army report arguing that in Iraq, "cultural understanding is an endless endeavor that must be overcome [by] *leveraging* whatever assets are available" (see Price 2008a), we have a rather frank statement of how the military conceptualizes the usefulness of anthropologists assisting occupying troops.

When the army's desire to leverage culture is added to Colonel Schweitzer's expression of the need to use anthropologists to "change the environments" of Iraq and Afghanistan, we see how the military envisions harnessing anthropology for soft counterinsurgency. No anthropologist-contractor need act surprised or chagrined three years (and well over a million tax-free dollars) later when they discover to what ends their work has been put; the army has been abundantly clear: it does not just want to understand the cultural environment it is working in, it wants to change it to its liking, and anthropologists are to be the tools leveraging needed cultural knowledge.

But the military has lacked not only specific cultural knowledge; it has lacked some basic skills needed to negotiate in any world. The army's Strategic Studies Institute recently published a paper by soldier Tyson Voelkel expressing that, after the shift toward counterinsurgency in Iraq, "No longer was it standard operating procedure to blow up the doors of suspect houses with C-4 or other explosives. Instead, we began knocking" (Voelkel 2007, 534–35). Why is anthropology needed for this? More would be gained from reading Emily Post or Mr. Rogers than reading Evans-Pritchard.

The Problem with Using Soft Power on the Soft Machine Is Manipulation

Soft and hard counterinsurgency campaigns share purposeful bonds of desired manipulation, and this manipulation creates serious ethical problems and raises fundamental questions about whom this anthropology serves.[5]

I can understand why the military wants anthropology for counterinsurgency; it makes sense. But few in the military understand the ethical and political basis of anthropology's resistance, as if ethical commitments to voluntary informed consent, disclosure, and protection were optional and our disciplinary understandings of power were epiphenomenal.

There is a long, if understudied history of efforts to harness anthropology for hard and soft forms of counterinsurgency. Historically, American approaches to the anthropology of manipulation have been directly influenced by warfare, although war's armistice later brought these skills (and ethical problems) to industry.

Most of the issues we confront today were faced by anthropologists in World War II, although that war occurred in vastly different political and ethical terrain: fighting fascism raised different political issues than our contemporary wars of occupation, and that war's anthropologists negotiated their decisions without formalized ethical codes.

World War II birthed a new form of applied anthropology that sought explicitly not only to understand culture, but to manipulate it. The Society for Applied Anthropology's 1941 wartime founders, Eliot Chapple and Conrad Arensberg, shared interests in designing forms of social control. At Harvard, Arensberg gravitated toward the work of Lloyd Warner, and, with Chapple, he established studies of industrial relations that benefited the managerial sectors of Fordist American workplaces. Arensberg believed that anthropological knowledge could be harnessed by leaders to alleviate societal problems, although explanations of who would determine which sectors of society would benefit were unclear. During the war, Arensberg served in the Military Intelligence Division, and he applied anthropology to the management of interned Japanese Americans.

It was as a reaction to these manipulative, rather than representative, forms of applied anthropology that Sol Tax later advocated for a less externally manipulative model of activist applied anthropology under the label of "action anthropology," which sought not to control and motivate cultural actors in ways desired by external groups but to use anthropology as a means of communicating the desires of the groups that anthropologists studied (see Tax 1952, 1975; Bennett 1996). Tax differentiated his efforts from those of mainstream applied anthropology by stressing an activist allegiance to the desires of the communities studied by anthropologists.

Under Tax's rubrics of "action anthropology" there could be no anthropologically informed counterinsurgency: soft or hard.

Historical Examples of Soft Counterinsurgency

There were plenty of anthropological contributions to World War II that did not involve counterinsurgency or the manipulation of studied populations—just as there are anthropological contributions to today's wars that do not involve counterinsurgency or nonconsensual manipulation of studied populations.

I note in passing that anthropology's commitments to studied populations might make it more naturally aligned with insurgency than with counterinsurgency, although it has historically participated in both. I would estimate that during World War II, anthropologists probably contributed more to insurgent than to counterinsurgent campaigns.

Some of these insurgent campaigns included things like Tom Harrisson's daring mission for the British Z Special Unit in which he parachuted into the Sarawak highlands to arm and train a Kelabit regiment for a bloody insurgency against Japanese occupiers along the coastal region. Edmund Leach armed, trained, and fought alongside Kachin guerrillas against the Japanese in Burma. Clyde and Florence Kluckhohn, Alexander Leighton, Ruth Benedict, and others at the Office of War Information oversaw the creation of native language pamphlets dropped behind Japanese lines encouraging occupied people to resist Japanese occupation. OSS agent Carelton Coon trained Maggrebi assassins and bombers targeting Vichy occupiers in North Africa (and so on).

To illustrate some of the ways that anthropologists have engaged with counterinsurgency in the past, I briefly summarize four episodes in which anthropologists contributed to or evaluated soft counterinsurgency programs. The first example comes from Philleo Nash's war work for the White House's Office of Facts and Figures; the second examines Gregory Bateson's assessment of Soviet counterinsurgency techniques. The third example considers Morris Opler's refusal to make interned Japanese American legible for his internment camp managers. The final cold war example describes how Walt Rostow and others secretly framed international aid programs as forms of counterinsurgency.

Philleo Nash

In 1943, Philleo Nash was appointed to a special White House post at the Office of Facts and Figures dedicated to monitoring domestic racial tensions that the Roosevelt administration feared could lead to widespread rioting that would disrupt America's civil order or industrial war production.

Nash was provided with his own newswire, air transport, and access to scholars and law enforcement personnel across the country to try and monitor and then quell racial disturbances. When Nash prevented labor actions such as wildcat strikes by black workers in Milwaukee (who were being subjected to the sort of humiliating and degrading conditions that led to collective actions during the civil rights movement over a decade later), he contacted local minority leaders and persuaded them to use their local credibility to de-escalate volatile situations. In rare instances, Nash called in police or national guard units to prevent uprisings by a show of force.

One way of looking at Nash's work would be that Nash helped the nation's war production by using applied anthropological research methods and counterinsurgency techniques to influence the actions of justifiably disgruntled domestic minority populations. To this end, Nash manipulated oppressed minority groups striving for equal rights, and his suppression of these uprisings slowed the progression of an insipient equal rights movement. Nash's mentor, Harold Lasswell, felt at ease with a high degree of social manipulations, but Lasswell also thought that democracy was too dangerous a tool be left to the populace.

Decades after the war, Phileo's wife Edith wrote that "Thurgood Marshall once told [Phileo] that if he'd, 'been at Lincoln's side there never would have been a Civil War . . . (and we'd all still be slaves)'" (Nash 1989, 34). Make no mistake, Phileo Nash opposed American racist policies. After the war he directly contributed to the army's successful desegregation, but, intended humor aside, Thurgood Marshall's point is well taken: social upheaval can be an indicator of the prevalence of injustice, and such movements are necessary for liberation.

War necessitates such choices, and given the conditions that would have been faced by racial minorities and all Americans under a Nazi victory, it was a strategic choice to finish a struggle against the Axis before undertaking a domestic civil rights struggle. But this gambit should not camouflage the reality that these techniques were developed to serve the interests of a powerful social sector moving against and manipulating the immediate desires of less powerful individuals. When reading accounts in wartime issues of the *Chicago Defender* of black Americans struggling for workplace equality, I am left uneasy knowing that Nash's counterinsurgency operations were monitoring these same reports and organizing means of suppressing uprisings.

Gregory Bateson

The second example of World War II counterinsurgency finds Gregory Bateson contemplating the powers of soft counterinsurgency for the OSS (see

Price 1998). Bateson's experiences in wartime colonial India and in assisting insurgent operations in Burma led him to write a classified 1944 report favorably analyzing soft counterinsurgency techniques used by the Soviets to coopt various indigenous peoples' movements in Central and Eastern Asia. In the following passage, Bateson outlines for the OSS how such soft counterinsurgency techniques work, and he notes how these techniques might be emulated to suppress indigenous uprisings elsewhere:

> The most significant experiment which has yet been conducted in the adjustment of relations between "superior" and "inferior" peoples is the Russian handling of their Asiatic tribes in Siberia. The findings of this experiment support very strongly the conclusion that it is very important to foster spectatorship among the superiors and exhibitionism among the inferiors. In outline, what the Russians have done is to stimulate the native peoples to undertake a native revival while they themselves admire the resulting dance festivals and other exhibitions of native culture, literature, poetry, music and so on. And the same attitude of spectatorship is then naturally extended to native achievements in production or organization. In contrast to this, where the white man thinks of himself as a model and encourages the native people to watch him in order to find out how things should be done, we find that in the end nativistic cults spring up among the native people. The system gets over-weighed until some compensatory machinery is developed and then the revival of native arts, literature, etc., becomes a weapon for use *against* the white man (Phenomena, comparable to Gandhi's spinning wheel may be observed in Ireland and elsewhere). If, on the other hand, the dominant people themselves stimulate native [revivalism], then the system as a whole is much more stable, and the nativism cannot be used against the dominant people.
>
> OSS can and should do nothing in the direction of stimulating native revivals but we might move gently towards making the British and the Dutch more aware of the importance of processes of this kind. (Bateson 1944, 6–7)

In 2008, the RAND Corporation published a working paper by Olga Oliker entitled "Soft Power, Hard Power, and Counterinsurgency: The Early Soviet Experience in Central Asia and Its Implications," which echoed points made by Bateson, and regardless of the ironies of RAND recommending the emulation of Soviet counterinsurgency tactics, the report's conclusion and recommendations linked its findings to current problems faced in Iraq.

During his wartime service, Bateson saw the possibilities that counterinsurgency offered those wishing to suppress uprisings—and while such thoughts were natural products of the war, Bateson's postwar assessment of his OSS years came to be tinged with deep regrets. In later years, he became increasingly concerned not about the failures but about the successes of his OSS work. He came to be "disturbed with the OSS treatment of the natives, . . . he felt that he was associated with a dishonest outfit," and viewed the OSS as having run "deceitful propaganda" campaigns (see Price 1998; Lipset 1980, 174; see also Yans-McLaughlin 1986, 202–3, Mabee 1987, 8). Bateson saw theoretical potential for soft counterinsurgency, but after the flames of war cooled, he was ethically and politically disturbed by such manipulations and wondered what would happen if, as Laura Thompson wrote in 1944, anthropologists simply "became technicians for hire to the highest bidder?" (1944, 12). Although Thompson's question informed applied anthropology's ethics code after the war, her question remains largely ignored today.

The Brothers Opler and the War Relocation Authority

A low point for World War II soft counterinsurgent anthropology was found at the War Relocation Authority (WRA), where anthropological skills were used to monitor and attempt management of interned Japanese American citizens (Price 2008b). Most of the dozen WRA anthropologists worked on tasks far more aligned with the business of manipulation and engineered conformity than with the sort of representational action anthropology to be later envisioned by Tax.

Alexander Leighton and his staff viewed Japanese American internees as potential insurgents needing to be managed—and many anthropologists working at the camps adopted this mind-set: filing ethnographic reports identifying troublemakers and tracking disturbances with hopes of preemptively stopping protests.

But the work of Morris and Marvin Opler exemplifies the sort of compassionate advocacy later envisioned by Tax; and Morris Opler's camp fieldwork and legal advocacy (he wrote a plaintiff legal brief in the Supreme Court case of *Korematsu vs. the U.S.*) challenged the managerial counterinsurgent views imposed by Leighton and others.

Morris Opler described the deplorable conditions in the camps and refused to contribute to the anthropology of cooption that his superiors at WRA desired—he was criticized for working too much "like an old-fashioned ethnologist" (Washington CAS 1944, 9), and bureaucrats took actions to relieve him of his duties (see Hansen 1995, 626). The WRA had little use or interest in anthropology's theories and explanations: they were hungry for disarticulated culture factoids and methods that could make these "others" legible and manageable. Anthropologists whose commitments to the interned were at odds with the WRA were marginalized and ignored.

Beyond the resistance of the Oplers, most WRA anthropologists gave administrators what they wanted: views of culture that helped the WRA manipulate detainees. As Orin Starn observed, under these conditions, field-based "WRA anthropologists reformulated the classic Boasian axiom: instead of confronting power with truth, anthropology was to supply information to power" (1986, 705).

Walt Whitman Rostow and Max Millikan's Modernization Dreams

The final historical example of soft counterinsurgency I will review is a familiar remnant of the cold war, and it is the most likely form of soft counterinsurgency that anthropologists will be recruited to facilitate: programs in which anthropologists design and implement development programs that will restore the vital services our armed forced obliterated while destroying villages to save villages.

The political and ethical issues of using anthropology in such programs are complex, and while not categorically declaring that all such work presents anthropologists with insurmountable ethical problems, the extent to which development programs in occupied countries are arms of American counterinsurgency presents ethical problems for anthropologists. Ridiculing, dismissing, or ignoring these ethical problems and the explicit historical links of development programs to counterinsurgency will not solve these dilemmas— but I think that is pretty much what we can expect from the military, aligned anthropologists, and the media.

To stress the historical links between the cold war creation of development programs and counterinsurgent concerns, I note not only the sort of soft counterinsurgency microloan aid programs Lansdale advocated but also focus on a 1954 CIA document I had released under the Freedom of Information Act (and have published and discussed elsewhere; see Price 2003) that finds Walt Rostow and Max Millikan bluntly describing to Director of Central Intelligence Allen Dulles their visions of international aid programs in terms of serving U.S. counterinsurgent interests.

In this document, Rostow and Millikan clearly conceived of development as a form of global counterinsurgency—with the primary benefits not flowing to nations receiving such aid but to the United States' security. While the "public" Rostow hawked his brand of development as an entrepreneurial opportunity for underdeveloped nations, privately he sold the CIA on the resulting political capital and the implicit advantage to be gained through the resulting markets and lines of debt, political servitude, and installation of counterinsurgent regimes of stability favoring American interests. In order to reduce the lure of socialism in potentially insurgent populations, Millikan and Rostow wrote that

> In the short run communism must be contained militarily. In the long run we must rely on the development . . . of an environment in which societies which directly or indirectly menace ours will not evolve. We believe the achievement of a degree of steady economic growth is an essential part of such an environment. (Millikan and Rostow 1998 [1954], 3)

Just as development programs of the cold war imposed neocolonial managerial stability on nations devastated by colonial ransacking, we can expect a host of development cultural and economic "stabilization" programs in Iraq and Afghanistan.

Historical examples such as the roles played by social scientists and intelligence agencies involved in 1960s to 1970 USAID agricultural and police programs in war-torn Vietnam and Thailand offer some guidance on how these pacification programs may work. And if history is prologue, we can expect soft violins to play in the foreground while we are told (always in the Haigian passive voice) that "mistakes were made" but that this is not the time to argue about how we got into this mess; we must (suddenly) worry about the people in harm's way and that these people will be harmed if we worry about the ethical and political issues raised by anthropologically informed soft counterinsurgency (Price 2008c).

But to ignore such fundamental analyses of power is to repress very basic anthropological analysis and ignores the reality that aid projects in occupied countries are necessarily soft counterinsurgency programs and are fundamentally different than aid projects in nonoccupied countries.

Sorting Ethics and Politics

These four historical soft counterinsurgency vignettes represent anthropologists facing hard choices, considering seductive visions, resisting the lure of counterinsurgency, and working for funders with undeclared intentions.

Nash's counterinsurgency raised ethical issues even in a "good war;" and when anthropology is used for manipulation in the wars of neocons and neoliberals, the ethical issues remain, while the political outcomes get worse. Bateson's analysis shows how seductive visions of anthropological manipulation in wartime can be—although these visions can later fade. The Opler brothers' resistance finds anthropologists marginalized for representing studied populations instead of facilitating their management; and Rostow and Millikan's memo reminds us of how past wars have used aid as soft weapons of control.

Desires to use anthropology for manipulation are as old as the discipline itself. Obviously, American anthropology has a politically mixed track record, but at least part of this record includes a history of resisting making vulnerable those we study. At its best, anthropology does something more than making those we study legible to power—although this legibility is what those advocating hard or soft counterinsurgency desire.

It makes sense that the military would strive for a more culturally nuanced occupation; after all, it is the nature of occupying armies to seek to subjugate and occupy with as little trouble as possible. But anthropology's assistance in this task moves the discipline away from the most basic anthropological ethical principle of representing and not harming those we study.

When the military says it wants anthropology, it really only wants parts of it—it wants knowledge of local customs, language, and manners that can help achieve immediate military goals. If the military can identify and gain specific anthropological theories or techniques that can be used to control occupied populations, it will be thrilled. But so far the specific theories pushed by those selling counterinsurgency are limited: there are drab versions of structural-functionalism that give new meaning to the term "army surplus," there are supposedly predictive forms of network theory that would make Philip K. Dick cringe, and there are versions of highly quantitative but crudely simplistic cost-benefit analysis models that will soon take us into the early 1970s (McFate 2005a; Renzi 2006; Weinberger 2008b; Sautter 2008).[6] The importance of these theories is not whether they work as advertised, it is that the dream can be sold while building cult-like reputations of the salespeople selling them in the closed, non-peer-reviewed settings of the military. As Robert Gordon observed in his important study on the counterinsurgent uses of bushmen ethnologists by South African armed forces, such conditions "bolster the status of the ethnologist as a ritual 'expert' since other . . . personnel have little chance of challenging his or her magical knowledge" (Gordon 1987, 446).

There is much of anthropology that the military does not want: the military does not want anthropological critiques of power, imperialism, or neocolonialism. It does not want empathetic understandings of "the other" unless this can be used as an "asset" for "leveraging." The military also does not want nonaligned anthropologists doing an anthropology of counterinsurgency, and Minerva's deep pockets should help this nicely.

Soft counterinsurgency dreams that culture can fix what thousands of tons of munitions broke; and we need to question how anthropology's imagined role as "fixer" is directly linked to the initial invasions and occupations spawning the needed counterinsurgency. The more the military comes to believe that culture-based counterinsurgency campaigns are possible, the more that anthropology will be called on to patch up their invasions and occupations. As Steve Niva observes, "we can now update Clausewitz to mean: anthropology becomes an extension of war by other means" (SN to DP, April 22, 2008).

But anthropology is not political science—if for no other reasons than our ethnological and ethical histories tie us to those we study and share our lives with. Selling mainstream anthropologists hard counterinsurgency will be difficult—if not impossible, but selling soft counterinsurgency should be easier. Market forces and a disciplinary comfort with past development projects can ease the discipline in these directions. It is the deceptively friendly or humanitarian surface of soft counterinsurgency that will make assistance in these schemes of domination attractive to some.

The failure of many anthropologists to confront how the military has in the past (and does in the present) conceived of and used anthropological knowledge leads (some like Jager, McFate, and others) to fantasies that anthropological knowledge will now be used for something other than the same forms of leverage of peoples studied by anthropologists.

Anthropologists must acknowledge the fundamental lack of control they have when engaging the military. But they should do this in ways that acknowledge their own agency in enabling the ends of conquest and occupation to which their assistance serves regardless of their own intentions and motivations.

The American public accepts the narrative that individual soldiers are not to blame for the atrocities collectively committed by our armed forces. We have culturally constructed a space in which we accept that soldiers are only following orders and doing their duty and are not to be blamed for decisions made by politicians. But what of anthropologists working in these settings? Do anthropologists voluntarily making the cultural ways of occupied people vulnerable to military occupiers expect they too will get a free pass because they did not break the societies they imagine they are fixing?

I worry that some postmodern strains have left anthropology so marked with Lyotard's "incredulity towards metanarratives" that the discipline is unprepared to counter recurrent episodes of military cooption and exploitation of anthropological knowledge.[7] While not wanting to essentialize the past, anthropologists today should have the collective foresight to know to what ends our work will be put. If we could not control how it was used in a good war like World War II, what are the chances of controlling it in this war of occupation based on lies?

It is true that the military does not set policy and that its tasks are limited—but anthropologists working in these environments must understand their role in providing the military with cultural tools to smooth out problems of conquest and occupation. Anthropology has more to offer at the policy level than it does at the level of the cultural etiquette classes we are being asked to provide. Rather than using anthropology to solve problems of occupation and insurgency, we should use anthropology to keep us out of these situations in the first place. But promises of functional anthropological counterinsurgency (even false promises) only encourage civilian and Pentagon planners to envision more of these invasion fiascos as problems that anthropologists can solve after the mess has been made.

:: **NOTES** ::

1. The ideas in this paper have benefited from ongoing discussions on the ethics and mechanics of counterinsurgency with Steve Niva, Thomas Anson, Jeff Birkenstein, Alexander Cockburn, Hugh Gusterson, Roberto Gonzales, Richard Langill, Laura Nader, Roger Snider, and the often divergent views of members of the American Anthropological Association's Commission on the Engagement of Anthropology with U.S. Security and Intelligence Communities.

2. Nye even argues that soft power is not just effective, it is *cost* effective (Nye 2005).

3. Examples of hard counterinsurgency could include activities undertaken by armed Human Terrain Teams today or Vietnam War Phoenix program units, the "hunter-killer teams" (Valentine 1990, 12), that used cultural and ethnographic knowledge to select targeted individuals for kidnapping or assassination. Soft counterinsurgency often strives to nurture goodwill by (re)establishing programs filling basic human needs by supplying things like crop loans, electricity, local health clinics, or irrigation systems.

4. I am sure the Huk people had the bejesus scared out of them when they found their comrade's corpse along the trail—and the faux vampire holes in his neck may not have been as significant as Lansdale would have us believe. A dead friend is pretty scary in its own right. But these sort of dramatic claims for counterinsurgency link past efforts to sell counterinsurgency to the military with similar efforts in the present (see McFate 2005a).

5. While differentiating manipulation from other forms or persuasion has its difficulties, studying other cultures in order to alter them to one's advantage undermines basic ethical principles of obtaining informed consent and protecting those studied—unless one openly negotiates these terms.

6. Sautter's "inferior goods" argument comes close to making a rationalist argument that good counterinsurgency will use development and aid programs as forms of bribes (Sautter 2008).

7. See Graeber (2004, 71).

17

Yes, Both, Absolutely

A Personal and Professional Commentary on
Anthropological Engagement with Military
and Intelligence Organizations[1]

:: KERRY FOSHER ::

A Choice?

At the 2008 meetings of the Society for Applied Anthropology
(SfAA), I spoke in a panel on anthropology and government. The
panel was largely focused on work with the military, a topic not
well understood in the anthropological community. Of the pan-
elists who worked directly with the military, each represented a
significantly different type of engagement. One speaker, Brian
Selmeski, described his work in reorienting professional military
education for an entire military service, the U.S. Air Force. Montgomery McFate discussed her work with the Human Terrain System, a U.S. Army pilot project to deploy people with social science
backgrounds as parts of teams providing sociocultural analysis to
military commanders. I spoke about my work with the Marine
Corps Intelligence Activity, where I help figure out an appropriate
approach to culture and am building an analyst development program to teach social science concepts to people involved with military intelligence. Each of us had worked out our alignment with
the American Anthropological Association's (AAA) *Code of Ethics*
(1998) in our own way. However, a common theme among us was a
desire to work for change from the inside.

During the question and answer period, a young woman asked

us all which was more important, working for change from the inside or maintaining critical distance to work for change from the outside. I thought about the range of topics and methods that our discipline has been able to encompass. I thought about the diversity of engagements we embrace, from textual analysis that can take place in a university office, to traditional field research, to action anthropology, advocacy, policy advising, and applied work. I thought about the tradition of rigorous debate about and monitoring of ethics that allows this breadth of work. In such a tradition, there is no reason to choose, and, in fact, there may be an imperative to refrain from making a choice that excludes entire areas of practice from the disciplinary discourse. I replied to her question with what I truly believe to be the best answer for the discipline: "Yes, both, absolutely."

There are two types of choices hinted at in this exchange. One is an individual choice about personal ethics and an assessment of where one's activities and relationships fall in a professional code of ethics. The other is a choice for the entire discipline. Which kinds of activities and engagements will we allow under the big tent our discipline has formed and which are simply too problematic?

This commentary describes my own choices and what I believe to be the key issues in navigating the ethical challenges I face. I also mention what I feel are the potential benefits to the discipline of having some anthropologists directly engaged, despite the problematic nature of the work. I do not propose my choices as a model for anyone else in the discipline. I simply use them to illustrate what I feel are some of the core questions that face any anthropologist addressing this topic, regardless of the degree to which they decide to engage with people working in military or intelligence organizations.[2]

Context: A Bit of Ethnography

Relatively little is available in the anthropological literature that describes the types of engagements that anthropologists have with people and organizations related to U.S. national security.[3] Consequently, it is necessary to provide a brief discussion of types of work, categories of employment, and domains of practice as a framework for the comments that follow. I do not pretend that these descriptions are based on rigorous research. They are merely observations, as much research remains to be done in the ethnography of the security sector in the United States.

Anthropologists employed by military and intelligence organizations work in many different capacities. Some teach in academies, colleges, and universities. Some work as researchers, administrators, analysts, and trainers. Some do planning, research, classified or unclassified analysis, fieldwork, and so on. Most work in offices and classrooms in the United States. Some work in offices overseas. A few are deployed with operating forces. Some spend their time traveling around to different bases and facilities delivering training or policy advice. Work may be geared toward understanding U.S. organizations, international organizations, nongovernmental organizations, the joint environment, allies, perceived adversaries, or perceived neutral groups. It may involve providing information on specific groups or, as is the case with my own, it may have more to do with trying to ground policy, education, and planning in solid social science concepts and methods.

These anthropologists often are employed as civil servants. Their positions are similar to others in the federal bureaucracy, although a number of organizations are trying to create positions that are tailored to the kinds of freedom of schedule and publication that anthropologists prefer. One consequence of the recent increased interest in anthropologists is that many anthropologists now do private consulting or work with a contracting company. Such private sector jobs can be created and dismantled more easily than civil service positions. They also offer considerably more freedom in terms of working conditions and pay. Of course, they also come with less job security and, for those who are deployed into conflicts, a certain amount of ambiguity about which laws apply. It is difficult to assess the numbers of anthropologists who are employed in these categories. Of course, some of that depends on whom one "counts" as an anthropologist based on a variety of criteria such as the type of work being done, level of education, professional membership, publication, and so on. It also depends on who wants to be counted. I know a number of anthropology Ph.D.s working for the government who have adopted a different professional identity and now consider themselves to be a different sort of professional, an analyst, a manager, an advisor, whose work is informed by their anthropological background.

It also is useful to think about the domains of practice. Although each overlaps or is entangled with the others, they help me think about one dimension in this discussion. It is important to remember that in almost all of these domains, one's audience is likely to include both uniformed and civilians members of these communities.

Education: work on long-term educational approaches, teaching; often in the academies, colleges, and universities of professional military and intelligence education.
Training: work on strategies for training, delivering training; often as part of predeployment preparations or professional development.

Policy: advising on or developing policy, sometimes at the national level, sometimes within specific organizations.
Direct support to operations: usually deployment in an advisory or analytic
   capacity, sometimes involves field research.
Intelligence: involves aspects of all other domains but is focused on providing
   information, both classified and unclassified, that supports decision making
   by elected officials, other policy makers, or military commanders.
Research and development: basic and applied research conducted through
   the national laboratories and research institutes, military and intelligence
   universities, or with Federally Funded Research and Development Centers[4];
   although traditionally these organizations tended to look at hard science
   and engineering topics, they increasingly are trying to address culture-related
   topics.

These domains are emically derived. Whereas anthropologists may be interested in degrees of secrecy and transparency, relationships leading to a potential for bias, the possibility of harm to research communities, and so on, as
Sahlins reminds us, "These people have not organized their existence in answer
to what has been troubling us lately" (Sahlins 1999). Instead, these domains
follow the distinctions important in the military and intelligence communities and help point toward the sorts of institutional contexts in which anthropologists work, although perhaps not the boundaries of the work they actually
do within those contexts.

Increasingly, anthropologists are taking on shaping roles, advising their
organization or larger parts of military and intelligence institutions on what
they should be doing with regard to culture. As seems to be so often the case,
anthropologists are troubling these domains, cross-cutting, talking to one another, and generally perturbing the waters. My own work touches on many of
these domains. My primary employment is in intelligence. I spend a good part
of every day dealing with educational and training issues as we try to figure out
how social science can be included in the professional development of members of the intelligence community. I also deal with training and education
issues at higher levels of policy, trying to help ensure that standards are developed based on social science and education theory rather than what is con-
venient and familiar. I work with people who want to model culture or some
aspect of human behavior, trying to point out the problems with technological
"solutions" to anything related to human life. I work with the organization's
leadership to develop an approach to incorporating more social science that is
based on sound scholarship and is sustainable over time, as the culture money

streams begin to dry up. I also provide limited guidance on how we can best provide direct support to operations, particularly questions of when it is appropriate to send somebody into a conflict zone to provide analytic support related to culture and when it is not. I provide no region or group-specific analysis. Almost everything I do is focused on generic concepts and methods. The common themes through all of my projects are that I provide advice on how to make better use of social science concepts in intelligence and how to encourage intelligence analysts to use different approaches in their work.

Questions

Point of Departure

How did I get into the position described in the paragraph above? As the audience member at the SfAA meetings pointed out, there is one individual question that marks a point of departure for all future questions for any academic. Should I stay in a traditional academic role, thereby preserving my autonomy and credibility as a source of objective assessment and critique? Alternatively, should I try consulting for or working within one of these organizations to see what I might be able to learn and accomplish from that vantage point? There are trade-offs in each case. When directly engaged, you risk absorbing the assumptions and biases of the organization(s) for which you work. In some cases, you may be risking causing harm to your research community or enabling harm caused by others. You almost assuredly are enabling flawed institutions. However, there also are risks if you choose the more traditional path. It is very challenging to try to learn about security-related organizations from the outside. Unless you are particularly careful and fortunate in your contacts, you end up having to craft your critique with the sorts of sources and information that are available to an investigative journalist rather than the ethnographic data upon which our discipline normally bases analysis and critique.

This also is a choice about the frame(s) in which I make my ethical decisions. At the macrolevel, the decision-making frame of the discipline focuses on the structural constraints produced by powerful institutions and discourses. This frame cannot be ignored, and I accept many of the critiques that emerge from it. However, I do not accept that this is the only frame in which to make choices. There also must be analysis and decision making at the level of human practice. Structures do not emerge, continue, and change as a result of a Kroeberian superorganic force. However powerful they may be, they rise and fall as aggregates of human agency. As illustrated in the following sections, some of my choices have been made in acceptance of constraining structures but with greater emphasis on human agency and the lives currently being lived within those structures.

Each of the questions below factors into this first choice. However, if the choice is made to engage in an enduring relationship with a military or intelligence organization, especially one where compensation is involved, the questions must be revisited on a near daily basis. Most anthropologists working for military and intelligence organizations are faced with choices about which projects to accept, which lines of advice to advocate, and how to draw lines. All of these decisions must begin with whether or not something is within the code of ethics of the appropriate professional organization, usually the AAA or the SfAA(Society for Applied Anthropology 1983; American Anthropological Society 1998).

To What Degree Am I Enabling a Flawed System?

Few would debate that any anthropologist who works with or for an organization engaged in U.S. national security is enabling a flawed system. While this does require vigilance, it is not unique to those engaged with the security sector. I have a hard time imagining any large institution that is not flawed. For example, anyone teaching in a traditional academic environment enables the replication of flawed and unjust systems that affect not only their students but also the communities in which anthropologists traditionally study. People who teach in those environments may work very hard in the classroom to counter those effects, but that does not erase them.

This is not to say that we should adopt a completely relativistic stance with regard to the security sector, only that its status as a flawed institution cannot serve as the sole basis for a robust disciplinary debate on ethics, scholarship, and practice. The choice to be part of or work with any large institution is always going to involve a balancing act as we judge how much good can be done from within as opposed to taking an outside stance. My decisions have tended to come down on the side of working within organizations, but those are choices I make for myself, not the discipline as a whole.

What Harm May I Cause?

The guideline to do no harm to one's research community, seemingly so simple, has been the most difficult guideline for me to navigate. I believe this part of the AAA *Code of Ethics* (1998) is critical to the discussions and internal decision-making process of any anthropologist considering any sort of work. While much of disciplinary attention has gone to the consequences of action, some of us also feel compelled to look at the consequences of inaction, especially in terms of individual lives. If I do nothing about a situation where I can help mitigate harm or give people more options, where does that fall in terms of the "do no harm" guidelines? The nine-year-old girl in Kabul and the nineteen-year-old Marine do not have the luxury of waiting for us to sort out our national debate on foreign policy. I believe their lives matter. In terms of my overall employment, I have decided that I have a personal ethical obligation to engage under these circumstances.

On another level, there is understandable fear in the discipline that anthropological information and techniques, whether willingly supplied or in the form of published materials, will be used to harm the communities in which anthropologists have traditionally studied. This is undoubtedly true, as it would be if they could only access what we had published. I believe that engagement offers at least some possibility of interpreting, offering other, nonviolent courses of action, and so on, but only if we are willing to accept that we will not always "win" in terms of how information is used. You have to be willing to persist over the long haul.

Anthropologists also worry, based on past experience, that security institutions will take anthropology cafeteria style, rather than understanding the need for the full package. Again, this is undoubtedly true, as it is with our students, readers from other disciplines, and lay readers of all kinds. As with information use, this concern is almost certain to become truth if none of us is in the room when the choices are made.

One of the ways I navigate these concerns involves institutional and organizational shaping. Sometimes this simply means educating my organization, the Department of Defense, or the intelligence community about the concerns of social scientists and suggesting ways that problems can be reframed and solved in an ethical manner. Sometimes it means trying to create institutional mechanisms to provide support for ethical decision making. One example of this sort of work is my efforts, now gaining traction, to establish an Institutional Review Board for the organizations at Quantico that do social science research. In terms of day-to-day activities, I sometimes decide to engage or assist security organizations and sometimes refuse based on what courses of action I feel will cause the least harm or do the most good. For example, thus far I have declined to provide assistance with region-specific information. Instead, I work on providing general cultural concepts and shaping overall approaches at the organizational level. That may change over time as I continually assess my situation and actions.

Is the Work Secret?

Types and degrees of secrecy vary among kinds of engagement. All aspects should be explored by anthropologists considering a new project or job: (1) concealing sponsorship, research activities, or results from the community under study; (2) kiva secrets—concealing some aspects of a community to maintain access for research purposes or so that you can, as Carolyn Fluehr-Lobban (2008) has termed it, "do some good" by working within it (this is problematized when the community to which access is being preserved is an employer or client and is a tertiary topic of study for the anthropologist); (3) not publishing or presenting the results of research in anthropological venues (or at all); (4) secrecy to protect informant confidentiality.

With the exception of the first type of secrecy, there are legitimate reasons for all of the others in various types of engagements (inside or outside of the security sector)—what matters is that those reasons and the consequences are carefully thought out with reference to the AAA *Code of Ethics* (1998) and, preferably, discussed with colleagues.

I work in an intelligence organization. Because of classification laws and organizational policies, if I write about the specifics of what I do or the operation of my employer, I am obliged to have that material reviewed. Thus far, I have decided I do not want to submit to that kind of review and have decided to draw a line between the details of my workday and the things about which I write for the discipline. This means a significant sacrifice in terms of my curriculum vitae, as it will severely limit what I can publish. However, I default to the ethical obligation described above. The obligation I feel to the lives and experiences of people currently in conflict trumps any concerns I might have about professional advancement.

This decision raises issues of whether or not what I do is actually anthropology if I cannot discuss it with colleagues and subject my work to peer review. This is a real concern. However, it also is a concern for anyone doing applied work or advocacy in which they withhold certain information. I am comfortable with the idea that I may be an anthropologist acting as an advisor or an advisor whose work is informed by anthropology rather than an anthropologist doing anthropology. Others may be less comfortable with that distinction. There is a larger disciplinary discussion that needs to happen on this issue, but it must first be disentangled from the exclusive focus on security.

Issues of classification and other restrictions on information sharing, such as the "for official use only" and "sensitive but unclassified" designations, present a continual challenge. Although it has not happened yet, it is likely that I will someday encounter restricted information that I believe the discipline or the public should know. I will follow the laws to which I am subject, but such an incident would be a trigger for me to revisit substantively my willingness to engage.

Daily Decision Making

There is no question that working within the security sector, especially working within an intelligence organization, has a high potential for ethical missteps. In the absence of disciplinary guidance, every anthropologist must design his or her own process for ensuring that his or her work falls within the AAA or SfAA codes and within their own guidelines for appropriate and ethical behavior. My process is convoluted but always includes the following aspects or mechanisms:

Preserve the Ability to Leave

This means some difficult choices about lifestyle and finances, but I believe it is essential for anyone working in the security sector, except those involved in professional military education, where the setting is similar to a university. This means that I must preserve the ability to get other kinds of jobs and must always have enough of a financial cushion to walk away if I am asked or expected to do things I consider unethical. For somebody paying off student loans, this is not easy. For somebody trying to raise a family, it might be impossible, something that should be given due consideration before accepting a position.

Be Systematically Vigilant

I believe it is not enough to make ethical choices once and then become passive. I make small choices constantly because my work changes frequently, but I do not believe that is enough either. On a weekly basis, I take time to revisit my larger choices. Should I be engaged in this way? In this situation? Are there better ways for me to be constructively engaged given my specific skills and knowledge? Is the slope getting too slippery even if what I am doing right now seems acceptable? On a monthly basis, I revisit these topics with one or more colleagues in my network. This attention may seem melodramatic, but I see it as the equivalent of flossing. It is a preventative measure, one that is necessary for those of us who are working within organizations that wield a great deal of power.

Maintain an Intellectual Bucket Brigade

Every anthropologist interested in security should maintain a network of colleagues up and down the spectrum of engagement, a sort of intellectual bucket brigade. This helps ensure that data, analysis, and critique from different perspectives circulate. There are benefits to this sort of communication for everyone in the network. For those in traditional academia, the material from those working within the security sector may not be readily available through documentary or ethnographic research. For those, like myself, who are working within military or intelligence organizations, the outside perspective is critical. I rely on those in my bucket brigade to provide hand holds on a potentially slippery slope, to help me realize when I start to lose sight of the impact of my setting on the choices I have available and on my decision-making process. On a more practical level, this network provides me with a group of people I can call when I am considering a new course of action. I use the differences among my colleagues to help make my decisions strong.

It is in this last mechanism that I believe we see the greatest potential benefit for the discipline as a whole.[5] Given that all these institutions are linked in some way to the capacity for collective violence, understanding how they are created, maintained, and transformed by the people within them should be an important topic in anthropology. As mentioned earlier, it is very difficult to get rich data from security-related organizations from the outside. It is possible to do interviews, policy analysis, and some degree of text analysis on documents that are released to the public. However, these need not be the only sources. It is quite possible for those of us who are working within military and intelligence organizations to act as something like informants, passing along data, perspectives, and research ideas that we do not have time or inclination to pursue on our own. We also can give insights into the lively arena of internal critique in these organizations. Of course, our ability to do this is constrained by all the legal and organizational factors described above. Like people in any community in which an anthropologist conducts fieldwork, we will be biased, tangled in our own narratives and those of the organizations in which we work. However, we may be able to help span a gap in knowledge that has proven very difficult for the discipline to cross.

For now, this system of questions, positionality, vigilance, and consultation seems to work for me. It is time-consuming and sometimes intellectually challenging and almost certainly not the most elegant solution. I am hopeful that the AAA and SfAA will emerge from current debates with a mandate not simply to revise codes of ethics but also to provide guidelines and support for anthropologists working in the many contexts, not just military and intelligence organizations, where ethical decision making has to be a rigorous, ongoing process.

:: **NOTES** ::

The views expressed in this commentary are the author's alone and do not represent Marine Corps Intelligence Activity or any other U.S. government agency.

1. This commentary is derived in part from conversations previously published in an interview. See Nuti and Fosher (2007).

2. This commentary does not address the larger historical and political contexts in which anthropological work with the military is currently taking place. Those contexts and their implications are addressed by other contributors far more eloquently than I could manage here. I also do not address to any great degree whether or not the work I do is or is not anthropology or the issue of "do no harm," as I am exploring these topics in other publications.

3. See AAA Commission on the Engagement of Anthropology with the US Security and Intelligence Communities (2007), McNamara (2007b), and Selmeski (2007).

4. Such as RAND, MITRE, Center for Naval Analysis, and the Lincoln Labs.

5. There also are possibilities in terms of the use of applied government work to drive development of middle-range theory. However, these are still at the speculative stage.

SECTION 5

CONSTRUCTIONS AND DESTRUCTIONS OF CONSCIENCE

:: JOHN D. KELLY ::

I n May 2007 the U.S. Department of Defense released the fourth report of its Mental Health Advisory Team, a report dated November 17, 2006. As the army's surgeon general emphasized to reporters, Operation Iraqi Freedom (as it is officially called) included an effort to monitor soldiers' mental health that was in many ways unprecedented. She declared an earlier mental health report, dated December 16, 2003, and released in March 2004, to be the first professional assessment of the morale and mental health of soldiers in a combat environment (U.S. Army Surgeon General, and HQDA G-1 2003). The fourth report in 2007 broke further new ground; it was the first to ask deployed soldiers detailed questions about battlefield ethics (Office of the Surgeon Multinational Force-Iraq and Office of the Surgeon General United States Army Medical Command 2006).

The findings of the report are stark. About 30 percent of the deployed soldiers (U.S. Army and Marines Corps) reported cursing or insulting noncombatants in their presence, 12 percent of the interviewed Marines and 9 percent of the soldiers (to use the report's language) reported damaging or destroying property unnecessarily, and 7 percent and 4 percent, respectively, hitting or kicking noncombatants without necessity. Only 38 percent of the Marines and only 47 percent of the soldiers agreed with the generalization that "[a]ll non-combatants should be treated with dignity and respect," while 17 percent of each group agreed that "[a]ll non-combatants should be treated as insurgents." Torture? Forty-four percent of the Marines and 41 percent of the soldiers agreed that "[t]orture should be allowed if it will save the life of a Soldier/Marine," while 39 and 36 percent, respectively, agreed that "[t]orture should be allowed in order to gather important info about insurgents." Only 24 percent of Marines and 25 percent of soldiers agreed with the statement, "I would risk my own safety to help a non-combatant in danger."

The report also showed that when soldiers and Marines reported that they had handled dead bodies or human remains or were in a unit that had suffered casualties, the percentage of those who reported that they would insult noncombatants, destroy property, and act violently without necessity rose significantly. This distinction of experience of death and violence was not used to interpret answers in the other categories. Nor did the report give detailed attention to the correlations among different answers, a shame, given how many superficial contradictions resided in the relations between the answers to the officially "ethical" questions. The acting surgeon general of the army, Major General Gale Pollock, drew her own conclusions for the press when releasing the report. To quote from the May 4, 2007, American Forces Press Services story by Sergeant Sara Wood, still posted as of August 2, 2008, on the U.S. Department of Defense Web site:

> These findings may seem alarming, Pollock said, but it is important to keep them in perspective. These troops have been seeing their friends killed and injured, and anger is a normal reaction, she said. However, what's important to note is that the troops who had these thoughts did not act on them and actually mistreat any noncombatants.
>
> "What it speaks to is the leadership that the military is providing, because they're not acting on those thoughts," she said. "They're not torturing the people. And I think it speaks very well to the level of training that we have in the military today." (Wood 2007)

Other interpretations can also be made of the apparent contradictions among the answers to these ethical questions provided by deployed military personnel. Eighty-seven percent of Marines and 88 percent of soldiers reported receiving clear training in how to behave toward noncombatants, and 81 percent and 78 percent, respectively, agreed that "[t]raining in proper treatment of non-combatants was adequate." But only about half the soldiers and a third of the Marines (47 and 34 percent) agreed that they would report a unit member for violating the Rules of Engagement, a clear requirement of those rules. Over half the soldiers, but only two in five Marines (55 and

40 percent) agreed that they would report a unit member for injuring or killing an innocent noncombatant. Leadership? Somewhere in between: two-
thirds (67 percent of Marines and 71 percent of soldiers) agreed that "NCOs
and Officers in my Unit made it clear not to mistreat non-combatants."

The report called for more education, "anger management classes" including battlefield ethics taught in the combat theater, and training including specific scenarios, "so Soldiers and Marines know exactly what behaviors are acceptable on the battlefield and the exact procedures for reporting violations."
The report also advised that after action reviews stress adherence to the rules
of engagement.

But to take the responses of the military personnel seriously suggests that
they already utilize at least two levels of rules: that they know the official Rules
of Engagement and are also aware of some others, more tacit and perhaps more
important. Adding Lewis Carroll–style rules to obey the rules might or might
not directly address such complexity in conscience. The soldiers' responses
suggest ethical decisions not to obey already known rules, when the interests
of peers in the unit contradict those of others in the world, a commonplace
among soldiers as comparatively assessed by John Keegan and others. It also
suggests situations in which, as the cliché has it, something has got to give,
where not all rules can be followed. Despite their confidence in the clarity of
their training, 31 percent of Marines and 28 percent of soldiers agreed that
they had "encountered ethical situations in which I did not know how to
respond."

Anthropologists and other social scientists have long studied the contradictions of ethics in context, how religious, social, and other formal ethical rules
in operate in relation to the complex values orienting actual practices. The discovery of complexity in response to official systems is not by itself evidence of
anomie or dysfunction and has been found in diverse social fields by scholars
as distant in theory and method as Pierre Bourdieu, Bruno Latour, and Alfred
Kroeber. However, the reported levels of anger, distrust, disrespect, and actual
violence against noncombatants in Operation Iraqi Freedom are harder to sustain as business as usual even for a battlefield (harder to say whether they are
commonplace in military occupation of territory) and require greater inquiry
to be more fully understood.

The papers in this section responded to an invitation from the "Science,
Technology, Society and the State" workshop for scholars with insight into
military affairs to address the issues raised in a classic anthropological article
on battlefield ethics, Marshall Sahlins's 1966 essay "The Destruction of Conscience in Vietnam." Sahlins was invited by the U.S. Army to see conditions
in Vietnam for himself after he helped lead "teach-ins" against that war at the

University of Michigan. In his article, Sahlins described what he saw on his tour and reflected on its implications for the soldiers. An American "advisor" helped lead a platoon, attempting a stealthy, nighttime ambush of Vietcong infiltrators outside a loyal village. They were interrupted by an old woman. "'You boys want some tea?' she asked, with plaintive ingratiation. 'Go away,' he said, 'we're waiting for someone.'" On his own visa form, Sahlins had to choose from a list of purposes and entered as "tourist." He asked, "was it any more irrelevant than the things other Americans were doing in Vietnam" (Sahlins 2000 [1966], 232)?

Sahlins's argument is reviewed and discussed in several of the papers in this section, especially that of Kevin Caffrey. (Elsewhere, see also what is possibly the first scholarly reflection on Sahlins's article in connection to the Iraq invasion, in Bennett forthcoming). This section begins with papers by Hugh Gusterson and Rochelle Davis that concern themselves with the U.S. military's efforts to construct conscience, by way of increasing the troops' cultural sensitivity and knowledge of others. Questions about the relationship of culture and ethics, the U.S. military's interpretation of the use of culture as an ethical and practical tool, and the prospects for ethical improvement by way of deployment of cultural knowledge are searchingly examined in these essays. The papers of Jeffrey Bennett, Kevin Caffrey, and Christopher Nelson then anchor this volume, with their riveting continuation of the primary theme that the rest of Sahlins's essay took on: the effects of deployment on American soldiers themselves.

The world would be a better place if we could believe the army's acting surgeon general when she assures us that military leadership keeps the troops from acting on "bad thoughts." Sahlins documented the use of threats, bribes, and, above all, trickery in interrogation techniques led by American "advisors" in 1966 Vietnam and the effects of all the levels of contradiction and sham upon the American interrogators themselves. Aware of the lies, in short, the interrogators developed a perverse respect for the more worthy opponents who resisted their efforts more strongly. Then, when asked about their expressions of such respect, the interrogators became liars of another kind, probably also liars to themselves:

> There is no question of Mr. X's admiration of the prisoner who will not be broken. "Tremendous," he says. "Just tremendous." Then he lies when I ask if he admires this man. And at the end he lies the ultimate lie of Americans in Vietnam. Notwithstanding that he had just described a specific prisoner who would not yield, he denies he was ever involved in such an interrogation: "because we're advisors—in every sense." (Sahlins 2000 [1966], 253)

If this process is the central moment that Sahlins presents as the destruction of conscience in Vietnam, the point at which increasing numbers of the values allegedly advanced and defended by the war effort get compromised and even destroyed in the heart and mind of the American soldier, what is happening to the conscience of Americans, starting with its soldiers, in what the military insists is Operation Iraqi Freedom? To be clear about our own ethics, this should be an ethnographic question. We asked these anthropologists to consider it and hope that their answers can engender further inquiry into one of the most important questions in this entire encounter between U.S. anthropology and the U.S. military.

18

The Cultural Turn in the War on Terror

:: HUGH GUSTERSON ::

They don't hate us for our freedom. They hate us for our fiefdom.
Bill Maher (*Late Night with Bill Maher,* March 21, 2008)

American forces in Iraq have been experimenting with different versions of the "phraselator"—a handheld device that translates between English and Arabic. One version has a repertoire of seven hundred complete phrases in its memory. This is useful as long as Iraqis only use the seven hundred approved phrases. Another uses mathematical algorithms to generate voice-synthesized translations between English and Arabic—although it only comes close to working as long as speakers confine themselves to one sentence of speech at a time and have the right accent (Merle 2006).[1]

I like the bizarre story of the phraselator because it shows how language and culture have become major problems for U.S. counterinsurgency forces, while also dramatizing the Pentagon's instinctive turn to inept, simplistic, and reductive fixes that seek algorithmic solutions to hermeneutic problems—in this case through a clumsy attempt at automation. The phraselator is an attempt to solve a problem that the nineteenth-century military strategist Clausewitz theorized as "friction." As Clausewitz construed it, this is the problem: on the battlefield, chance, irrationality, human quirks, and poor communication derange the heavily rationalized plans of strategists and generals. In Clausewitz's words, "Everything is very simple in War, but the simplest thing is difficult. These difficulties accumulate and produce a friction which no man can imagine who has not seen War. . . . Friction is the only conception which in a general way corresponds to that which distinguishes real War from War on paper . . . Every War is rich in particular facts, while at the same time each is an unexplored sea, full of rocks which the general may have a suspicion of, but which he has never seen with his eye, and round which, moreover,, he must steer in the night . . . It is therefore this friction . . . which makes that which appears easy in War difficult in reality" (1982, 164–7).

The U.S. national security bureaucracy has come to recognize that culture is a source of friction in the so-called War on Terror.[2] U.S. troops find themselves fighting an intimately violent guerrilla war and trying to discern friend from foe in a country that speaks a different language and worships a different god, where real men hold hands, where free and open American body language can lead to serious trouble, where familiar hand signals can have unfamiliar meanings, where loyalties defy American intuitions, and where the political map is one in which Republicans and Democrats have no place. In journalist George Packer's words, in Iraq "the Americans were moving half-blind in an alien landscape."[3] Confronted by unanticipated insurgencies in Iraq and Afghanistan, the U.S. military is beginning to think of cultural knowledge (which General Petraeus has described as a "force multiplier") as a sinew of war much like airlift capability or ammunition stockpiles. The result has been a sharp cultural turn in the War on Terror. Nor is this cultural turn purely rhetorical or doctrinal. In 2006, the secretary of defense, Robert Gates, allocated $11.4 million in funding to Human Terrain Teams in Iraq and Afghanistan. By 2008 this funding had grown to $131 million. And in 2008 Gates announced the allocation of $50 million to Project Minerva—an unclassified research initiative, not unlike the ill-fated Project Camelot of the 1960s, mobilizing social scientists to comb through documents captured from Saddam Hussein's regime; to research the connections between religion, especially Islam, and terror; and to think more generally about the cultural roots and dynamics of terror. The initial announcement of the Minerva initiative was soon followed by an announcement of a further $8 million a year for a subsidiary National Science Foundation Minerva program.[4]

The symptoms of this cultural turn in the War on Terror are abundant. Many anthropologists already know about the $4 million Pat Roberts Intelligence Scholars Program—a sort of ROTC for spies that has been condemned by Britain's Association of Social Anthropologists but not by the American Anthropological Association (Gusterson and Price 2005). But most anthropologists are less aware that in the world of military colleges, think tanks, and contractors there has been a sudden efflorescence of workshops, military journal articles, grant competitions, and job solicitations designed to leverage military use of cultural knowledge. Examples include "Culture Summits" in 2007, 2008, and 2009 sponsored by Training and Doctrine Culture Center (TRADOC); a workshop on "Cross-Cultural Understanding" at the Naval Postgraduate School in Monterey; the Office of Naval Research's solicitation of proposals to study "Sociocultural Modeling to Understand Asymmetric Threat Environments"; and a request for contractor bids to develop a "rapid ethnographic assessment program." Job vacancies for anthropologists (and other social scientists) have also been advertized by the Central Intelligence Agency (CIA), the Marine Corps, TRADOC, the Eighteenth Airborne Corps, the Air Force Culture and Language Center, the Counterinsurgency Center for Excellence, the University of Foreign Military and Cultural Studies, the U.S. Army Special Operations Command, the "sociocultural cell" at U.S. Africa Command, the U.S. Army's Fourth Psychological Operations Group, and the contractors Science Applications International Corporation, Alelo Corporation, Archimedes Global, and the Consortium for Strategic Communication. And there are faculty positions for anthropologists at the Air War College, Air University, the National Defense Intelligence College, the Army Logistics Management College, and the Army War College. In addition to a growing gray literature on culture and military operations that is proliferating on various military and contractor Web sites, these investments are now beginning to produce publications in journals such as *Military Review* and *Small Wars Journal* and books such as Paula Holmes-Eber's *Operational Culture for the Warfighter* and the Marine Corps' *Counterinsurgency Field Manual.*

This cultural turn has been partly enmeshed with a turn to simulations. James Der Derian has been documenting simulated Iraqi/Afghani villages and towns built at the U.S. military base in Twentynine Palms, California, where soldiers practice counterinsurgency in environments peopled by actors playing scripted roles as community leaders, police chiefs, Muslim clerics, and so on (Der Derian, Udris, and Udris 2009). Forterra Systems has been hired by the U.S. military to produce multiplayer online environments populated by avatars representing U.S. troops, insurgents, police, and civilians (Gregory 2008).

Meanwhile the Defense Threat Reduction Agency has undertaken a $5 million initiative on "computational culture modeling." The goal is to use cultural data to develop computer models that can predict the collapse of states and the eruption of terrorist movements, genocide, and insurgencies. This project, a computer-age stepchild of the Human Relations Area Files, is the idée fixe of

Stephen Younger, the former director of nuclear weapons development at the
Los Alamos National Laboratory. Younger has spent recent years developing
computer models of the emergence of norms of reciprocity in Polynesia and,
unusually for a nuclear weapons designer whose Ph.D. is in physics, is now
listed as adjunct faculty in the anthropology department at the University of
Hawaii (see Younger 2005, 2007).

Wallet-Sized Culture

The military's cultural turn has what we might think of as negative and positive modalities. I mean "negative" and "positive" here more in a Foucauldian
than in an evaluative spirit. A negative modality is one that resorts to open
violence and coercion—the tools of the sovereign in Foucault's terms—in its
use of cultural knowledge against the other. Examples would be the alleged
use of anthropologist Raphael Patai's book *The Arab Mind* by interrogators
at Guantanamo and Abu Ghraib. According to Seymour Hersh (2004a), U.S.
interrogators used their Cliff Notes knowledge of Arab cultures to develop
strategies for breaking prisoners' resistance that made use of forced public nu-
dity and homosexual acts, smearing prisoners with fake menstrual blood, and
using scantily clad women as interrogators.[5]

"Positive" instantiations of the Pentagon's cultural turn use cultural knowledge not for overt coercion but to smooth away misunderstandings between
occupiers and occupied and produce frictionless interactions. Examples would
include the Iraqi Culture Smart Card[6] and the Marine Corps Primer on Cultural Sensitivity in Arab Lands. The Iraqi Culture Smart Card—wallet-sized
Arab culture—provides a portable orientation to Islam, Iraqi ethnic and cultural groups, female dress codes, and so on. It also has a section on Iraqi hand
gestures, explaining that, in Iraq, the thumbs-up sign is an obscene gesture.[7]
This might have been useful for *Fox News* commentators to know when they
marveled in the early days of the occupation at all the thumbs-up signs American troops were getting from Iraqis.

Like the Iraqi Culture Smart Card, a Marine Corps handout on Iraqi cul-
ture, introduced in 2003,[8] gives a condensed, simplified rendering of Iraqi culture as a set of rules and norms. It is the cultural equivalent of the phraselator.
Some of the norms as they are stated may not offer such a good orientation to
Iraqi culture. The primer starts well, offering that "touching among the same
sex is not considered homosexual," advising discretion in interactions with
Arab women, and warning that our hand gesture for "stop" means "hello" in
Iraq—a source of confusion that has led to many shootings of Iraqi civilians
at checkpoints. But it goes on to say, "Arabs do not believe in cause and effect

Cultural Groups

ARABS

- Arabs view Kurds as separatists within Iraq and are wary of their desire for autonomy.
- Arabs view the Christian Assyrians and Chaldeans as Iraqis, but recent Islamic extremism has sparked some hostility towards them.
- Arabs look down upon the Turkoman because Arabs generally view Turkish culture as inferior.
- Arabs view Iranian Persians negatively and fear the historically strong political and cultural influence of Persia.

SHIA AND SUNNI ARAB

- Tension exists between Shia and Sunni Arabs over access to political and economic power.
- Sunnis blame Shia for undermining the mythical unity of Islam and they view them as less loyal to Iraq.
- Shia blame Sunnis for marginalizing the Shia majority and resent Sunni attempts to question their loyalty to Iraq.

KURDS

- Kurds are openly hostile toward Iraqi Arabs and seek to assert their political and cultural independence.
- Kurds are distrustful of the Turkoman, as they have competing claims over Kirkuk.
- Kurds do not interact much with Assyrians and Chaldeans.

ASSYRIANS

- Assyrians experienced persecution by both Kurds and Arabs.
- Assyrians recognize their minority status as a religious and ethnic group.
- Assyrians believe they have much in common with the Chaldeans, including ethnic and Christian religious heritage.

CHALDEANS

- Chaldeans rejoined the Catholic Church in the 18th century and do not believe that they are similar to Assyrians.
- As a religious and ethnic minority, the Chaldeans distrust both Kurdish and Arab intentions.
- They have peaceful relations with Turkoman.

TURKOMAN

- Turkoman view themselves as a marginalized repressed minority and seek greater influence in Iraq.
- Turkoman fear Kurds, and there has been a long history of conflict between the two groups.
- Turkoman identify closely with Turkey and the Ottoman period of Iraqi history

Figures 18a–18d The Iraq Culture Smart Card has 16 panels and is waterproof and tear-resistant. It is designed to fold up so it can be carried in a soldier's pocket for easy reference. Panels contain information on Iraqi history, customs, religion and social structure."

but rather in isolated incidents or the will of Allah," and "Arabs perceive problems as someone's plot to make their life more unpleasant. We may view this as paranoia," and "Arabs make group decisions. Do not try to force an individual to make a decision. . . . If forced to make a quick decision . . . they feel no commitment to abide by it."

Cultural Customs

HONOR AND SHAME

Admitting "I don't know" is shameful for an Iraqi.

Constructive criticism can be taken as an insult.

Women will often wear head scarves as a show of respect, even if wearing Western clothing. Women are rarely without a male relative or friend for escort.

FAMILY

Family is the center of honor, loyalty, and reputation.

Men are always the head of the family. No direct attention should be given to female relatives.

PERSONAL SPACE

Iraqis do not share an American concept of "personal space" in public situations, and in private meetings or conversation. It is considered offensive to step or lean away from an Iraqi.

Women are an exception to this rule. One should not stand close to, stare at, or touch women.

SOCIALIZATION AND TRUST

When conducting business, it is customary to first shake the hand of all the males present, taking care to grip neither too firmly nor too meekly.

Allocate plenty of time for refreshments before attempting to engage an Iraqi in business conversation. It is important to first establish respect and trust.

Figures 18a–18d (continued).

Human Terrain

Within anthropology most of the controversy about the military's cultural turn has been focused on the Pentagon's new Human Terrain Team program—a program condemned by the AAA Executive Board in fall 2007 (AAA Executive Board 2007). In 2007, one team was deployed to Afghanistan and five to Iraq. The Pentagon soon announced plans to deploy about twenty more.[9] As

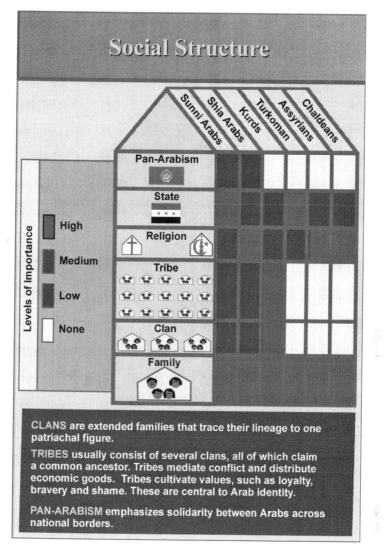

Figures 18a–18d (continued).

originally conceptualized, each team was made up of five members, with the team leader, the human terrain research manager, and the human terrain analyst being military personnel and the other two members (the regional studies analyst and the cultural analyst) civilian social scientists. Over time the teams have grown larger and their internal organization has evolved.

The Human Terrain Team program has become particularly identified with the anthropologist turned military consultant Montgomery McFate. Follow-

Don't Do This

- Don't use your left hand for contact with others, eating, or gestures. It is considered unclean.

- Don't point with a finger; it is a sign of contempt. Instead, point with your entire hand.

- Don't ask for a single opinion on an issue, as Iraqis often first reply with the answer they think you want to hear, rather than an honest response.

- Don't slouch, lean, or appear disinterested when conversing with Iraqi men. Do not expose the soles of feet or shoes.

- Don't back away from an Iraqi during conversation. Close personal interaction is customary and distance is considered rude.

- Don't offer a Muslim food or drink or consume either publicly during Ramadan. Never offer a Muslim alcohol or pork.

- Don't engage in religious discussions.

- Don't make the "OK" or "thumbs up" signs; they are considered obscene.

- Don't praise an Iraqi's possessions too much. He may give them to you and expect something of equal value in return

Figures 18a–18d (continued).

ing appearances on the *Diane Rehm Show, Charlie Rose,* and *BBC World News* as well as profiles in *Elle Magazine* and the *San Francisco Chronicle,* McFate is arguably *the* public face of anthropology today, the new Margaret Mead on a mission to leverage anthropology in the policy world and the public domain. Writing in the journal *Joint Force Quarterly,* McFate (2005b, 43/8) says that "the ongoing insurgency in Iraq has served as a wakeup call to the military that adversary culture matters. . . . The more unconventional the adversary, and the further from Western cultural norms, the more we need to understand the society and underlying cultural dynamics. To defeat non-Western opponents . . . we need to improve our capacity to understand foreign cultures." McFate says, "a federal initiative is urgently needed to incorporate cultural and social knowledge of adversaries into training, education, planning, intelligence, and operations. Across the board, the national security structure needs to be infused with anthropology, a discipline invented to support war fighting in the tribal zone. Cultural knowledge of adversaries should be considered a national security priority." You will note here the theoretically antiquarian assumption that anthropology is the study of the non-Western other. We will return to this later.

In recent public appearances before anthropological and other audiences, McFate has used quite different arguments in support of Human Terrain Teams than she uses when writing for the military's own specialized journals. Speaking to anthropologists, she has eschewed the forcefully neocolonial language she uses for military audiences and made a consequentialist argument structured around the pragmatist ethics of harm reduction. Saying that she opposed the original invasion of Iraq, she has suggested that, for better or worse, we are now stuck with the bad situation in Iraq and has argued that, if anthropologists have specialized knowledge that would reduce casualties in a situation that cannot be undone, then they have a moral obligation to use that knowledge to save lives. Failure to do so implicates anthropologists in the deaths of Iraqis killed in hostilities exacerbated by cultural friction. "Does writing op-eds and being angry at the government help? Isn't it better to do something?" she asked in a 2007 talk at George Mason University. "You have a choice of helping to reduce harm or feeling pure doing nothing."[10]

Borrowing counterinsurgency guru David Kilcullen's[11] description of culture-centric counterinsurgency as "armed social work," McFate has portrayed the Human Terrain Teams as Emily Posts and Albert Schweitzers in uniform. They teach U.S. troops the elements of local good manners, explaining how to search houses for weapons with more cultural sensitivity, for example, and they converse with local populations to discern their needs. A front-page *New York Times* article (Rohde 2007) mentioned a Human Terrain Team in Afghanistan that discovered that one village wanted a volleyball net—which the U.S. military duly supplied—and that destitute widows in another village were being drawn toward the Taliban by their financial needs, which the U.S. military stepped in to satisfy with a job-training program.

A whistleblower, Zenia Helbig, who was expelled from the Human Terrain

System when she made remarks indicating her opposition to an attack on Iran, has suggested that the Human Terrain Teams are far less competent than the TRADOC public relations apparatus would have us believe. She points out that TRADOC has found it hard to recruit anthropologists and, despite salaries rumored to go up to $300,000 per year, has often had to settle for recruits with masters degrees in such fields as international relations instead of the Ph.D. anthropologists they seek. According to Zelbig, the anthropologists recruited have been specialists not in Middle Eastern culture but in such areas as the Caribbean, Native American culture, the Philippines, and Latin American archaeology. These cultural specialists are, hence, dependent on interpreters in the field, and, according to Helbig, their training at Fort Leavenworth gives them only a superficial introduction to Middle Eastern culture. With three deaths so far among Human Terrain Team social scientists, they also seem to have a disproportionately high mortality rate, raising questions about the adequacy of their training for a battlefield environment.[12]

Critics worry that, as Derek Gregory (2008) puts it, "cultural knowledge [i]s not a substitute for killing but also a prerequisite for its refinement." We know that Human Terrain Teams are to construct databases of information on political leadership, kinship relations, economic systems, and agricultural output in military areas of operation. In Vietnam a similar initiative, known as CORDS (Civil Operations and Revolutionary Development Support) was, through the infamous Phoenix program, associated with the targeted assassination of 26,000 suspected Vietcong. In this context, it is ominous that Jacob Kipp, one of the architects of the cultural turn, has labeled Human Terrain Teams a "CORDS for the twenty-first century" (see Kipp et al. 2006). Roberto Gonzalez quotes a blog entry by Lieutenant Colonel Gian Gentile rebuking Human Terrain Team anthropologist Marcus Griffin for his naiveté about Human Terrain Teams:

Don't fool yourself. These Human Terrain Teams whether they want to acknowledge it or not . . . do at some point contribute to the collective knowledge of a commander which allows him to target and kill the enemy in the Civil War in Iraq.

I commanded an Armored Reconnaissance Squadron in West Baghdad in 2006. Although I did not have one of these HTTs [Human Terrain Teams] assigned to me (and I certainly would have liked to), I did have a Civil Affairs Team that was led by a major . . . I often used his knowledge to help me sort through who was the enemy and who was not and from that understanding that he contributed to I was able to target and sometimes kill the enemy. So stop sugarcoating what these teams do.[13]

Misrecognition

Besides the very real possibility that Human Terrain Team anthropologists collecting ethnographic information for Pentagon databases and intelligence analysts will, even if inadvertently, provide fuel for the machinery of killing in Iraq and Afghanistan, there is in the Pentagon's cultural turn a sort of epistemological danger too. One dimension of the problem is hinted at in the following quote from Master Sergeant Rachael Ridenour, a cultural analyst for a Human Terrain Team in Afghanistan. *Military Times* quotes Ridenour as saying that "[c]ulture is a multifaceted thing, and our goal is to make the product as user-friendly as possible (Cavallaro 2008.)." As Robert Albro has pointed out,[14] the kind of culture the Pentagon wants—a "product" that can be condensed, objectified, and deployed—is the kind of culture Margaret Mead and Ruth Benedict trafficked in, culture that was—like other enemy communications—a code to be cracked, not the kind of culture generated today by post-Geertzian ethnographers, many of whom are terrified to use the word "culture" at all. In such a situation the danger to the Pentagon is that, quite apart from the political costs of working with the military, the epistemology of its culture project may deter more sophisticated anthropologists from participating. The costs of depending on cultural analysts who have not absorbed postcolonial and postmodern critiques of anthropology are made clear in a brilliant article by Derek Gregory. Gregory foregrounds troubling tropes in some of the cultural analyses that have been generated by the Pentagon's culture warriors, particularly David Kilcullen, in the Afghan and Iraqi theaters of war. He points out that these analyses tend to treat Iraq and Afghanistan as interchangeable (hence the generic Islamic villages used for training at Twentynine Palms), that their frequent invocations of T. E. Lawrence index Orientalist tropes of unchanging Middle Eastern cultures, and that they overemphasize tribe and clan to the detriment of other principles of affiliation and mobilization. Such analytic errors are not just a matter of academic quibbling. They have real-world consequences.

But there is a still more serious sense in which the Pentagon's deployment of anthropology ends up, perversely, entrapping U.S. forces in a profound misrecognition of their relationship with the Other. Under the guise of dispelling cultural misunderstanding, anthropology ends up being implicated in the production of what it used to be fashionable to call false consciousness, in this case neocolonial false consciousness. The problem is hinted at in this story from the *Washington Post:*

The American troops took some care to be polite when entering Iraqi homes. During Thursday's six-hour patrol, they handed out Iraqi newspapers and packets of gum and attracted an eager following of young children. But machine-gun-toting Americans rooting through bedrooms, inspecting weapons and demanding identification cards, clearly unsettled some residents. . . .

One soldier, on his second tour in Iraq, said, . . . "I was here last time, in the beginning. Now it's totally changed. They don't even respect us anymore. They spit at us, they throw rocks at us. It wasn't like that before." (Partlow 2007)

"Why do they hate us?" is a question that has been asked many times by American policy makers and pundits. A 2004 Defense Science Board Study concluded that hostility to the United States was being driven by cultural misunderstanding. And the cultural turn, undergirding a misconstrual of occupation as "armed social work," holds out the hope that they will cease to hate us if only we engage in "cultural mitigation." But the reason they hate us is not just that our soldiers often show the soles of their feet and do not understand the difference between a Sunni and a Shi'ite but that, in general, people do not like their countries occupied by foreign militaries. They do not like their national affairs being directed by foreign leaders; they do not like being stopped at checkpoints by foreign soldiers who point guns at them and rifle through the contents of their cars; and they do not like foreign soldiers searching their bedrooms and asking questions about their associations, no matter how polite and culturally informed those soldiers might be. As seven sergeants argued in a remarkable op-ed in the *New York Times,* "we need to recognize that our presence may have released the Iraqis from the grip of a tyrant, but that it has also robbed them of their self-respect. They will soon realize that the best way to regain dignity is to call us what we are—an army of occupation—and force our withdrawal" (Jayamaha et al 2007). While a little cultural knowledge is doubtless useful in greasing the wheels of occupation, the military's new culturalist paradigm evaporates political grievances into cultural grievances and holds out the fantasy that American soldiers will be loved in Iraq if only they get their hand signals right and learn to show respect for Arab women.

Derek Gregory (2008) points out that the Iraqi avatars in U.S. military training simulations speak in ways that are scripted by the U.S. military "and so they cannot ask awkward questions about US foreign policy or military operations." The silence of the avatars here mirrors a question forbidden to their interlocutors, a question whose very asking would undermine the salvation narrative of American manifest destiny. And so instead we have, in Gregory's (2008,) words, a situation in which

the emphasis on cultural difference—the attempt to hold the Other at a distance while claiming to cross the interpretive divide—produces a diagram in which violence has its origins in 'their' space, which the cultural turn endlessly partitions through its obsessive preoccupation with ethno-sectarian division, while the impulse to understand is confined to 'our' space, which is constructed as open, unitary and generous: the source of a hermeneutic invitation that can never be reciprocated.

Conclusion: Future Anthropologies

The War on Terror is deepening the militarization of American society. It is enabling the national security state to build new constituencies and to penetrate disciplines and practices that were formerly off limits. As part of this process, disciplines such as public health are being remade through the power of homeland security money. And now suddenly there is money for us too, if we are willing to engage in "human terrain mapping" and "computational culture modeling" and to analyze captured Iraqi documents. If we say yes on any significant scale, our discipline will never be the same again.

Although most of the debate about anthropology and the War on Terror has focused on anthropological participation in Human Terrain Teams, in many ways these teams are the least of our problems, and the debate about them is even a distraction from our real problems. First of all, only a marginal handful of anthropologists are participating in the teams. And, second, the ethical barriers to participating in such teams are so transparently clear to most anthropologists that there is little to debate. That is why the AAA was able to make a clear, forceful statement condemning the Human Terrain Teams, while its commission on the relationship between anthropology and the military, on the other hand, has so far been unable to draw bright lines in regard to other issues raised by the military's attempted rapprochement with anthropology.[15]

A deeper, more fundamental and insidious militarization of our discipline is underway that will be harder to recognize, let alone contest. This is in some ways a replay of a match the national security state lost in the 1960s—the last time it tried to mobilize anthropology for counterinsurgency. Seeing the furious reaction in anthropology to Project Camelot and the Thai village study, and confronted with the 1971 AAA ethics code that condemned counterinsurgency work in the strongest terms, the national security state retreated, taking with it a small cadre of militarized anthropologists (Wakin 2008). Many of these anthropologists kept a low profile in the discipline, working for government agencies, not publishing in anthropology journals, and avoiding national meetings, at which, as one anthropologist who works for an intelligence agency told me, they were made to feel unwelcome (often in ways, incidentally, that I do not condone).

Now, in a context in which the AAA ethics code has been weakened, the rise of practicing anthropology has changed the topography of our discipline, and 9/11 has created a new opening for a militarized anthropology, the national security state has reentered anthropology's world. At the 2007 AAA meeting, TRADOC personnel could be seen engaged in their own ethnographic study of us, busy taking notes at many of our panels. Military agencies have begun contacting anthropology professors asking whether, for example, they would like to write reports on tribal cultures in Syria and the occupied territories or help construct detailed neighborhood maps of Havana. The CIA has, for the first time in decades, tried to place a job ad in *Anthropology News*. It has also invited professors from my department on a tour of the CIA in the hope that they will direct their students to careers there. And the Human Terrain Team bureaucracy, unlike its predecessors in the 1960s, has reacted to the AAA's keep-out sign by defiantly posting a recruitment ad on the AAA Web site, by holding an informational session at the 2008 AAA meeting, and by mounting an e-mail recruitment campaign targeted at anthropologists all over the country. They have made it clear that this time they do not intend to go away.

In parallel with the rise of an applied military anthropology, we can also expect shifts in academic anthropology. In her book *Creating the Cold War University*, Rebecca Lowen maps the profound ways in which the cold war remade Stanford University. The government threw vast amounts of money at the physics department to build a particle accelerator and train a reserve labor force of physicists for the weapons labs; the political science department moved away from its older interest in high theory and ethically driven debate toward area studies, development studies, and a positivist conception of knowledge more in line with Pentagon epistemology; the communications department shifted toward surveys and polls useful for the study and manipulation of mass opinion at home and abroad; and the psychology department developed interests in obedience to authority, brainwashing, and influence of a kind that aligned nicely with the interests of intelligence agencies. Meanwhile, fracture lines opened up within disciplines between those who had clearances and those who did not.

Thus a possible future for anthropology is one in which the military becomes a principal funder of anthropology, where our high-status academic research is increasingly oriented to the Middle East, the new epicenter for area studies, and other aspects of the War on Terror, while a new apparatus of applied military anthropology soaks up the Ph.D.s who cannot find academic jobs. Many departments would adjust their curricula accordingly, especially at the Masters of Arts level. There would be specialized conferences and journals for securitized anthropologists, some closed to foreign nationals or those without security clearances. And the ethics code, especially its constraints on secret research, would be weakened to accommodate these developments.

Such developments are difficult for a community such as ours to resist. The AAA is a decentered organization that does not license, and therefore cannot delicense, its members. I am not sure that is inappropriate, but it makes it hard to impose a professional code of practice on AAA members in more than an exhortary way. Anthropology is also an undercapitalized discipline that has, in recent years, generated a sizeable lumpen proletariat of unemployed or semiemployed Ph.D.s. And this makes anthropology quite vulnerable to reshaping by government agencies with even relatively small (by government standards) sums of money. In such circumstances, the evident difficulties in recruiting anthropologists that the Human Terrain System and the Minerva Initiative are experiencing is little short of extraordinary, and they leave me proud of my professional colleagues.

The Network of Concerned Anthropologists (http://concerned.anthropologists.googlepages.com/), of which I am one of the founders, is an attempt to counter the prospective militarization of anthropology, especially with regard to U.S. military intervention in the Middle East, within the decentered logic of our disciplinary apparatus. Its pledge campaign (mobilizing the discipline around a signed pledge not to participate in counterinsurgency work) is an attempt to make these subterranean processes of disciplinary militarization more visible, to incite debate about them, and to mobilize and dramatize principled opposition to them within the discipline. It takes a stand for the principle, so passionately articulated by Franz Boas in 1919,[16] that anthropologists should not study others in order to facilitate their subjugation or occupation.

I urge anthropologists not just to sign the pledge and debate these issues but also to consider engaging in a sort of countermilitarized anthropology, a critical ethnography of the military and the War on Terror, in the spirit of the sustained ethnographic work that has already been undertaken by anthropologists such as Holly Barker, Andrew Bickford, Brian Ferguson, Leslie Gill, Roberto Gonzalez, Barbara Rose Johnston, Catherine Lutz, Joseph Masco, Carolyn Nordstrom, Mark Pedelty, David Price, Antonius Robben, Marshall Sahlins, Jeff Sluka, and David Vine.[17] In such a scenario, an alternative future for our discipline, we might use our ethnographic skills to answer questions such as these: what was it in the organizational culture of the U.S. intelligence community that led to the false prediction of weapons of mass destruction in Iraq? What was it in the organizational culture of the Pentagon that allowed it to invade another country with a plan most senior officers believed inadequate to occupation? How was it possible to take a professional army committed, on paper at least, to human rights and create organizational subcultures where torture and human rights abuses thrived? What is it in the culture of American decision making, saturated as it is with rational-choice models and cost-benefit analyses, that fosters a misplaced confidence in our ability to predict and manage events? Good answers to such questions would do more to enhance American national security than wallet-sized culture cards cartooning Arab culture.

: : NOTES : :

My thanks to John D. Kelly, Beatrice Jauregui, Sean T. Mitchell, and Jeremy Walton for their hard work in assembling this volume and for their patience in regard to this chapter. Versions of the ideas in this chapter were presented at the Smithsonian Institute, at Brown University's Watson Institute, at the University of Chicago's conference on Anthropology and Global Counterinsurgency, and at Brandeis University's anthropology department. My thanks to everyone who responded to those presentations. And special thanks to Joe Masco for referring me to the funny video of the phraselator in action.

1. The limitations of the phraselator are nicely dramatized in an amusing video of a reporter testing it out on the streets of his neighborhood in Brooklyn: http://blog.wired.com/defense/2008/06/brooklyn-test-d.html.

2. At the time of writing, the Obama administration seems to be moving away from the "War on Terror" toward the clumsier locution "Overseas Contingency Operations" (Wilson and Kamen 2009). "War on Terror" is retained here, partly because it seems unlikely that the new locution will catch on, partly because this struggle—whatever name we affix to it—was known as the War on Terror at the moment when cultural friction emerged as a major reverse salient for the Pentagon to deal with, and partly because the American people have, whether we like it or not, learned to call it that.

3. Packer (2005, 233) quoted in Gregory (2008). Colonel Martin Schweitzer, in a March 26, 2008, news briefing thanked social scientists who were working with the U.S. military in Afghanistan, saying, "social scientists . . . help us out here understand and properly maneuver within the Afghan community. So we can reduce the civilian casualties. We reduce the friction" (Office of the Assistant Secretary of Defense 2008).

4. The Human Terrain System budget figures come from an e-mail to my colleague David Price from Harvey Perritt at TRADOC on August 15, 2008. Robert Gates announced Minerva in an April 14, 2008, speech: http://www.defenselink.mil/speeches/speech.aspx?speechid=1228. The Pentagon's call for proposals under Minerva can be found at http://www.arl.army.mil/www/DownloadedInternetPages/CurrentPages/DoingBusinesswithARL/research/08-R-0007.pdf. On May 28, 2008, AAA president Setha Low wrote to Gates and others expressing concern about aspects of the Minerva program: http://www.aaanet.org/issues/policy-advocacy/upload/Minerva-Letter.pdf. At this point, the definitive source for information and opinion on Minerva is the excellent Web site assembled by the Social Science Research Council at http://www.ssrc.org/essays/minerva/. Thomas Asher's essay there (http://www.ssrc.org/essays/minerva/home/asher/) gives a particularly helpful overview of the program.

5. For a disputation of Hersh's claims by an anthropologist, see McNamara (2007a).

6. The Iraqi Culture Smart Card has been archived at http://www.fas.org/irp/doddir/usmc/iraqsmart-0506.pdf. For a discussion of the smart card, see Nuti (2006).

7. According to the U.S. Army's Defense Language Institute, the Iraqi meaning of the thumbs-up is, however, more complicated, since many Iraqis may have assimilated the Western meaning. See Koerner (2003).

8. http://www.harpers.org/archive/2004/06/0080063. My thanks to Kerry Fosher for helping me to clarify that this was not an older Marine Corps primer with which some accounts confuse it.

9. For more on the Human Terrain Team system, see Gonzalez (2009), http://humanterrain system.army.mil/; and Kipp et al., http://usacac.leavenworth.army.mil/CAC/milreview/English/SepOct06/kipp.pdf. See also the collection of articles at http://blog.wired.com/defense/human_terrain/index.html and the series of articles online by the independent journalist John Stanton: http://cryptome.info/0001/hts-joke.htm; http://cryptome.info/0001/hts-farce.htm; and http://english.pravda.ru/opinion/columnists/23-07-2008/105853-us-army-0.

10. Montgomery McFate talk at George Mason's Department of Sociology and Anthropology on October 24, 2007.

11. Kilcullen, an Australian lieutenant colonel, has been described in the *New Yorker* and the *Washington Post* as an anthropologist, but his degree is in politics. He is special advisor to general David Petraeus. For more on his worldview see his "28 Articles"—a cult counterinsurgency text posted online at http://usacac.army.mil/CAC/milreview/English/MayJun06/webpdf/BoB_Insights_Reviews_Letters_MJ06.pdf—and Kilcullen (2009).

12. Zenia Helbig letter to the Project on Government Oversight, March 28, 2008. See also Ephron and Spring (2008). For another critique of the program by an insider, see Connable (2009). As journalist Noah Schachtman observes, Connable's article could have been titled "We Don't Need No Stinkin' Anthropologists."

13. Gian Gentile, Response to Marcus Griffin blog entry, posted at http://marcusgriffin.com/blog/2007/10/why_is_the_use_of_anthropology.html, quoted in Gonzalez (2008). This blog entry was removed within a few days of Gonzalez publicly quoting it.

14. Panel on Anthropology, U.S. Intelligence and the U.S. Military, Elliott School of International Affairs, George Washington University, April 13, 2007.

15. The Commission's report can be found at http://www.aaanet.org/_cs_upload/pdf/4092_1.pdf.

16. Boas (1919).

17. Let me apologize in advance to anyone I left off this list who thinks they should have been on it.

19

Cultural Sensitivity in a Military Occupation

The U.S. Military in Iraq

:: ROCHELLE DAVIS, *with* DAHLIA EL ZEIN *and* DENA TAKRURI ::

At the time of the U.S. invasion of Iraq, there was no cultural training policy or unified training plan in either the U.S. Army or Marine Corps to prepare troops to serve in the Middle East.[1] The planning, conception, and implementation of the invasion of Iraq and subsequent occupation have revealed, among other things, the absence of a long-term vision by the U.S. government for the role of the U.S. military and government in the country.[2] Similarly, criticisms of the U.S. military show how the leadership envisioned toppling the Saddam Hussein government and did not prepare for the long-term military occupation and rebuilding of the country.[3] This longer term role, of course, has required the U.S. military and governmental forces to interact much more with Iraqis, in particular as they train Iraqi troops and rebuild the country's infrastructure. The logical considerations in such a plan would encompass an understanding by U.S. troops of the communities, societies, cultures, and people of the country they are occupying, administering, restructuring, and rebuilding. Rather than an overall U.S. governmental policy, individuals and unit commanders have found ways to brief their troops about Iraqis from the outset, and varying written and aural material has been developed to hand out to troops on their way to Iraq.[4]

As a cultural anthropologist of the Arab world working in the United States, I became aware of and concerned by the types of knowledge about Muslims and Iraqis that were being produced and disseminated among U.S. servicemen and women and to the American population following the 2003 invasion. This chapter grows out of a subsequent research project about the U.S. military in Iraq that was conceived out of the desire to understand the U.S. war in Iraq generally and specifically the experiences of U.S. military personnel with Iraqis and their views about Iraqi culture and society and the future of Iraq. The interviews for this research were conducted in 2007 with active- and reserve-duty U.S. military servicemen and women as well as veterans, from a wide range of ages, ranks, locations in the United States, and backgrounds. The project consisted of forty in-depth interviews ranging in length from forty-five minutes to two hours covering fifteen demographic questions and seventeen open-ended questions. We interviewed twenty-one army, seventeen marine, one navy and one air force personnel. Interviewees ranged in rank from E-3 (private first class [army] or lance corporal [marines]) up to O-6 (colonel) who had served in Iraq between 2003 and 2007 and ranged in age at time of service from twenty-one to fifty-eight. Participants came from a wide variety of military occupation specialties, duty positions, and branch specialties, including intelligence, infantry, military police, logistics, civil affairs, and medical personnel. The interviewees were recruited via word of mouth, referrals of friends and relatives, on-base requests, and listservs from all over the United States, and the interviews were conducted face-to-face and over the telephone. The limitations of a sample size consisting of just forty interviews, when there have been at least three quarter of a million U.S. troops serving in Iraq, are obvious. At best, we hope, in the tradition of in-depth qualitative work, to illuminate some of the issues that emerged from these conversations about how these soldiers and marines were trained to think about Iraqi culture and society and the ways they independently developed to understand and interact with Iraqis and also to gain from their experience an understanding of some of the larger issues about military culture and the U.S. occupation of Iraq.

We must emphasize that the material we collected from these interviews is what the soldiers and marines recall and not necessarily what actually took place in terms of training they received or knowledge they developed in Iraq; rather, it is what they remembered and then reported to us. Thus, the issues discussed here suggest more about the military personnel's experiences and how successful the cultural training programs were (or were not) than about the actual content of the cultural training programs.[5] We argue in this paper, based on the interviews, that the knowledge about Iraq and Iraqis passed on by the U.S. military establishment to its troops is largely seen as insufficient and not useful; thus military personnel on the ground turn to other sources—other troops and translators—to gain what they define as "useful information." Thus, instead of the U.S. military being the source for understanding the country and people of Iraq, most of our interviewees reported that they gained the most useful knowledge about Iraqis—both for what they define as "mission effectiveness" and for interacting with Iraqis—once in Iraq from other military personnel, from civilian Iraqis and translators, and from knowledge they gained prior to going to Iraq.

Cultural Sensitivity and the Military Occupation of Iraq

As an example of U.S. military policy regarding cultural sensitivity, the practice of separating the males and females during house raids was cited by many of the interviewees as part of cultural consideration.[6] A twenty-two-year-old infantry captain remarks, "The fact that we . . . didn't take females, that was conscious early on. Nor did we search them. We did have women military police that were with us who would do searches of the females. So that was taken into consideration." A twenty-six-year-old infantry sergeant mentions similar experiences: "Well I mean, of course men would never deal with women as far as searching them and stuff like that."

These considerations of "local culture" were referred to by the project's participants as components of Iraqi culture without the acknowledgement that such practices would be common even in the United States. From our own experiences, we know that when going through any type of security either in an airport or elsewhere, female searchers are always provided to search women. However, in the context of house raids and military occupation, these servicemen and women view this practice as part of Iraqi cultural sensitivities. In part this has to do with all Iraqis being seen as enemies, and thus the women are not civilians to be searched as if at an airport but are all instead seen as potential insurgents or aiding insurgents (which, of course, some of them are and do). Thus because of the military occupation of Iraq, U.S. soldiers and marines are in situations in which, owing to military reasons, no Iraqi is to be trusted until proven trustworthy or harmless; thus, even when dealing with civilians this exception (men do not search women) to a military principle (secure the area) is justified as a "cultural consideration."

The concept of "cultural training" as expressed by the military suggests that culture can be taught to others. However, in teaching culture, someone must determine what constitutes the teachable components of a specific culture. Thus by choosing what subjects and information it wants soldiers and marines to know about Iraqi culture, the U.S. military is taking on both an authoritative and determining role of what Iraqi culture is and which of its features are most important and can be taught to American servicemen and women. For the U.S. military as a whole, cultural training is administered to its servicemen and women with the intention of increasing operational effectiveness, which it believes can also be achieved by not offending Iraqis (see, e.g., Baker 2003). However, for many of the servicemen and women, cultural training and the emphasis on cultural considerations help them, as individuals, to reconcile the morality of their interactions by providing them with certain ways of performing their actions that are seen to be culturally sensitive. The fact that these participants took note of the "culturally considerate" nature of these raids speaks to this larger contradiction of a culturally sensitive occupation. Hence, cultural consideration becomes a way for these individuals to view their actions, such as a house raid, which some acknowledge to be very difficult for Iraqis to accept, in ways that in their minds soften the violence and invasiveness of them. One soldier recalled that "if the raids went peacefully and nothing happened and nobody was hurt and we had no reason to feel anything suspicious was going on, the women would make us tea, which was delicious, which was cool. I guess I can relate to that. Tea brings everyone together . . . " Framing what is by its very nature a violent and invasive house raid, for example, in terms of short-term accomplishment of objectives (finding the bad guys, not upsetting the family), disconnects the raids from their role in the larger military invasion and occupation. In his telling, the hospitality offered by the family to those who have violently entered their home can only be accepted if there is nothing suspicious going on. Once the soldiers feel the situation is secure, a cultural interaction can happen between Iraqis and Americans, one that this soldier reports enjoying. Cultural training also leads soldiers and marines to think that culture in general and cultural sensitivity in particular can be part of achieving the goal of "winning the hearts and minds" of the Iraqi people—part of the liberation discourse of the Iraq War.

However, not all of our participants agreed with these cultural considerations toward women, and one participant expressed dismay at this practice by pointing out that not being able to search women was militarily inefficient. An infantry first lieutenant, aged thirty-one, remarked that " . . . the U.S. army does some cultural things that aren't very military. Like you don't search them. And so, are they wearing a bomb, are they hiding stuff? Could easily be! But I'm not allowed to do anything." This response is representative of a group of respondents who found cultural consideration in operations militarily inefficient and, as this interviewee emphasizes, simply in conflict with the military's mission. How then do soldiers and marines evaluate the cultural training they receive, the role it plays in how they do their jobs and how they think of Iraqis?

Cultural Training Knowledge in the U.S. Military

According to the interviewees, U.S. military personnel gain information about Iraqi culture and society through different sources: formal military cultural training; advice and stories from other U.S. military personnel; and advice from Iraqi, Arab, and/or other interpreters. Of the forty interviewees in our study, thirty-three reported that they received some sort of formal cultural training prior to deployment to the Middle East, which in their recollections ranged from a half-hour lecture by the chaplain of the unit to periodic lectures as part of predeployment training to a three-day intensive course on the history and religions of Iraq to manuals and CDs on the country and language. Of the seven who did not receive any sort of cultural training, they reported that they were "expected to figure it out themselves when they got there." One air force captain in the medical corp reported that

> I was told there is too much to do for the mission. So you show up at your job and do it. . . . The group commander said, "Hit the ground running, just go do what you need to do," because most people at our installation were not going to interact with Iraqis at all. Even any of the work being done on the installation was done by third country nationals but not Iraqis, a lot of Indians, a lot of Pakistanis.

The majority of military personnel who were interviewed felt that the information they received in the formal training situations offered in the military was oftentimes extremely basic. One infantry army soldier who served throughout all of 2005 described the training as "minimal."[7]

> You certainly sort of receive the cultural dos and don'ts, you know—don't do anything with your left hand, don't show anybody the soles of your feet, [. . .] that things go slow there. [. . .] I think that the training was absolutely aimed at [. . .] Arab culture for dummies. You know, here are three or four things that you can do to not offend people.

The interviewees described their formal training as largely consisting of this type of knowledge: a list of dos and don'ts, which embody behaviors that can be obeyed like orders. In this sense, the military training portrays culture as a basic skill with which to interact with Iraqis and something that both the military and its personnel can define as knowable and tangible.

The interviewees, however, found the formal training and the type of cultural information they received in it to be of little to value to them. Of those who received formal cultural training by either the army or marines, only five of the thirty-three reported it to be useful. A thirty-five-year-old army infantry company commander described his cultural training as " . . . really useful, I mean the things that they said were important. However, there was a lot of stuff you had to discover. But the things that we were told were in their own way, very useful. I mean it's important not to show your feet to an Iraqi, not to show the soles of your feet to an Iraqi, it can really make them uncomfortable." This captain thought that one of the advantages of such cultural training was that it helped the U.S. military do things that wouldn't offend the Iraqis they had contact with. Of the remaining twenty-eight interviewees, fifteen described it as "somewhat useful," eleven said it was not useful at all, and two were ambivalent. One U.S. Marine Corps intelligence officer described the training as not exactly what they needed: "Yes, it was like, what things to do and what not to do, and most of it didn't even apply, like the 'don't shake with the left hand' that kind of stuff, that doesn't really apply. I didn't find that any of the cultural training prepared me in any way." The generally negative assessment by our interviewees of this cultural training reflects on both the content of the training material as well as its pedagogical conception.

In examining the U.S. military definitions of culture and cultural training as recalled by the interviewees, "culture" was defined as and confined to a list of dos and don'ts that the soldiers and marines widely considered insufficient and not particularly useful. And yet at the same time, this list of dos and don'ts is what they hold to be real truths about Iraqis and constitutes the basic and essential information that they know about Iraqi culture and society.[8] This seeming contradiction reveals a fundamental element in the perspectives of the U.S. servicemen and women: what they learned may be how Iraqis "really are," but that information was not seen as useful for the U.S. soldiers' and marines' needs in their roles as military occupiers. Thus, their criticisms of the cultural training they receive are not about whether it is accurate or not, because they may believe the information they receive. Rather, their criticisms tend to reflect that they think the information they are provided formally is not useful for them in the jobs they do in the military in their interactions with Iraqis.

Given these reactions to the cultural training that the military provided, soldiers and marines sought knowledge about Iraqi culture through interactions with other military personnel who had previously served in Iraq or had begun their tours prior to their colleagues. One navy corporal equipment operator said, "We didn't learn until we got there and we either learned from the guys who had been there longer than us or from our superiors who had gotten word from their superiors." The interviewees' assessment of the technique of "swapping stories," as they called it, in their telling is a more useful method of learning about Iraqi culture than the formal training. This may be due in large part to the perceived credibility of a fellow military colleague who is both trusted and respected for already having served in Iraq and who witnessed and learned about Iraqis and the situation there firsthand.

But what kinds of knowledge did this story swapping consist of? In some cases, the interviewees learned basic information about Iraqi society and power structures. A twenty-two-year-old army captain recalled that trading information was crucial for learning the differences in local social and power structures in the rural and urban areas.

> The intelligence guys, we met a couple times a week and then we met with the operations guys. So, yeah, you pass stories. The one thing was in the cities, in Baghdad, shaykhs were early on, were not really considered that important. I know they are important in the countryside and we learned that although they were shaykhs in the city, they didn't have the authority that you would think in most communities. I remember that we traded stories about, you know, a shaykh who would show up and say, "I am the shaykh of this area," and you would think this guy is the man and then you would talk to people and they would be like, "No, we don't deal with him." So that was one of the things we learned about shaykhs.

In this case, the Baghdadi shaykh himself tried to gain power by playing on the stereotypes about the dominant role of shaykhs in all of Iraqi society that the U.S. military and government has incorrectly absorbed (that is, "tribal society is dominated by shaykhs"). The officer himself says, "They didn't have the authority that you would think in most communities" indicating that what they learned about shaykhs, what one would think, could be generalized across an entire country. Of course, no one country is homogenous, and such a view of culture and society erases all differences among class, education, religion, and geographical location, among many other things. Ultimately, the officer learned about some of the most basic differences between urban and rural society in Iraq and simple lessons about how people attempt to gain power for themselves.

In addition to the general information about Iraqi society and dos and don'ts, these tips often related to how to do the jobs they were trained for in the context of Iraqi insurgents, military, and civilians. Thus, the advice focused around how the insurgents fight, what to do about women and children during raids, and how best to get information from Iraqis. This they defined as the type of cultural information that was useful to them—knowledge and techniques that helped them do their jobs as military personnel in Iraq.

Other knowledge they gained came in the form of relatively nuanced information and insight into multiple facets of Iraqi culture, society, and politics, including religious differences in Iraq, the brutality of Saddam's regime, Iraqis' love for soccer, and how to speak persuasively with Iraqis. What some of the interviewees suggested was that knowing something about Iraqis and Iraq—such as the ancient history of Iraq, how they had suffered under Saddam, or the names of famous Iraqi soccer players—was important not necessarily for specific mission success but for creating some sort of connection or relationship with Iraqis that allowed the U.S. servicemen and women to understand the situations they were in, allay Iraqi suspicions, and show respect for Iraqis, all of which, in theory, would allow them to better do their jobs. The reactions of Iraqis when Americans had this kind of knowledge were described by a thirty-eight-year-old army first lieutenant:

> I think the theme that stuck out throughout a lot of training was that this is kind of the foundation of modern civilization and that we were shown slide after slide regarding the technologies, the knowledge, the resources that have been developed in Mesopotamia and that general area. I think our jaws dropped. We brought that up with the Iraqis who we advised and they were very proud of it, and they were, I think, very impressed that we knew that this was where modern civilization really came from.

The third way in which the interviewees learned about Iraqi culture was through the military personnel's interactions with translators, who were either in-country Iraqis or Iraqi or Arab expatriates or, in a very few cases, Americans who spoke Arabic. Like the jobs of the military personnel whom our interviewees learned information from, for the most part the translators' job also included imparting credible information to the servicemen and women.[9] Moreover, the idea of using translators as cultural brokers or sources of knowledge also hinged on them being seen as trustworthy. Many servicemen and women expressed their inability to trust Iraqis as they said Iraqis lied constantly or were looking to gain from every interaction. These qualms about trust were circumvented by the close relationships that developed between military personnel and their interpreters, who in most cases after 2003 lived on the same base. A fifty-eight-year-old mustang sergeant in the army expressed his admiration of his Iraqi interpreter whom he also attributes to saving his life more than once:

> Probably the smartest interpreter I had had worked for the Indian embassy. She was in the diplomatic service, probably for I think it was fifteen years. She

knew the history of Iraq printed in six books, she knew those books cover to cover, and over probably a three- to four-month period, she really gave me a great understanding of what Iraq was all about, which that was a real plus for us. [Because of that we developed] respect for her, and we were willing to listen. But she really educated us in the society norms, the dos and don'ts, and she became a very integral part of our mission planning, so she was very important. All three of the interpreters that we dealt with, the F2 section dealt with, were very educated: they at least had a two-year college education, and the lady that I spoke about had a four-year college degree. So they were a huge asset to us.

The soldiers' and marines' interactions and closeness to Iraqi and/or Arab translators afforded them useful native knowledge that transcended, in most cases, their fears of untrustworthy Iraqis.[10] One army infantry lieutenant, when asked about the cultural training he received, replied that they relied on their interpreters for that kind of information:

And we truly believed that our interpreters should be the ones teaching this course in the future. Mostly after events would happen we would kind of run through them with the interpreters and say, you know, "What did this mean? How could we do this better? He said this, did it really mean this?" Most of our interpreters would bring up with us if we did something that either struck a good note or bad note. For us, that was our bread–and-butter cultural interaction.

The translators provided the U.S. soldiers and marines an opportunity to not just learn behaviors but to ask questions such as "What did this mean" and to understand the contextual meaning of actions and the results of certain behaviors. In contrast, the formal cultural training about dos and don'ts was given without much understanding of the larger social context and environment in which these behaviors were embedded. One serviceman described the cultural training he received as what " . . . you would tell a tourist, which was not really, I don't think, at the depth of what we needed." He continued with an assessment of its weaknesses:

There wasn't a whole lot of "let's understand how Arabs or Iraqi culture works" or how to understand or plan for, really train for, the kind of interactions you are going to have with them. It was much more at a surface level of, you know, like I said, here's the four things you can do to avoid offense, but not so much how to pursue it . . .

That the military issues commands in the forms of dos and don'ts, what David Price (this volume) calls "disarticulated culture factoids," on how to act properly without elaborating or substantiating why points to the larger motives behind cultural training. The U.S. military's priority, of course, is to complete missions and enhance mission effectiveness, which means for them that cultural issues should help advance military priorities and objectives. The soldiers and marines, however, found that formal cultural training did not provide them with this nor did it provide them a more comprehensive explanation of Iraqi culture. "Culture" is taught to them as a fixed behavior, the right reaction to a certain situation, enumerated as are so many other military responses to situations (rules of engagement), when to fire a weapon, who to salute and how, etc.). Thus, Iraqi culture as defined by the military, like military culture as taught to initiates, becomes a knowable thing. Unlike how culture is lived by people and defined by anthropologists, culture for the U.S. military is not thought of as a process or as flexible systems and behaviors that are constantly changing and adapting. Thus, the ways the soldiers and marines are taught about culture formally by the U.S. military fails to provide them with the ability to understand or behave according to how Iraqis themselves live and understand their culture. So U.S. soldiers and marines end up turning to other sources—translators, other troops, and even Iraqis themselves—to understand behaviors and meanings. The interviewees found that knowledge of Iraqi history, culture, society, and subjects of interest to Iraqis aids U.S. military personnel in building relationships with Iraqis and engendering among them a sense of respect by the occupying forces toward the country they occupy and its people. Ultimately, the interviewees expressed that even the simplest cultural considerations and basic formal behavior seem to be appreciated by Iraqis.

Defining Culture

The responses to the kinds of cultural training the U.S. military provided reveal the difficulties of offering a blanket introduction about the large and varied country that is Iraq to such a diverse group of military personnel. It seems that in trying to make such cultural information accessible to all, the information becomes diluted and overly practical. In essence, when culture is reduced to a list of dos and don'ts, all diversity, subtlety, and variation are erased so that broad generalizations are made to represent the entire populace, without regard to economic level, educational level, rural and urban differences, geographic location, gender, travel experience, and so on. Even among the interviewees, depending on the level of their interaction with Iraqis and time spent in Iraq, we found a range of diversified responses. A fifty-one-year-old marine colonel with three tours of duty in Iraq points out, "Don't show them the bottom of your feet, don't eat with your left hand, and I'm left-handed, don't talk about women, sex, religion, politics . . . and that's all they wanted to talk about once they got to know you! They are more like us than they are different."

However, with increased contact with Iraqis, particularly when the U.S. military personnel lived closely with Iraqi soldiers and police, some of the U.S. military personnel came to realize the specificity of certain behaviors and how they were not so much about "Iraqi" culture as they were about formal and informal behavior, generational issues, respect, rural and urban differences, and so on.[11] One U.S. Army National Guard captain battalion intelligence officer in Baghdad recalled that the cultural training he received was the same as everyone else's but that "once you get there you learn—everybody was all freaked out about touching with the left hand and, you know, when you sit down, don't show the bottom of your foot. That's all true, but it's all in context. If it's a friend or someone you've known for a while, they are not going to give a shit."

The U.S. military's list of dos and don'ts also suggests that there is one static culture spread all across Iraq and that it does not change. As we have shown, some servicemen and women knew better: one marine first lieutenant reported that it did not really matter if he learned the culturally appropriate hand gestures, because after four years of the U.S. military presence in Iraq, the Iraqis had gotten used to them. He concluded that "the whole thing about not showing them the palm of your hand or your feet is not necessarily considered a sign of disrespect." Cultures, of course, change, adapt, and rework global influences. It should not be surprising that Iraqis, as people do everywhere, adapt to and adopt other cultures. As an army captain explained, "They [the Iraqis] understand that, at least the guys that I interacted with, that Americans have a whole different set of customs and don't understand their customs. However, just doing stuff as simple as pulling your feet back or whatever, makes them feel a lot better."

Given the military occupation of Iraq, the overwhelming military force and power shown by the U.S. armed forces, and the rebuilding and security role taken on by the U.S. military, Iraqis are adapting to the dominant powers, learning about American culture and how to deal with the U.S. soldiers and marines as a military power, an occupying army, potential employers, providers of security, and people with power to help and hurt them. The power dynamics suggest that cultural awareness and the drive to adapt or accept are often left to those whose very life and death, life ways, and incomes depend on learning the cultural mores and practices of the powerful.

Finally, what we found consistently throughout these interviews is the struggle of our subjects in understanding the role of cultural considerations in the context of a military occupation.[12] The individual interviewees had varied emphases on the need for cultural consideration in executing military operations that dealt regularly with civilians—some saw it as an unnecessary burden on them as they tried to achieve their military objectives, while others saw it as playing a major role in their ability to achieve their military objectives. This contextualized and commonsense application of cultural information is, of course, how Americans (and everyone else) learn to apply our own cultural knowledge. It is true that sitting with one's foot on one's knee so that the bottom of the shoe is turned to face the person on one's left or right is rude and disrespectful in Arab society. However, the importance placed on this offensive but forgivable behavior, this oft-repeated "don't," and the singularity with which the U.S. military personnel whom we interviewed recalled it, when asked what they learned about Iraqi culture, seems misplaced. In the context of a military invasion by the most powerful country in the world, the deaths of tens of thousands of Iraqis, the destruction of Iraqi civil institutions, the continued nonfunctioning of the government, the economy, the water and electricity systems, and so many other elements of the Iraqi state, the emphasis by the interviewees about avoiding showing others the soles of their shoes as an important Iraqi cultural practice seems to be something that they themselves can control in a situation that has become uncontrollable. The ironies of cultural training and culturally sensitive practices in the context of the military occupation do not deny or belittle individual efforts to recognize humanity through cultural differences and thereby define a more humanistic role for themselves within the destruction of the U.S. military invasion and occupation.[13] However, the ways in which the U.S. military defines culture and the types of information that U.S. soldiers and marines define as useful fundamentally reinforces the dominance of the U.S. military power in Iraq to control and circumscribe all aspects of Iraqis' lives.

The study was led by Dr. Rochelle Davis, and research was also conducted by Georgetown MA students Rola Abimourched, Dahlia Elzein, Elizabeth Grasmeder, R. Brian Seibeking, Dena Takruri, and BA student Jonathan Ouellette. Funding was provided by grants from Georgetown University's School of Foreign Service, the Oman Faculty Grant from the Center for Contemporary Arab Studies, and the Georgetown Undergraduate Research Opportunities Program (GUROP). The survey was conducted anonymously and any names mentioned in the interviews, American and Iraqi, have been changed. Our appreciation and thanks is extended to the U.S. servicemen and women who agreed to be interviewed and took the time to help us understand their views and experiences.

:: **NOTES** ::

1. The United States established major military bases in the Middle East (Saudi Arabia, Qatar, and later Kuwait) following August 1990 when Iraq invaded Kuwait and the United States invaded during the first Gulf War in 1991 and thus had had a presence in the Middle East for more than twelve years at the time of the invasion of Iraq. Veterans of this war recall that certain units had developed informational and training materials at this time concerning Arab and Muslim societies for their own specific uses, including a small pamphlet or "smart card" (cf. Gusterson, this volume). In addition, an Army War College paper prepared in February 2003 provides a prescient discussion of post-invasion Iraq and the various local Iraqi issues that the U.S. invasion force would have to take into consideration, which it clearly did not. See Crane and Terrill (2003).

2. The U.S. National Security Strategy issued in September 2002 presents a reformulation of U.S. foreign policy that expresses the Bush administration's willingness to use military power unilaterally without international considerations but does not delimit specific actions or plans. (U.S. National Security Council 2002). Numerous journalistic accounts and documentary films chronicle the results of such a strategy and the absence of a long-term plan for the U.S. presence in Iraq, including writings by Seymour Hersh in his regular *New Yorker* column, "Annals of National Security." See also Packer (2005), Rosen (2004), Ricks (2006), Woodward (2004), Kirk (2004), and Ferguson (2007).

3. In addition to the extensive accounts in Woodward and Ricks, a Human Rights Watch report (2003) confirms the absence of on-the-ground planning and the resulting complications:

> U.S. combat troops in Baghdad like the 82nd Airborne and 1st Armored Division are being asked to perform law enforcement and policing tasks for which they are not prepared. According to soldiers and commanders, there was inadequate training and equipment for what the military calls SASO (Stability and Support Operations) and an inadequate supply of Arabic interpreters. The problem was articulately presented by an unnamed U.S infantry commander in an After Action Report filed April 24, 2003 and since declassified [...] "After less than 48 hours after the first battlefield engagement," the commander said "members of this company team were tasked to conduct checkpoint operations southwest of al-Najaf. With no training, soldiers were expected to search vehicles, interact with civilians with no CA [Civil Affairs] or PSYOPS [Psychological Operations] support, detain EPW's [Enemy Prisoners of War], and confiscate weapons. Less than 48 hours after this, the unit was again heavily engaged in combat operations. The radical and swift change from combat operations to SASO and back to combat operations over and over again causes many points of friction for the soldiers and their leaders. With the exception of a class given to the platoon leaders, there were no formal classes or training conducted by CA prior to the operation. No training on checkpoint operations or dealing with civilians was received."

4. This has resulted in mixed reviews as to the accuracy of the content or the appropriateness. One interviewee deployed in the initial invasion reported that his chaplain gave a briefing on Islam in which, inaccurately, the Muslim god was portrayed as being different from the Christian god. Soldiers are now given "smart cards," which are pocket-sized sixteen-page informational cards with cultural information and Arabic sayings on them (Iraq Cultural Smart Card: Guide for Cultural Awareness, http://www.fas.org/irp/doddir/usmc/iraqsmart-0506.pdf), in addition to CDs and online training material. See the University of Military Intelligence (http://www.universityofmili taryintelligence.us/main.asp), the U.S. Army Training and Doctrine Culture Center, the U.S. Army Battle Command Knowledge System (https://bcks.army.mil), and a variety of secure U.S. military training Web sites (see in particular http://www.au.af.mil/au/aul/bibs/culture.htm).

5. A number of other scholars are working on the subject of U.S. military cultural training programs, including Georgetown University M.A. student Rudy Ghareeb. Military personnel have

also been writing articles advocating for the importance of cultural training. See Elder (2007) and Elkhamri (2007).

6. These responses were to the question, "In your opinion, was local culture taken into consideration when you or your unit planned/executed its operations?"

7. Only fourteen of the forty reported that they received some training in the Arabic language.

8. For example, the 2004 and May 2006 Iraq Culture Smart Card states, "Admitting 'I don't know' is shameful for an Iraqi," and in a section called "Islamic Flag Meanings," it states that "Muslims often fly colored flags to observe various holidays or dates of personal significance. Each color carries a specific meaning." The first of these is so generalizing as to cast everything Iraqis say with suspicion, and the second provides no information other than to say that they fly flags for nonmilitary reasons.

9. Early in the invasion and occupation, the translators came from areas close to the bases and went home at night. U.S. military thought many of these people to be corrupt and untrustworthy. It was when the local translators were brought to the bases to live, because they and their families had become targets of the growing Iraqi insurgency, that different kinds of relationships developed in which the American soldiers became more trusting of the local translators.

10. At the same time they are considered untrustworthy by American troops, they are also suspected and targeted for assassination by Iraqi insurgents. See Associated Press (2005).

11. This issue is explored more fully in Davis and Grasmeder (n.d.).

12. The variation among our interviewees in terms of how we contacted them, rank, political leanings, and so on rule out that our interview sample is overly biased toward "culturally sensitive" people. In terms of political leanings, our sample included thirteen moderates, eight conservatives, five liberals, one libertarian, one progressive, and fourteen unreported.

13. My students and I have had long discussions about our own conceptions of the value of cultural training in the course of a military occupation. By suggesting that U.S. soldiers and marines individually try to make sense of their missions and be culturally sensitive is not to be soft on the U.S. military's role in the occupation of Iraq. Instead, what we are trying to do is to be fair and honest to our informants, the forty or so men and women that we interviewed for this project, and to reflect on the sense of how many of them understood Iraqi culture and reported their own behavior.

20

The "Bad" Kill

A Short Case Study in American Counterinsurgency

:: JEFFREY BENNETT ::

We had been losing a lot of people without doing anything . . . My sergeant Major told me he wanted to produce more kills, and I was the guy to make it happen.

Staff Sergeant Michael Hensley, 1/501st (A) scout/sniper platoon

He [Hensley] asked me if I was ready. I had the pistol out. I heard the word shoot. I don't remember pulling the trigger. It took me a second to realize that the shot came from the pistol in my hand.

Sergeant Evan Vela, 1/501st (A) scout/sniper platoon

It's a terrible war out there and you have to make tough decisions. This war doesn't provide you that luxury to be perfect.

Sergeant Anthony Murphy, 1/501st (A) scout/sniper platoon

If you've never been outside the wire, . . . you don't have a basis to judge what I do or what I don't do.

Sergeant Richard Hand, 1/501st (A) scout/sniper platoon

Introduction

"Small wars" or insurgencies have plagued conquering states since the days of the Roman Empire. To end these wars, states have adopted strategies ranging from national annihilation, at one end of the brutality[1] spectrum, to simply paying insurgent leaders to demobilize their units at the other. More times than not, however, state-sponsored counterinsurgency campaigns have relied upon heavy doses of violence to achieve their aims. There are many reasons for this, but Gil Merom notes that foremost among them is the fact that the manifold costs involved in counterinsurgency warfare all go up as the conquering state attempts to impose limits upon the killing and displacement of innocents (Merom 2003, 46). In other words, in counterinsurgency warfare, identifying and protecting innocents is much more time and resource intensive than labeling large segments of the population "hostile" and utilizing violence indiscriminately to either destroy or pacify those segments.

> From an expedient point of view, then, the movement on the strategic scale from selective eradication to indiscriminate annihilation is tempting. In that sense, counterinsurgency is inherently degenerative . . . Indeed, the most disturbing conclusion from our current moral vantage point is that brutality pays [in counterinsurgency warfare] . . . at least as long as altruistic moral restraints are absent. (Merom 2003, 47)

In fact, Merom argues that large democracies like the United States, France, and Israel all understood this well during the twentieth century. Thus, they all attempted to create a climate of opinion both within and outside the theater of military operations that would free their armed forces from "the moral restraints that prevent the use of excessive brutality," in Algeria, Vietnam, and Lebanon (Merom 2003, 79). More specifically, these conquering states actively churned out propaganda and attempted to carefully manage information related to the conflicts they were involved in to ensure that the brutality they relied upon to pacify insurgents was thoroughly compartmentalized—that is, either hidden from public view or ideologically legitimized. However, Merom claims that this strategy ultimately failed in all the cases just mentioned because the educated middle classes back "home" were able to shift the war's center of gravity from the battlefield to the "marketplace of ideas," putting increased pressure on the state to align its use of violent force with the moral temperament characteristic of the society it represented—and ultimately, this moral pressure had a destabilizing effect on both the conduct of counterinsurgency warfare and the political field more generally (Merom 2003, 79). Merom has described this process and its consequences in the following terms:

> As time passes, society becomes better aware of the implications of the war, including its human cost. Because casualties, particularly in non-existential wars,

threaten to undercut support for the war, the state is tempted to rely on more firepower and higher levels of brutality [to end the conflict quickly and avoid a slow erosion of public support]. . . . The ensuing brutality, however, invigorates moral opposition to the war [which is normally spearheaded by the educated middle classes]. Depicted as immoral, the war objectives and casualties seem even less sensible. . . . In such a case, the war initiative shifts to the insurgents, and retreat becomes only a matter of time. However, the state may decide to try to overcome the erosion of support for the war and remain aggressive on the battlefield. But then it must become more deceptive and/or coercive at home, and this in turn creates a secondary detrimental expansion of the normative gap [between state and society]. The war then becomes synonymous with a threat to the democratic order, and the government consequently loses its legitimacy. At the end, then, democracies fail in small wars because they cannot find a winning balance between the costs of war in terms of human lives and the political cost incurred by controlling the latter with force. (Merom 2003, 24)

This seems like an apt description of what occurred in the wake of the U.S. invasion and occupation of Iraq in 2003. The intent of this paper, however, is not to trace the way moral outrage generated by incidents such as the Abu Ghraib prison scandal, the Haditha massacre or abuses committed by private security contractors, have forced U.S. military commanders in Iraq to adopt more creative and costly strategies for ending the insurgency. Rather, using Merom's observations as a starting point, this paper asks how, six years into the conflict, the U.S. government's difficulty in balancing military expediency and moral tolerance in Iraq has affected the American combat soldiers on the ground there. After all, if Merom is correct, it is the American soldiers and Iraqi civilians (not the educated middle classes in the United States) who are the most vulnerable to the convulsions and contradictions associated with Iraq-related crises and policy changes.

To support this point and help suggest some answers to the question I have just posed, I will focus on a single story drawn from last winter's headlines that I believe reveals much about the war and American attempts to manage its myriad costs. The story revolves around the actions of a handful of scout/snipers from Alaska who were sent to the "Triangle of Death"[2] as the troop surge got underway in early 2007.

The "Bad" Kill

On the morning of May 11, 2007, an Iraqi national named Genei Nesir Khudair al-Janabi walked into a "hide site" occupied by a scout/sniper team from the 1-501st airborne infantry operating in Jurf as Sakhr, a Sunni strong-hold about thirty-five miles south of Baghdad. Sergeant Evan Vela, a ranger-qualified sniper and veteran of numerous combat missions, had been tasked with guarding the hide site while the other team members slept, but he failed to react as the Iraqi farmer approached. In the brief chaos that ensued, Ge-nei al-Janabi was captured, bound, and covered with a poncho. Staff Sergeant Michael Hensley, the mission leader, then ordered the rest of the team, with the exception of Vela, to exit the hide site and pull security while he radioed his platoon leader, First Lieutenant Matthew Didier. In his initial radio call, Hensley reported that a local national (LN) armed with an AK-47 had been spotted on a trail about one hundred meters away. Didier subsequently or-dered Hensley to monitor the LN's actions to see if he might lead the sniper team to a weapons cache.

A short while later, Sergeant Robert Redfern, another member of the five-man team conducting the mission, spotted a "kid" between twelve and seventeen years old approaching the hide site and quickly "waved him in" for questioning. According to Redfern, "the immediate concern was whether this was an enemy tactic . . . having someone walk right into a hide site had never happened before" (Consolidated Article 32 Report, September 30, 2007, 87). The kid turned out to be Genei al-Janabi's seventeen-year-old son, Mustafa. The boy later testified that he had just learned that a cousin had been killed by Shi'ite militia members, and he had gone to tell his father the news. Un-fortunately, the Americans were oblivious to these developments. Instead, Hensley later reported that after the kid was detained, Genei al-Janabi "started making a lot of noise. He started crying, at times, he was yelling. I was trying to shut him up" (Parker 2008). Meanwhile, a group of "military aged" men began gathering approximately 150 meters from the hide site, giving Hensley good reason to fear that the captive's animated sobbing was placing his small, exhausted, and lightly armed team at risk.

Finally, Hensley decided to release the boy. He then radioed First Lieuten-ant Didier again to request permission to conduct a "close kill" (a kill made within ten feet) under the false pretense that the still wandering and armed Iraqi national was about to make contact with his team. First Lieutenant Di-dier informed Hensley that he had permission to make the kill if necessary. In Hensley's words, after that, "I asked him [Vela] if he was ready . . . I moved out of the way. I pulled the head rag over his [the Iraqi's] head . . . and told Vela to shoot" (Parker 2008). Vela hesitated for a few seconds and then fired a 9 mm round into Genei al-Janabi's head, but the Iraqi did not die immediately. The massive brain hemorrhage he suffered caused him to convulse on the ground and choke on his own blood. Vela later testified that Hensley, "kind of laughed about it and hit the guy in the throat and said shoot again" (Kratovac 2007). Vela responded by firing a second round, and the captive's body went limp. The execution was complete. Vela had finally chalked up his first kill. Hensley then proceeded to pull an AK-47 from his rucksack and plant it on the body, telling Vela "this is what we are going to say happened" (Kratovac 2007).

Nine months later, an eight-person military panel meeting at Camp Liberty in Iraq convicted Sergeant Vela of committing murder and planting incriminating evidence. Vela had openly confessed to the killing, but the conviction still disappointed Vela and his comrades, who concluded that they had been betrayed by their chain of command. During the trial, Hensley and his men had reported that the team had been under constant pressure from the "top" to produce "kills" during the spring of 2007, pressure that was accompanied by the suggestion that the team adopt a more relaxed version of the standard rules of engagement (ROE). As a result, in the buildup to Genei al-Janabi's murder, 1-501 snipers had engaged several other, unarmed Iraqis, but without any negative repercussions. Specifically, Vela's best friend, Sergeant Anthony Murphy, had killed an unarmed Iraqi man probing near his position with a lead pipe. Specialist Michaud had shot an unarmed man he believed was tinkering with command wire. SSG Hensley had killed an unarmed farmer working with his family in a field close to an irrigation canal. And just weeks before the May 11 incident, SPC Sandoval had shot an unarmed man in the head as he crouched in a farm field with a rusty sickle. In the end, all of these killings were deemed legitimate by investigators—that is, they were all justified on the grounds that the victims' behaviors could have been interpreted as suspicious or "threatening" in some way. Thus, it was difficult for most of Vela's supporters to comprehend why he was being punished for a killing that had been authorized by his platoon leader and directly ordered by Hensley to ensure the safety of the team in hostile territory. This sentiment was probably best expressed by Vela's former platoon sergeant, Sergeant First Class Steven Kipling, who likened the trial to a witch hunt, saying, "if all U.S. combat soldiers in Iraq were subjected to the same scrutiny applied to Vela, 'we would have thousands' of [similar] cases" (Moore 2008).

The Snipers and the Counterinsurgency

American snipers in Iraq are not tasked with "meeting and greeting" Iraqis. Their job does not involve rapport-building activities, civil affairs, or contributing to reconstruction efforts. Instead, their job is to hunt and kill insurgents, and their collective worth is measured largely in terms of the enemy body count they generate. Moreover, due to the operational environment in

Iraq and the kinds of missions sniper teams are regularly assigned, the line that separates combatants from noncombatants and legitimate engagements from illegitimate executions[3] are relatively fuzzy and manipulable. Therefore, much depends on the operational style and ethical climate manufactured by commanders at multiple levels, who are themselves under constant pressure to produce measurable results.

To be more specific, sniper teams typically set up in hide positions and survey sectors of key terrain with high-powered optics. They then generate real-time reports regarding the human activity unfolding in their sectors, and they engage and destroy targets in those sectors that have been reclassified as real or potential threats based upon firsthand observations. Thus, sniper teams provide the units they support with tactical intelligence and security. However, in the course of doing so they also psychologically affect local populations in powerful and perverse ways. Put simply, Iraqis living or moving through territory where American snipers are active must (1) assume that they are being watched; (2) know that displaying interest in irrigation canals, street gutters, trash cans, and so on, carrying shovels, pipes, or boxes and so on, using hand signals, video cameras, or binoculars and so on, running or walking off designated paths, lingering in windows and so on might all be considered suspicious or potentially threatening behaviors, and (3) know that they will be killed by snipers if they display those behaviors. Of course, it is not clear *how* Iraqis are supposed to understand the behavioral mandates that American sniper teams routinely impose on them, but in theory the panoptic killing scheme I just described is supposed to result in fewer rather than more civilian casualties because the precision weaponry snipers utilize is so much more discriminating than the other forms of direct and indirect fire American troops have at their disposal.

The 1-501st Parachute Infantry Regiment (PIR) deployed to Iraq in October 2006 and operated in Jurf as Sakr, Iskandariya, Karbala, and Fallujah as the Bush administration began the troop surge. These are some of the most dangerous areas in Iraq, and within a few months of being in-country more than twenty soldiers from the brigade the 1-501st was part of had been killed and many more wounded in insurgent attacks. Meanwhile, the unit seemed unable to find and kill insurgents or limit the number of improvised explosive device (IED) attacks occurring in its area of operations. In fact, a full seven months into the deployment, kill teams from the 1-501st sniper section had only managed to shoot two Iraqis. Thus, at the apex of the surge, the battalion leadership made a change. They gave almost full control of the scout/sniper platoon to SSG Michael Hensley, an army ranger, former all-services sniper competition winner, and Afghanistan combat veteran. In the simplest terms, his superiors,

LTC Balcavage and CSM Knight, told Hensley that they wanted to increase enemy body count, that he would be reporting directly to them rather than to his platoon leader, and that his men were to kill any Iraqi they felt presented a threat to American troops or equipment. In fact, Hensley later claimed that he was told on more than one occasion, "You guys don't need to worry if you feel threatened for a second, don't hesitate to engage" (Parker 2008).

On the first mission Hensley led in April 2007, his team produced five confirmed kills, and more followed. The dramatic turnaround boosted the unit's morale and the battalion's company commanders and first sergeants began openly praising Hensley's men for taking the fight to the enemy. Meanwhile, a steady stream of gossip and rumors regarding the killings began to circulate among the battalion's lower enlisted soldiers, raising questions about Hensley's methods.

The Privates, the Box, and the Charges

SSG Hensley participated in every mission the unit ran after assuming control of the sniper section. However, some of the lower enlisted soldiers in the unit, especially soldiers who were not well liked or highly regarded, were rarely taken "outside the wire," and when they were, their incessant complaining and inability to perform to the high standards that Hensley had set created problems for the unit. For example, after a routine call to provide security for engineers on June 20, two of these soldiers, Private First Class Flores and Private First Class Petta received counseling statements from Sergeant Vela for falling asleep and jeopardizing the safety of the other men on the mission. The following is an excerpt from testimony[4] provided by SPC4 Michaud, who was also on the mission:

Q. So how—how big of deal (*sic*) is that to fall asleep out there in sector?

A. You don't do that.

Q. So these guys were about to get in big trouble?

A. Roger.

Q. And what was their response to this?

A. Sergeant Vela had called them in and Sergeant Vela came to me afterwards and said that, you know, "hey listen to this. Flores and Petta said that they were going to come out with whatever they know if I go through with this counseling statement and UCMJ action." I said, "What are you talking about?" He's like, "They're saying we're killing innocent civilians and planting shit on them." I was like, "Okay, let 'em do it."

Q. Was this kind of blackmail for having been—

A. I considered it as blackmail. I thought blackmail kind of had to be truthful though, you had to actually have some basis behind it to be able to do that. I mean, that's why Vela was just like, "Okay, go ahead." He didn't do anything wrong. They were getting UCMJ action, they had fallen asleep. Bottom line. (Consolidated Article 32[b] hearing, 73)

Flores and Petta, who would later be described as "untrustworthy" and "worthless" by other members of their unit, left the counseling session with Vela and went directly to the unit Chaplain to report "moral problems" they had with the way the scout/sniper platoon was operating (Consolidated Article 32[b] hearing, 73). On June 22, Flores and Petta provided formal statements to the Army's Criminal Investigation Division. A few days later, Sandoval, Vela, and Hensley were all detained and interrogated by military detectives. Later, they would all stand trial for murder and planting incriminating evidence at kills sites based upon the statements Flores and Petta had provided.

As it turns out, Flores, Petta, and several other lower enlisted soldiers in the unit had been talking for some time about the "box" that SSG Hensley kept in his room, and several soldiers claimed they had seen an AK-47 in Hensley's wall locker. None of these soldiers had been officially read in on the Asymmetrical Warfare Group's bait and shoot program, as the details of the program were secret and disseminated on a need-to-know basis. Therefore, they were unaware that Hensley had inherited the box of "bait" when he took over as the sniper section leader in April. So in their imaginations the dummy explosives, mortar rounds, and command wire that their noncommissioned officers ordered them to take out on patrol could only have existed to cover up illegitimate kills. Moreover, Hensley had ordered Flores to place a roll of command wire (ostensibly from the bait box) in the pocket of an Iraqi killed by Sandoval in April 2007, seemingly confirming this suspicion—and Flores had shared this information with at least two other soldiers. Thus, when the disgruntled privates met with the Criminal Investigation Division investigators at the end of June, they had plenty to say. And although the accusations they made were based almost entirely on speculation, their complaints ultimately resulted in numerous criminal charges being filed against their fellow platoon members.

The Rules of Engagement and the Question of Murder

Sandoval, Hensley, and Vela were all accused of murder in Iraq because their actions in the field seemed to have violated the standard ROE. But how exactly did they understand those rules, especially given that LTC Balcavage and CSM Knight had allegedly issued a "nonorder"[5] to the sniper section to increase the enemy body count? In this section, I will attempt to answer this question by providing several examples of the way soldiers from the 1-501st scout/sniper platoon understood an actual shooting incident. The testimony pertains to SPC Sandoval's killing of the "squirter" on April 27, 2007. Sandoval killed the man (on Hensley's order) because he was suspected of having fired on Iraqi army troops earlier in the day; however, at the time of the killing the Iraqi man was unarmed, taking a break from the grass cutting he had been doing moments before.

Here is the testimony from Sergeant Richard Hand, 1-501st scout/sniper platoon:

> Q. Sergeant Hand, what kind of mental state do you snipers need to be in when you go out on a mission?
>
> A. Mentally we have to be prepared to engage and destroy anything or anyone at any given point in time.
>
> Q. Might that include women?
>
> A. It includes women, small kids, dogs, cats, donkeys, cows, anything and everything that can be perceived as a threat.
>
> Q. Because if they are a threat, then you have PID [positive identification] and the ROE says you can shoot, correct?
>
> A. Yes, sir.
>
> Q. That evaluation of the threat you rely on everything you know about the circumstances, correct?
>
> A. Yes. You take in all the information that's on-scene. Unfortunately a lot of people bring in passive things too, which in my opinion, I think is a good thing, you bring in a lot of positive with all of your experiences and you use that to sort through the information that you've gathered while you're on the ground and you use that to come up with a decision to either kill or not to kill.
>
> Q. Would part of that, a small part of that, evaluation include the age of that person?
>
> A. Because we're all human, I mean, you don't want to shoot a little girl, you just don't want to do it. It looks bad for us and—I mean, if you have to, you have to though.
>
> Q. Does a military age male create a greater threat in your mind?
>
> A. Yes.
>
> Q. Greater potential for threat?
>
> A. Yes, there is definitely a greater potential for threat from roughly 14 to 30-year old Iraqi male versus a young female or even a younger male.
>
> Q. Now the woman you were pulling security on by the water pump at the

house, she was getting close to the point where she was going to be taken down, correct?

A. Yes. Because of her mannerisms, her vocalizations, and the heightened— and the adrenaline pumping through me, I was really close to putting her down.

Q. And that heightened sense was present for that whole scene, correct?

A. I would have to say yes. Anyone who was there, if their heart wasn't pumping just a little bit more and they weren't just a little more aware then they weren't mentally there.

Q. If that woman had made a move for a weapon to an area where you couldn't see if there was a weapon, would you have taken her down?

A. Yes.

Q. Any hesitation there?

A. No.

Q. As you understand the ROE, if any person runs from an engagement with the Iraqi Army, do you have PID on them even if they are unarmed?

A. If—okay, could you restate that a little bit?

Q. If somebody engages the Iraqi Army. Flees. And are unarmed. As you understand the ROE, can you engage that person even though they are unarmed?

A. Yes.

Q. Clear, no question about it?

A. No question. If they were combative and they decided to flee the area and they drop their weapon, which is one of their SOPs, Standard Operating Procedures, they break contact and they drop everything and they just take off running. That is PID. (Consolidated Article 32[b] hearing, 373)

Here is the testimony of SP4 Michaud, 1-501st scout/sniper platoon:

Q. What was your ROE for engaging targets?

A. Basically reasonable certainty. Positive ID. If the guy is doing something wrong, hostile act, hostile intent. At the time they were really pushing for if you felt threatened.

Q. Who was it that was pushing that? The feel threatened?

A. The battalion commander, our sergeant major. Leadership in general.

Q. Were they pushing it hard?

A. Yeah.

Q. Why do you think they were pushing it so hard?

A. Umm—

Q. Did they want some kills?

A. I think—I mean we all want kills. I mean there's a lot of bad guys out here that need to be killed. And with—

Q. And kills means results out here?

A. Exactly. It's our job out here is to lay people down who are doing bad things. And we were losing a lot of guys in our brigade and I'm not saying that's the reason, but what I am saying is that we lost a lot of guys. I don't want to call it revenge, but we needed to find a way so that we could get the bad guys the right way and still maintain the right military things to do. But if we push this a little bit more, you know, "hey, did you feel threatened?" Bottom line, "Yeah I felt threatened." Then it's okay then.

Q. And those are the actual words that the sergeant major and battalion commander used, "do you feel threatened"?

A. Roger.

Q. And as you understood the ROE, "squirter" running, even if they are unarmed and even if they take some cover or pretend job as cover, you still have PID, right? As far as you understand?

A. It depends. It depends on the area you're in.

Q. What about this area? Right after an engagement with the Iraqi Army?

A. Well this area, I mean, yeah. I mean to me that's PID. But I believe everyone else that is PID. But if you go to an area where that's not normal or— basically it all depends on the situation and the area in your in. If you're at a Tier 1 IED spot and there's a guy digging on the side of the road at two in the morning, he's probably putting in an IED.

Q. And your evaluation of this situation was that this was a bad guy? This was PID?

A. Roger.

Q. This was a legit kill?

A. Roger. If I was there it's what I would have done too.

Q. What was the atmosphere in the scout platoon as far as getting in trouble for doing your job? Skip—Was there fear of being investigated after every— every kind of shot?

A. I think—I don't think so. I mean, we always joked about it, stuff like that, but as far as us actually thinking that we were getting—the thought never crossed our mind because every dude that we put down is bad. You know if we were out there murdering—murdering innocent civilians then yeah, I would be a little scared that I would go to jail. But I don't think any of us were worrying at all. The fact was we thought this dude was bad and—yeah, I don't think anybody was really worried about it. (Consolidated Article 32[b] hearing, 68)

Before concluding, I want to note one final case of the ROE being followed properly. In 2005, Marcus Luttrell was serving as a sniper on SEAL Team 10 in

Afghanistan during the same time period that Michael Hensley was deployed there. Luttrell's team was hunting for a Taliban commander when it was compromised by a small group of Afghan goat herders. The team was operating in a remote, hostile region with minimal support and insufficient weaponry to engage a large enemy element, thus their discovery by the Afghan locals put them at great risk. The pressing question then was what should the team do? Ultimately, Luttrell's team decided to follow the ROE and release the unarmed locals. However, not long thereafter, SEAL Team 10 was attacked by thirty to forty Taliban fighters who had been tipped off by the fleeing goat herders. Luttrell was the only man on his team to survive the ensuing firefight, and when a Special Operations helicopter flew in to help extract him, it too was attacked resulting in the deaths of all sixteen men on board.

This incident provoked a debate within the military about how such scenarios ought to be handled in the future. Most military experts agreed that, barring other options, in a repeat scenario it would be better to kill the innocent detainees than to risk failing the mission and endangering the lives of the American troops. However, this solution clearly violates the rules of war, and for that reason it cannot be adopted as doctrine. So the Luttrell case propels us in a very direct way into the heart of the problem Merom has described: in small wars, combat leaders are routinely forced to choose between militarily expedient and morally acceptable solutions, which are often at odds with one another. Moreover, they must take full responsibility for their choices. This is a large part of what makes small wars unwinnable by liberal, democratic governments; in wars such as these, military victory usually comes at the cost of moral defeat and vice versa. Or, as Sahlins suggested in his study of the Vietnam conflict, winning such a war comes at the cost of losing American hearts and minds (Sahlins 2000[1966], 245). Having noted that, I will conclude by offering one more piece of Article 32 testimony from Sergeant Anthony Murphy who was transferred to D Company in the wake of the murder allegations leveled against Hensley, Sandoval, and Vela:

Q. Just one question, Sergeant Murphy. Has this investigation of what's going on had an effect on Soldiers pulling the trigger in any way?
A. Yes, absolutely. I talk to guys all the time.
Q. And what effect is it?
A. *They're confused. They don't know if their command is going to have their back if they're faced with a situation. Do I need to pull the trigger or not?* . . . I just came to a unit, Delaware [D Company], that they will not pull the trigger on people. And that's all they want to do, they think that it's like that, but now they're like, "what's going to happen if?" and I'm like, I don't know, I

can't tell you. If you feel threatened, take the shot, and I hope—I pray that your command takes your back, because you have milliseconds to make decisions like this. (Consolidated Article 32[b] hearing, 268; emphasis added)

The Outcomes

Jorge Sandoval was tried on murder charges and for planting incriminating evidence connected to the April 27 shooting. His court martial took place in Iraq in September 2007. He was cleared of murder charges but convicted of conspiring to plant incriminating evidence. As a result, he was reduced in rank to E-2 and sentenced to 150 days of confinement, 106 of which he had already served by the time of his sentence. Today Sandoval is a civilian.

Michael Hensley was tried on multiple counts of murder and planting incriminating evidence. His court martial took place in Iraq in October 2007. He was cleared of all murder charges but was found guilty of planting incriminating evidence and disrespecting and disobeying a superior officer. Hensley was reprimanded, reduced to the pay grade of E-5, and sentenced to 135 days of confinement, which he had already served by the time of the sentence. Today Sergeant Hensley is an instructor at the Florida Phase of the U.S. Army Ranger School.

The 1-501st PIR redeployed to Fort Richardson, Alaska, in December 2007. However, in an almost unprecedented turn of events, Evan Vela was flown back to Iraq for his court martial, which took place at Camp Liberty, Iraq, in February 2008. Part of the apparent justification had to do with the fact that Mustafa al-Janabi was permitted to testify at the proceedings and face the man who had killed his father. Here it is interesting to note that in August 2007, when Sandoval, Hensley, and Vela were all in pretrial confinement, their battalion commander, LTC Balcavage, invited senior members of the al-Janabi tribe—one of the most powerful Sunni tribes in Iraq—to FOB ISKAN (Forward Operating Base Iskandariya) to sign an agreement that would prevent factions of the tribe who had admitted to attacking Americans and working with al-Qaeda from doing so in the future—by paying them. I am not certain which faction of the al-Janabi tribe Genei al-Janabi might have belonged to or whether obtaining justice for his killing figured into the agreement Balcavage signed in August 2007. However, I do know that Evan Vela was subsequently found guilty of murder, stripped of his rank and pay, and sentenced to ten years confinement in the military prison in Fort Leavenworth, Kansas, where he remains today. After receiving his sentence, his only question was whether he would be allowed to remain in the U.S. Army after serving his time.

Conclusion

I believe this story graphically highlights the way the U.S. government's attempts to establish a working balance between military expediency and moral restraint are affecting combat troops on the ground in Iraq. As Curtis Carnahan (Evan Vela's father) said, "it's like the U.S. government unleashes the war machine when things get tough, and then handcuffs it when things get messy" (personal communication). As a result, many of the lower enlisted soldiers who serve on the cutting edge of that war machine are coming home with blood on their hands, or in handcuffs, or in Evan Vela's case, both.[6] The story also makes it clear that Iraqis of all stripes are affected by the same vicissitudes, often fatally. It is thus understandable why Hensley and many other American combat soldiers in Iraq have adopted the practice of carrying "insurance" (such as spools of command wire or foreign weapons) on their missions: if they fail to pull the trigger in uncertain situations, they risk being killed by the enemy,[7] but if they pull the trigger and fail to convince the sensitive site exploitation teams that it was justified, they risk being charged with murder. Although Merom's study suggests that this double-bind situation signals a looming U.S. defeat in Iraq, I want to suggest that the killing of Genei al-Janabi and imprisonment of Evan Vela, a double sacrifice of sorts, is better viewed as a complex metaphor for the ongoing counterinsurgency. Ironically, Evan Vela's story failed to generate much discussion in the United States because it was almost completely eclipsed by news and interviews related to the publication of the U.S. Army's new counterinsurgency manual,[8] a text that promises victory if U.S. troops can somehow learn to tolerate the paradoxical, frequently unjust nature of the conflict.[9]

:: **NOTES** ::

1. "Brutality" is a vague and highly rhetorical term, but in this case it might be measured in terms of the destruction and/or internal displacement of noncombatants, the destruction of property and productive resources, and documented violations of the rules of war.

2. Since the 2003 invasion of Iraq, American military officials have referred to the region south of Baghdad connecting the towns of Yusufiyah, Jurf as Sakr, and Salman Pak as the "Triangle of Death." The predominantly Sunni region has been plagued by both sectarian and anti-American violence since 2003.

3. One could argue that legitimate sniper kills satisfy all the criteria necessary to be labeled executions.

4. All of the quoted testimony from 1/501st soldiers used in this paper derive from a verbatim transcript of the Article 32 hearing held at FOB ISKAN on July 24, 2007, to determine whether SSG Michael Hensley and SPC Jorge Sandoval would be subject to Article 39 court martial proceedings. These documents were supplied by a private source, and to my knowledge are currently not available via the Freedom of Information Act.

5. An order communicated in an informal way with the tacit understanding that the chain of command would refuse to take responsibility for problems arising from its execution but that failure to execute the order would have negative consequences for the soldiers tasked with the "getting the job done."

6. This point is further supported by the testimony provided by U.S. soldiers and marines at the recent Winter Soldier conference.

7. One informant I interviewed while researching the Evan Vela case made it clear that neither he nor his fellow soldiers felt that Iraq was "worth dying for." If this sentiment is widely shared by U.S. troops in Iraq, it helps to explain why so many soldiers and marines have seemingly adopted a "shoot first, ask questions later" disposition when on patrol.

8. The fact that this field manual has been made available to the general public for free via the Internet suggests that it was created largely for public consumption rather than military education.

9. For more information about this case, see Junod (2008).

21

The Destruction of Conscience
and the Winter Soldier

:: KEVIN CAFFREY ::

Winter Soldier

This essay examines testimony at the Winter Soldier 2008 antiwar event as an ethnographic case of veterans' attempts to communicate with the American people. Soldiers' narratives of rules of engagement (ROE), and especially how they change over time, emerge as an indicator for damage done to American conscience. Mindful of Sahlins's 1966 observation that the Vietnamese counterinsurgency (COIN) necessarily destroyed conscience, this argument concludes that COIN is incompatible with liberal democracy. The human realities of Algeria, Vietnam, and now Iraq have been bloody documentation of a trial and error learning process that leaves us wondering if America had already lost the war once Iraq became a generalized COIN. The insight offered by the veterans who spoke at Winter Soldier 2008 gives us ethnographic purchase on this issue.

Following the Clausewitzian convention that politics and war are a kind of kin, the status of combat ROE in Iraq here appears as a general indicator of conscience in the same way that the degree of adherence to a moral code is a general indicator of any ethical climate. Conscience being something having to do with the relationship between practice and the moral code to which it is supposed to adhere, the condition of the conventional moral code in play can be taken as a general indicator of ethical condition. This paper argues that the destruction of conscience for soldiers in Iraq can be documented through the indicator of degradation in the ROE over time. Further, signs of a similar destruction for the American public can be seen where the propaganda fabric of legitimation for the Iraqi occupation is contradicted by video material available online—scattered images that throw light on the contradictions that energize the malformations of politicomilitary engagement in Iraq.

The 2008 Winter Soldier event was held March 13–16 just outside of Washington, D.C., to remind Americans of lessons not yet learned. Now constituting a pattern for U.S. imperial practice, it first occurred under eerily familiar circumstances in 1971. Over one hundred members of Vietnam Veterans Against the War gathered in Detroit of that year to share their stories with fellow citizens—to deny the enduring fiction that atrocities in Vietnam were the work of "a few bad apples." Atrocities like the My Lai massacre had fanned flames of popular opposition to the Vietnam conflict, but political and military leaders continued to insist that such crimes were isolated exceptions to an overall successful policy. By invoking this trope of rotting fruit, the military and that era's "stay the course" punditry had denied accusations of systematic atrocity to avoid political accountability. The argument was that "this insane soldier" or "that malcontent"—secretly worm-ridden to begin with—could not singularly constitute an indictment against policy action.[1] Thus, Winter Soldier 1971 brought together their numbers, qualifications, decorations, and vivid experiences to graphically demonstrate that the excesses of war were a result of a system of war rather than a few malcontents. Honored veterans of action at the point of occupation assembled to verify what each other said in order to convince ordinary people that the realities of atrocity could not be denied and that representatives of U.S. forward-deployed power were carrying out these actions as a structural product of policy. They were largely ignored by mainstream media, but the event had a powerful impact on those who attended.

Twenty-seven-year-old, decorated Navy Lieutenant John Kerry later took his case to Congress, and spoke before the Senate Foreign Relations Committee. Television cameras lined the walls and veterans packed the seats to hear Kerry, in one of the most famous antiwar speeches of the era, describe the Winter Soldier events in 1971.

> [T]he emotions in the room, and the feelings of the men who were reliving their experiences in Vietnam . . . They relived the absolute horror of what this country, in a sense, made them do . . . Someone has to die so that President Nixon won't be—and these are his words—"the first president to lose a war." We are asking Americans to think about that . . . how do you ask a man to be the

last man to die in Vietnam? How do you ask a man to be the last man to die for a mistake?[2]

The same sentiment was heard at Winter Soldier 2008, and the refrain of numbing atrocity reminds us that in modern COIN war, conscience is destroyed. Indeed, it must be if this type of conflict is to continue. This particular casualty of war is incrementally wrought in day-to-day engagement experiences that have been structurally malformed into "atrocity producing situations" (Hedges and Al-Arian 2009)—a demise manufactured by otherwise reasonable sentiments of fear and rage that are put into visceral crisis. The idea that conscience is destroyed seems obvious to anyone who has heard the commonsense notion that war makes one "hard." Upon hearing this suggestion, for example, an Israeli veteran of the first Intifada admonished the author for suggesting the obvious. The thought that conscience *must* be destroyed, however, is a rather more fugitive notion. Like the Israeli veteran, some resist it because one possible next step down that path is a view of war as conspiracy theory in which someone is purposefully wearing down the natural resistance people have to atrocity, possibly with the likes of Dick Cheney, Halliburton, and the military-industrial complex pulling the strings. Obscured by this fear of unlikely agency is the chance that destruction of conscience is an iterative by-product of the very nature of COIN action. Perhaps more compelling is the notion that each new war may be something like a familiar but sui generis order that, once energized, exerts a transformational influence on the societies involved—right down to the disciplining of soldiers' sentiments and self-understandings. For this discipline is a necessary component of the broad-spectrum information adjustment that make crucial popular support for modern military politics possible; and its contradictions, given the political realities of the societies involved, are revealing.

Sahlins's observations on Vietnam demonstrated that the destruction of conscience is not a new development in American misadventure. His 1965 fact-finding trip there, where he interviewed military personnel charged with extracting information from captured insurgents, resulted in his "The Destruction of Conscience in Vietnam" argument (2000[1966], 232). The claim was that the conflict was so polluted by lies and contradictions, that American soldier-"advisors" were losing *their* hearts and minds rather than winning those of the local people. He argued that the Americans were in this process victimizing innocent Vietnamese in order to advertise U.S. military power and political will to the Chinese and that along the way they were committing the very crimes they claimed to be preventing the Chinese from perpetrating. This reality was not something American advisors could afford to face, and they could only deny it by finding and destroying Vietnamese communists—even where they did not exist. To Sahlins, "It is Vietnam's tragedy to have been chosen the battleground for America's stand against the forces of evil"—a contradiction in which the place and the people were irrelevant, and "all the compromises and the self-deceptions of the Americans, and all the brutalization, originate" (2000[1966], 238, 233). Unfortunately, this lesson seems to be yet another thing about which we must have constant vigilance—like the potential for a predictable erosion of our freedoms in the face of fear. We do not seem to learn this lesson once and for all, and the inherited experience of the thoughtful seems no match for the Machiavellian will of the powerful—no matter how intimate their experience with the erosion of conscience.[3] If as a country we cannot learn from our mistakes, we should entertain Sahlins's advice on this topic. We can take the Winter Soldier 2008 gathering as an opportunity to document the extent to which a familiar destruction of conscience can be seen haunting Iraq, so that we might again learn this remedial lesson for the new century.

Once again, a major reason for Winter Soldier 2008 was to answer the intellectual cowardice demonstrated by claims that extralegal violence perpetrated in military occupation was the work of "a few bad apples." This time it was the crimes committed in Abu Ghraib that prompted the gathering, and soldiers had to once again lean on one another for support as they struggled to publicly articulate their testimonies. Again it was an emotional ordeal; again it was largely ignored by the mainstream media; and again the motivation for its participants was (among other things) an unyielding patriotism. A spokesman for the soldiers insisted on this fact, first and often: "We are fighting for the soul of our country. We will demonstrate our patriotism by speaking out with honor and integrity instead of blindly following failed policy. Winter Soldier is a difficult but essential service to our country."[4]

There was much about the Iraq occupation for them to talk about. Veterans' testimonies spoke of U.S. troops raiding home after home in which no insurgent, illegal activity, or evidence was found—while nonetheless terrorizing the families inside. There were also repeated and systematic accounts of U.S. troops kicking, abusing, and randomly assaulting Iraqi prisoners of war whom they were disciplined to always call "detainees" so that Geneva conventions "did not apply." Pettiness was on display when U.S. soldiers recounted being commanded to destroy boxes containing entire archives of birth certificates in Fallujah after a scorched-earth program there in 2004. In first-person narratives of fear and revenge, U.S. troops appeared spraying machine-gun fire into homes after hearing a single shot from somewhere in a village. Careless escalation in the fog of war was demonstrated in narrated episodes in which soldiers recounted shooting farmers working in their fields at night simply because they were out after occupation-mandated curfew, even despite the soldiers' knowing that this was the only time when the farmers could take advantage of the random electricity supply to run their irrigation pumps. Appalling indifference to civilian life was recounted in stories in which U.S. troops were commanded to not stop for pedestrians and to run over anyone or anything in the road as their convoys sped down highways. These narratives allowed the audience to feel something of the rage soldiers felt when improvised explosive devices killed or maimed comrades and friends and to perhaps understand the conditions in which this rage was directed over time toward innocent civilians thought to be supporting the insurgents.

The excesses and atrocities reported during the testimonies reinforced and sharpened hazy images that have otherwise been slow to clear. The world saw the pictures of Abu Ghraib, and the Winter Soldier testimonies reminded us that conditions got much worse. The widespread abuse of "special rendition" was made easier to believe by what was recounted at Winter Soldier 2008, especially after what we know from the Arar case,[5] the grotesque details of which now suggest that what was being attempted was not so much information gathering as perhaps the purposeful fracturing of minds under the watchful eye of military physicians and psychologists. Rape and indiscriminate killing in Iraq, along with the inability or unwillingness to bring the perpetrators to justice, demonstrate a U.S. failure to take responsibility for its military activities in forward deployment. The neoliberal habit of privatizing much of the occupational activity, thereby injecting yet another layer of insulation from responsibility, seems to cement this failure of will. Meanwhile, a beholden mainstream media faithful more to their economic commitments than to their duty as the fourth estate serves as backdrop for many of the testimonies heard, and a constant antagonism for many who need to know.

"No, No Peace of God Be with You . . . "—The Destruction of Conscience and ROE

The posted topics for the Winter Soldier event were instructive about what was most in need of testimony.[6] The fact that "Rules of Engagement," like "Racism and War: The Dehumanization of the Enemy," needed two full testimonial panels shows an awareness of ROE as a key indicator of struggle with soldiers' own consciences as returning combatants, and we should take this signal seriously. Testimony regarding ROE in Winter Soldier 2008 displays revelatory patterns that speak to the realities of COIN war in Iraq, and it indicates processes of patriotism malformed, honor in crisis, and brotherly love twisted in a crucible of the "atrocity-prone situations" that characterize this type of conflict. The mention of ROE was a shifting refrain that pointed repeatedly to the steady degradation of these rules once boots hit the ground. Even in the best of situations, the point was repeatedly made that the very fact of U.S. soldiers' presence in Iraq resulted in the simple and iterative slide of ROE from clear and hard to vague and malleable. Jason Lemieux, a marine sergeant for four years, articulated precise reasons for the importance of ROE:

> Proper rules of engagement serve an important strategic purpose, which is to legitimize military force. By projecting an image of restraint and professionalism, militaries seek to reinforce the idea that they are protecting local residents rather than oppressing them. Not only do these rules undermine any support for any local opposition, they also deflect accusations of occupation and oppression from foreign countries and in some cases the people of the country the military is supposedly serving.

As laws designed to limit the use of force in military situations, ROE constitute a written code of moral behavior—the script of a language of ethical convention that sees its speech in military action. If ROE are this index of moral economy, adherence to them demonstrates support for the mission cause and maintenance of the methods for executing the mission. But in the fog of war and its tendency toward extremes, especially when there is an unclear enemy and unclear objectives, these rules have a way of being slowly pushed out of consideration by fear, the need for defense, and the desire for revenge. The incremental loosening of these rules and muddying of their preexisting clarity is also a communicative act, and what it says is that support of the mission cause and confidence in the methods of executing the mission itself are failing. The resulting change in the conscience of individual soldiers marks not a destruction born of individual intent but rather one that is a necessary consequence of life in COIN occupation.

This evidence still may not convince someone dedicated to our recent brand of spasmodic security, so what is needed is an account of how conscience is destroyed. Examples of this iterative destruction were demonstrated in Winter Soldier 2008 by narratives of the incremental dissolution of ROE over occupational combat time—a fact voiced in the "We changed ROE more than we changed underwear"[7] catchphrase found in the testimonies. One narrative that reflected it in memorable terms was the way that Jason Herd, a veteran from a family with a long tradition of soldiering, matter-of-factly recounted the dissolution of adherence to preconflict ROE. He began by noting that when his unit first showed up in Iraq, most of what it was doing was "walk and greet" missions in safe areas. This was a strategy of winning hearts and minds by walking around, greeting people, and asking whether his unit's soldiers could be of some assistance. In the early part of his deployment there was little else to what he was doing. People were friendly, if wary. Yet the joy at having Saddam gone gave way to the realities of harassment by the American presence as an occupying force, and people's attitudes changed. Even in quiet areas, the effect of the occupation was felt. This was driven home to Herd when an Arabic greeting ("The peace of God be with you") he offered to one elderly woman was met with the harsh response of "No . . . no peace of God be with you." The interpreter explained that her son had been arrested for no good reason, and although he was eventually released, his mistreatment at the hands of coalition forces soured the mother on Americans for the duration. As time went on, Herd pointed out that relationships between Americans and Iraqis continued to deteriorate, often resulting in refusals by Iraqis to even minimally acknowledge the Americans who appeared before them. Estrangement toward the soldiers from the civilian side of the occupation thus began as a self-protective unwillingness to engage at all. Providing the example of how soldiers were supposed to follow the "steps of reaction" procedure[8] for any approaching unknown individual or vehicle, Herd noted that this rule was followed for only a few weeks. After the stresses and contradictions of military occupation (what he called "the absurdity of war") took its toll, he then noted, "You start to deal with the predicament by indiscriminate fire." The realization that he had been irreparably altered by the facts of Iraqi COIN came home to him when he nearly killed an eighty-year-old woman driving her car toward him when she repeatedly failed to stop after being motioned to do so. Later it was made clear to him that with eighty-year-old eyesight she simply could not see him because he was "wearing desert colors standing against a desert colored wall." His assessment of occupation was simple: "We react out of fear for our lives, and we cause complete and utter destruction . . . Not only are we disrupting their lives, we are disrupting our lives as well." This was an immanent astuteness that was heard repeatedly throughout the testimonies.

Clifton Hicks, an army soldier with the First Cavalry in Iraq, reported that on the night of January 21, 2004, a civilian was run over and left for dead by a humvee in front of his. The soldiers in that vehicle had just wanted to go back to base and get some sleep, and that goal had become more important to them than stopping to see if they could do something for the man they had run over. What had started for them as strict adherence to regulations for any such incidents had been loosened and then finally sidelined by the constant anxiety, workload, and fear of simply being in Iraq—an aspect of a precapitalist alienation of the soldier that Kelly, citing Weber, mentions elsewhere in this volume. These factors had worn down on their endurance until Iraqi life was not worth stopping for . . . literally. Hicks's humvee did stop to help the victim, and it took three hours of waiting—out in the open, in the dark, in occupied Iraq—for the issue to be properly addressed through official channels. During this time Hicks's soldiers could not go to sleep, were targets for insurgent snipers, and were terrifyingly aware of their precarious mortality. Their seemingly exemplary behavior proved a starkly brutal rule: the lesson, he pointed out, was that the next time they would not stop either. This is the sad general lesson of the occupation for U.S. soldiers: do not act on your American conscience in Iraq; do not even have one, or you will pay an Iraqi price.

Visibly struggling to avoid certain topics on the advice of event lawyers[9] and trying to forestall shutting down completely, Steve Mortillo's testimony was one that impressed upon the audience that rules in Iraq degenerate over time. In Andaluja, his mission was to conduct "presence patrols" designed to show a military presence as a deterrent to insurgent activity. At first he reported that his squad hardly ever returned fire at anything, and the few incidents that did occur were met with a precisely controlled response. After they started taking casualties, the nature of this response changed, and "suppressive fire" became less precise. Mortillo said this was a process in which "[w]e started getting resentful. There was an understanding that we were going to do what we needed to do in order to make sure everyone else made it home." He also faulted the American practice of raiding houses on the flimsiest of evidence as the one most contributing to Iraqi resentment toward the American soldiers, saying it was an aspect of the conflict that was reproducing itself because "you want so badly to avenge your friends that you get caught up in the cycle of war."

Jesse Hamilton, a former soldier who was against the war but volunteered to train the Iraqi army because he thought he could do some good, worked in Falluja from 2005 to 2006. Chalking the contradictions of Iraqi insurgency up to the quirks of the Iraqis, he explained it as a clash of cultures—but the imagery of his message revealed much. In what may have been a productively misunderstood (but very accurate) example of projection, he suggested: "They have a different culture than we do, different morals . . . Iraqis can be very brutal . . . they treat their people badly." After making these comments about Iraqis that could also easily and accurately be said of Americans, his closing comments resonated with the theme of Winter Soldier: "I just stopped caring." In an effort to make sense of the transformation in himself over time from thinking he could "do some good" into a state of indifference, he suggested, "You can only take so much when people take pot shots at you . . . it begins to wear down on your mind."

An especially clear report of incremental ROE erosion was from Sergio Kochergin, who mentioned simply that "as time went on the rules started getting more lenient." His squad had started out with clear rules stating that a "target" had to be identified as holding a weapon in order to be so declared, after which the soldier would call post for permission to engage. Later this sequence was relaxed to not needing to call post for the engagement decision to take place. Then it became a simpler matter of anyone carrying suspicious items (like a heavy bag, binoculars, or a shovel) being a legitimate target. Finally, it reached the point where it was entirely up to the individual soldier to make the decision to fire based solely on whether the soldier felt threatened. In an insurgency-counterinsurgency conflict, one is forced to wonder whether *anyone* ever feels anything but threatened. Threat and fear mutually perpetuate until the malformed end of this path—the darkness of conscience destroyed—was the decision to leave a "drop weapon" when assessing the results of a weapons-fire incident that might leave the legitimacy of the kill open to interpretation.[10]

Jason Washburn's statements about ROE reconfirm their moving target status in Iraq. Saying, "ROE changed a lot . . . it seemed like every time we turned around the ROE were changing," he mentioned that his squad had been told that the changes depended on the climate of the area and the threat level; the higher the threat, the more viciously they were permitted to respond. Uncompromising viciousness soon became the norm, he reported, indicating that he was involved in or witnessed the physical harassment of locals, the careless shooting of a woman who was bringing them food, and the shooting of taxi drivers for driving. This dangerous lack of clarity regarding ROE guaranteed a lessened adherence even to the rules that were enunciated and thereby further qualified Iraq as a truly modern war—the defining quality of which seems to be that radically more civilians than military personnel die in its unfolding.

In order to drive home the structural element of these occurrences, there is perhaps no better way than to recite Vincent Emanuelle's repeated mantra by way of clarification after recounting multiple, egregious examples. He and others struggled to state, restate, and then restate again that "This was not an isolated incident, and these things took place over the entire course of my deployment."

The testimony continued, and evidence mounted. As the consequences of COIN warfare for its involved societies began to take shape in the by-product, much of the focus was on atrocities seen and committed. This is to say that early ROE not followed by way of later flexibility was such a powerful component to the narratives that one wonders at its decision-making mechanics. Much recent investigation into the processes regarding moral decision making extends what we may have already suspected after noting the Milgram and Stanford prison experiments. A good guess is that people are not deliberative when faced with a moral choice unless they (1) immediately recognize it as a moral choice and (2) have the time to explicitly consider its implications.[11] Without these two conditions being met, decisions are made where emotion and context exert determining effects. In such situations, factors like copying leadership behavior and the impulse to act based on immediate sentiments most often predominate. In extreme situations like military occupation, the clear delineation between "us" and "them" gets taken up in the sentiments of fear and revenge to result in a very hostile environment for ethical decision making, which is why ROE were developed in the first place. Few people immediately visible to the ordinary soldier are recognizably guilty of outright action against American troops, so the next degree of abstraction comes into play. On this next level all Iraqis are collaborators and the soldiers are occupiers, both guilty in the eyes of the other. Atrocity, aggression, and mindless violence then accompany military action, and they are arranged on a slope canted toward extremes. We have seen through soldiers' testimony that ROE, the written equivalent of a code of moral conduct and a reflection of social ethics, tend to give way in the face of the situations necessitated by military occupation. A presence patrol cannot remain merely a presence patrol when its audience is suffering a thousand associated, incremental infringements on their lives. "Presence" mutates into unwelcome harassment after a time and then becomes a malformed aggression as occupation wears on. Ethical will in leadership continues to fail, and ROE grow more amorphous. In the logic of COIN, the "fog" of war has a predictable schedule.

This example is a very powerful part of what Clausewitz (2007) meant when he said that "war tends to extremes," but this extreme may hide more nefarious detail. In Iraq conscience must be destroyed for the fiction of justification in occupation, neocolonialism, and unwarranted aggression to take place. This is work for a true master of suspicion to chew on in order to fully illuminate the political economic elements of the situation, but it seems clear that any assistance provided in legitimizing COIN wars—whether it is in the form of intellectually and morally feeble legal opinions from Professor Yoo or the "shoot from the hip" clichés from the Bush-Cheney-Rumsfeld clique days—stems from a failure to take the reality of COIN war seriously.

Global Destruction—The Dog of War in Iraq

Another aspect of how conscience is destroyed is geographically removed but in direct line of sight to Iraq. COIN wars are now global, each one a kind of miniature world war in terms of its potential audience. A massive media operation must be mounted to support the conflict, otherwise the various voices of conscience, moderation, and responsibility dilute support for the war effort. One part of this military-media endeavor must have the effect of destroying conscience in the United States so that COIN warfare can occur in Iraq. We are reminded that the French hit upon the term "global war on terror" first, and for similar domestic sentiment manipulation purposes. Yet, craven media notwithstanding, the varied and heterogeneously disciplined U.S. population is also not so uniformly numbed. While the mainstream feeds a steady stream of soporific misdirection packaged as "necessary" and "reality," there seems still to be too much conscience left—although it too can be strangely malformed in expression.

The disillusionment that washed over the U.S. popular audience when reports of Abu Ghraib came out was a serious blow to overall popular support. The sense of horror and disgust at these crimes was insufficient to shock Americans from their stupor, but it showed signs that the great wall of American (self)censorship was failing. Abu Ghraib's arbitrary atrocities filtering through the military-media firewall piled up, and it was perhaps indicative of the state of our society that the next crack in the wall was an atrocity made for YouTube. The workings of this disillusionment (symbolically at least) were seen in a short video that was something like a cross between LOLcats and Faces of Death, with the hypercuteness of small animals and the senseless violence of shock and awe. The video appeared on the Internet in the first week of March 2008, and it showed a young U.S. Marine killing a puppy. It echoed a story (possibly fiction)[12] from a former soldier in Vietnam of how his comrades—who had witnessed, perpetrated, and endured all manner of human violence—reacted with ostracizing disgust at how one of them, as a bored young man numbed by war, detonated a claymore mine after strapping a small dog to it . . . as a joke. His fellows' disgust at him, and subsequent avoidance of him, was a sign of his having gone too far.

Here was a pattern worthy of note. This bit of conscience had not been destroyed, but it was malformed. It was an example that gave hope by suggesting the possibility that we were not lost but damned us further by showing that Iraqi pain, suffering, and death were less shocking in American eyes than the death of a dog. The comparison is understandably infuriating. The epitome of innocence cannot be much better symbolized than by the image of a puppy, held by the scruff of its neck as if by its mother, physiologically calmed by the nature of the grasp. Having it then flung over a cliff by a young U.S. Marine as a joke to be filmed is an act charged with meaning. The pornography of violence that this represents has to do with the marine's demonstration of himself as hard. He seems to demonstrate that he is so prepared for the horrors of war, so hardened to killing, that he can kill innocence itself. Other marines present at the performance judged this act mean, but got the joke. The YouTube audience suffered something like shock and awe that one of "the good guys" could be so horrible, and the response was almost unanimously negative[13]—vocal to the point of being shrill, with even the Marine Corps investigating. One wonders how they dealt with the matter, for something about the American response to this video hinted at a dangerous confusion of priorities.

Why was it that the video of the killing of a small dog generated a more immediate, unquestioning, and unified revulsion among Americans than was the case with the torturing and killing of Iraqi civilians? The short answer must have been that the action was very meaningful in a way that clashed with the process of war in Iraq—like the Vietnam veteran ashamed of having gone too far in killing a puppy. Symbolically, its significance was in the fact that, minor as it was, it caused a general furor in the Marine Corps and across the country. This was because it drove home the "Madison Avenue by other means" (Sahlins 2000[1966]) nature of the Iraq War, and the fundamental contrivance its political argument of images revealed came dangerously close to reminding a somnambulant American public that Iraq and Iraqis had nothing to do with 9/11 or al-Qaeda. Believing that Iraq has weapons of mass destruction and al-Qaeda was going to follow soldiers home from Iraq if the U.S. left was something that most Americans seemed willing to lie to themselves about and suffer the consequences—although most of the immediate suffering was Iraqi. But the senseless killing of a cute little puppy for display was akin to shooting mom and napalming the apple pie. That this archetypal image of injustice was associated with the Iraq occupation connected U.S. military behavior in Iraq with the notion of heinous crime, and the video became a full frontal assault on the fabric of the Global War on Terror fiction. It tore a hole in the notion that America and its soldiers were always on the side of right, and for the right reasons.[14]

Note again the persistent malformation of conscience here, however. It was not the actual heinous crimes that shocked the conscience. Rather, the death, torture, and human suffering wrought by the U.S. occupation and its unavoidable tendencies toward extremes were obscured, while the dog's horrible demise was not. Its brutal death indexed the other killing in a theater that had been ignored by the American public. Once torn, the propaganda fabric was compromised. The reality of this more important killing of Iraqi noncombatants and the Hollywood quality of the puppy killing was a recapitulation of the truth of the U.S. Iraq presence: the United States was once again involved in a forward-deployed, neoimperial enterprise in which Americans kill and terrorize a people in order to demonstrate to terrorists (who were not there before) that they should not threaten "us"—the advertisement function of blood. It amounted to the divination of secret underworld realities of neoliberal war by way of animal sacrifice.

Americans know what occupation is down deep in their historical psyche. When they look at the camera obscura of the Iraqi present, they see something familiar in the act of fighting for freedoms and self-determination against an occupying force—and it causes dissonance to resist this recognition. U.S. revolutionary Thomas Paine, writing in 1776 when Americans were defending their homeland against an occupying force, said, "These are the times that try men's souls. The summer soldier and sunshine patriot will, in this crisis, shrink from the service of his country; but he that stands it now, deserves the love and thanks of man and woman."

The sentiments of courage and sacrifice found herein naturally alight on those Iraqis who find the occupation unbearable, and it takes a willing ignorance to not notice how the nature of COIN and occupation makes these sentiments immediately useful to the cause of resistance. Perhaps the similarity of Iraqis who find the occupation unbearable to other courageous, patriotic citizens can be instructive. The Winter Soldiers Paine was calling on to endure the hardships of fighting for independence have much in common with the Winter Soldiers of the present, who are fighting against the dangers of the United States' own imperial impulse. George Washington famously refused to entertain the idea that he could become monarch of the new United States on the logic that he "did not fight this war against George the third in order to become George the first;" but George the forty-third is not so sure of this historical lesson. Even President Obama is reported to be packing his new Pentagon with cheerleaders of COIN convinced of its political utility, so the struggle against Paine's "sunshine patriots" will likely continue. To be sure, this fight is in no way straightforward. The enemy in this case is us, and it calls upon both an intellectual and passionate patriotism that makes the modern soldier's fight all the more difficult in that it is a struggle for American souls.

"Charlie Mike": Continuing and Conclusions

Sustaining a counterproductive, disastrous occupation in Iraq has shown all indications of being a failure. Once Iraqis stopped welcoming the United States and thanking us for deposing Saddam (if they ever did) and started an insurgency answered by COIN techniques, America lost. Even if "we" win, America loses because it will have caused the country to lose too much of itself in order to win. The military is predisposed toward continuing its mission and will do so as a matter of honor until given the order to cease—were things any other way, it would not be a professional military. And indeed, the soldiers participating in Winter Soldier invoked "charlie mike" ("continue mission") as the order given from above whenever something happened that needed addressing, no matter how violent. Yet conscience must be destroyed by the nature of occupation and COIN. Vietnam, Northern Ireland, Algiers, and Iraq provide the evidence for this claim, and there is an inverse relation between the integrity of conscience and the length of time with boots on the ground. The stark honesty from these soldiers' testimonials shows this, as does the general fog of malaise and apathy that characterizes the American public. So stark is this dissonance that events such as the YouTube puppy killing stand out as brute reminders of the reality of an occupation where "good" Americans fighting "evil" are becoming evil and destroying the good around them, and perhaps in them.

Other signs of an ethical devastation closer to home were also reported at Winter Soldier 2008. Mr. and Mrs. Lucey, whose son Jeffrey returned from Iraq and spiraled away into an abyss of self-annihilating depression, were sensitive to this destruction of conscience. After spending the last weeks of his life with a flashlight at night looking for camel spiders he was sure he heard scurrying around his room, he left a suicide note saying, "I am truly embarrassed of the man I have become" His mother could only conclude after the fact that "his spirit died somewhere in Iraq . . . [from] . . . a cancer that ravaged his soul."[15]

Anthropology and COIN: Rules of Engagement

In the context of continuing violence in occupied Iraq, the U.S. military has taken a newfound interest in culture and ethnography. Their hope is to revitalize COIN theory and practice by getting anthropologists to produce knowledge of the cultural terrain. Intended use of this knowledge for tactical purposes has occurred simultaneously with the emergence in anthropology of global war and governance as objects of serious ethnographic and theoretical interrogation. Some scholars are of the opinion that a middle ground can be reached where anthropology can serve America in this tactical fashion—perhaps by facilitating the in-country aspects of policy decisions. The prevailing evidence suggests that this is shortsighted, misguided, and, most of all, intellectually timid. As data that have been brought to bare on this question mount, we can only conclude that we "took our marbles and went home" after World War II for very good reasons (see Yans-McLaughlin 1986, 214, and the introduction to this volume). When it became clear that the number and proportion of civilian deaths in the execution of COIN warfare would inescapably put us on "the wrong side" if we were to assist in military means or ends—no matter what side of the war we were on—we collectively found a position as a check against the careless involvement in such a war. Nuclear fire, colonial wars, and the imperatives of a military-industrial thirst have given us enough ethnographic and other material to have learned this lesson for all time, but we do not appear to have done so.

Anthropologists are again looking for a professional and scholarly response to an unnecessary war while looking for a position on war more generally—even though we already have one where we voted with our feet, our hearts, and our minds. We exercise our abilities and training to further understand contemporary war, American power, and the logics of domestic and international security. We seek an ethnographic understanding of global responses to recent use of U.S. military action. We read military theory as social theory and try to understand why all of a sudden the military wants our expertise in studying culture in the face of insurgency. These are all good ends, to be sure. But we have already been taught many of these lessons; and while we always learn new things each time we look, it seems we know enough to act in this matter. The classroom may be new, and the trappings may be different, but the lesson must strike us as familiar. By now we should have developed an acute allergy to the temptation to contribute anything other than criticism of the most incisive kind to this matrix of neoimperial war; for our only reasonable contribution if we want to avoid complicity is at the level of strategy. And strategically, it has become anthropologically clear that such a war should not be waged. COIN war is incompatible with liberal democratic values of justice and responsibility. For the inevitable contradiction between tactical necessity and liberal values must end in the fatal erosion of one. To fail in this strategic responsibility is to, however unwittingly, be "whored by our commitment" where we can only lose ourselves in Iraq and lose the war—whatever the military outcome (Sahlins 2000[1966]).

Winter Soldier testimonies provide additional ethnographic insight into this from the human point of imperial occupation, and our disciplinary focus on the human beings involved provides an inescapable reason to take a clear position on COIN. Those brave men and women who testified are the Winter Soldiers in this crisis, and they refuse to shrink away from service to their country now—although it means facing up to the terrifying shadow in themselves and being called traitors by lesser men and women. Having learned their lesson the hard way, most no longer serve their country tactically. Now they are critics, checking strategy concocted by intellectually uncourageous leaders. They may not get the love and thanks that Thomas Paine said they should—and we certainly will not. But we can do no less than them.

: : NOTES : :

1. It would not be the last such attempt to hijack the notion of "preexisting condition" as a money-saving insurance strategy, as many traumatized soldiers were to learn to their great detriment. See Priest and Hull's "The Other Walter Reed" exposè series, http://www.washingtonpost.com/wp-srv/nation/walter-reed/index.html, and many other similar inquiries.

2. John Kerry, testifying on April 22, 1971; see Record: BC0019.10, Pacifica Radio Archive, Washington Report, no. 10.

3. Iraq is not exactly Vietnam, but some of the similarities are outweighing the differences these days; and a serious comparison of these two tokens of an imperial behavior type must be made despite their differences. A firm and noble conviction that America is a "good" country on the side of right is no excuse for willful ignorance in light of the obvious errors of our imperial ways. Sahlins reminded us of the threat to our collective and individual consciences that emerged from committing, or having allowed, acts of torture/aggressive interrogation in Vietnam. Something very similar to that threat endures today because of our Global War on Terror activities, and we are again fighting in a foreign country not because of anything they did to us. We are again allowing fear mongering foisted upon us to motivate us; again our war fighting is neither declared nor justified by international consensus; again the conflict is causing massive civilian casualties compared with military casualties; and once again the primary goal of the conflict is something more akin to Madison Avenue rather than diplomacy and statecraft. This time there is more of an overt resource manipulation that factors largely into the interests of the Wall Street–neoconservative axis; and there is also a much more nefarious façade of religious clash masking the event's other political mechanics.

4. Iraq Veterans against the War, http://www.ivaw.org.

5. See CBC News, "In Depth: Maher Arar-Timeline." http://www.cbc.ca/news/background/arar/.

6. Panels included "Rules of Engagement (Part One)," "The Crisis in Veterans' Healthcare," "Corporate Pillaging and Military Contractors," "Rules of Engagement (Part Two)," "Divide to Conquer—Gender and Sexuality in the Military," "Racism and War—The Dehumanization of the Enemy (Part One)," "Racism and War—The Dehumanization of the Enemy (Part Two)," "The Cost of War in Iraq and Afghanistan," "The Cost of the War at Home," "The Breakdown of the Military," and "The Future of GI Resistance."

7. Sergeant Adam Kokesh, Marine Civil Affairs Battalion. Winter Soldier 2008 testimony.

8. The required steps are commonly thought to be a verbal challenge, a second verbal challenge, a third verbal challenge with warning shot, and finally a shot for effect at center of mass.

9. Presumably this was to avoid legal self-incrimination.

10. See Bennett, this volume, for a description of these circumstances.

11. Examples are the work of Professors Treviño and Nelson (2003) and Forsyth (2003), although these are established positions in social and organizational psychology.

12. Tim O'Brien, who writes fiction that is more than a little autobiographical, reports this story in his 1990 novel, *The Things They Carried* (1998 [1990]).

13. Occasionally, however, a response was concerned with the need to work out a logical apology for this event.

14. Still, it is perhaps interesting that this terrible little video indicates something not entirely damning. It seems to suggest that the destruction of conscience necessitated by the Iraq military-political matrix has its limits in that it cannot readily extend to something so fundamental that it shocks the core of homefront conscience too openly—breathless attempts of Fox Entertainment notwithstanding.

15. His parents asked the question of whether post-traumatic stress disorder was a mental problem or whether it was a normal reaction to a completely abnormal situation where all conventions of sociality are burnt away.

22

No Better Friend, No Worse Enemy

History, Memory, and the Conscience of a Marine

:: CHRISTOPHER T. NELSON ::

So hope for a great sea-change
On the far side of revenge.
Believe that a further shore
Is reachable from here.
Believe in miracles
And cures and healing wells.

Seamus Heaney, *The Cure at Troy*

Over the winter holiday in 2007, I immersed myself in the books, articles, and films that I hoped would help me to prepare for a class on the anthropology of war.[1] Apart from ethnographies of conflict and violence, I concentrated on books concerned with the wars in Iraq and Afghanistan. I was particularly interested in those written and read by the soldiers and Marines who fought there.[2] Many of the texts were new to me: critical studies by Thomas Ricks (2006), Jeremy Scahill (2007), Dave Grossman (1998), and T. X. Hammes (2007); popular accounts by Bing West (2005) and Marcus Luttrell and Patrick Robinson (2008); doctrinal proposals by David Petraeus (see U.S. Army/Marine Corps 2007) and John Nagl (2005). However, among the books that were read and discussed by the soldiers themselves were many that had been extremely familiar to me when I was a Marine. Bernard Fall's *Street without Joy* and *Hell in a Very Small Place,* Robert Taber's *War of the Flea,* Mao Zedong's

On Guerilla Warfare, the *Marine Corps Small Wars Manual.* Reading books
as different Jonathan Shay's remarkable and provocative *Achilles in Vietnam*
and Colby Buzzell's *My War: Killing Time in Iraq* inspired me to return to
the classics as well, and I spent a long weekend caught up in Marcus Aurelius,
Xenophon, and Homer. After more than two decades, the books that I read
were quite different from those that I remembered. However, Odysseus was
still the compelling figure that I once admired so much. Of course, in the years
since I first read the Odyssey, I had not completely forgotten him. I met him
in Horkheimer and Adorno's *Dialectic of Enlightenment,* Seamus Heaney's *The
Cure at Troy,* and Barry Unsworth's *The Song of Kings.* Still, it was a real pleasure to discover him again in the pages of Homer's poem.

I found myself focusing less on the cunning and persuasive Odysseus than
on the aging and melancholy warrior. I particularly felt his sadness and despair as I read once again of his visit to the Kingdom of the Dead. Determined
to return to Ithaca, Odysseus offered a sacrifice to summon the seer Tiresius,
hoping to enlist his aid and advice. Tiresius responded, but he was also joined
by the spirits of Odysseus's companions slain nearly a decade earlier before the
walls of Troy. I paused as I read this, memories of my own comrades returning
to me like the specters that greeted Odysseus. Unlike Odysseus, who met the
shades of Agamemnon, Ajax, and Achilles, I felt as if I could also see my own
younger self among the remembered images of my old friends and Marines.
If that young Marine lieutenant were to see me as I am now, I suppose that I
would appear to be the ghost—bereft of arms and stripped of command. And
yet, I also feel a real measure of surprise as I recall him.

I do not mean to say that I have otherwise forgotten about the past. The
narrative that describes the path that leads from where I began to where I am
today is always with me. Childhood in an industrial town in western Pennsylvania, an ROTC scholarship to a state university, service in the Marines,
graduate school and fieldwork, teaching and research at a university. However,
remembrance—the deep and critical act of memory that both hurls me back
to a moment in the past and draws that moment forward into the present—
interrupts this comfortable notion of a personal history. Brought face-to-face
with the man I once was, with the things that I once did, I am compelled to
ask, Was that truly me? If I am who I think myself to be, how should I understand the person who was the author of those actions in the past? Must the
man that I am today be called to account for the man that I once was?

Paul Ricoeur wrote that he found great possibility in the feeling of astonishment that a person experiences when they truly remember the past. For
Ricoeur, surprise is more than a simple recognition of temporal distance, of
details that have become obscured with the passage of time. It speaks to a ruth-

less critique of the self. Remembrance subjects the past to the ethical judgment of the present, requires that we accept responsibility for our past actions and commit ourselves to making right the wrongs that we have caused. Because the feeling of astonishment is also an index of the moral development of the remembering actor, Ricoeur (2006) viewed this experience with hope. Perhaps he was right.

Not all acts of memory yield this deep and critical reflection. Often the image that we recall simply evokes the pleasure of recognition. It is reminiscence without remembrance, as memory is diverted to comfortable paths and predictable forms or interrupted by new experiences. In this way, memories of my time in the Marines often return to me unbidden, stirred by a newspaper headline, a television commercial, the glimpse of a uniform across a campus quadrangle. Each an opportunity for reflection, a moment that is often lost to the flow of everyday life.

There is, however, an obligation to critical remembrance that I am reminded of whenever I meet an old friend from the Marines. As our conversation draws to a close, one or the other of us will inevitably say, "Semper Fi." This is the motto of the Marine Corps: Semper Fidelis, or "always faithful." Faithful to the Constitution, faithful to the example and the judgment of every Marine who ever marched to the colors, faithful to your comrades. It is spoken with pride and with resignation and with anger and with disgust. It acknowledges many things, from a burden to be borne to an obligation neglected. It is also a pledge to remember.

I have often reflected on the choice of this phrase as the motto of the Marine Corps. However, as I prepared for class, I came across references to a newer motto, one that seems to be much more grounded in the conditions of our current wars: No Better Friend, No Worse Enemy. I had first learned of this phrase several years before in newspaper accounts of an Article 32 investigation[3] into the actions of Marine Lieutenant Ilario Pantano. As one might expect from its title, it also figures prominently in Pantano's autobiography *Warlord: No Better Friend, No Worse Enemy,* which I read as I was thinking about ways to discuss killing in combat and war crimes with my students.

In April 2004, Pantano and the Marines of his platoon conducted a raid on a house near Baghdad. Two Iraqi men captured at the site were interrogated by Marine intelligence operators and released. Pantano again detained them and, with gestures and fragmentary Arabic, ordered them to search their car, then to search it once more. During the second search, Pantano testified that the two men stepped toward him in a threatening way. Here is Pantano's own account—in intimate and dramatic detail. In many ways, it resonates with popular war films, novels, and memoirs of the post-Vietnam years. At the same time, it is dependent on passive locutions and without the clear indexicality of the personal pronouns that would link the narrator with the remembered actor:

"Kuff! Stop!"

Can the others see this? Ten meters down the broken gravel road in each direction, Doc Gobles and Coburn are guarding a narrow, defensive perimeter.

A beat of time . . . one second, half that . . . a microsecond. Freezing hot adrenaline, A rifle is firing.

The butt of the M-16 is snugged against a shoulder stiffened by dried sweat and fear. The salt stains on the flak jacket trace a history like the tree rings of war. A new ring is forming.

The selector switch is on burst. Each press of the trigger sends three metal-jacketed 5.56 mm bullets slashing into flesh. They are close. Real close. The bullets go right through the men into the car, into the trees. Into Iraq.

More a continuous blast than a drumbeat as the rifle pounds. A shower of brass shell casings glints in the fading daylight.

The butt thuds, hollow now against the stained jacket. Empty mag.

Fuck.

The index finger, the only bare skin on the gloved right hand, hits the button to drop the empty magazine while the left deftly snatches a new one from a pouch on the web gear. The fresh magazine with twenty-eight more rounds slams home. The bolt releases, driving a round into the chamber. More three round bursts.

Seconds later the weapon is empty, quickly reloaded and the muzzle begins to sweep for new threats. The men are twisted, their bodies finally still. Blood from their wounds smears down the car's white doors and soaks into the dry mud.

A radio squawks, static, words and numbers . . . another IED on Tampa. Another bomb. How many today?

"Doc, Coburn. Mount up. IED." (Pantano 2007)

Pantano's carefully worded account fails to mention that he hastily scrawled "No Better Friend, No Worse Enemy" in English on a piece of cardboard and left it on the wrecked car in that ruined street. An annotation to the mute bodies of the dead.

Beyond its immediate political and moral references, the account of Pantano's actions has an almost mythic dimension to it, recognizable to both students of military history and aficionados of war films and novels. He is the son of divorced immigrant parents, raised on the edge of poverty in Hell's Kitchen.

He was a respected former Marine Sergeant, a veteran of the first Gulf War, a Marine sniper. He is also an alumnus of Horace Mann, a well-known Manhattan prep school, and a former Goldman Sachs trader and media producer, inspired by 9/11 to return to the Marine Corps as an officer. Pantano had been in command of his platoon for only about three months and in Iraq for less than a month when the killings occurred. The incident was reported by his own platoon sergeant, Sergeant Daniel Coburn, a Marine regularly described as a weak and ineffective leader. The relationship between lieutenant and sergeant, their respective characters, the killings, and the betrayal are classic tropes: you need look no further than Jeff Bennett's paper in this volume to find resonances in his account of U.S. Army sniper Evan Vila's trial.

I could go on to describe Pantano as an exemplar of the U.S. military in Iraq—a man like any other man, put into an untenable position, his conscience compromised by the demands and contradictions of his mission. We might also let this shooting stand for the relationship between colonizer and colonized in Iraq. I could portray him as a young, inexperienced leader overwhelmed by fear and responsibility, operating with inadequate guidance and vague rules of engagement. I could as easily describe him as a hard man, a seasoned combat Marine who did what had to be done. It might also be useful to consider the formal construction of his text more closely, to think about a narrative organization in which chapters drawn from court transcripts alternate with those based entirely on Pantano's remembrances. However, for now, I am more interested in the macabre sign that he posted on the dead men's car. "No Better Friend, No Worse Enemy." Why these words at this moment? To whom is this message addressed?

The phrase was well-known throughout the Marine Corps of the early 2000s. In fact, it served as the motto of the First Marine Division under the command of General James Mattis. At the time of the shooting, Pantano's battalion was assigned to Mattis's division. More than twenty years ago, I served in the First Marine Division myself. If the division had a motto then, I do not remember what it was. We never operated as a division—no Marine unit had since Vietnam—and everyone I knew identified much more closely with their battalion and their regiment. The closest thing that I can remember to a motto was represented on the division's insignia. Although it was no longer worn on uniforms, the insignia was a red numeral "1" set on a blue diamond-shaped field. The red "1" was surrounded by the stars of the Southern Cross, and the inscription "Guadalcanal" was written vertically along its length. This detail had its own personal significance for me since two of my uncles fought with the Marines on Guadalcanal. There is always a debt to the past.

Popular writers as diverse as Thomas Ricks (2006) and Bing West (2005)

have described Mattis as the greatest living Marine combat officer, the finest
Marine of his generation. He commanded a battalion in the first Gulf War, a
brigade and task force in Afghanistan, and the First Marine Division in the
invasion and occupation of Iraq. He is also known to be deeply interested in
history. In fact, his motto is adapted from Lucius Cornelius Sulla's epitaph,
rendered in my old copy of Plutarch as "No friend ever surpassed him in kind-
ness; no enemy in mischief" (Plutarch 1916, 415). A strange choice perhaps
for a general in the service of this republic, the words of a consul who led his
army into Rome, establishing the precedent invoked by Julius Caesar when he
crossed the Rubicon.

And yet, as any conscientious student of history and politics would recognize, Sulla provides a critical example of leadership for Machiavelli, that most
influential and perhaps elusive of political theorists. In *The Art of War,* Machiavelli (2001 [1521]) writes of Sulla's cunning in deceiving both his enemies
and allies, manipulating each to accomplish his objectives. Plutarch's citation
of Carbo grounds this assessment of Sulla in a metaphor familiar to readers
of *The Prince:* "in making war on the fox and lion in Sulla, [I] was more an-
noyed by the fox" (Plutarch 1916). Machiavelli brings these images together,
first in his reference to Achilles' tutor, Chiron the centaur—both man and
beast, capable like his kin of wildness and ferocity, yet a gentle, refined being
who schools Achilles in the arts. That which is beast for Machiavelli is, like
Sulla, both lion and fox: bold and clever, the strengths of one supplementing
the weaknesses of the other. We have then an image of a leader who is the master of his times—refined and compassionate if the situation allows it; cunning
and brutal if conditions demand it (Machiavelli 2008 [1513]).

"No Better Friend, No Worse Enemy" is indeed a powerful sign. It is Mattis's commander's guidance, the strategic principle by which he expects his
Marines to act. It is an index of his philosophical and ethical commitments.
It is also a practical example of his understanding of historical practices—a
pragmatic, thoughtful, and reflexive leader transforming the examples of the
past in order to meet the demands of the present.

Marines have a kind of obsession with the past. Here is Mattis again, cited
in Ricks's *Fiasco:*

> For all the "4ᵗʰ Generation of War" intellectuals running around today saying
> that the nature of war has fundamentally changed, the tactics are wholly new,
> etc., I must respectfully say, "Not really": Alexander the Great would not
> now be in the least bit perplexed by the enemy that we face right now in
> Iraq, and our leaders going into this fight do their troops a disservice by not
> studying—studying, vice just reading—the men who have gone before us. We

have been fighting on this planet for 5000 years and we should take advantage of their experiences. "Winging it" and filling body bags as we sort out what works reminds us of the moral dictates and the cost of incompetence in our profession. (Ricks 2006, 317)

Of course, Marine training is more than a history seminar. In fact, it is something very different. Marines are fond of the maxim, "be technically and tactically proficient," and this commitment to developing the knowledge and skill necessary for their profession begins early in training. A host of disciplinary practices also encourages Marines to be obedient, aggressive, and resourceful.[4] They are taught to get the job done and to put the welfare of their comrades before their own. And they learn to kill.[5] At the same time, young Marines are also reminded of their obligation to the Constitution of the United States and their duty to uphold the law—from the law of war to the detailed instructions that they receive from their leaders. They also find themselves in an environment in which formal religiosity—particularly Christianity—is treated favorably. While it is undoubtedly true that far less emphasis is placed on ethics and morals than on other training, Marines are still expected to draw upon these lessons in making decisions under fire.[6] Taking into account the earlier lives of the Marines, it also serves to ensure a kind of deep ambivalence and sense of contradiction. Killing is valorized and routinized; at the same time it is subject to a host of qualifications and regulations, changing and contradictory. Stitching together man and beast is a difficult task.[7]

It is clear that the disciplinary construction of a soldier is complex and carried out at many levels. Integral to this transformation of the subject—of civilian into Marine—is an intense and affective appropriation of the past, one that is accomplished across an enormous variety of practices ranging from the habitual to the contemplative. It would be simplistic to believe that the social being that the Marine was before training began was either fully reduced or repressed, replaced by a kind of martial automaton. Instead, the Marine is offered access to a different history, a different genealogy, one that is superior to the one to which he already belongs.

This process is framed by a kind of spatiotemporal separation, a severing of old ties and a suppression of established quotidian relationships and practices that create an opportunity to move into the past while the Marine is also being prepared for the future. At first, the recruit or the candidate for commissioning is opened to the history of the Marine Corps itself. The newly reorganized bodily hexis—modes of dress and movement—is grounded in historical lessons that link this expressiveness to other images of the past. Voice, posture, gait, facial expressions, articles of clothing, and manner of dress are not simply reconfigured but linked to historical examples. Some references are indefinite. Boots are laced left over right, a belt can only extend a specific length beyond the buckle, those in authority speak in a certain way because, they are told, that is the way that Marines have always done it. Other historical references are quite specific. Recruits are taught that members of the Fifth and Sixth Marine Regiments wear the fourragère, a braided cord wrapped around the left shoulder, because those regiments were awarded the French Croix de Guerre for bravery during World War I. Finally, some are oddly ambiguous. Marines learn that stories claiming that the scarlet stripe that trims the dress trousers of commissioned and noncommissioned officers symbolizes the blood shed in the battle of Chapultepec are apocryphal; however, the effect of this disclaimer still creates a relationship between uniform ornamentation and courage in combat.

Even beyond deportment and bodily adornment, references to the past are ubiquitous. Barracks and office walls are covered in posters, photographs, and paintings; streets and buildings are named after famous Marines and decisive battles. Unit signs and banners are marked with lists of the engagements in which the organization distinguished itself—from St-Michel to Fallujah, analogous to the ribbons and medals worn by individual Marines. The physical space of a training base is itself a manifold of representations of Marine Corps history—dotted with the hulks of tanks, amtracks, and aircraft, the statues of a century or more of leaders.

When I was a lieutenant, a hike through the woods at The Basic School[8] would lead you through a long abandoned network of trenches, still marked with broken and rusted strands of barbed wire, to mock-ups of World War II amphibious landing craft and cargo nets, past an empty clearing that was designated the "Asian Ville"—perhaps Vietnam—and to a newly completed Soviet-style system of barriers and fortifications. My company commander at Officer Candidates School told us that when he was a candidate, he was given a photograph of a Marine Lieutenant who had been posthumously awarded the Medal of Honor. The solemn black and white photograph gazed at him from the door of his locker, an exemplar of Marine leadership and yet another judge of his own efforts. Recruits and candidates running on sandy trails and asphalt roads in Parris Island or Quantico or San Diego sing "Give Me That Old Marine Corps Spirit," enumerating old battles and famous Marines to the tune of "Give Me That Old Time Religion." Appropriation of the hymn is both ironic and powerful. Like a convert to a new faith, recruits proclaim their commitment to the self-transformation necessary to be a part of the lineage that they both narrate and enact.

The past is also encountered in what we might more formally recognize as history. Officers and enlisted Marines at every level study military history in quiet classrooms, squad bays, tree-lined clearings, and crowded shipboard berthing. These lessons extend beyond Marine Corps history as such—the first commandant's reading list issued by General Alfred Gray in 1998 (and revised by subsequent commandants) is made up of scholarly and popular studies in military history and tactics, divided into groups of those thought to be appropriate for each rank (Trainor 1989). These graphic representations are not limited to print media: they extend to films and music as well. The films *Breaker Morant* and *Twelve O'Clock High* were part of my training at the Basic School; in his novel *Jarhead,* Anthony Swofford gives a bitterly humorous portrayal of the consumption of what he calls "war porn." Quite aware that the films themselves might have been created as antiwar texts, Swofford and his fellow Marines literally devoured films like *Apocalypse Now* and *Platoon* with a kind of fierce exuberance.[9]

The study of history also extends to other educational genres: map studies, staff rides, and field exercises. At a certain point, the boundaries become blurred. One moves easily from reading Guderian's account of the blitzkrieg to studying Napoleon's Iberian campaign to practicing the interception of a North Korean armored assault into South Korea. It is not critical history as such but an aggressive and directed survey of material that one might be able to add to one's own repertoire of knowledge and practices. The reader—a young corporal with Steven Pressman's *Gates of Fire,*[10] a lieutenant with Rommel's *Attacks,* a lieutenant colonel with Aurileus's *Meditations*—searches for what will be useful to him. This produces a strange engagement with the past. Napoleon's battalion carré, Lewis Puller's pursuit of Sandino, Xenophon's assumption of command, Galula's morphology of reactionary warfare against decolonization are all fair game, regardless of their ostensive situation. Marines relentlessly rummage through the historical record, paying little heed to the ideological or political context from which the lessons were drawn. What is certain is that this appropriative reading assumes that the reader, the subject, is already capable of mastering the lesson itself. Mattis's citation of Alexander the Great is quite clear on this. He does not write wistfully about Alexander's generalship; instead, he aligns himself with Alexander, rather than with his less capable (presumably U. S. Army) colleagues

Which brings me back to Mattis's motto, "No Better Friend, No Worse Enemy." It expresses a variety of possible attitudes toward an external population: from the altruism of humanitarian aid (Graeber 2007) to the forced reorganization of a colonized society (Galula 2006 [1964]; U.S. Army/Marine Corps 2007; Nagl 2005). In any case, it defines the assumption of an ethical position. The Marine stands at a point from which he may deal kindly or brutally, a choice completely dependent on his evaluation, his judgment. As one of the former Marines in the recent Winter Soldier testimony has said, his commanding officer told him that we are going to Iraq to "Kill those who need to be killed and save those who need to be saved."[11] The ability to make this distinction may be shaped by training and experience, but this ability to do so is never questioned. Mattis himself said as much, pleasurably reflecting on his experiences in Afghanistan and Iraq:

> Actually, it's a lot of fun to fight. You know, it's a hell of a hoot. It's fun to shoot some people. I'll be right upfront with you, I like brawling... You go into Afghanistan, you got guys who slap women around for five years because they didn't wear a veil... You know, guys like that ain't got no manhood left anyway. So it's a hell of a lot of fun to shoot them. (cited in E. Schmitt 2005)

Mattis's comments were scandalous, provoking a tepid admonition from General Michael Hagee, then commandant of the Marine Corps. However, the real scandal was Mattis's honesty, expressed in his choice of speech genres. We prefer public utterances about war to be couched in euphemism, to be spoken with reluctance and sorrow. Mattis's direct remarks point to what we have already discussed: a subject that knows itself to have the right to judge and the capacity to act.

And yet, the appropriation of a martial past can never fully replace the habits of a lifetime already lived. The judgment of, as Mattis said, the men who have gone before us cannot sweep away the lived experiences that preceded that judgment. The pleasure and the pride that one might take in actions in the present are still subject to the evaluation of conscience. Reversing Ricoeur's critical juxtaposition of past and present, we ask, How could the man that I remember myself to have been be responsible for the acts that I commit today? From Jonathan Shay's *Achilles in Vietnam* to the testimony at the recent Winter Soldier hearings to media reports that as many as 25 percent of Marines and soldiers suffer from post-traumatic stress disorder, we must consider those who are overwhelmed by the past and by their judgment of themselves.

At the same time, we should be attentive to those who have worked through their pasts. In 1984, William Broyles published an essay entitled "Why Men Love War."[12] In it, Broyles struggles to explain that, in spite of its horrors, there was a joy and a beauty to combat that was unequaled by anything that he had experienced before or since. His essay has been reprinted and has become a mainstay in critical courses about the experience of war; I first read it in my cramped office in a Quonset hut at Camp Pendleton, California. One afternoon after training had ended, my First Sergeant handed me the issue of *Es-*

quire in which the essay had recently appeared. He told me that Broyles had been his platoon commander during his second tour in Vietnam. Broyles was a good and conscientious lieutenant, he said. Then, the First Sergeant talked about his own experiences as a small unit leader. He told me that those memories were what steadied him through life in the garrison-bound Marine Corps and gave him the forbearance to train young lieutenants despite their obvious and extensive flaws.

I remember the violent and profane stories told by salty veterans in barracks and wardrooms and bars. I remember standing duty as a captain at Officer Candidates School, listening to a morning news account of the invasion of Panama with my commanding officer—an old warrior, a veteran of Korea and Vietnam—who put a fatherly hand on my shoulder and looked at me with compassion. *Don't worry, you'll get your war.*

I also remember Achilles' words to Odysseus in the Kingdom of the Dead. Odysseus had praised Achilles, reminding him of his valor and honor. Achilles—student of Chiron the centaur—replied, "No winning words about death to me, shining Odysseus! By god, I'd rather slave on earth for another man—some dirt poor tenant farmer who scrapes to keep alive—than rule down here over all the breathless dead. But come, tell me the news of my gallant son (Homer 1999, 265)."

And yet, Achilles' renunciation of valor and glory is tempered by his concern with the martial success of his son and his desire to avenge himself on those who had troubled his aging father. In the end, nearly a decade in the Kingdom of the Dead seems to have made him regret the fact that his end came rather than reject the path that led him to that end.

What of Pantano and his inscription—"No Better Friend, No Worse Enemy?" The question of justification and responsibility for the killings was decided by General Richard Huck, who received the report of the Article 32 investigation and dismissed all charges against Pantano.[13]

What of the message itself? Perhaps it was addressed to the Iraqis who lived in the surrounding neighborhood. However, given the fact that Pantano himself writes about training his men in functional Arabic so that they can communicate with the Iraqis whom they meet, this does not seem convincing. Perhaps he intended it to defend his actions to his comrades. This also seems unlikely. With the exception of his platoon sergeant, there seemed to have been little concern about the incident among his fellow Marines. In fact, it was the sign itself that drew criticism: the investigating officer reviewing Pantano's case suggested that there was something unseemly in an officer posting a sign on the bodies of the dead. Perhaps it was directed to audiences in America and beyond. Pantano was, after all, a media consultant before returning to the Marines. Or perhaps it is a message to a future self, written on a scrap of cardboard, deposited in the media and in memory, protection against acts of remembrance and conscience in a moment yet to come. Regardless of Pantano's intent, it is a message that we can read and interpret as well. The question remains: Having done so, how will we act?

: : NOTES : :

1. I have recently begun teaching a class about the anthropology of war. Although I was a Marine infantryman before I became an anthropologist, I never thought this experience gave me any special license to speak about warfare. I never served in combat. However, the fact that my students could find themselves on battlefields in Iraq or Afghanistan before another year passes convinced me that I had to add my voice to the critical debate.

2. The *Small Wars Journal* (http://www.smallwarsjournal.com) has been a particularly useful guide.

3. A preliminary hearing to determine whether a court martial is necessary.

4. See Ricks (1998) for the most recent account of Marine training (although a host of other novels, memoirs, and films—such as Kubrick's *Full Metal Jacket* also take up this theme); see also the critical analysis of dressage in the work of Mauss, Lefebvre, and Foucault.

5. While written from a psychological perspective, Grossman (1998) is the most critical and incisive study of this element of military training I have found.

6. At Pantano's Article 32 hearing, the score that he received on a Basic School examination in the law of war was admitted as evidence.

7. See Kevin Caffrey's essay in this volume for a detailed critique of the rules of engagement in Iraq and Afghanistan.

8. The blandly named course in which newly commissioned lieutenants spend six months training in the skills necessary for basic infantry operations before moving on to more specialized schools.

9. Jeff Bennett also pointed out a recent *New York Times* report in which young soldiers assigned to a frontier patrol base in Afghanistan watched the HBO series *Rome,* finding parallels to their own beleaguered situation.

10. The novel is about the Spartan defense of Thermopylae and has been extremely popular among Marines, who see parallels between their own training and that of the Spartans. In fact, Pressman is a former Marine officer whose own experiences of military training are interwoven with the historical material he drew upon.

11. Videos of the Winter Soldier testimony are available on the Iraq Veterans against the War Web site: http://ivaw.org/wintersoldier/testimony.

12. Broyles, a Hollywood writer and producer known for his television series *China Beach* as well as his work on *Flags of Our Fathers, Jarhead, Apollo 13,* and *Cast Away.*

13. Pantano has since resigned his commission.

REFERENCE LIST

AAA Commission on the Engagement of Anthropology with the US Security and Intelligence Communities. 2007. *Final Report American Anthropological Association.*

Abrahams, Fred. 2004. *Razing Rafah: Mass Home Demolitions in the Gaza Strip.* New York: Human Rights Watch.

Ackerman, Spencer. 2008. A Counterinsurgency Guide for Politicos. *Washington Independent,* July 28. http://washingtonindependent.mypublicsquare.com/view/the-cricketers.

Agamben, Giorgio. 1998 [1995]. *Homo Sacer: Sovereign Power and Bare Life.* Translated by Daniel Heller-Roazen. Stanford: Stanford University Press.

———. 2005. *State of Exception.* Translated by Kevin Attell. Chicago: University of Chicago Press.

Air Force. 1997. *Air Force Magazine: Journal of the Air Force Association* 80 (4), April. http://www.afa.org/magazine/April1997/0497perry.asp.

Allen, George W. 2001. *None So Blind: A Personal Account of Intelligence Failure in Vietnam.* Chicago: Ivan R Dee.

Allen, Lori. 2009. Martyr Bodies in the Media: Human Rights, Aesthetics, and the Politics of Immediation in the Palestinian Intifada. *American Ethnologist* 36 (1): 161–80.

Almeida, Paulo Roberto de. 2000a. *Dossier Amazônia 1: Primeira Onda de Boatos, Maio-Junho de 2000.* http://www.pralmeida.org/docs/01DossierAmazonia1.html.

———. 2000b. *Dossier Amazônia 2: Segunda Onda de Boatos, Outubro-Novembro de 2000.* http://www.pralmeida.org/docs/02DossierAmazonia2.doc.

———. 2001. *Dossier Amazônia 3: Terceira Onda de Boatos, Novembro de 2001.* http://www.pralmeida.org/docs/03DossierAmazonia3.html.

American Anthropological Association. 1998. *AAA Principles of Professional Responsibility.* http://www.aaanet.org.

American Anthropological Association Executive Board. 2007. Statement on the Human Terrain System Project. October 31. http://www.aaanet.org/issues/policy-advocacy/Statement-on-HTS.cfm.

American Anthropological Society. 1998. *Code of Ethics of the American Anthropological Association, American Anthropological Society.*

Amnesty International. 2007. *Amnesty International Report 2007: Republic of the Maldives.* http://thereport.amnesty.org/eng/Regions/Asia-Pacific/Maldives.

An-Na'im, Abdullahi Ahmed. 2007. A Brief Comment on the Maldives Penal Code Project: Failure to Take Shari'a Seriously, Not "Codifying" It. *Journal of Comparative Law* 2 (1): 54–60.

Anderson, Benedict. 1991 [1983]. *Imagined Communities.* New York and London: Verso.

Anderson, Christopher. 2004. Heartbreak in the Tropics. *US News & World Report* 136 (9): 37–8.

Anderson, John Ward. 2004. Top Militant among Five Killed in Raid in West Bank. *Washington Post,* July 7, A13.

Andrade, Dale, and Lt. Col. James H. Willbanks. 2006. CORDS/Phoenix: Counterinsurgency Lessons from Vietnam for the Future. *Military Review* (March-April): 9–23.

Ankersen, Christopher, ed. 2008. *Civil-Military Cooperation in Post-Conflict Operations: Emerging Theory and Practice.* London: Routledge.

Aranguren Molina, Mauricio. 2001. *Mi Confesion: Carlos Castaño Revela sus Secretos.* Bogotá: Editorial Oveja Negra.

Arendt, Hannah. 1951. *The Origins of Totalitarianism.* New York: Harcourt.

———. 1972. *Crises of the Republic.* New York: Harcourt, Brace, Jovanovich.

Arnold, Mark. 2004. *Anatomy of a Tragedy: From Nablus to the North Shore.* http://www.jewishjournal.org/archives/archiveSept10_04.htm.

Aronstein, David C., and Albert C. Piccirillo. 1997. *Have Blue and the F-117: Evolution of the "Stealth Fighter."* Reston: American Institute of Aeronautics and Astronautics.

Arthur, Charles. 2003. About 10,000 People Marched in the Capital on Friday to Call for the Resignation of President Jean-Bertrand Aristide. *Haiti Support Group, News Briefs,* December 26. http://haitisupport.gn.apc.org/fea_news_main24.html.

———. 2004. Haiti's Army Turns Back the Clock. *Znet,* April 2. http://www.zmag.org/znet/viewArticle/8801.

Asad, Talal, ed. 1973. *Anthropology and the Colonial Encounter.* London: Ithaca Press.

Associated Press. 2005. Translators Dying by the Dozens in Iraq. *USA Today.* May 21. http://www.usatoday.com/news/world/iraq/2005-05-21-translator-deaths_x.htm.

Association for the Prevention of Torture . 2007. Defusing the Ticking Bomb Scenario: Why We Must Say No to Torture, Always. http://www.apt.ch/component/option,com_docman/task,doc_details/gid,281/Itemid,59/lang,en/.

Austin, John. 1995. *The Province of Jurisprudence Determined.* Cambridge: Cambridge University Press.

Baba, Marietta. 1998. The Anthropology of Work in the Fortune 1000: A Critical Retrospective. *Anthropology of Work Review* 18 (4): 17–28.

Bacevich, Andrew J. 2004 *American Empire: The Realities and Consequences of U.S. Diplomacy.* Cambridge: Harvard University Press.

Bachelet, Pablo. 2004. Should the U.N. Run Haiti? Some See Little Alternative. *Miami Herald,* December 12.

Baker, Jason B. 2003. Winning Hearts with Cultural Awareness. *Soldiers* 58 (July): 29.

Bateson, Gregory. 1944. Gregory Bateson to Dillon Ripley, OSS Southeast Asia Command, Memorandum, November 15, 1944. Released by CIA under FOIA in August 1944.

Beck, Leda. 2000. Internet Cria Rumor Sobre Internacionalização da Amazônia (article from the *Estado de São Paulo,* May 12, 2000). In *Dossier Amazônia 1: Primeira Onda de Boatos, Maio-Junho de 2000,* edited by Paulo Roberto de Almeida, 71–4. http://www.pralmeida.org/docs/01DossierAmazonia1.html.

Benedict, Ruth. 1946. *The Chrysanthemum and the Sword.* Boston: Houghton Mifflin.

Benjamin, Walter. 1968. *Illuminations.* Translated by Harry Zohn. New York: Schocken Books.

———. 1978. Critique of Violence. In *Reflections: Essays, Aphorisms, Autobiographical Writings,* edited by Peter Demetz, translated by Edmund Jephcott, 277–300. New York: Schocken Books.

Bennett, Jeffrey S. Forthcoming. Abu Ghraib: A Predictable Tragedy? In *"Over There": Living with the U.S. Military Empire,* edited by Seungsook Moon and Maria Hoehn. Durham: Duke University Press.

Bennett, John. W. 1996. Applied and Action Anthropology: Ideological and Conceptual Aspects. *Current Anthropology* 36: S23–S53.

Benton, Barbara, ed. 1996. *Soldiers for Peace: Fifty Years of United Nations Peacekeeping.* American Historical Publications, Facts on File, Inc.

Bergerud, Eric. 1993. *The Dynamics of Defeat: The Vietnam War in Hau Nghia Province.* Boulder, CO: Westview Press.

Bhatia, Michael. 2008. Fighting Words: Naming Terrorists, Bandits, Rebels and Other Violent Actors. In *Terrorism and the Politics of Naming,* edited by Michael Bhatia, 5–22. London and New York: Routledge.

Bibring, Edward. 1943. The Concept of the Repetition Compulsion. *Psychoanalytic Quarterly* 12 (1943): 75–97.

Bishara, Amahl. 2005. The Targeted and the Untargeted of Nablus. *Middle East Report* (235): 8–11.

———. 2008. Watching U.S. Television from the Palestinian Street: The Media, The State and Representational Interventions. *Cultural Anthropology* 23 (3): 488–530.

Blaufarb, Douglas F. 1977. *The Counterinsurgency Era: U.S. Doctrine and Performance, 1950 to the Present.* New York: Free Press.

Bloch, Ernst. 1977 [1932]. Nonsynchronism and the Obligation to the Dialectics. *New German Critique* 11: 22–38.

Blumenthal, Max. 2004. The Other Regime Change: Did the Bush Administration Allow a Network of Right-Wing Republicans to Foment a Violent Coup in Haiti? *Salon.com,* 16 July, http://www.salon.com/news/faeture/2004/07/16/haiti_coup.

Boas, Franz. 1919. Scientists as Spies. *Nation,* December 20.

Bobbitt, Philip. 2002. *The Shield of Achilles: War, Peace, and the Course of History.* New York: Anchor Books.

Bohning, Don. 2004. An International Protectorate Could Bring Stability to Haiti: Nation in Chaos. *Miami Herald,* November 22.

Bolívar, Ingrid. 2006. *Discursos Emocionales y Experiencias de la Política: las Farc y las Auc en los Procesos de Negociación del Conflicto* (1998–2005). Bogotá: Ediciones Uniandes, Centro de Investigación y Educación Popular.

Boyer, Paul. 1985. *By the Bomb's Early Light: American Thought and Culture at the Dawn of the Atomic Age.* New York: Pantheon.

Brasil, Ame-o ou Deixe-o. 2000. Retratação. Brasil, Ame-o ou Deixe-o. http://brasil.iwarp .com/retrata.htm.

Brigham, Robert K., and Martin J. Murray. 1994. Conflicting Interpretations of the Vietnam War, 1945–1975. *Bulletin of Concerned Asian Scholars* 26 (January-June): 111–18.

British Broadcasting Corporation. 2008. New Maldives President Sworn In. http://news.bbc .co.uk/2/hi/south_asia/7721335.stm.

Brogden, Mike, and Preeti Nijhar. 2005. *Community Policing: National and International Models and Approaches.* Devon: Willan Publishing.

Broyles, William. 1984. Why Men Love War. *Esquire* (November).

Bruneau, Thomas C., and Scott D. Tollefson, eds. 2006. *Who Guards the Guardians and How: Democratic Civil-Military Relations.* Austin: University of Texas Press.

Brush, Peter. 1994. Civic Action: The Marine Corps Experience in Vietnam. In *Vietnam Generation* 5:1–4, 127–32. http://www2.iath.virginia.edu/sixties/HTML_docs/Texts/Scholarly/Brush_CAP_01.html.

Brzezinski, Zbigniew. 2007. Five Flaws in the President's Plan. *Washington Post,* A19, January 12.

B'Tselem (The Israeli Information Center for Human Rights in the Occupied Territories). 2004. The Forbidden Roads Regime (Map). http://www.btselem.org/Download/Forbbiden_Roads_Map_Eng.pdf.

Buchan, James. 2003. Miss Bell's Lines in the Sand. *Guardian,* March 12.

Buchanan, Patrick J. 2003. Whose War? *American Conservative* 24. http://www.amconmag.com/03_24_03/cover.html.

Burns, E. Bradford. 1995. Brazil: Frontier and Ideology. *Pacific Historical Review* 64 (February): 1–18.

Butterfield, Fox. 1983. The New Vietnam Scholarship. *New York Times Magazine,* February 13.

Buzzanco, Robert. 1996. *Masters of War.* New York: Cambridge University Press.

Cable, Larry. 1986. *Conflict of Myths: The Development of American Counterinsurgency Doctrine in the Vietnam War.* New York: New York University Press.

Cala, Andres. 2003. Former Haitian Police Chief and Four Others Suspected of Plotting against Haiti's Government Released. *Associated Press,* May 8.

Caldeira, Teresa Pires do Rio. 2000. *City of Walls: Crime, Segregation, and Citizenship in São Paulo.* Berkeley: University of California Press.

Calhoun, Craig, Frederick Cooper, and Kevin W. Moore, eds. 2006. *Lessons of Empire: Imperial Histories and American Power.* New York: New Press.

Callwell, Charles. 1996 [1906]. *Small Wars: Their Principles and Practices.* 3d ed. Lincoln, NE: University of Nebraska Press.

Caplan, Jane, and John Torpey. 2001. Introduction. In *Documenting Individual Identity: The Development of State Practices in the Modern World,* edited by J. Caplan and J. Torpey, 1–12. Princeton: Princeton University Press.

Caroit, Jean-Michel. 2003. Haiti, la Lois des Milices. *Le Monde,* November 5.

———. 2004. Comment Jean-Bertrand Aristide a été poussé par les Etats Unis à quitter le pouvoir en Haiti. *Le Monde,* March 6.

Carroll, James. 2006. *House of War: The Pentagon and the Disastrous Rise of American Power.* Boston: Houghton Mifflin.

Carvalho, José Murilo. 1998. O Motivo Edênico no Imaginário Social Brasileiro. *Revista Brasileira de Ciências Sociais* 13 (38).

Castells, Manuel. 1996. *The Rise of the Network Society, The Information Age: Economy, Society and Culture.* Vol. 1. Cambridge, MA; Oxford, UK: Blackwell.

Castro, Celso, ed. 2006. *Amazônia e Defesa Nacional.* Rio de Janeiro: FGV.

Caton, Steven C. 1990. *"Peaks of Yemen I Summon": Poetry as Cultural Practice in a North Yemeni Tribe.* Berkeley: University of California Press.

Cavagnari Filho, Geraldo Lesbat. 2003. O Argumento do Império. *Política Externa* 12 (1): 75–83.

Cavallaro, Gina 2008. Ending the Culture Clash: Human Terrain Teams Are Making Iraq and Afghanistan Safer, Commanders Say. *Army Times,* March 31.

Center for Defense Information. 1996. *U.S. Military Spending, 1945–1996.* http://www.cdi.org/Issues/milspend.html.

Center for Strategic and Budgetary Assessments. 2008. Classified Funding in the FY 2009 Defense Budget Request. http://www.csbaonline.org/4Publications/PubLibrary/U.20080618.Classified_Funding/U.20080618.Classified_Funding.pdf.

Cervo, Amado Luiz. 2000. Sob o Signo Neoliberal: as Relações Internacionais da América Latina. *Revista Brasileira de Política Internacional* 43 (2): 5–27.

Chomsky, Noam. 1968. *American Power and the New Mandarins.* New York: Pantheon.

Chomsky, Noam, Paul Farmer, and Amy Goodman. 2004. *Getting Haiti Right This Time: The U.S. Military and the Coup.* Monroe, ME: Common Courage Press.

Chu, Julie. 2008. Card Me When I'm Dead: Identification Papers and the Pursuit of the Good Afterlife in China. Paper Presented at the Department of Anthropology, University of Chicago.

CINEP, Centro de Investigación y Educación Popular. 2007. http://www.cinep.org.co/editorial.htm.

Clausewitz, Carl von. 1982 [1832]. *On War.* Edited by Anatol Rapoport. Translated by J. J. Graham. New York: Penguin Classics.

———. 1989 [1832]. *On War.* Edited and translated by M. Howard and P. Paret. Princeton: Princeton University Press.

Coffey, Maj. Ross. 2006. Revisiting CORDS: The Need for Unity of Effort to Secure Victory in Iraq. *Military Review* (March-April): 24–34.

Cohen, Lizabeth. 2003. *A Consumer's Republic: The Politics of Mass Consumption in Postwar America.* New York: Knopf.

Cohn, Bernard, and Teri Silvio. 2002. Race, Gender, and Historical Narrative in the Reconstruction of a Nation: Remembering and Forgetting the American Civil War. In *From the Margins: Historical Anthropology and Its Futures,* edited by Brian Axel. Durham: Duke University Press.

Colby, William E. 1989. *Lost Victory.* Chicago: Contemporary Books.

Comaroff, Jean, and John L. Comaroff. 2003. Transparent Fictions; or, the Conspiracies of a Liberal Imagination: An Afterword. In *Transparency and Conspiracy: Ethnographies of Suspicion in the New World Order,* edited by Harry G. West and Todd Sanders, 287–99. Durham and London: Duke University Press.

———. 2006a. Criminal Obsessions, after Foucault: Postcoloniality, Policing, and the Metaphysics of Disorder. In *Law and Disorder in the Postcolony,* edited by Jean Comaroff and John Comaroff, 273–98. Chicago: University of Chicago Press.

———. 2006b. Law and Disorder in the Postcolony: An Introduction. In *Law and Disorder in the Postcolony,* edited by Jean Comaroff and John Comaroff, 1–56. Chicago: University of Chicago Press.

———. 2006c. Figuring Crime: Quantifacts and the Production of the Un/Real. *Public Culture.* 18 (1): 209–46.

———. 2006d. *An Excursion into the Criminal: Anthropology of the Brave Neo South Africa.* Carl Schlettwein Lectures. Lit Verlag.

Commission Citoyenne de Réflexion sur les Forces Armées. 2005. *Rapport Préliminaire.*

———. 2006. *Rapport Final.*

Commission on Presidential Debates. 2000. The Second 2000 Gore-Bush Presidential Debate. http://www.debates.org/pages/trans2000b.html.

Compact Edition of the Oxford English Dictionary. 1971. Oxford: Oxford University Press.

Connable, Ben. 2009. All Our Eggs in a Broken Basket: How the Human Terrain System is Undermining Sustainable Military Cultural Competence. *Military Review* (March-April): 57–64.

Çoşkun, Mustafa. 2008. Faşizme Tehlikesi. *Radikal Gazetesi,* July 7. http://www.radikal.com .tr/Default.aspx?aType=HaberDetay&ArticleID=886999&Date=09.07.2008.

Couto, Ruy de Paula. 1999. A República Ianomâmi. http://brasil.iwarp.com/republica.html.

Crane, Conrad, and W. Andrew Terrill. 2003. Reconstructing Iraq: Insights, Challenges, and Missions for Military Forces in a Post-Conflict Scenario. February 2003. http://www .strategicstudiesinstitute.army.mil/Pubs/Display.Cfm?pubID=182.

Crickmore, Paul. 2003. *Combat Legend: F-117 Nighthawk.* Shrewbury, UK: Airlife.

Cunha, Manuela Carneiro da. 1993. *Legislação Indigenista no seculo XIX* . São Paulo: Editora da Universidade de São Paulo and Comissão Pro-Indio.

Cunningham, David. 2004. *There's Something Happening Here: The New Left, the Klan, and FBI Counterintelligence.* Berkeley: University of California Press.

Cushing, Frank Hamilton. 1967 [1882–3]. *My Adventures in Zuni.* Palmer Lake, CO: Filter Press.

Daraghmeh, Ali. 2004. Palestinian Professor, Son Killed in Israeli Raid. July 6 Associated Press.

Das, Veena. 1990. *Mirrors of Violence.* Oxford: Oxford University Press.

Das, Veena, and Arthur Kleinman. 2000. *Violence and Subjectivity.* Berkeley: University of California Press.

Davis, Rochelle, and Elizabeth Grasmeder. n.d. Nationalist Sentiments and Military Occupation: U.S. Military Personnel and Their Experiences with Iraqis (2003–2007). Unpublished manuscript. Submitted to *Political Science Quarterly.*

Deflem, Mathieu, and Suzanne Sutphin. 2006. Policing Post-War Iraq: Insurgency, Civilian Police and the Reconstruction of Society. *Sociological Focus* 39:4 (November): 265–83.

Dehghanpisheh, Babak, and Evan Thomas. 2008. Scions of the Surge. *Newsweek,* March 15.

Der Derian, James, David Udris, and Michael Udris. 2009. *Cultural Warriors.* Providence: Udris Film.

Derrida, Jacques. 1991. Force of Law: The Mystical Foundations of Authority. *Cardozo Law Review* 11:920–1045.

Diane Rehm Show. 2007. Radio Broadcast: Anthropologists and War. October 10. http://wamu.org/programs/dr/07/10/10.php

Dixon, Ivan, dir. 1973. *The Spook Who Sat by the Door.* Obsidian.

Doumani, Beshara. 1992. Rediscovering Ottoman Palestine: Writing Palestinians into History. *Journal of Palestine Studies* 21 (2): 5–28.

Dreyfuss, Robert. 2005. *Devil's Game: How the United States Helped Unleash Fundamentalist Islam.* New York: Metropolitan Books.

Drinnon, Richard. 1980. *Facing West: The Metaphysics of Indian-Hating and Empire-Building.* New York and London: Meridian Book.

Duffield, Mark. 2001. *Global Governance and the New Wars: The Merging of Development and Security.* London: Zed Books.

Dumas, Pierre-Raymond. 1994. *Haiti, une Armée dans la Mêlée.* Port-au-Prince: L'Imprimeur II.

Dupuy, Alex. 2005. From Jean-Bertrand Aristide to Gérard Latortue: The Unending Crisis of Democratization in Haiti. *Journal of Latin American Anthropology* 10 (1): 186–205.

———. 2007. *The Prophet and the Power: Jean-Bertrand Aristide, the International Community, and Haiti.* Lanham, MD: Rowman & Littlefield.

Easton, Marleen. 2006. Reconsidering the Process of Demilitarization: The Case of the Belgian Gendarmerie. *Asian Policing* 4 (September): 19–30.

El Tiempo. 2008. Se Pagará Recompensa a "Rojas" Tres Guerrilleros Más por Información sobre "Iván Ríos." March 18. http://www.eltiempo.com/archivo/documento/CMS-4011485 FARC-EP.

Elder, Ralph E. 2007. Arab Culture and History: Understanding Is the First Key to Success. *Armor* 116 (January-February): 42–44

Elkhamri, Mounir. 2007. Dealing with the Iraqi Populace: An Arab-American Soldier's Perspective. *Military Review* 8 (January-February): 110–13.

Elliot, David. 2003. *The Vietnamese War: Revolution and Social Change in the Mekong Delta, 1930–1978.* New York: M. E. Sharpe.

Embree, John F. 1944. Community Analysis—An Example of Anthropology in Government. *American Anthropologist* 46 (3): 277–91.

Ephron, Dan, and Silvia Spring. 2008. A Gun in One Hand, a Pen in the Other. *Newsweek,* April 21.

Escobar, Arturo. 1995, *Encountering Development. The Making and Unmaking of the Third World.* Princeton, NJ: Princeton University Press.

Esposito, Michele K. 2006. Various Organizations, Losses on the Five-Year Anniversary of the Al-Aqsa Intifada, Comparative Statistical Table. *Journal of Palestine Studies* 35(2): 194–99.

Evans-Pritchard, E.E. 1940. *The Nuer: A Description of the Modes of Livelihood and Political Institutions of a Nilotic People.* New York: Oxford University Press.

Fanon, Franz. 1976. *The Wretched of the Earth.* Translated by Constance Farrington New York: Penguin Books.

FARC. 2007. FARC-EP Ejército del Pueblo. Informes de Guerra. http://www.farc-ep.org. Accessed in April 2007. This page no longer exists.

Faria, Tales. 2007. Bantustans, Chiapas e Curdistões no Brasil. *Jornal do Brasil,* January 29.

Fatton, Robert, Jr. 2002. *Haiti's Predatory Republic: The Unending Transition to Democracy.* Boulder, CO: Lynne Rienner Publishers.

Fausto, Boris. 1999. *A Concise History of Brazil.* Translated by Arthur Brakel. New York: Cambridge University Press.

Feaver, Peter. 2005. *Armed Servants: Agency, Oversight, and Civil-Military Relations.* Cambridge, MA: Harvard University Press.

Feldman, Allen. 1994. On Cultural Anaesthesia: From Desert Storm to Rodney King. *American Ethnologist* 21 (2): 404–18.

Ferguson, Charles, dir. 2007. *No End in Sight.* Red Envelope Entertainment.

Ferguson, Niall. 2004. *Colossus: The Price of America's Empire.* New York: Penguin Press.

Ferguson, R. Brian, and Neil L. Whitehead, eds. 2000. *War in the Tribal Zone: Expanding States and Indigenous Warfare.* School of American Research Advanced Seminar Series. Santa Fe: SAR Press.

Feuchtwang, Stephen. 1973. The Colonial Formation of British Social Anthropology. In *Anthropology and the Colonial Encounter,* edited by Talal Asad, 71–100. London: Ithaca Press.

Finer, Samuel E. 2002 [1962]. *Man on Horseback: The Role of the Military in Politics.* Piscataway: Transaction Publishers.

Fisas, Vicenç. 1995. *Blue Geopolitics: The United Nations Reform and the Future of the Blue Helmets.* Pluto Press with Transnational Institute.

Fisk, Robert. 2001. Palestine: Death in Bethlehem, Made in America. *Independent,* April 15.

———. 2005. Turning a Blind Eye to Murder and Abuse in Basra. *Counterpunch/The Independent,* September 24/25.

Fitch, Noël Riley. 1999. *Appetite For Life: The Biography of Julia Child.* New York: Anchor Books.

Folha de São Paulo. 1999. Comandante Ve Risco de Intervenção Externa . *Folha de São Paulo,* June 19.

Foresta, Ronald. 1992. Amazonia and the Politics of Geopolitics. *Geographical Review* 82: 128–42.

Forsyth, D. R. 2003. Individual Moral Philosophies (IMPs) and Ethical Thought and Action. In *The Psychological Study of Morality,* edited by L. Begue, N. Przygodski, and C. Blatier. Paris: Inpress Publisher.

Foucault, Michel. 1978. *The History of Sexuality.* Translated by Robert Hurley. New York: Pantheon Books.

———. 2003 [1976]. *Society Must Be Defended: Lectures at the Collège de France, 1975–1976.* New York: Picador.

Franklin, Bruce. 2000. *Vietnam and Other American Fantasies.* Amherst: University of Massachusetts.

Fraser, Genevieve Cora. 2004a. Palestinian American Calls for US Investigation into Israeli Assault. http://archive.ramallahonline.com/modules.php?name=News&file=article& sid=2114.

———. 2004b. Palestinian Family Ensnared in Israeli Death Trap. http://sandiego.indymedia. org/en/2004/07/105034.shtml.

———. 2005. Palestinian American Calls for US Investigation into Israeli Assault. http:// archive.ramallahonline.com/modules.php?name=News&file=article&sid=2114.

Freud, Sigmund. 1915. Thoughts for the Times in War and Death. Delivered at B'nai Brith club in Vienna. And Appendix to paper: Letter to Dr. van Eedan, 28 December 1914. In *The Standard Edition of the Complete Psychological Works of Sigmund Freud.* Edited by James Strachey. Vol. XIX. London: Hogarth Press and the Institute of Psychoanalysis.

———. 1960 [1920]. *Beyond the Pleasure Principle.* New York: Norton.

Fukuyama, Francis. 1989. The End of History? *National Interest* 16:3–18.

Fulbright, William. 1967. A Point of View. *Science,* December 22, p. 1555.

Galula, David. 2006 [1964]. *Counterinsurgency Warfare: Theory and Practice.* Santa Barbara, CA: Praeger Security International.

Gardner, Lloyd C., and Marilyn B. Young, eds. 2008. *Iraq and the Lessons of Vietnam: Or, How Not to Learn from the Past.* New York: New Press.

Garfield, Seth. 2004. A Nationalist Environment: Indians, Nature, and the Construction of the Xingu National Park in Brazil. *Luso-Brazilian Review* 41 (1): 139–67.

Gélin-Adams, Maryle, and David M. Malone. 2003. Haiti: A Case of Endemic Weakness. In *State Failure and State Weakness in a Time of Terror,* edited by Robert I. Rotberg, 287–304. Washington, DC: Brookings Institute Press.

Gill, Lesley. 2004. *The School of the Americas: Military Training and Political Violence in the Americas.* Durham: Duke University Press.

Glenn, David. 2007. Former Human Terrain System Participant Describes Program in Disarray. *Chronicle of Higher Education,* December 5.

Goebel, Michael. 2007. Introduction: Nationalism, the Left and Hegemony in Latin America. *Bulletin of Latin American Research* 26 (3): 311–18.

Gonzalez, Fernán, Ingrid Bolivar, and TeófiloVasquez . 2003. *Violencia Política en Colombia— De la Nación Fragmentada a la Construcción del Estado.* Bogotá: Centro de Investigación y Educación Popular.

Gonzalez, Roberto, ed. 2004. *Anthropologists in the Public Sphere: Speaking Out on War, Peace, and American Power.* Austin: University of Texas Press.

———. 2008. From Anthropologists to Technicians of Power. Paper Presented at Society for Applied Anthropology Meetings, Memphis, March 28.

———. 2009. *American Counterinsurgency: Human Science and the Human Terrain.* Chicago: Prickly Paradigm Press.

Gordillo, Gastón. 2006. The Crucible of Citizenship: ID-Paper Fetishism in the Argentinean Chaco. *American Ethnologist* 33 (2): 162–76.

Gordon, Robert. 1987. Anthropology and Apartheid: The Rise of Military Ethnology in South Africa. *Cultural Survival Quarterly* 11.4. http://www.cs.org/publications/CSQ/csq-article .cfm?id=740.

Gottman, Jean. 1986 [1943]. Bugeaud, Galliéni, Lyautey: The Development of French Colonial Warfare. In *Makers of Modern Strategy: Military Thought from Machiavelli to Hitler,* edited by Edward Mead Earle. Princeton: Princeton University Press.

Graeber, David. 2004. *Fragments of an Anarchist Anthropology.* Chicago: Prickly Paradigm Press.

———. 2007. Army of Altruists. *Harper's* (January).

Grandin, Greg. 2004. *The Last Colonial Massacre: Latin America in the Cold War.* Chicago: University of Chicago Press.

———. 2006. *Empire's Workshop: Latin America, the United States, and the Rise of the New Imperialism.* New York: Metropolitan Books.

Grant, Zalin. 1991. *Facing the Phoenix: The CIA and the Political Defeat of the United States in Vietnam.* New York: Norton.

Gravel, Mike, ed. 1971. *Pentagon Papers.* Vol. 4. Boston: Beacon Press.

Green, Linda. 1999. *Fear as a Way of Life. Mayan Widows in Rural Guatemala.* New York: Columbia University Press.

Greene, Graham. 1955. *The Quiet American.* London: Heinemann.

Greenlee, Sam, dir. 1969. *The Spook Who Sat by the Door.* Allison and Busby.

Greenspan, Alan. 2007. *The Age of Turbulence: Adventures in a New World.* New York: Penguin Group.

Gregory, Derek. 2008. "The Rush to the Intimate": Counterinsurgency and the Cultural Turn. *Radical Philosophy* 150 (July/August). http://www.radicalphilosophy.com/default.asp? channel_id=2369&editorial_id=26755.

Greider, William. 1998. *One World Ready or Not: The Manic Logic of Global Capitalism.* New York: Simon & Schuster.

Griffin, Marcus. 2007. From an Anthropological Perspective. http://www.marcusgriffin .com/blog.

Grimmett, Richard F. 2007. *Conventional Arms Transfers to Developing Nations, 1999–2006.* Washington, DC: Congressional Research Service.

Grossman, Dave. 1998. *On Killing: The Psychological Cost of Learning to Kill in War and Society.* New York: Back Bay Books.

Guha, Ranajit. 1982. On Some Aspects of the Historiography of Colonial India. *Subaltern Studies* 1:1–8. New Dehli: Oxford University Press.

Gupta, Asha, ed. 2003. *Military Rule and Democratization: Changing Perspectives.* New Dehli: Deep & Deep Publications, Pvt., Ltd.

Gusterson, Hugh. 1996. *Nuclear Rites: A Weapons Laboratory at the End of the Cold War.* Berkeley: University of California Press.

Gusterson, Hugh, and David Price. 2005. Spies in Our Midst (with David Price). *Anthropology Newsletter* 46 (6): 39–40.

Haass, Richard. 1999. *Intervention: The Use of American Military Force in the Post-Cold War World.* Revised Edition. Washington, DC: Brookings Institution.

Hammes, Thomas X. 2006. *The Sling and the Stone: On War in the 21st Century.* St. Paul: Zenith Press.

Hanafi, Sari, and Linda Tabar. 2005. *The Emergence of Palestinian Globalized Elite: Donors, International Organizations, and Local NGOs.* Jerusalem: Institute of Jerusalem Studies.

Hansen, Arthur A. 1995. Oral History and the Japanese American Evacuation. *Journal of American History* 82 (2): 625–39.

Haraway, Donna. 1997. *Modest_Witness@Second_Millennium. FemaleMan©_Meets _OncoMouseTM.* New York: Routledge.

Hardt, Michael, and Antonio Negri. 2000. *Empire.* Cambridge, MA: Harvard University Press.

Harrison, John P. 1955. Science and Politics: Origins and Objectives of Mid-Nineteenth Century Government Expeditions to Latin America. *Hispanic American Historical Review* 35 (2): 175–202.

Harvey, David. 2005. *The New Imperialism.* New York: Oxford University Press.

Hayden, Tom. 2007. Harvard's Humanitarian Hawks. *Nation,* July 14.

Hedges, Chris, and Laila Al-Arian. 2009. *Collateral Damage: America's War against Iraqi Civilians.* New York: Nation Books.

Helbig, Zenia. 2007a. Interviewed by Roberto Gonzalez, December 4.

———. 2007b. Personal Perspective on the Human Terrain System. Unpublished manuscript posted at http://blog.wired.com/defense/files/aaa_helbig_hts.pdf.

Hemming, John. 1978. *Red Gold: The Conquest of the Brazilian Indians.* London: Macmillan.

Hernandez, Sandra. 2004. Top U.S. Officer Tells Aristide to Stay Quiet: Intervention Needed to Avert Bloodbath. *South Florida Sun-Sentinel,* March 19, 21A.

Hersh, Seymour. 2004a. *Chain of Command: The Road from 9/11 to Abu Ghraib.* New York: Harper Collins.

———. 2004b. The Grey Zone. *New Yorker,* May 17.

Higgs, Robert. 2007. The Trillion-Dollar Defense Budget Is Already Here. *Independent Institute,* March 15. http://www.independent.org/newsroom/article.asp?id=1941.

Hillen, John. 2000. *Blue Helmets: The Strategy of UN Military Operations.* London: Brassey's.

Hinton, Mercedes S., ed. 2008. *Policing Developing Democracies.* New York: Routledge.

Hobbes, Thomas. 1968 [1651]. *Leviathan.* New York. Penguin Classics.

Hobsbawm, Eric. 1995. Nationalism and National Identity in Latin America. In *Pour une histoire economique et sociale internationale: melanges offerts a Paul Bairoch,* edited by Bouda Etemad, Jean Baton, and Thomas David, 312–23. Geneva: Editions Passe Present.

Hofstadter, Richard. 1965. *The Paranoid Style in American Politics and Other Essays.* New York: Knopf.

Holanda, Sergio Buarque de. 2000. *Visão de Paraíso.* São Paulo: Publifolha.

Holland, Ryan. 2004. *Securing Dystopia: Gangs and Terror in Chicago's Urban Imaginaries.* B.A. thesis. Department of Anthropology, University of Chicago.

Holmes-Eber, Paula, and Barak A. Salmoni. 2008. *Operational Cultures for the Warfighter: Principles and Applications.* Quantico, VA: Marine Corps University Press.

Homer. 1999. *The Odyssey.* Translated by Robert Fagles. New York: Penguin Classics.

Horsman, Stuart. 2008. Themes in Official Discourses on Terrorism in Central Asia. In *Terrorism and the Politics of Naming,* edited by Michael Bhatia. London and New York: Routledge.

Hosmer, Stephen, Konrad Kellner, and Brian Jenkins. 1986. *The Fall of South Vietnam.* New York: Krane, Russak.

Howell, Georgina. 2006. The Remarkable Life of Gertrude Bell. *Guardian,* September 3.

Human Rights Watch. 2002. *Israel, the Occupied West Bank and Gaza Strip, and Palestinian Authority Territories.* http://www.hrw.org/wr2k2/mena5.html.

———. 2003. *Hearts and Minds: Post-War Civilian Deaths in Baghdad Caused by U.S. Forces.* October. http://www.hrw.org/reports/2003/iraq1003/iraq1003full.pdf.

———. 2005. *Israel/Occupied Palestinian Territories.* http://hrw.org/english/docs/2005/01/13/isrlpa9806.htm.

Hunt, David. 2003. Revolution in the Delta. *Critical Asian Studies* 35, 4: 599–620.

Hunt, David, and Jayne Werner. 1993. *The American War in Vietnam.* Ithaca: Cornell University Press.

Hunt, Richard A. 1995. *Pacification: America's Struggle for Vietnam's Hearts and Minds.* Boulder: Westview Press.

Hunter, Wendy. 1997. *Eroding the Military Influence in Brazil: Politicians against Soldiers.* Chapel Hill: University of North Carolina Press.

Huntington, Samuel. 1957. *The Soldier and the State: The Theory and Politics of Civil-Military Relations.* Cambridge: Belknap/Harvard University Press.

———. 1996. *The Clash of Civilizations and the Remaking of World Order.* New York: Simon & Schuster.

Hussain, Nasser. 2003. *Jurisprudence of Emergency: Colonialism and the Rule of Law.* Ann Arbor: University of Michigan Press.

Hutchinson, Sharon E. 1996. *Nuer Dilemmas: Coping with Money, War, and the State.* Berkeley: University of California Press.

Hymes, Dell H., ed. 1999. *Reinventing Anthropology.* Ann Arbor: University of Michigan Press.

Ignatius, David. 2003. Think Strategy, Not Numbers. *Washington Post.* August 26, A13. http://www.washingtonpost.com/wp-dyn/articles/A45136-2003Aug25.html.

Iriye, Akira. 2002. *Global Community: The Role of International Organizations in the Making of the Contemporary World.* Berkeley: University of California Press.

Ives, Kim. 1995. Haiti's Second U.S. Occupation. In *Haiti: Dangerous Crossroads,* edited by Deidre McFadyen and Pierre LaRamée, 107–18. Boston: South End Press.

Jacobsen, Kurt. 2001. Afghanistan and the Vietnam Syndrome. *Economic and Political Weekly* 35, November 3.

———. 2004. The Passion of Robert McNamara, or Sympathy for the Devil? *New Politics* X (Summer): 147–50.

Jager, Sheila Miyoshi. 2007. *On the Uses of Cultural Knowledge.* Washington, DC: Strategic Studies Institute.

James, Wendy. 1973. The Anthropologist as Reluctant Imperialist. In *Anthropology and the Colonial Encounter,* edited by Talal Asad, 41–69. London: Ithaca Press.

Jauregui, Beatrice. 2004. *Rethinking State Coercion with the Armed and the Civil: Theorizing Legitimacy through Law Enforcement.* M.A. thesis. University of Chicago.

————. Forthcoming. *Shadows of the State, Subalterns of the State: Police and "Law and Order" in Postcolonial India*. Ph.D. diss. University of Chicago.

Jayamaha, Buddhika, et al. 2007. The War as We Saw It. *New York Times,* August 19, p.11.

Jefferson, Thomas. 1803. Transcript: Jefferson's Instructions for Meriwether Lewis. Rivers, Edens, and Empires: LEWIS & CLARK and the Revealing of America (Library of Congress Exhibition). http://www.loc.gov/exhibits/lewisandclark/transcript57.html.

Johnson, Chalmers. 1997. The CIA and Me. *Bulletin of Concerned Asian Scholars* 29, 1 (January–March): 34–37.

————. 2000. *Blowback: The Costs and Consequences of American Empire.* New York: Henry Holt.

————. 2004. *The Sorrows of Empire: Militarism, Secrecy, and the End of the Republic.* Owl Books.

————. 2008. Mission Creep: America's Unwelcome Advances. *Motherjones.com.* August 22.

Jorgensen, Joseph G., and Eric Wolf. 1970. Anthropology on the Warpath in Thailand. *New York Review of Books* 15 (9), November 19.

Junod, Tom. 2008. The Six-Letter Word That Changes Everything. *Esquire,* June 11. http://www.esquire.com/features/michael-hensley-0708.

Kalyvas, Stathis N. 2006. *The Logic of Violence in Civil War.* New York: Cambridge University Press.

Kalyvas, Stathis N., and Matthew Kocher. 2003. Violence and Control in Civil War: An Analysis of the Hamlet Evaluation Study. Paper given at University of Chicago.

Kasfir, Nelson. 2004. Domestic Anarchy, Security Dilemmas, and Violent Predation: Causes of Failure. In *When States Fail: Causes and Consequences,* edited by Robert I. Rotberg, 53–76. Princeton, NJ: Princeton University Press.

Kelly, John D. 2002. Alternative Modernities or an Alternative to "Modernity": Getting Out of the Modernist Sublime. In *Critically Modern: Alternatives, Alterities, Anthropologies,* edited by Bruce M. Knauft, 258–86. Bloomington: Indiana University Press.

————. 2003. U.S. Power, after 9/11 and before It: If Not an Empire, Then What? *Public Culture* 15 (2): 347–69.

————. 2006. Who Counts? Imperial and Corporate Structures of Governance, Decolonization and Limited Liability. In *Lessons of Empire: Imperial Histories and American Power,* edited by Craig Calhoun, Frederick Cooper, and Kevin W. Moore. New York: New Press, 157–74.

Kelly, John D., and Martha Kaplan. 2001a. Nation and Decolonization: Toward a New Anthropology of Nationalism. *Anthropological Theory* 1 (4): 419–37.

————. 2001b. *Represented Communities: Fiji and World Decolonization.* Chicago: University of Chicago Press.

————. 2004. "My Ambition Is Much Higher Than Independence": US Power, The UN World, The Nation-State, and Their Critics. In *Decolonization: Perspectives from Now and Then,* edited by Prasenjit Duara, 131–51. Routledge.

————. 2009. Legal Fictions after Empire. In *Art of the State: Sovereignty Past and Present,* edited by Douglas Howland and Luise White, 169–95. Bloomington: University of Indiana Press.

Kelly, Lawrence C. 1980. Anthropology and Anthropologists in the Indian New Deal. *Journal of the History of the Behavioral Sciences* 16:6–24.

————. 1984. Why Applied Anthropology Developed When It Did: A Commentary on People, Money, and Changing Times, 1930–1945. In *Social Contexts of American Ethnology, 1840–1984,* edited by J. Helm, 122–38. Proceedings of the American Ethnological Society.

Kelly, Tobias. 2006. Documented Lives: Fear and the Uncertainties of Law During the Second Palestinian Intifada. *Journal of the Royal Anthropological Institute* 12:89–107.

Kenyatta, Jomo. 1938. *Facing Mt. Kenya*. London: Secker and Warburg.

Khalidi, Rashid. 2004. *Resurrecting Empire: Western Footprints and America's Perilous Path in the Middle East*. Boston: Beacon Press.

Kifner, John. 1988. Israel's New Violent Tactic Takes Toll on Both Sides. *New York Times*, January 22, A10.

Kilcullen, David. 2004. *Countering Global Insurgency*. Unpublished manuscript posted at http://smallwarsjournal.com/documents/kilcullen.pdf.

———. 2007. *Two Schools of Classical Counterinsurgency*. Unpublished manuscript posted at http://smallwarsjournal.com/blog/2007/01/two-schools-of-classical-count.

———. 2008. *Anatomy of a Tribal Revolt*. Unpublished manuscript posted at http://smallwarsjournal.com/blog/2007/08/anatomy-of-a-tribal-revolt/.

———. 2009. *The Accidental Guerilla: Fighting Small Wars in the Midst of a Big One*. Oxford: Oxford University Press.

Kinzer, Stephen. 2006. *Overthrow: America's Century of Regime change from Hawaii to Iraq*. New York: Henry Holt and Company, LLC.

Kipp, Jacob, Lester Grau, Karl Prinslow, and Don Smith. 2006. The Human Terrain System: A CORDS for the 21st Century. *Military Review* (September–October): 8–15.

Kirk, Michael, dir. 2004. *Rumsfeld's War*. Frontline/Washington Post Television Documentary. Airdate: October 26.

Klein, Naomi. 2007. *The Shock Doctrine: The Rise of Disaster Capitalism*. New York: Metropolitan Books.

Koerner, Brendan I. 2003. What Does a "Thumbs Up" Mean in Iraq? *Slate*, March 28. http://www.slate.com/id/2080812/

Kolbe, Athena R., and Royce A. Huston. 2006. Human Rights Abuse and Other Criminal Violations in Port-au-Prince, Haiti: A Random Survey of Households. *Lancet* 368(9538): 864–73.

Kolko, Gabriel. 1971. The Political Significance of the Center for Vietnamese Studies and Programs. *Bulletin of Concerned Asian Scholars* 4, 2 (February): 39–49.

Koonings, Kees, and Dirk Kruijt, eds. 2002. *Political Armies: The Military and Nation Building in the Age of Democracy*. New York: Palgrave Macmillan.

Kratovac, Katarina. 2007. Army Sniper Acquitted of Murder in Iraq. *USA Today*, September 27.

Kristensen, Hans M. 2006. *Global Strike: A Chronology of the Pentagon's New Offensive Strike Plan*. Washington, DC: Federation of American Scientists. http://www.nukestrat.com/.

Laguerre, Michel. 2005. Homeland Political Crisis, the Virtual Diasporic Public Sphere, and Diasporic Politics. *Journal of Latin American Anthropology* 10(1): 206–25.

Lansdale, Edward. 1972. *In the Midst of Wars An American's Mission to Southeast Asia*. New York: Harper and Row.

Lapham, Lewis. 1997. *Waiting for the Barbarians*. London: Verso.

Laqueur, Walter. 1976. *Guerrilla: A Historical and Critical Study*. Boston: Little, Brown.

Law and Society Trust. 2007. State of Human Rights in the Maldives. *Law and Society Trust Review* 17 (January): 231. Colombo, Sri Lanka.

Légitime, Général François Denys. 2002 [1879–1918]. *L'Armée Haïtienne, sa Nécessité, son Rôle*. Port-au-Prince: Les Éditions Lumière.

Leslie, Stuart. 1993. *The Cold War and American Science: The Military-Industrial-Academic Complex at MIT and Stanford*. New York: Columbia University Press.

Lessig, Lawrence. 1999. *Code and Other Laws of Cyberspace*. New York: Basic Books.

Levy, Gideon. 2004. Death in a Cemetery. *Ha'aretz*, July 23.

Lewy, Guenther. 1980. *America in Vietnam*. New York: Oxford University Press.

Lindsay, Reed. 2006. Peace Despite the Peacekeepers in Haiti. *NACLA Report on the Americas* (May/June): 31–6.

Lipset, David. 1980. *Gregory Bateson: The Legacy of a Scientist*. Englewood Cliffs, NJ: Prentice Hall.

Long, Ngo Vinh. 1971. Land Reform? *Bulletin of Concerned Asian Scholars* 4, 2 (February): 50–54.

———. 1973. *Before the Revolution*. Cambridge, Mass: MIT Press.

Longman, Timothy. 2001. Identity Cards, Ethnic Self-Perception, and Genocide in Rwanda. In *Documenting Individual Identity: The Development of State Practices in the Modern World*, edited by J. Caplan and J. Torpey, 345–57. Princeton: Princeton University Press.

Lourenção, Humberto Jose. 2007. *Forças Armadas e Amazônia*: (1985–2006). Ph.D. diss, State University of Campinas.

Lowen, Rebecca. 1997. *Creating the Cold War University: The Transformation of Stanford*. Berkeley: University of California Press.

Luban, David. 2005. Liberalism, Torture, and the Ticking Bomb. *Virginia Law Review* 91 (6): 1425–61.

Luttrell, Marcus, and Robinson, Patrick. 2008. *Lone Survivor: The Eyewitness Account of Operation Redwing and the Lost Heroes of SEAL Team 10*. New York: Back Bay Books.

Luttwak Edward. 2007. Dead End: Counterinsurgency Warfare as Military Malpractice. *Harper's*, February. http://www.harpers.org/archive/2007/02/0081384.

Lutz, Catherine. 2001. *Homefront: A Military City and the American Twentieth Century*. Boston: Beacon Press.

———. 2002. Making War at Home in the United States: Militarization and the Current Crisis. *American Anthropologist* 104 (3): 723–35.

———. 2006. Empire Is in the Details. *American Ethnologist* 33 (4): 593–611.

Lyons, J. F. S. 1971. *Ireland Since the Famine*. London: Weidenfeld & Nicolson.

Lyotard, Jean-François. 1984. *The Postmodern Condition: A Report on Knowledge*. Translated by Brian Massumi. Minneapolis: University of Minnesota Press.

Mabee, Carleton. 1987. Margaret Mead and Behavioral Scientists in World War II: Problems in Responsibility, Truth, and Effectiveness. *Journal of the History of the Behavioral Sciences* 23: 3–13.

MacDonald, Elizabeth P. [a.k.a. EP McIntosh]. 1947. *Undercover Girl*. New York: MacMillan.

Machiavelli, Niccolo. 2001 [1521]. *Art of War*. Translated by Ellis Farneworth. Cambridge, MA: Da Capo Press.

———. 2008 [1513]. *The Prince*. Translated by Luigi Ricci. New York: Modern Library.

Madariaga, Patricia. 2006. *Matan y Matan y Uno Sigue Ahí. Control Paramilitary Vida Cotidiana en un Pueblo de Urabá*. Bogotá: Ediciones Uniandes.

Maldivian Democratic Party. 2007. *A Tourist Paradise: The Dictatorship Continues*. Internal Report on the Events leading to the November 10th Demonstration by the Maldivian Democratic Party. Malé: Maldivian Democratic Party.

Mamdani, Mahmood. 2004. *Good Muslim, Bad Muslim: America, the Cold War and the Roots of Terror*. New York: Three Leaves Press, Doubleday.

Manning, Robert. 1989. We Could Have Won Vietnam. *New York Times*, November 12.

Mansour, Camille. 2005. The Palestinian Perception of America After 9/11. In *With Us or against Us: Studies in Global Anti-Americanism,* edited by T. Judt and D. Lacorne, 157–71. New York: Palgrave McMillan.

Marques, Adriana Aparecida. 2007. *Amazônia: Pensamento e Presença Militar.* Ph.D. diss, University of São Paulo.

Martin, Percy Alvin. 1918. The Influence of the United States on the Opening of the Amazon to the World's Commerce. *Hispanic American Historical Review* 1 (2): 146–62.

Martins Filho, João Roberto. 2005. The Brazilian Armed Forces and Plan Colombia. *Journal of Political and Military Sociology* 33 (Summer): 107–23.

Martins Filho, João Roberto, and Daniel Zirker. 2000. Nationalism, National Security, and Amazonia: Military Perceptions and Attitudes in Contemporary Brazil. *Armed Forces and Society* 27 (October 1): 105–29.

Marx, Karl. 1977. *Capital, Volume One.* Translated by Ben Fowkes. New York: Vintage Books & Random House.

———. 1978 [1852]. The Eighteenth Brumaire of Louis Bonaparte. In *The Marx-Engels Reader,* edited by Robert C. Tucker. 2d ed. W. W. Norton.

Masco, Joseph. 2006. *The Nuclear Borderlands: The Manhattan Project in Post–Cold War New Mexico.* Princeton: Princeton University Press.

Mason, Ann. 2003. Colombia's Democratic Security Agenda: Public Order in the Security Tripod. *Security Dialogue* 34: 4.

May, Elaine-Tyler. 1988. *Homeward Bound: American families in the Cold War Era.* New York: Basic Books.

Mayer, Arno. 2002. *The Furies: Violence and Terror in the French and Russian Revolutions.* Princeton: Princeton University Press.

Mayer, Jane. 2007. The Black Sites. *New Yorker,* August 13.

Mbembe, Achille. 2006. On Politics as a Form of Expenditure. In *Law and Disorder in the Postcolony,* edited Jean Comaroff and John Comaroff, 299–336. Chicago: University of Chicago Press.

McChesney, Robert. 2004. *The Problem of the Media: U.S. Communication Politics in the 21st Century.* New York: Monthly Review Press.

McCormick, John P. 1997. *Carl Schmidt's Critique of Liberalism: Against Politics as Technology.* Cambridge: Cambridge University Press.

McCrocklin, James. 1956. *Garde D'Haiti, 1915–1934: Twenty Years of Organization and Training by the United States Marine Corps.* Annapolis, MD: United States Naval Institute.

McFate, Montgomery. 2005a. Anthropology and Counterinsurgency: The Strange Story of Their Curious Relationship. *Military Review* (March–April): 24–38.

———. 2005b. The Military Utility of Understanding Adversary Culture. *Joint Force Quarterly,* July issue no. 38. http://calbears.findarticles.com/p/articles/mi_m0KNN/is_38/ai _n15631265.

McFate, Montgomery, and Andrea Jackson. 2005. An Organizational Solution to the DoD's Cultural Knowledge Needs. *Military Review* 85 (4): 18–21.

McNamara, Laura. 2007a. Notes on an Academic Scandal: Seymour Hersh, Abu Ghraib, and The Arab Mind. *Anthropology News* 48(7):4–5.

———. 2007b. Where Are the Anthropologists? *Anthropology News* 47 (7): 13.

McNickle, D'Arcy. 1979. Anthropology and the Indian Reorganization Act. In *The Uses of Anthropology,* edited by W. Goldschmidt, 51–60. Washington, DC: American Anthropology Association.

Meek, C. K. 1937. *Law and Authority in a Nigerian Tribe: A Study in Indirect Rule.* Oxford: Oxford University Press.

Mendelson Forman, Johanna. 2004. The Nation-Building Trap: Haiti after Aristide. *Open-Democracy,* March 11, 2004. http://www.opendemocracy.net.

Merle, Renae. 2006. First Ears, Then Hearts and Minds. *Washington Post,* November 1, p.D1.

Merom, Gil. 2003. *How Democracies Lose Small Wars.* Cambridge: Cambridge University Press.

Miller, Christopher. 1994. Unfinished Business: Colonialism in Sub-Saharan Africa and the Ideals of the French Revolution. In *The Global Ramifications of the French Revolution,* edited by Joseph Klaits and Michael H. Haltzel, 105–26. Cambridge, UK: Cambridge University Press.

Miller, Nicola. 2006. The Historiography of Nationalism and National Identity in Latin America. *Nations and Nationalism* 12 (2): 201–21.

Miller, Richard B. 2008. Justifications of the Iraq War Examined. *Ethics and International Affairs* 22 (Spring): 43–67.

Millikan, Max F., and Walt Rostow. 1998 [1954]. Notes of Foreign Economic Policy. In *Universities and Empire,* edited by Chris Simpson, 39–55. New York: New Press.

Mindich, David T.Z. 1998. *Just the Facts: How "Objectivity" Came to Define American Journalism.* New York: New York University Press.

Mitchell, Sean T. 2008. *Relaunching Alcântara: Space, Race, Technology and Inequality in Brazil.* Ph.D. diss. University of Chicago.

Molano, Alfredo. 2001. La Justicia Guerrillera. In *El Caleidoscopio de las Justicias en Colombia, Análisis Socio-Jurídico,* vol. II, edited by Boaventura Sousa Santos and Mauricio Garcia Villegas, 331–88. Bogotá: Colciencias, Instituto Colombiano de Antropología e Historia, Universidad de Coimbra, Universidad de los Andes.

Mooney, James. 1973. *The Ghost-Dance Religion and Wounded Knee.* New York: Dover Publications.

Moore, Soloman. 2008. G.I. Gets 10-Year Sentence in Killing of Unarmed Iraqi. *New York Times,* February 11.

Morris, Errol, dir. 2003. *The Fog of War: Eleven Lessons from the Life of Robert S. McNamara.* Sony Pictures.

Moyar, Mark. 1997. *Phoenix and the Birds of Prey: The CIA's Secret Campaign to Destroy the Viet Cong.* Annapolis, MD: Naval Institute Press.

———. 2006. *Triumph Forsaken: The Vietnam War 1954–65.* New York: Cambridge University Press.

———. 2007. *Phoenix and the Birds of Prey: Counterinsurgency and Counterterrorism in Vietnam.* 2d ed. Omaha: University of Nebraska.

Myre, Greg. 2004. Mideast Clashes Kill 6 Palestinians and Israeli Officer. *New York Times,* July 7, A3.

Nagl, John A. 2005. *Learning to Eat Soup with a Knife: Counterinsurgency Lessons from Malay and Vietnam.* Chicago: University of Chicago Press.

———. 2007. Foreword to the University of Chicago Press Edition. *The US Army/Marine Corps Counterinsurgency Field Manual,* xiii–xx. Chicago: University of Chicago Press.

Nash, Edith. 1989. Philleo Nash and Georgetown Day School. In *Applied Anthropologist and Public Servant: The Life and Work of Philleo Nash,* 34–41. National Association for the Practice of Anthropology, Bulletin, no. 7. Washington, DC: American Anthropological Association.

Nash, June. 1993. *We Eat the Mines and the Mines Eat Us: Dependency and Exploitation in Bolivian Tin Mines.* New York: Columbia University Press.

Navaro-Yashin, Yael. 2002. *Faces of the State: Secularism and Public Life in Turkey.* Princeton and Oxford: Princeton University Press.

Nevill, Capt. H. L. 1999 [1912]. *Campaigns on the North-west Frontier.* Nashville: Battery Press.

Niva, Steve. 2008. The New Walls of Baghdad: How the U.S. Is Reproducing Israel's Flawed Occupation Strategies in Iraq. *Foreign Policy in Focus, FPIF Policy Report.* April 21. http:// www.fpif.org/fpiftxt/5162.

Nordstrom, Carolyn. 1997. *A Different Kind of War Story.* Philadelphia: University of Pennsylvania Press.

Nugent, Stephen. 2007. *Scoping the Amazon: Image, Icon, and Ethnography.* Walnut Creek, CA: Left Coast Press.

Nuti, Paul. 2006. Smart Card: Don't Leave Military Base without It. *Anthropology News* 47 (7): 15–6.

Nuti, Paul, and Kerry Fosher. 2007. Reflecting Back on a Year of Debate with the Ad Hoc Commission. *Anthropology News* 48 (7): 3–4.

Nye, Joseph S. 2005. *Soft Power: The Means to Success in World Politics.* New York: Public Affairs.

O'Brien, Tim. 1998 [1990]. *The Things They Carried.* New York: Broadway Publishers.

Office of the Assistant Secretary of Defense. 2008. DefenseLink News Transcript: DoD News Briefing with Col. Schweitzer and Sgt. Maj. Flowers from the Pentagon Briefing Room, Arlington, VA, March 26. http://www.defenselink.mil/transcripts/transcript.aspx? transcriptid=4180.

Office of the Surgeon Multinational Force-Iraq, and Office of the Surgeon General United States Army Medical Command. 2006. *Mental Health Advisory Team (MHAT) IV, Operation Iraqi Freedom 05-07: Final Report.* November 17. http://www.armymedicine.army .mil/reports/mhat/mhat_iv/MHAT_IV_Report_17NOV06.pdf.

Oliker, Olga. 2008. Soft Power, Hard Power, and Counterinsurgency: The Early Soviet Experience in Central Asia and Its Implications. RAND Working Paper. RAND Corporation. WR-547-RC. February http://www.rand.org/pubs/working_papers/2008/RAND _WR547.pdf.

Oliveira, Roberto Monteiro de. 2001. A Iminente Conquista Estrangeira da Amazônia. http://www.militar.com.br/artigos/artigos2001/robertomonteirodeoliveira/ iminenteconquistaamazonia.htm.

Opler, Morris. 1987. Comment on "Engineering Internment." *American Ethnologist* 14 (2): 383–84.

Orwell, George. 1961 [1956]. Politics and the English Language. In *The Orwell Reader,* edited by George Orwell, 355–66. New York: Harcourt and Brace.

Packer, George. 2005. *The Assassins' Gate: America in Iraq.* New York: Farrar, Strauss and Giroux.

Palacios, Marco. 1995. *Entre la Legitimidad y la Violencia. Colombia 1875–1994.* Bogotá: Editorial Norma.

Pamuk, Orhan. 2004. *Snow.* Translated by Maureen Freeley. New York: Alfred Knopf.

Pantano, Illario. 2007. *Warlord: No Better Friend, No Worse Enemy.* New York: Threshold Press.

Pape, Robert. 2006. *Dying to Win: the Strategic Logic of Suicide Terrorism.* New York: Random House.

Paret, Peter. 1964. *French Revolutionary Warfare from Indochina to Algeria: The Analysis of a Political and Military Doctrine*. New York: Frederick A. Praeger Publishers.

Parker, Ned. 2007. Sniper Accused of Murder Disputes Statement. *Los Angeles Times,* December 8.

———. 2008. Sniper Unit Leader Tells of Ordering Shooting. *Los Angeles Times,* February 9.

Partlow, Joshua. 2007. U.S. Unit Walks 'A Fine Line' in Iraqi Capital. *Washington Post,* February 6, A1.

Passage, David. 2007. Speaking Out: Caution, Iraq Is not Vietnam. *Foreign Service Journal* (November): 13–16.

PASSIA. 2008. *Palestine Facts and Figures.* Jerusalem: PASSIA.

Pattillo, Donald M. 1998. *Pushing the Envelope: The American Aircraft Industry.* Ann Arbor: University of Michigan Press.

Pecaut, Daniel. 1988. *Crónica de Dos Décadas de Política Colombiana, 1968–1933.* Bogotá: Siglo XXI Editores.

Peixoto, João Paulo Machado. 2003. Statecraft: o Legado do Governo Fernando Henrique e os Desafios de Lula. In paper presented at the *VIII Congreso Internacional del CLAD sobre la Reforma del Estado e de la Administración Pública.* Panama. http://unpan1.un.org/intradoc/groups/public/documents/CLAD/clad0047109.pdf.

Perusek, Glenn. 2005. The US Occupation and Resistance in Iraq. *New Politics* X (Winter): 36–52.

Peters, Ralph. 2000. The Human Terrain of Urban Operations. *Proceedings* 30 (1): 4–12.

Peterson, Scott. 2007. US Army's Strategy in Afghanistan: Better Anthropology. *Christian Science Monitor,* September 7, p. 1.

Petraeus, David H. 2006. Observations from Soldiering in Iraq. *Military Review* (January–February): 2–11.

Pincus, Walter 2007. A Potentially Winning Tactic, with a Warning. *Washington Post,* August 27, A11.

Pino, Nathan, and Michael D. Wiatrowski, eds. 2006. *Democratic Policing in Transitional and Developing Countries.* Interdisciplinary Research Series in Ethnic, Gender and Class Relations. Hampshire, UK; Burlington, VT: Ashgate Publishing.

Pirnie, Bruce R., and William E. Simons. 1996. *Soldiers for Peace: Critical Operations Issues.* Santa Monica, CA: National Defense Research Institute, RAND.

Plato. 2008 [ca. 360 B.C.E.]. *Republic.* Translated by Robin Witerfield. Oxford: Oxford University Press.

Pletsch, Carl E. 1981. The Three Worlds, or the Division of Social Scientific Labor, circa 1950–1975. *Comparative Studies in Society and History* 3/23(4):565–90.

Plutarch. 1916. *Lives: Alcibiades and Coriolanus, Lysander and Sulla.* Cambridge: Loeb Classical Library.

Podhoretz, Norman. 2004. World War IV: How It Started, What It Means, and Why We Have to Win. *Commentary* (September): 17–54.

Polgreen, Lydia, and Tim Weiner. 2004. Haiti's Rebel Says He Is in Charge, and Political Confusion Deepens. *New York Times,* March 3, A1.

Pontecorvo, Gillo, dir. 1966. *The Battle of Algiers.* The Criterion Collection.

Porch, Douglas. 1986. Bugeaud, Galliéni, Lyautey: The Development of French Colonial Warfare. In *The Makers of Modern Strategy: From Machiavelli to the Nuclear Age,* edited by Peter Paret, 376–407. Princeton: Princeton University Press.

Presidential Commission, The Republic of the Maldives. 2003. Investigative Findings on the Incident of Shooting at Maafushi Jail. December 29. Malé: The President's Office, Republic of the Maldives.

Price, David. 1998. Gregory Bateson and the OSS. *Human Organization* 57 (4): 379–84.

———. 2003. Subtle Means and Enticing Carrots: The Impact of Funding on American Cold War Anthropology. *Critique of Anthropology* 23(4): 373–401.

———. 2007. Pilfered Scholarship Devastates General Petraeus' Counterinsurgency Manual. *CounterPunch* 14 (18): 1–6.

———. 2008a. The Military "Leveraging" of Cultural Knowledge: The Newly Available 2004. Stryker Report Evaluating Iraqi Failures. *CounterPunch,* March 18. http://www.counterpunch.com/price03182008.html.

———. 2008b. *Anthropological Intelligence: The Deployment and Neglect of American Anthropology during the Second World War.* Durham: Duke University Press.

———. 2008c. Anthropology's Third Rail: Counterinsurgency, Vietnam, Thailand, and the Political Uses of Militarized Anthropology. Paper presented at School for Advanced Research seminar on "Scholars, Security and Citizenship." July 24–25, Santa Fe.

Prochnau, William. 1995. *Once upon a Distant War.* New York: Vintage.

Project for a New American Century. 2000. *Rebuilding America's Defenses: Strategy, Forces, and Resources for a New Century.* http://www.newamericancentury.org/RebuildingAmericas Defenses.pdf.

Race, Jeffrey. 1972. *War Comes to Long An.* Berkeley: University of California.

Raffles, Hugh. 2002. *In Amazonia: A Natural History.* Princeton: Princeton University Press.

Rashid, Ali. 2005. Citizens' Brutality. *Minivan News.* Comment and Opinion Section. May 31. http://www.minivannews.com/news/news.php?id=725.

Reeves, Tom. 2003. Between a Sharp Tongue and a Blind Eye: The Politics of Criticism and Propaganda. *NACLA Report on the Americas* (July/August).

Regan, Jane. 2003. Haiti: Burning Slums Signal Gang Rule. *IPS/GIN,* October 1.

Renzi, Fred. 2006. Networks: Terra Incognita and the Case for Ethnographic Intelligence. *Military Review* (September/October):16–22.

Restrepo, Jorge, and Spagat, Michael. 2004. *Civilian Casualties in the Colombian Conflict: A New Approach to Human Security.* London: Royal Holloway College, University of London.

Rich, Ben R., and Leo Janos. 1994. *Skunk Works: A Personal Memoir of My Years at Lockheed.* New York: Little, Brown, and Company.

Ricks, Thomas E. 1998. *Making the Corps.* New York: Touchstone Books.

———. 2006. *Fiasco: The American Military Adventure in Iraq.* New York: Penguin Press.

Ricoeur, Paul. 2006. *Memory, History, Forgetting.* Chicago: University of Chicago Press.

Robinson, Paul. 2006. *Final Report of the Maldivian Penal Law and Sentencing Codification Project.* Volumes 1 and 2. Commissioned by the Office of the Attorney General of the Maldives and the United Nations Development Programme.

Robinson, Paul H., Zulfiqar, Adnan, Kammerud, Margaret, Orchowski, Michael, Gerlach, Elizabeth A., Pollock, Adam L., O'Brien, Thomas M., Lin, John C., Stenson, Tom, Katirai, Negar, Lee, J. John and Melzer, Marc Aaron. 2007. Codifying Shari'a: International Norms, Legality and the Freedom to Invent New Forms. *Journal of Comparative Law* 2(1):1–53.

Rodríguez, Edwin. 2007. Los Estudios Sobre El Paramilitarismo En Colombia. In *Análisis Político* (60):117–34.

Rofel, Lisa. 1999. *Other Modernities: Gendered Yearnings in China after Socialism*. Berkeley: University of California Press.

Rohde, David. 2007. Army Enlists Anthropology in War Zones. *New York Times*, October 5.

Rohter, Larry. 2002. Deep in Brazil, a Flight of Paranoid Fancy. *New York Times*, June 23.

Rosaldo, Renato. 1986. From the Door of His Tent: The Fieldworker and the Inquisitor. In *Writing Culture: The Poetics and Politics of Ethnography*, edited by James Clifford and George E. Marcus, 77–97. Berkeley: University of California Press.

Rose-Ackerman, Susan. 2004. Establishing the Rule of Law. In *When States Fail: Causes and Consequences*, edited by Robert Rotberg, 182–221. Princeton, NJ: Princeton University Press.

Rosen, Nir. 2004. How the Middle East Is Really Getting Remade. *Asia Times Online*, May 21. http://www.atimes.com/atimes/Middle_East/FE21Ak01.html.

———. 2008. The Myth of the Surge. *Rolling Stone*, March 6.

Rotberg, Robert, ed. 2003. *State Failure and State Weakness in a Time of Terror*. Washington, DC: Brookings Institute Press.

———. ed. 2004a. *When States Fail: Causes and Consequences*. Princeton, NJ: Princeton University Press.

———. 2004b. The Failure and Collapse of Nation-States: Breakdown, Prevention, and Repair. In *When States Fail: Causes and Consequences*, edited by Robert I. Rotberg, 1–45. Princeton, NJ: Princeton University Press.

Rousseau, Jean-Jacques. 1968. New York: *The Social Contract*. Translated by Maurice Cranston. Penguin Classics.

Rubinstein, Robert A. 2008. *Peacekeeping under Fire: Culture and Intervention*. Boulder, CO: Paradigm Publishers.

Rumsfeld, Donald H. 2002. Transforming the Military. *Foreign Affairs* 81 (3): 20–32.

Saada, Imad. 2004. Israeli Officer, Four Palestinians Killed as Quartet Discuss Peace Process. Nablus: Agence France Presse.

Sahlins, Marshall. 1999. Two or Three Things That I Know about Culture. *Journal of the Royal Anthropological Institute* 5:399–422.

———. 2000 [1966]. The Destruction of Conscience in Vietnam. In *Culture in Practice: Selected Essays*, 229–60. New York: Zone Books.

Said, Edward W. 1984. Permission to Narrate. *Journal of Palestine Studies* 8 (3): 27–48.

Sampaio, Fernando G. 1994. *O Dia em que Napoleão Fugiu de Santa Helena*. Porto Alegre: S, M & B Editores.

Sautter, John A. 2008. The Two Sides of Economic and Democratic Change: An Economic Model of Terrorism and Insurgency. *Small Wars Journal*. February 7. http://smallwarsjournal.com/mag/2008/02/an-economic-model-of-terrorism.php.

Schleifer, Yigal. 2005. Sure It's Fiction. But Many Turks See Fact in Anti-US novel. *Christian Science Monitor*, February 15. http://www.csmonitor.com/2005/0215/p01s04-woeu.htm.

Scahill, Jeremy. 2007. *Blackwater: The Rise of the World's Most Powerful Mercenary Army*. New York: Nation Books.

Scales, Robert. 2004. Army Transformation: Implications for the Future. Testimony before the U.S. House Armed Services Committee, July 15.

Schlight, John. 1996. *A War Too Long. The USAF in Southeast Asia, 1961–1975*. Air Force History and Museums Program. http://www.scribd.com/doc/1451050/US-Air-Force-a-war-too-long.

Schmidt, Hans. 1971. *The United States Occupation of Haiti, 1915–1934*. New Brunswick, NJ: Rutgers University Press.

Schmitt, Carl. 2005 [1922]. *Political Theology: Four Chapters on the Concept of Sovereignty*. Translated by George Schwab. Chicago: University of Chicago Press.

Schmitt, Eric. 2005. General Is Scolded for Saying, "It's Fun to Shoot Some People." *New York Times*, February 4, sec. Washington.

———. 2006. 2,000 More M.P.'s Will Help Train the Iraqi Police. *New York Times*, January 16, International Section.

Schrecker, Ellen. 1998. *Many Are the Crimes: McCarthyism in America*. Boston: Little, Brown.

Schuller, Mark. 2008. "Haiti Is Finished!" Haiti's End of History Meets the Ends of Capitalism. In *Capitalizing on Catastrophe: Neoliberal Strategies in Disaster Reconstruction*, edited by Nandini Gunewardena and Mark Schuller, 191–214. Lanham, MD: AltaMira Press.

Schulzinger, Robert D. 1997. *A Time for War: The US and Vietnam*. New York: Oxford University Press.

Sedrez, Lise. 2000a. E-mail to brasanet@unm.edu (sent May 2000). In *Dossier Amazônia 1: Primeira Onda de Boatos, Maio-Junho de 2000*, edited by Paulo Roberto de Almeida, 29. http://www.pralmeida.org/docs/01DossierAmazonia1.html.

———. 2000b. Earlier Images of the Amazon in the USA. In *Forest History: International Studies on Socioeconomic and Forest Ecosystem Change: Report Number 2 of the UURFO Task Force on Environmental Change*, edited by M. Agnoleti and S. Anderson, 93–108. Wallingford: CABI Publishing.

Seitz, Charmaine. 2003. ISM at the Crossroads: The Evolution of the International Solidarity Movement. *Journal of Palestine Studies* 32(4): 50–67.

Selden, Mark. 1969. The NLF and the Transformation of Vietnamese Society. *Bulletin of Concerned Asian Scholars* 2 (October): 34–43.

Selmeski, Brian. 2007. Who Are the Security Anthropologists? *Anthropology News* 48 (5): 11–12.

Semana Magazine. 2005. Sí Hay Guerra Señor Presidente. No. 1221, February 7.

Sharp, Jeremy M. 2008. *CRS Report for Congress: U.S. Foreign Aid to Israel*. Washington, DC: Congressional Research Service.

Sheehan, Neil. 1988. *A Bright, Shining Lie: John Paul Vann and America in Vietnam*. New York: Vintage.

Shirts, Matthew. 2001. Mentiras Amazônicas. *Estado de São Paulo*, December 3.

Siegel, James T. 1998. *A New Criminal Type in Jakarta: Counter-Revolution Today*. Durham: Duke University Press.

Sifry, Micah, and Christopher Cerf, eds. 2003. *The Iraq War Reader: History, Documents, Opinions*. New York: Simon & Schuster.

Sikkink, Kathryn. 1991. *Ideas and Institutions: Developmentalism in Brazil and Argentina*. Ithaca: Cornell University Press.

Silverstein, Paul A. 2000. Regimes of (Un)Truth: Conspiracy Theory and the Transnationalization of the Algerian Civil War. *Middle East Report* 214.

———. 2002. An Excess of Truth: Violence, Conspiracy Theorizing and the Algerian War. *Anthropological Quarterly* 75 (Autumn): 643–74.

Simpson, Christopher. 1994. *Science of Coercion*. New York: Oxford University Press.

Skogan, Wesley G. 2003. *Community Policing: Can It Work?* The Wadsworth Professionalism in Policing Series. Belmont, CA. Wadsworth Publishing.

Slater, Candace. 2003. *Entangled Edens: Visions of the Amazon*. Berkeley: University of California Press.

Smith, Dan. 1994. Just War, Clausewitz and Sarajevo. *Journal of Peace Research* 31(2): 136–42.

Society for Applied Anthropology. 1983. *Professional and Ethical Responsibilities.*

Soderland, Walter C. 2006. U.S. Network Television News Framing of the February 2004 Overthrow of Haitian President Jean-Bertrand Aristide. *Journal of Haitian Studies* 12(2): 78–111.

Sorley, Lewis. 1999. *A Better War: The Unexamined Victories and Final Tragedy of America's Last Years in Vietnam.* New York: Harcourt Brace & Company.

Spicer, Edward H. 1979. Anthropologists and the War Relocation Authority. In *The Uses of Anthropology,* edited by W. Goldschmidt, 217–37. Washington, DC: American Anthropology Association.

Starn, Orin. 1986. Engineering Internment: Anthropologists and the War Relocation Authority. *American Ethnologist* 13 (4): 700–20.

Steward, Julian. 1969. Limitations of Applied Anthropology: The Case of the Indian New Deal. *Journal of the Steward Anthropological Society* 1 (1): 1–17.

Stocking, George W. Jr. 1992. *The Ethnographer's Magic and Other Essays in the History of Anthropology.* Madison: University of Wisconsin Press.

———. 2001. *Delimiting Anthropology: Occasional Inquiries and Reflections.* Madison: University of Wisconsin Press.

Strauss, Leo. 1964. *The City and Man.* Chicago: Rand McNally.

Summers, Frank. 2007. The American Psychological Association, and the Involvement of Psychologists at Guantanamo Bay. *Psychoanalysis, Culture and Society* 12 (April): 83–92.

Summers, Harry G. 1982. *On Strategy: A Critical Analysis of the Vietnam War.* Novato, CA: Presidio Press.

———. 2007. Preface. *Phoenix and the Birds of Prey: Counterinsurgency and Counterterrorism in Vietnam* by Mark Moyar. 2d ed. Omaha: University of Nebraska.

Suzuki, Peter T. 1980. Case Study: A Retrospective Analysis of a Wartime "National Character" Study. *Dialectical Anthropology* 5 (1): 33–45.

———. 1981. Anthropologists in the Wartime Camps for Japanese Americans: A Documentary Study. *Dialectical Anthropology* 6 (1):23–60.

———. 1986. The University of California Japanese Evacuation and Resettlement Study: A Prolegomon. *Dialectical Anthropology* 10 (3):189–231.

Sweetman, Bill. 1999. *Inside the Stealth Bomber.* Osceola, WI: Motorbooks International.

Tacitus. 1894. *The Agricola and Germania.* Translated by R. B. Townshend London: Metheun & Co.

Tambiah, Stanley J. 1997. *Leveling Crowds: Ethnonationalist Conflicts and Collective Violence in South Asia.* Comparative Studies in Religion and Society, 10. Berkeley: University of California Press.

Tang, Truong Nhu. 1985. *Viet Cong Memoir.* New York: Harcourt, Brace, Jovanovich.

Taussig, Michael. 1991. *Shamanism, Colonialism, and the Wild Man: A Study in Terror and Healing.* Chicago: University of Chicago Press.

Tax, Sol. 1950. Action Anthropology. *América Indígena* 12: 103–9.

———. 1975. Action Anthropology. *Current Anthropology* 16: 514–17.

Thompson, Edward Palmer. 1971. The Moral Economy of the English Crowd in the 18th Century. *Past & Present* 50:76–136.

Thompson, Laura. 1944. Some Perspectives on Applied Anthropology. *Applied Anthropology* 3:12–16.

Thompson, Scott, and Donaldson Frizzell, eds. 1977. *The Lessons of Vietnam*. New York: Krane, Russak.

Todd, Lin et al. 2006. *Iraq Tribal Study: Al Anbar Governorate*. Unpublished report commissioned by the U.S. Department of Defense. http://www.comw.org/warreport/fulltext/0709todd.pdf.

Toohey, Brian, and William Pinwell. 1989. *Oyster: The Story of the Australian Secret Intelligence Service*. Victoria: Heinemann.

Trainor, Bernard E. 1989. Order of Battle Is Set In Campaign to Mold Well-Read Marines. *New York Times*, August 10.

Treviño, Linda K., and Katherine A. Nelson. 2003. *Managing Business Ethics: Straight Talk about How To Do It Right*. Hoboken, NJ: Wiley Publishers.

Trouillot, Michel-Rolph. 1990. *Haiti, State against Nation: The Origins and Legacies of Duvalierism*. New York: Monthly Review Press.

Trujillo, Marco. 2004. "Cannibal Army" Rebels Seize Haitian City. *National Post*, February 7, A14.

Trullinger, James. 1980. *Village at War*. New York: Longman.

Tsing, Anna. 2005. *Friction: An Ethnography of Global Connection*. Princeton: Princeton University Press.

Uçar, Orkun and Burak Turna. 2005. *Metal Fırtına*. İstanbul: Timaş Publishing.

Unger, Roberto Mangabeira. 2007. *The Self Awakened*. Cambridge: Harvard University Press.

United Nations. 2005. *Haiti-MINUSTAH-Mandate*. http://www.un.org/Depts/dpko/missions/minustah/mandate.html.

———. 2008. *Report Number 63: Implementation of the Agreement on Movement and Access and Update on Gaza Crossings*. http://www.ochaopt.org/documents/AMA_63.pdf.

Universidad del Rosario. 2006. *Monitoreo Mensual—Cooperación Internacional para el Desarrollo Andino*. Bogotá and Madrid: CIDÁN.

Uribe, Álvaro. 2002a. No Igualar a la Fuerza Pública con Actores del Conflicto. Speech delivered on December 5. Presidencia de Colombia. http://www.presidencia.gov.co/prensa_new/sne/2002/diciembre/05/12122002.htm.

———. 2002b. Clausura del Foro Conflicto Armado: La Cara Urbana. Speech delivered on November 27. Presidencia de Colombia. http://www.presidencia.gov.co/prensa_new/discursos/discursos2002/noviembre/conflicto.htm.

———. 2002c. Encuentro con Directores de Escuelas de Formación y Academia Superior de la Policía. Speech delivered on October 3. Presidencia de Colombia. http://www.presidencia.gov.co/prensa_new/discursos/discursos2002/octubre/policia.htm.

———. 2003. Palabras del Presidente durante la Ceremonia de Ascenso en la Escuela General Santander. Speech delivered on June 20. Presidencia de Colombia. http://www.presidencia.gov.co/prensa_new/sne/2003/junio/20/14202003.htm.

U.S. Army Surgeon General, and HQDA G-1. 2003. *Operation Iraqi Freedom (OIF) Mental Health Advisory Team (MHAT): Report*. December 16. http://www.armymedicine.army.mil/reports/mhat/mhat/mhat_report.pdf.

U.S. Central Intelligence Agency. 2008. *Maldives: The World Factbook*. https://www.cia.gov/library/publications/the-world-factbook/geos/mv.html#Military.

U.S. Department of the Army. 2006. *Counterinsurgency Field Manual No. 3-24*. Washington, DC: Government Printing Office. http://www.fas.org/irp/doddir/army/fm3-24fd.pdf.

———. 2007. *U.S. Army/Marine Corps Counterinsurgency Field Manual*. Chicago: University of Chicago Press.

U.S. Department of Defense. 2006. *Measuring Stability and Security in Iraq.* Quarterly Report to Congress in accordance with the Department of Defense Appropriations Act 2006 (Section 9010), Public Law 109–148, August 29.

———. 2007. *2008 Global War on Terror Amendment.* Washington: Government Printing Office.

U.S. Department of State. Bureau of Democracy, Human Rights, and Labor. 2007. *Country Report on Human Rights Practices: Maldives.* http://www.state.gov/g/drl/rls/hrrpt/2007/100617.htm

U.S. House Un-American Activities Committee. 1967. *Guerrilla Warfare Advocates in the United States.* Washington, DC: Government Printing Office.

U.S. Joint Chiefs of Staff. 2000. *Joint Vision 2020.* Washington, DC: Government Printing Office. http://www.dtic.mil/jointvision/jvpub2.htm.

U.S. Marine Corps. 2006. Iraq Cultural Smart Card: Guide for Cultural Awareness (revised). Marine Corps Intelligence Activity, Quantico, VA. http://www.fas.org/irp/doddir/usmc/iraqsmart-0506.pdf.

U.S. National Security Council. 2002. *The National Security Strategy of the United States of America.* Washington, DC: Government Printing Office. www.whitehouse.gov/nsc/nss.pdf.

U.S. Office of the Secretary of Defense. 2007. *OSD RDT&E Budget Item Justification.* Washington, DC: Department of Defense.

U.S. *v.* Michael Hensley and U.S. *v.* Jorge Sandoval. 2007. Consolidated Article 32(b) hearing, Forward Operating Base Iskandariyah, Iraq, 24 July. Verbatim transcript.

Valentine, Douglas. 1990. *The Phoenix Program.* New York: Morrow.

Villacres, Edward. 2007. Interview on the *Diane Rehm Show,* October 10. WAMU-FM 88.5, Washington DC. http://wamu.org/programs/dr/07/10/10.php.

Voelkel, Tyson. 2007. Counterinsurgency Doctrine FM 3-24 and Operation Iraqi Freedom: A Bottom-Up Review. In *The Interagency and Counterinsurgency Warfare: Stability, Security, Transition, and Reconstruction Roles,* edited by Joseph R. Cerami and Jay W. Boggs 551–56. Carlisle, PA: U.S. Army's Strategic Studies Institute. http://www.strategicstudiesinstitute.army.mil/pdffiles/pub828.pdf.

Wakin, Eric. 2008. *Anthropology Goes to War: Professional Ethics and Counterinsurgency in Thailand.* Madison: University of Wisconsin Press.

Warner, Michael. 1992. The Mass Public and the Mass Subject. In *Habermas and the Public Sphere,* edited by Craig Calhoun, 377–401. Cambridge, MA: MIT Press.

———. 2002. *Publics and Counter-Publics.* New York: Zone Books.

Washington CAS. 1944. Community Analysts Section Annual Report July 1-December 31, 1943. Washington, DC.

Wax, Dustin M. 2008. Introduction. In *Anthropology at the Dawn of the Cold War,* edited by Dustin M. Wax, 1–16. London: Pluto Press.

Weber, Max. 1958a. Bureaucracy. In *From Max Weber: Essays in Sociology,* translated and edited by H. H. Gerth and C. Wright Mills, 196–244. Oxford: Oxford University Press.

———. 1958b. Politics as a Vocation. In *From Max Weber: Essays in Sociology,* translated and edited by H. H. Gerth and C. Wright Mills, 77–128. Oxford: Oxford University Press.

———. 1958c. Science as a Vocation. In *From Max Weber: Essays in Sociology,* translated and edited by H. H. Gerth and C. Wright Mills, 129–156. Oxford: Oxford University Press.

———. 1978 [1919]. *Economy and Society.* Edited by Guenther Roth and Claus Wittich. Berkeley: University of California Press.

Weinberger, Sharon. 2008a. Gates: Human Terrain Teams Going through "Growing Pains." *Wired Blog Network.* April 16, http://blog.wired.com/defense/2008/04/gates-human-ter.html.

———. 2008b. Pentagon Looks to Network Science to Predict Future. *Wired Blog Network.* April 5, http://blog.wired.com/defense/2008/04/pentagon-looks.html.

Welch, Claude E., ed. 1976. *Civilian Control of the Military: Theory and Cases from Developing Countries.* Albany: State University of New York Press.

Welsh, David. 1968. Pacification in Vietnam. In *Ramparts: A Vietnam Primer,* edited by Robert Scheer, 61–79. San Francisco: Ramparts.

West, Bing. 2005. *No True Glory: A Frontline Account of the Battle for Fallujah.* New York: Bantam Books.

West, Harry, and Todd Sanders, eds. 2003. *Transparency and Conspiracy. Ethnographies of Suspicion in the New World Order.* Durham and London: Duke University Press.

White, Josh, and Bradley Graham. 2005. Military Says It Paid Iraqi Papers for News. *Washington Post,* December 3.

White, Josh, and Ann Scott Tyson. 2006. Rumsfeld Offers Strategies for Current War. *Washingtonpost.com,* February 3.

Willbanks, James H. 2007. *The Tet Offensive: A Concise History.* New York: Columbia University Press.

Wilson, Scott, and Al Kamen. 2009. Global War on Terror Is Given a New Name. *Washington Post,* March 25, A4.

Wolf, Naomi. 2007. Fascist America, in 10 Easy Steps. *Guardian,* April 24. http://www.guardian.co.uk/world/2007/apr/24/usa.comment.

Wood, Sara. 2007. Defense Department Releases Mental Health Assessment Findings. American Forces Press Service. May 4. http://www.army.mil/-news/2007/05/07/3005-defense-department-releases-mental-health-assessment-findings/ .

Woodward, Bob. *Plan of Attack.* 2004. New York: Simon & Schuster.

Wright, Robin M., and Manuela Carneiro da Cunha. 2000. Destruction, Resistance, and Transformation—Southern, Coastal, and Northern Brazil (1580–1890). In *The Cambridge History of the Native Peoples of the Americas,* edited by Bruce G. Trigger, Wilcomb E. Washburn, and Richard E. W. Adams, 287–381. Cambridge: Cambridge University Press.

Yalnız, Murat. 2008. Öcalan da Ergenekon'un Adamı ve Bu Görevi Sürüyor. *Yeni Aktuel,* Sayı 135, February 7–13: 22–28.

Yans-McLaughlin, Virginia. 1986. Science, Democracy, and Ethics: Mobilizing Culture and Personality for World War II. In *Malinowski, Rivers, Benedict and Others: Essays on Culture and Personality,* edited by George Stocking, 184–217. Madison: University of Wisconsin Press.

Young, Marilyn. 1991. *The Vietnam Wars, 1945–1990.* New York: Harper Perennial.

Younger, Stephen M. 2005. Simulating the Dynamics of Simple Societies. *Los Alamos Research Highlights,* April.

———. 2007. *Endangered Species: How We Can Avoid Mass Destruction and Build a Lasting Peace.* New York: Ecco.

Zartman, I. William. 1995. *Collapsed States: The Disintegration and Restoration of Legitimate Authority.* Boulder, CO: Lynne Riener.

Zaverucha, Jorge. 2005. FHC, Forças Armadas e Polícia: Entre o Autoritarismo e a Democracia, 1999–2002. Rio de Janeiro: Editora Record.

Zizek, Slavoj. 1989. *The Sublime Object of Ideology.* New York and London: Verso.

CONTRIBUTORS

GREG BECKETT is Harper Fellow and Collegiate Assistant Professor in the Social Sciences Collegiate Division at the University of Chicago. His current book project, *The End of Haiti,* explores the intersection of environmental collapse, political struggle, and state failure in contemporary Haiti, with a focus on the social experience of crisis during the so-called "unending" transition to democracy.

JEFFREY BENNETT is an assistant professor of anthropology and religious studies at the University of Missouri–Kansas City. He is currently working on a book about religion and politics in early twentieth-century Portugal. He was enlisted in the U.S. Army between 1986 and 1992. During that time he served as a team leader in the 1/501ˢᵗ scout platoon and as a weapons sergeant in the First Special Forces Group (Airborne).

AMAHL BISHARA is an assistant professor in the Department of Anthropology at Tufts University. She published "Watching U.S. Television from the Palestinian Street: The Media, The State, and Representational Interventions" in *Cultural Anthropology* (2008). She is currently completing an ethnography of the production of U.S. news in the West Bank.

KEVIN CAFFREY is lecturer in the Committee on Social Studies at Harvard University. His work focuses on China, religion, culture, and politics.

PAOLA CASTAÑO is a Ph.D. candidate in the Department of Sociology at the University of Chicago. Her dissertation examines practices of categorization of the victims of the armed conflict in Colombia in the National Commission of Reparation and Reconciliation and the role of understandings of violence in this process. She has degrees in political science and history from the Univerisdad de los Andes in Bogotá-Colombia and is the author of *La Construcción de un Campo de Conocimiento: La Historia Mundial* (Universidad de los Andes, 2005).

ROCHELLE DAVIS joined the Center for Contemporary Arab Studies at Georgetown University in the fall of 2005 as an assistant professor of Arab culture and society. She completed her Ph.D. in 2002 at the University of Michigan in cultural anthropology and modern Arabic literature. Her book manuscript in progress deals with village books published by Palestinian refugees about their villages that were destroyed in 1948. Her current research is about the U.S. military's conception of culture in the current war in Iraq. Her coauthors, Dahlia Elzein and Dena Takruri, graduated in 2008 from Georgetown University's Center for Contemporary Arab Studies with M.A.s in Arab studies. Dahlia currently works at Human Rights Watch in New York and Dena is an assistant producer at al-Jazeera Arabic in Washington, D.C.

KERRY FOSHER is a social anthropologist who focuses on practice, process, and change within U.S. security institutions. She works in an applied capacity as the Command Social Scientist for Marine Corps Intelligence Activity, where she is responsible for shaping how the command learns about and addresses social science concepts and data. She is the author of *Under Construction: Making Homeland Security at the Local Level* (University of Chicago Press, 2008).

ELIZABETH GARLAND is assistant professor of anthropology at Union College. She received her Ph.D. in cultural anthropology from the University of Chicago in 2006 and is currently completing a book on wildlife conservation, tourism, and the neoliberal state in Tanzania.

ROBERTO J. GONZÁLEZ is associate professor of anthropology at San Jose State University. He is the author of *Zapotec Science: Farming and Food in the Northern Sierra of Oaxaca* (University of Texas Press, 2001) and editor of *Anthropologists in the Public Sphere: Speaking Out on War, Peace, and American Power* (University of Texas Press, 2004). His recent articles, "Towards Mercenary Anthropology?" and "Human Terrain: Past, Present, and Future Applications" (published in *Anthropology Today*) critically examine anthropological collaboration in counterinsurgency.

MARCUS B. GRIFFIN received his Ph.D. in anthropology from the University of Illinois in 1996. After seven years as a professor at Christopher Newport University in Newport News, Virginia, he deployed to Iraq to support U.S. Army and Marine stability operations in Baghdad and Anbar Province. He now is a Senior Social Science Advisor to the U.S. Army's Human Terrain System, a program of the Training and Doctrine Command.

HUGH GUSTERSON is professor of anthropology and sociology at George Mason University. He is the author of *Nuclear Rites* (1996) and *People of the Bomb* (2004) and coeditor of *Why America's Top Pundits Are Wrong* (2005) and *The Counter-Counterinsurgency Manual* (Prickly Paradigm, 2009). He also writes a regular column for the *Bulletin of the Atomic Scientists*. Gusterson is cofounder of the Network of Concerned Anthropologists.

JAMES L. HEVIA is professor of international history at the University of Chicago and associate editor of the journal, *positions*. His current research concerns British India army intelligence and the construction of geo-strategic Asia.

KURT JACOBSEN is a research associate in the Program on International Politics, Economics and Security (PIPES) in the Political Science Department at the University of Chicago. He is the author or editor of half a dozen books including, most recently, *Experiencing the State* (Oxford, 2006), coedited with Lloyd Rudolph. Forthcoming are *Freud's Foes: Psychoanalysis, Science and Resistance* (Rowman & Littlefield) and *Pacification and Its Discontents* (Prickly Paradigm Press).

BEATRICE JAUREGUI is a visiting fellow at the Center for the Advanced Study of India, and received her Ph.D. in the Department of Anthropology at the University of Chicago. Her dissertation, "Shadows of the State, Subalterns of the State: Police and 'Law and Order' in Postcolonial India," is an ethnographic study of police life and work in northern India.

JOHN D. KELLY is professor of anthropology in the college and chair of the Department of Anthropology at the University of Chicago. He has written extensively about decolonization and Pax Americana, his work including *Represented Communities: Fiji and World*

Decolonization (with coauthor Martha Kaplan; University of Chicago Press 2001), *The American Game: Capitalism, Decolonization, World Domination and Baseball* (Prickly Paradigm, 2006), and, most recently, "Legal Fictions after Empire" (with Martha Kaplan, in *Art of the State: Sovereignty Past and Present,* edited by Douglas Howland and Luise White).

JOSEPH MASCO teaches anthropology and science studies at the University of Chicago. He is the author of *The Nuclear Borderlands: The Manhattan Project in Post-Cold War New Mexico* (Princeton University Press, 2006). He has published widely on U.S. national security culture in venues such as *Cultural Anthropology, Public Culture, American Ethnologist, Radical History Review,* the *Bulletin of the Atomic Scientists,* and *Cabinet.* His current projects explore the intersections of national security, technology, affect, and the public sphere in the United States.

SEAN T. MITCHELL is visiting assistant professor in the Department of Anthropology at Vanderbilt University. His current book project, *Relaunching Alcântara: Space, Race, Technology and Inequality in Brazil,* an ethnographic study of the conflicts surrounding Brazil's principal satellite launch base, analyzes the changing politics of race, inequality, and technomilitary development in Brazil.

CHRISTOPHER T. NELSON is a cultural anthropologist at the University of North Carolina at Chapel Hill. A graduate of the University of Chicago, his interests include history, memory, and the critique of everyday life. His book, *Dancing with the Dead* (Duke University Press, 2009), is a study of Okinawan comedians, storytellers, and ethnographers. From 1983 until 1990, he was a Marine infantry officer.

MIHIR PANDYA is a doctoral student in the Department of Anthropology at the University of Chicago. His dissertation research focuses on the cultural life of the aerospace industry in Southern California.

DAVID H. PRICE is a professor at St. Martin's University in Lacey, Washington, where he teaches courses in anthropology and social justice. His research uses the Freedom of Information Act, archives, and interviews to document historical interactions between anthropologists and intelligence agencies. He is the author of *Threatening Anthropology* (Duke University Press, 2004) and *Anthropological Intelligence: The Deployment and Neglect of American Anthropology during the Second World War* (Duke University Press, 2008).

JEREMY WALTON is an assistant professor in the religion program at New York University. His book manuscript, *Constructing Civic Virtue in a Secular State: Islam, Civil Society and Liberal Piety in Contemporary Turkey,* explores the relationship between secular and religious dispensations in Turkey with an eye toward questions of aesthetics, publicness, and practices of historicity.

DUSTIN M. WAX teaches anthropology and women's studies at both the College of Southern Nevada and the University of Nevada, Las Vegas. He is a founding member of the anthropology weblog *Savage Minds* (http://www.savageminds.org), selected as a top twenty science blog by *Nature* in 2006, and is the editor of the recently released book *Anthropology at the Dawn of the Cold War: The Influence of Foundations, McCarthyism and the CIA* (Pluto Books, 2008).

Abu Ghraib Prison, 282, 313, 330, 331, 337; as portrayed in Turkish media, 106, 113
action anthropology, 251, 255, 262
Adana, 111
Afghanistan: in Caldwell manual, 169, 171; development programs in, 257; preemptive strikes in 1990s, 3. *See also* Afghanistan, conflict in (2001–)
Afghanistan, conflict in (2001–), 1, 4, 36, 66n6, 96, 174–75, 197; books about, 343; destruction of conscience during, 13; failure for U.S. to achieve stability in, 15n2, 196, 201; HTT in, 215, 231, 234–36, 246, 249–50, 284, 287, 289; insurgency in, 194, 280; as a retaliatory war, 200; U.S. soldiers' experience in, 316, 322 348, 352, 354n9
Africa, 12, 176; Central, 117–23; East, 242–43; North, 35, 69, 170, 195, 252; South, 170–72, 258. *See also* Algeria; Rwanda; Sudan
African Americans, 150, 203–5
Agamben, Giorgio, 7, 19, 34, 47, 50n3, 51n5
Aktuel (magazine), 111–13
Alcântara Launch Center, 90, 103n5
al-Janabi, Genei, 313–15, 323–24
Algeria: French counterinsurgency tactics in, 70, 72, 173, 200, 239, 312, 327; insurgency in, 181, 194–95, 203, 205
Almeida, Paulo Roberto de, 95, 98, 99, 103n12–13

al-Qaeda, 3, 107 338; and terrorist activities, 79, 194, 210; U.S. attempt to eliminate, 75, 196–98, 241, 323
Amazonia: environmentalist concerns about, 93–94, 100–1; fears of U.S. invasion of, 89–101
America. *See* United States
American Anthropological Association (AAA), 280, 293
American Army. *See* U.S. military
American Political Science Association, 9
American Power: ethnography of, 2, 6–7, 12, 341; fantasies/imaginaries of, 85–87, 105–10, 113–15, 196–202, and full spectrum dominance/global projection of, 1, 100, 149, 150, 181, 196, 199–200; in Israeli-Palestinian conflict, 125–35; material Projections of, 86, 119, 125–35, 137–45; opacity of, 41, 79, 87, 90, 99, 101, 102n3; ubiquity of, 85, 150, 181; during the War on Terror, 85, 87, 117, 193–206
American Psychological Association, 4, 186
Americans: African-, 150, 203–5; internment of Japanese-, 156–61, 164; mobilization through fear, 198; Native-, 154–55, 157–59. *See also* citizens/citizenship
Anderson, Benedict, 110
Ankara, 107, 108, 111
anthropological ethics. *See* ethics, of anthropology

anthropologists, 19, 20, 21, 85, 129, 134; as
"community analysts" for Japanese internment camps, 150, 156, 159, 161–64,
255–56; as employees of the British colonial administration, 236–39, 242; as employees of the U.S. government, 153–62,
209–13, 244n1, 245, 261–71, 292–93; on
Human Terrain Teams (HTT), 214–29,
231, 234–36, 246, 249–50, 288; as taking "shaping" roles, 263–65
anthropology, 149, 166–67; and alliance
with counterinsurgency initiatives,
153–67, 252–57; and colonial rule,
236–39; and the counterinsurgency field
manual, 74, 239–40, 248; and debate
over collaboration with the military,
1–13, 21, 68, 209–13, 234–36, 257–60,
291–94; and interest in U.S. military as
site of study, 2, 8, 293; and the political
role of, 1–16, 20, 69, 81, 82n3; and
renewed interest in global war, violence,
and ethics, 1–3, 7, 16n6, 275–77, 293,
343, 354n1; and resistance to military
recruitment, 5, 7, 212, 251, 280, 284,
288, 289, 291–94, 340–41; savage slot
and, 210–11; theoretical orientations of,
9, 162–66, 306; use as a "translator" or
cultural travel guide for military, 165,
211, 234–36, 255–60. See also action
anthropology; political anthropology;
research; soft counterinsurgency
Applied Anthropology Unit (AAU), 156,
157, 161
Arabs. See Iraqi culture; Islam; Middle East
Arendt, Hannah, 19, 186
Aristide, Jean-Bertrand, 39–48, 51n7, 51n9
armed actors, 41, 53, 55–58, 60,
62–65, 66n5. See also insurgency;
terrorism/terrorists
Arslan, Alparslan, 115n5
Ashcroft, John, 120
assimilation; of Japanese Americans, 159,
163; of Native Americans, 150, 157, 158
asymmetrical warfare, 57, 170, 175, 176, 318.
See also counterinsurgency; violence
Ataturk, Mustafa Kemal, 108–9

B2 bomber, 142, 143, 146n10–12, 147n15
BAE Systems, 234
Baghdad, 144–45, 216–18, 221–29

Barker, Holly, 293
Battle of Algiers, The (film), 150, 173,
193–95, 201, 204–5
Beckett, Greg, 20, 54, 68
Benedict, Ruth, 9–11, 252, 289
Benjamin, Walter, 19, 51n5, 107
Bennett, Jeffrey, 76, 276, 342n10, 347, 354n9
Bell, Gertrude, 236, 238–39, 242
Bickford, Andrew, 293
biopower, 7, 114, 246
bin Laden, Osama, 3, 197
Bishara, Amahl, 86
Bloch, Ernst, 146n3
blowback, 3, 10, 150, 202, 206. See also
Johnson, Chalmers
Blue: in blurry relationship to Green, 18,
20, 27, 74, 76; as characterized by
policing powers, 12, 29, 78, 79; in
Haiti, 40, 49; in the Maldives, 29, 32;
as symbol of rule of law, 18, 78, 80; 78;
transition from Green to, 68–69, 73, 75.
See also Blue in Green; police; United
Nations (UN)
Blue in Green, 9, 12, 17–21, 21n1, 22n2, 149;
definition of, 18; in Haiti, 40, 41, 49; implications in development and humanitarian initiatives, 21; in the Maldives,
23, 32; as security paradigm of liberal
democracies, 18–19, 34–36, 65, 78
Boas, Franz, 81, 157, 164, 256, 293,
295n16
Bobbitt, Philip, 14–15n1
Bourdieu, Pierre, 7, 275
Brazil, 12, 86, 89–101, 102n3, 103n5–7,
146n5; armed forces of, 91; embassy of,
95; leader of MINUSTAH in Haiti, 41,
47, 48; nationalism in, 89, 91, 100, 101,
102n4, 103n6
Brazil, Love it or Leave it (Web site), 91,
94–96
Bruckheimer, Jerry, 107
Bureau of Indian Affairs (BIA), 150, 157–59,
161
Busey, Gary, 113
Bush Administration, 15n3, 102n1, 102n3,
105, 180; and investigation of Hutu
Rebels, 117–22; and Iraq War strategy,
76, 177n3; and strategy for the War on
Terror, 79, 196–202, 205–6, 207n6,
309n2, 316

Bush, George W., 14n1, 207n9; calling War on Terror "the long war," 69; contempt for nation-building, 76; declaring right to declare citizens "enemy combatants," 201; denouncing "evildoers," 96; during 2000 campaign, 103n15; justification for war in Iraq, 75, 80

Caffrey, Kevin, 276
Caldeira, Teresa, 16n6
California, 12, 87, 352; simulated Iraqi/ Afghan villages in, 281; as site of U.S. Weapons industry, 12, 139, 142, 143, 146n12
Callwell, Charles E., 150, 169–74, 176
Cannibal Army, 39, 40, 42, 49
Casey, George W. Jr., 17
Castaño, Paola, 20, 33, 75, 172
categorization: of people, 20, 32, 53–65, 86, 144, 171, 201, 312; of states as "failed," 20, 40, 43–50
Central America, 3, 100, 102n3, 182, 196
Central Intelligence Agency (CIA): development of weaponry, 139; during the Cold War, 174; during the War on Terror, 200, 202, 233, 234, 236, 281; factbook, 29, 37n7; and failures in Vietnam, 182; imagined conspiracy in Turkey, 112; in *The Spook Who Sat by the Door,* 204–5
Chertoff, Michael, 120
Chicago, 150, 203–5, 207n10
Chomsky, Noam, 186
Churchill, Winston, 238
Ciência Hoje (magazine), 95
citizens/citizenship, 78, 198, 205, 339; as informants in Colombia, 58–64, 66n5; invocation of U.S. Citizenship, 117–18, 120, 130–33, 135; revocation of U.S. citizenship, 201–2
Civil Operations and Revolutionary Development Support (CORDS), 174–75, 177n3, 180, 187, 232, 288
Civil security. *See* Blue in Green
Civil-military relations. *See* Blue in Green
Clausewitz, Carl von: "Friction" in War, 279; moral economy of war, 76, 82n1; war as "politics by other means," 18, 22n3, 67, 210, 259, 327; war is unpredictable, 136n9; war tends to extremes, 336
Clinton, Bill, 3, 121

Clube Militar, 91
coercion: in anthropology, 163–64; in counterinsurgency practice, 180–81, 246; economic coercion, 59–60, 119, 240, 260n6, 276; institutional means of, 17–21, 77–78, 282; legitimate forms of, 18–21
cold war: and academia, 174, 292; anthropology during 209–10, 256–67; counterinsurgency during, 3; development of Stealth technology during, 137–45; and implications for War on Terror, 68–81, 197–99; ideology of, 101, 203, 205, 207n10, 207n11; post cold-war context, 6, 14n1, 45, 94, 211; as the third world war, 102n2
Collier, John, 157, 158, 162
Colombia, 11, 20, 53–65, 65n4, 98
colonialism: American occupation of Iraq (neo), 114, 196–201, 239–41, 336; and anthropology, 155, 210, 236, 239, 242, 341; British rule of Mesopotamia, 236–38, 240–41; conflicts during, 169–72, 233, 341; counterinsurgency during, 149, 195; critiques of, 7, 242–43, 258; decolonization, 19, 46, 49, 70, 72, 173, 181, 194, 195, 203, 209, 351; European, 19, 35, 150, 170, 176, 177n1; forms of ruling, 49, 166; French, 72, 73, 81, 195; in India, 37n4, 171, 254. *See also* postcolonialism, theory
Comaroff, Jean, and John L., 16n6, 56, 61, 63
commodity fetishism, 106, 115n2
computational culture modeling, 281, 291. *See also* U.S. military, cultural turn of
conscience: destruction of, 13, 76, 212, 243, 273–77, 327–40, 342n14; modes of, 1, 2, 151; of U.S. soldiers, 13, 212, 273–77; during Vietnam War, 13, 76, 243, 275–77; during War on Terror, 13, 190, 273–5, 327–40, 342n3, 342n14
conspiracy, 86, 99, 329; as a mode of imperial epistemology, 89–101, 111–15; of threats to Turkish sovereignty, 111–5, 115n9; of U.S. takeover of the Amazon, 89–101. *See also* fantasy
cooperants: role of civilians as in Colombian conflict, 55–64, 65n4, 66n5
CORDS, 174–75, 177n3, 180, 187, 232, 288
Corrie, Rachel, 131

counterinsurgency, 1–12, 14n1, 69, 193–206;
and the "Blue in Green," 21, 32, 34–36;
definitions of, 69–70, 153, 166, 179–80,
248; during the history of the U.S., 149–
51, 246–57; and HTT, 231, 234, 236;
and incompatibility with anthropology
and democracy, 155–56, 162–66, 212,
257–60, 327, 291–94; incorporation of
anthropological insights into, 210, 216,
279; Israeli, 126–32; in Maldives, 20, 23,
32, 34; Project Camelot, 163, 174, 280,
291; reaction in other countries to U.S.,
85–86; strategies/tactics of, 80–81, 312,
315; Thailand Affair, 163, 291; theory,
1, 2, 12, 20, 69–76, 169–76, 177n4,
195–96, 202, 241–42, 246–49; U.S in
Central America, 3, 100, 102n3; U.S.
domestic programs/effects of, 200–5,
233, 252–55; in Vietnam, 180–88, 232.
See also long war
COIN guide. See Counterinsurgency Field
Manual, the (2007)
Counterinsurgency Field Manual, the (2007),
4, 15n3, 68, 201, 281, 324; approach to
"culture," 5, 68, 175, 239–40; definitions
cited within, 153, 179; influence of Small
Wars, 74, 169–71, 175; prehistory of,
69–74, 149, 151, 196; use by Human
Terrain Teams, 218–21, 239–41, 248
counterterror. See counterinsurgency
court martial, 323, 325n4, 354n3
cultural sensitivity, 276, 282, 287, 297, 299,
300
cultural training, 297–302, 305–8, 309n5,
310n13
cultural turn (of the U.S. military),
1–7, 15n2, 175, 196, 209, 234, 249–50,
276–77, 279–91 340, 341
culture, 7, 8, 13, 27, 37n4, 85, 137, 138, 143,
145n1, 158; Indian, 158–61; institutional, 82n1, 218, 293 (see also moral
economy); intelligence and, 169, 175,
176, 177n3; Iraqi, 221–29, 240–41,
283–86, 301–8, 334; Middle Eastern,
282, 288, 309n4; military interest in,
1–2, 216–29, 234, 246–51, 256–59,
279–94, 340–41; military notions of,
175, 239–40, 261, 264–65, 276, 279–91,
298–8; of the "Other," 210–12. See also
U.S. military, cultural turn of

Das, Veena, 16n6, 79
Davis, Rochelle, 276
defense economy. See U.S. military; U.S.
weapons industry
decolonization. See colonialism;
postcolonialism
demilitarization, 17, 20, 23, 35
democracy, 76, 188, 201, 206, 253; anthropology's role in fomenting debate within,
243, 341; efforts to instill in Haiti,
40–50; liberal ideals of, 10, 17–19, 22n4,
23, 34, 40, 74, 313, 322, 327, 341; in
Maldives, 20, 24–34; violence/coercion
in the name of, 9–10, 22n2, 37n5, 58, 76,
99, 196, 202, 312. See also Blue in Green;
Democratic Security Policy (DSP)
Democratic Convergence (CD), 39, 43–44,
51n5, 51n10
Democratic Republic of Congo, 118, 120
Democratic Security Policy (DSP), 58–60,
63
Derrida, Jacques, 19, 51n5
development: in Brazil, 100, 103n5; as a
postcolonial project, 21, 46, 49, 173–75,
240; as a tool of soft counterinsurgency,
248–49, 256–59, 260n6
Dink, Hrant, 111–12
direct support to operations, 264–65
Do no harm principle, 266–67, 271n2. See
also ethics, of anthropology
domestic security, 205
Duffield, Mark, 16n6
Durkheim, Émile, 113

empire, 171, 311; of Brazil, 91–93; British,
150, 155, 171, 173, 234; European, 11;
Ottoman, 170, 238; Pax Americana and,
49, 81, 239; Roman, 105, 311; theories of
American Empire, 15n1, 19, 77, 107, 114.
See also Hardt, Michael; imperialism;
Negri, Antonio
England, Lynndie, 106
Erdoğan, Recep Tayyip, 106, 115n6
Ergenekon, 111, 112, 114, 115n5, 115n6
ethical decision making, 265, 267, 271, 275,
336. See Also ethics
ethics: of anthropology in a military context
(embedded anthropology), 4, 163–67,
209–13, 236, 239–43, 245–59, 261–71,
291–94; battlefield, 273–77, 311–24, 336,

349; of the HTS, 234, 236, 284, 287, 291. *See also* American Anthropological Association (AAA); anthropologists, employed by the U.S. government; conscience, destruction of; do no harm principle; Human Terrain Systems; informed consent; Rules of Engagement (RoE)
ethnography, 101, 115n3, 177n4, 293, 340; of American power, 2, 86; of Kenya, 242–43; "salvage," 157, of the U.S. military, 1–3, 5–11, 262. *See also* anthropology
Europe/European Union (EU), 11, 19, 107, 150, 172, 173, 182; and admission of Turkey to the EU, 111, 115n6; colonial role in the Middle East, 237–39; coverage of the Hood Event, 108; feudalism, 78; as a site of conflict, 172–73
Evans-Pritchard, E. E., 80, 155, 160, 250
evil, 18, 57, 96, 101, 183; axis of, 96; people as, 57, 340
execution, 56, 136n8, 315, 316, 324n3

F-117, 138–45, 146n10–2, 147n15–6. *See also* U.S. weapons industry
failed states: Haiti declared a, 43–46; invocation of category, 20, 40, 45–50; patterns of violence in, 56; theories of, 45–50, 50n3; U.S. complicity in creating, 68, 81
fanatic, 171–72, 211. *See also* terrorism/terrorists
Fanmi Lavalas (FL), 39, 40, 43, 51n8, 51n10
Fanon, Frantz, 7, 16n7
fantasy, 73, 81, 82n4; of domestic African-American insurgency, 150, 196, 200–5; of future soldiers, 199; of seeing Red, 73–76, 81, 82n4; of U.S. takeover of Amazon, 89–102; of U.S. takeover of Turkey, 105–15, 115n4, 115n7. *See also under* American power; cold war; film, cinematic imaginaries; Zizek, Slavoj.
Fawry, Mathew, 91, 92
Federal Bureau of Investigation (FBI), 118–21
Ferguson, Brian, 16n6, 293
film: and aesthetics of self-annihilation (Turkey), 105–10; cinematic imaginaries, 12, 150–51, 182, 193–206, 207n10; as training tools for U.S. military, 150, 173, 193–96; about war, 309n2, 337, 343–51, 354n4

Finer, Samuel E., 17
FINRAF, 97, 98, 100
First World, 209–13
FM, 3–24. *See* Counterinsurgency Field Manual, the
"fog of war," 18, 71, 330, 332, 336. *See also* ethics; green; violence
force of law, 19. *See also* Derrida, Jacques
Foucault, Michel, 7, 16n4, 18, 22n3, 77, 78, 282, 354n4
Fosher, Kerry, 212, 295n8
Freud, Sigmund, 183, 191
France, 7, 35, 39, 47, 146n5, 312; colonization, 35, 73, 170; counterinsurgency in Algeria, 70, 72, 173, 193–95, 200, 239, 312, 327; as the originators of counterinsurgency theory and practice, 69–72, 81, 337
Fritz, Samuel, 91
full spectrum dominance, 68, 76, 77, 100, 198–99
Fulbright, William, 243
Fulton, Robert, 92

Galliéni, Simon, 35, 73
Galula, David, 69–75, 80–81, 149, 195, 351. *See also under* counterinsurgency, during the history of the U.S.
Garland, Elizabeth, 12, 86
Gates, Robert, 15n2, 68, 280, 294n4
Gayoom, Maumoon Abdul, 23–26, 28–34, 36n1, 36n2, 36n8
Gaza Strip, 126, 131, 135n1
Germany, 107, 139, 146n5
Gill, Lesley, 16n6, 293
globalization, 14n1, 85–87, 114
Global War on Terror (GWOT). *See* War on Terror
Gonzalez, Roberto, 11, 19, 66n6, 150, 212, 288, 293, 309n9, 295n13
Grandin, Greg, 102n3
Green: in blurry relationship to Blue, 18, 20, 21n2, 27, 32, 34, 74, 76, 78; in Maldives, 32, 34; project to define political violence as, 12, 80; as symbol of "Fog of War," 18; as symbol of security by military force, 12, 18, 68, 79; transition to Blue, 68–69, 73, 75; and the "War on Terror," 78–80
Griffin, Marcus, 4, 13, 164, 212, 288, 295n13

Group, 184, 39, 43, 44, 47, 51n5, 51n9, 51n10
Gül, Abdullah, 115n6
Gulf War, 110, 308n1, 347, 348; Stealth technology in, 138, 143, 144, 145. *See also* Iraq
Gusterson, Hugh, 15n2, 68, 137, 147n14, 151, 260n1, 276

Habermas, Jürgen, 109
Haiti, 11, 20, 39–50, 51n5–7, 102n3
hard counterinsurgency, 246–51, 254, 258–59, 260n3. *See also* counterinsurgency
Hardt, Michael, 114. *See also* Empire
hearts and minds, 45, 73, 106, 184, 187, 247, 300, 322, 329. *See also* counterinsurgency
Helbig, Zania, 232, 234, 287–88, 295n12
Hensley, Michael, 311, 314–19, 322–24, 325n4
Hevia, James L., 69, 150, 151
Hobbes, Thomas, 22n3, 80, 180
Hofstadter, Richard, 101
house raid, 299, 300, 330
humanitarianism, 65n4, 259; aid, 62, 351; intervention, 46–47, 93–94; military and, 21, 46–47, 246; workers, 126, 200
human rights: abuses in the Maldives, 25, 33, 36n1; counterinsurgency undermines, 201, 206, 293–94; investigation in Colombia, 62–63; in Iraq, 17
Human Terrain System (HTS), 68, 176, 196, 206n2, 239, 249, 293, 295n9; activities of, 4–5, 13, 153, 212, 215–29, 231, 249, 260n3, 261, 244n1–3, 284–89; anthropological opposition to, 5–6, 150, 162, 212, 231, 236, 246, 284, 291, 293; deaths of HTT social scientists, 66n6, 244n2, 288; debatable ethical standards of, 163–66, 231–36, 239, 242, 288–89; funding of the, 232, 244n3, 280, 288, 291, 294n4; origins of, 154, 231–36, 239. *See also under* anthropologists; counterinsurgency; U.S. military
Human Terrain Teams (HTT). *See* Human Terrain System (HTS)
Hussein, Saddam, 197, 280, 297, 304, 333, 339; collaborators now working with

U.S. military, 182, 191. *See also* Iraq; Iraq, war in (2003–)

imperialism, 15, 182, 258; belief in, 237, 239; and conspiracy theory, 110–15; counterinsurgency as a war against, 70, 74; U.S., 90. *See also* American Power; empire
Incirlik Airforce Base, 111
incriminating evidence, 315, 318, 323
Indian "New Deal" (Indian Reorganization Act), 156–59, 162
indigenous peoples, 172, 254, in Brazil, 91–92; in colonies, 171–73
informed consent, 163, 251, 260n5. *See also under* ethics
insurgency (insurgents): analysis of, 171–76, 195, 203, 252, 254, 260, 281, 341; causes of, 166, 171–76, 181, 241, 248; definition of, 69–72, 153, 165, 311; domestic, 24–36, 203–5; in Haiti, 44–49; identification of, 20, 21, 24, 33–34, 75, 175, 274, 299 (*See also* categorization); Iraqi, 150, 182, 191, 193–94, 210–11, 233, 236, 238, 286, 303, 310n9–10, 315–16, 331, 334, 339 (*See Also* Iraq, War in (2003–); Maoist, 149; Taliban/Afghan, 194, 233, 236, 249, 322; U.S. battle against, 2, 14n1, 15n3, 128, 150, 187, 191, 193, 216, 232, 312, 315–16, 331, 334, 339; Vietnamese, 187–89, 329. *See also* counterinsurgency; intifada; pacification; rebels; uprising
intelligence, 1, 4, 5, 199, 203, 245, 316, 345; agencies (U.S), 261–71, 293; and anthropology, 155, 166, 169–75, 291; consequences of "bad" intelligence, 182, 185, 191; and controlling elections, 72; gathering in global counterinsurgency, 232–36, 287–89
Intelligence Branch, War Office (UK), 170
Internet: and the U.S. military, 281, 309n4, 325n8, 328, 337 spread of rumors on, 89–101, 103n14
internment, Japanese, 150–61, 162, 164, 252. *See also* Americans, internment of Japanese; War Relocation Authority (WRA); World War II
interpreters, 333; as key site of cultural knowledge for U.S. soldiers, 301, 304, 305, 309n3; working with HTT (or in Iraq), 217, 228, 288. *See also* translator

Intifada, 86, 125–30, 134, 136n3, 136n4, 136n8, 329

Iraq, 83n5, 120, 138, 174, 175, 177n3, 179; British control over, 237–41; nation-building in, 76, 191; Security Forces in, 17–18, 217, 219, 222, 223; *See also* Counterinsurgency; Iraq War (2003–); Iraqi culture; Iraqis; *Iraq Tribal Study*

Iraq War (2003–), 1, 4, 13, 15n1, 15n2, 17, 36, 69, 75, 77, 196–202, 279–93, 298–308; counterinsurgency in, 246–50, 257, 298–308, 343–354; cultural sensitivity during, 298–308; as fourth world war, 102n2; HTS in, 212, 215–29, 231–36, 246–50 (*see also* Human Terrain System (HTS); impact on U.S. soldiers, 273–77; 327–41; insurgency in (*see under* insurgency, Iraqi); as a mistake, 68, 76, 181, 190, 196, 200, 201, 242; and Turkey, 108–12; use of phosphorus bombs, 190; *See also* counterinsurgency

Iraqi culture: Smart Card, 282, 283, 295n6, 309n4 309n8; U.S. military initiatives to understand, 279–87, 298–308

Iraqis, 144, 236; civilians terrorized by U.S. military, 313–20, 330–39; encounters with U.S. military, 217, 221–24, 228–29; 298–300, 302–6, 313–20; fantasies of docility, 191; indices of economic wellbeing of, 221–29; religious practices, 228; resentment toward U.S., 181, 333–34, 336, and torture, 184, 338

Iraq Tribal Study, 240–41

Ireland, 254, 340

Islam: battle against extremism/insurgency, 33, 117, 232, 280; in Maldives, 24, 26, Shari'a, 26; Shia, 217, 228, 238, 241, 290; Sunni, 24, 217, 223, 228, 238, 241, 290, 314, 323, 324n2; in Turkey, 106, 115n6, ; understandings by the U.S. military, 106, 280–82, 298, 308n1, 309n4, 309n8, 310n8. *See also* Iraqi culture; Middle East

Israel, 125–35, 135n1–2, 136n3–5, 136n9, 139, 146n7, 312

Istanbul, 105, 107, 110, 111, 114

Jacobsen, Kurt, 69, 82n4, 150, 151, 196, 232

Japan, 1; counterinsurgency in Burma, 239, 247, 252

Japanese Americans, 150, 156–61, 162, 164, 251. *See also* internment, Japanese

Jauregui, Beatrice, 11, 40, 50, 50n2, 54, 68, 78, 115n1

Jefferson, Thomas, 153–54

Johnson, Chalmers, 3, 10, 190, 202, 207n5. *See also* blowback

Johnson, Lyndon Baines, 190

Johnston, Barbara Rose, 293

justice: departments/ministries/courts of, 15n3, 51n10, 60, 120, 122, 200; peace without, 75–81; privatization of, 60; theories of, 75–81, 135, 154, 186; and the U.S. investigation of Hutu Rebels, 117–22; and the U.S. military intervention in Iraq, 75–81, 82n1, 323, 331, 341

Kagame, Paul, 120

Kampala, 118–19

Kant, Immanuel, 20

Kelly, John D., 5, 15n4, 20, 21n1, 49, 149, 333

Kenyatta, Jomo, 242–43

Kerinçsiz, Kerim, 111

Kluckhohn, Clyde, 9–11, 252

knowledge: anthropological, 6, 9, 10, 162, 165, 270, 276, 287, 340; gathering in counterinsurgency, 1, 13, 35, 172, 175–76, 234, 269, 280, 288, 298–306; of local culture to suppress resistance, 153–55, 160, 171–73, 234–36, 246–60, 276, 282, 301–3; production of, 55, 63, 112, 129, 292, 301; Soviet, 142; and the state, 5, 15n4, 78, 137, 140, 145, 196 *See also* coercion; cultural training; culture; intelligence; leveraging culture; research

Küçük, Veli, 111

Kurdistan, 108, 110

Kurdistan Worker's Party (PKK), 108, 111, 112

Kurtlar Vadisi Irak (film), 105–14

labeling. *See* categorization

land reform, 188

Latheef, Jennifer, 32, 33

Latin America, 47–49, 50n4, 53–65, 89–102, 103n6, 176; and U.S. counter-insurgency, 74, 92, 94, 99, 100, 102n3, 174, 288

Latortue, Gérard, 47, 51n9
Lawrence, T. E., 236–9, 242, 289
Lessa, Luis Gonzaga, 93, 94
leveraging culture, 246–60, 276, 280–82, 287–90. *See also* culture; knowledge
logic of necessity, 20
Lockheed Corporation, 139–43
London, 113, 171, 242,
long war, 14n1, 69, 74, 85, 102n1, 167, 200, 207n8-9, 211. *See also* counterinsurgency; War on Terror, the
Los Angeles, 86, 142, 146n12. *See also* California
low-intensity conflicts. *See* counterinsurgency
Luttwak, Edward, 169
Lutz, Catherine, 16n6, 102, 293

Machiavelli, Niccolo, 18, 19, 78, 191, 330, 348
Maldives, 11, 20, 23–36, 36n1, 37n4; Black Friday, 26
malform- (-ed, -ation), 328, 329, 331, 335–38
manifest destiny, 92, 182, 290
manipulation. *See* categorization; coercion; knowledge; leveraging culture
Mao Tse Tung, 70, 149; fetishism of, 67, 69, 75, 81, 149
Masco, Joseph, 7, 15n4, 150, 151
mass media: coverage of HTS, 6, 162–65, 231; lack of coverage for Winter Soldier, 328–31; portrayals of war, 237, 256, 343–44; responses to American Power in Turkey, 105–15; U.S. coverage of Israeli-Palestinian conflict, 132–35; and the War on Terror, 193–206, 219, 242, 336–38, 352–54. *See also* film; internet; propaganda campaigns
Mattis, James, General USMC, 347, 348, 351, 352
Maury, Matthew Fontaine, 92, 93
McFate, Montgomery, 162, 165, 210–11, 234, 261, 285–87, 295n10
McNamara, Robert, 186, 190
Mead, Margaret, 1, 286, 289
memory, 343–54; as data, 141, 279; institutional, 171; military, 82, 105; public, 82, 137, 151
Merom, Gil, 312, 313, 322, 324
Metal Firtina (Metal Storm), 105–14

Middle East: British colonial occupation of, 190, 192n9, 236–9; ignorance/conceptions of culture of, 234, 279, 282–83, 288–90, 294, 301, 305, 308; increased interest of academics, 292, 297; U.S. intervention, policy in, 12, 102n3, 112, 125, 200, 207n9, 293, 297, 301, 308n1. *See also* Iraq; Israel; Nablus; Palestinian territories/Palestinians; Tel Aviv; Turkey; West Bank
military-industrial complex, 137–39, 143, 146n4 150, 198, 329, 341. *See also* U.S. weapons industry
military policy. *See* U.S. military
Minerva Project, 5, 14, 68, 82n2, 206n2, 258, 280, 293, 294n4
MINUSTAH, 39–41, 47–48
Mitchell, Sean T., 86
modernization theory, 211
Monroe Doctrine, 92
Mooney, James, 154–55, 158
moral economy: of the state, 77–78; of war, 67, 72, 79–80, 82n1, 332. *See also under* culture, institutional
Muslims. *See* Islam

Nablus, 86, 125–35, 136n7
Nasheed, Mohamed ("Anni"), 24, 26, 37n7
nation (-states): democratic ideals of, 10, 14n1, 29, 34, 69, 71, 76, 110, 154; "host" nation, 75, 176; instability/problems of; 45–46, 81, 173, 210; insurgencies and the, 2, 14n1, 174, 195, 203–5, 233; sovereignty of, 47, 49, 74, 102n3, 103n6, 110, 196; theories of, 45–46, 82n3, 195. *See also* failed states; imperialism; Pax Americana
national security: in Colombia, 58, 65n4; in Haiti, 42; in the Maldives, 20, 23–35; U.S., 5, 15n4, 49, 137, 165, 198–201, 206, 262–66, 280–94, 309n2
National Security Service (NSS), 23–26, 28–33
nationalism: African, 242–43; as a focus of anthropology, 6; Brazilian, 89, 91, 100, 101, 102n4, 103n6; Maldives, 24–35, Turkish, 107–13; uprisings against foreign occupation, 72, 181, 189, 194, 233, 290, 339; U.S. weapons industry, 138. *See also* colonialism; intifada

nation-building: anthropology and, 10, 209, 256–57; in Haiti, 43–50; in Maldives, 23–35; U.S. and, 3, 43, 46, 49–50, 75, 76, 176, 181, 202, 256–57. *See also* development; Pax Americana

Native Americans, 150, 154–59, 182

NATO, 105, 112

Navaro-Yashin, Yael, 110, 115n1

Negri, Antonio, 114. *See also* empire; Hardt, Michael

Nelson, Christopher T., 276

Neoliberalism, 7, 94, 257, 331, 339; resistance to, 101; privatization impetus, 191

Network of Concerned Anthropologists, 5–7, 245, 293

New York, 93, 113, 196

Nevada, 142, 143, 146n12

New York Times, The, 90, 94, 132, 133, 249, 287, 290, 354n9

9/11. *See* September 11, 2001

Nixon, Richard, 184, 190, 328

NLF (National Liberation Front), 184–89

noncombatants, 13, 180; Palestinian, 128–34; as a source of information, 53–57, 61, 172; unethical treatment of, 273–75, 316, 324n1, 338. *See also* categorization

nonsynchronicity, 137, 145, 146n3

Nordstrom, Carolyn, 16n6, 293

Obama, Barack, 15n3, 81, 191, 294n2, 339

Öcalan, Abdullah, 111–12

Office of Special Plans, 185

Ohio, 140, 142, 143, 207n9

Operation Infinite Reach, 3. *See also* Iraq, War (2003–)

Operation Iraqi Freedom, 273, 275, 277 *See also* Iraq, War (2003–)

Opler, Marvin, 161, 255–58

Opler, Morris, 159, 161, 252, 255–58

Orakoğlu, Bülent, 112

pacification: in Fallujah, 194; in French Algeria, 193–95; of Vietnamese populations, 150, 180–90. *See also* counterinsurgency; CORDS; peace; Phoenix program; Vietnam War

Paine, Thomas, 339, 341

Palestinian territories/Palestinians, 86, 125–35, 136n3. *See also* Islam; Middle East

Palestinians, 125–35, 136n3

Pamuk, Orhan, 115n7

Pandya, Mihir, 87

Pantano, Ilario, 1st Lt. USMC, 345–47, 353–54, 354n6, 354n10

paranoia, 283; of U.S. military, 101, 102n3. *See also* conspiracy

passports, 18, 125–27, 130–33

Pax Americana, 6–14, 20, 49, 50, 67, 81, 82n2, 90, 101, 114, 199, 211. *See also* American Power

peace, 87, 92, 180, 207n9; military means of achieving, 10, 12, 20, 35, 43, 72, 75–78, 81; "no peace of god be with you," 331, 333; scholarship on, 7, 8, 16n6; secured by civil means, 17, 71, 80; UN ideology of, 27; U.S. as self-proclaimed broker of, 134. *See also* pacification; Pax Americana

Pedelty, Mark, 293

Pentagon Papers, 188, 190

Pentagon, 14n1, 79, 245, 260, 339; development of airborne weaponry, 140–44; development of HTS, 231–34, 239–43, 284; epistemology of culture, 279, 282, 289–93, 294n2; film screenings for policymakers, 193–96, 203; and Vietnam, 174, 187, 190. *See also* Human Terrain Systems (HTS); U.S. military

Peters, Ralph, 233

Petraeus, Gen. David, 1, 15n2, 232, 280, 295n11, 343; beliefs on counterinsurgency, 73–74, 76, 221; and the Counterinsurgency Field Manual, 75, 175–76; strategy in Iraq, 240–42

Phoenix program, 175, 182–84, 191n5, 232, 245, 260n3, 288. *See also* Vietnam War

phraselator, 279, 282, 294n1

PKK, the, 108, 111, 112

Pletsch, Carl, 210, 211

police: Colombian, 58–63; Haiti, 39–42, 51n6; Iraqi, 17, 182, 219, 222, 228, 281, 307; Maldives, 20, 23–35, 37n4; Rule of Law and, 18–20, 21n2 78; Turkish, 108, 111–12; Ugandan, 119; UN Peacekeepers as, 48; U.S., 253; in Vietnam, 257; women, 299. *See also* under Blue; Blue in Green; civil security; coercion

political anthropology, 1–8, 11–13, 69, 82n3, 149, 209–13, 260, 293–94
political science, 2, 4, 6, 8, 9, 210, 259, 292
populace, 29, 97, 182, 219, 253, 306
Portugal, 91
postcolonialism, 2, 163; theory, 6, 19, 289; focus on nationalism, 6; forms of war, 19. *See also* colonialism; development; nation (-state); nation-building; Pax Americana
Powell, Colin, 3, 10
Price, David, 150, 163, 212, 293, 294n4, 306
propaganda campaigns, 71, 97, 182, 195, 202, 205, 236, 255, 312, 328, 338. *See also* mass media
psychoanalysis, 179, 183. *See also* repetition compulsion
psychologists, 4
publicness, 107, 109, 110
Putin, Vladimir, 114

rational choice analysis, 186, 189, 294
rationality, 109, 143, 211
Reagan, Ronald, 100
rebels: Huk Communist Rebels, 247–48; Hutu, 117–23. *See also* insurgency (insurgents); terrorism/terrorists
Red, as in seeing Red, 12, 67, 69, 74, 75, 81
rendition, 142, 331; of Hutu Rebels, 120–21; during War on Terror, 200, 206
repetition compulsion, 12, 179, 181, 185, 190. *See also* psychoanalysis
research, 4–6, 11, 55, 82n3, 115n3, 129, 133, 137, 139, 146n12, 174, 298, 344; classified, 165–66, 268–69; ethnographic, 101, 102; fieldwork, 90, 163–66, 262; problem-based (applied), 156–61, 262–70; for the U.S. military, 209–13, 216–29, 262–71; 280, 285, 291–93. *See also* anthropology; HTS; intelligence; knowledge; Minerva Project
Rice, Condoleezza, 106, 113
Rio de Janeiro, 91, 93, 95
Robben, Antonius, 293
Rotberg, Robert, 45–46
rule of law: in Africa, 122; appeals to the, 31; as a sphere of the "Blue," 18, 20, 22n4; in Haiti, 43–46. *See also* Blue in Green; justice
Rules of Engagement (RoE), 19, 274, 275,

306, 315, 318, 327, 331, 332, 340, 342n6, 347, 354n7. *See also* ethics, battlefield
rumor, 90–95, 136n8, 140, 247, 317. *See also* conspiracy; fantasy; paranoia
Rumsfeld, Donald, 1, 15n2, 197, 207n6, 234, 336; as portrayed in Turkish media, 105, 106, 110, 113, 114; and Iraq war, 182, 190
Rwanda, 46, 86, 117–23; genocide in, 118, 120, 121; relations with the U.S., 120–22; security forces, 120–22. *See also* Africa

Sahlins, Marshall, 13, 14, 76, 182, 264, 293, 322, 327, 329, 330, 342n3; destruction of conscience, 76, 243, 275, 277; fieldwork in Vietnam, 275–77. *See also* conscience
Salah, Khaled, 129–34
Salah, Salam, 129, 132–34, 136n6
Sampaio, Fernando G., 91
Schmitt, Carl, 19, 48, 50n3, 51n5
second world, 210
secrecy, 198, 200; in building Stealth technology, 140, 143, 145n1, 147n14; as a problem in anthropological research, 165, 264, 268. *See also* ethics; knowledge
security, 75, 80, 179, 182, 184, 232, 256, 280, 316, 341; anthropological study of, 2, 11, 15n4, 262, 270; Blue-in-Green paradigm of, 16–21, 21n2, 23–36; concerns in building, 76, 80, 307; and failed states, 45–46, 50n3, 75; forces/officials, 17, 21n2, 24–32, 118, 121, 128, 182, 217, 219–20, 223, 249; global, 45, 49, 50n3; homeland, 291; in Maldives, 23–34; policy of Colombia, 56–65; policy of U.S. pre-9/11, 99, 137, 142–45, 150, 256; policy of U.S. post-9/11, 76, 196, 198–206, 222, 232, 287, 291–94, 317; private forms of, 21, 21n2, 41, 313; "pulling" security, 314, 316, 317, 319 (*see also* sniper); restoration in Haiti, 40–49; state, 15n4, 150, 199, 205–6, 291–92; U.S. institutions of, 262–70, 279. *See also* Blue in Green; national security; U.S. military
September 11, 2001, 3, 7, 60, 79–80, 125, 292, 338, 347; conceptions of American power since, 107, 114; conspiracy theory and, 112; and the establishment of a security state, 196–201. *See also* al Qaeda; New York

Shari'a. *See* Islam
sheikh, 240
Shirts, Matthew, 100
Siegel, 16n6
Silverstein, Paul, 99, 115n1
Skunk Works, 140–42
slavery, 83n4, 91, 103n7, 253
Sluka, Jeff, 293
Small Wars, 169–76, 311, 313, 322
sniper, 311, 313–21, 324n3, 334, 347
social science/social scientists: debate over
    role in U.S. military, 4, 8, 21, 151, 239,
    242, 243, 264–67; as embedded in the
    U.S. military, 1, 154 (HTS), 160, 163,
    165, 174, 244n2, 257, 263; within the
    HTS, 154, 196, 215, 231–35, 285–88,
    294n3, and the Minerva project, 5, 280;
    study of counterinsurgency, 20, 65, 275.
    See also anthropologists; cultural turn
    (of the U.S. military); Human Terrain
    System (HTS)
sociology, 4, 6, 210
Soft Power, 246, 250, 254, 260n2. *See also*
    counterinsurgency
soft counterinsurgency, 246–59, 260n3. *See
    also* counterinsurgency
Solimões River, 91
sovereignty: in Afghanistan, 235; Brazilian
    notions of, 91, 92, 99, 100, 101, 103n5,
    n6, n15; claims to violate, 40, 47, 50n3;
    imagined threats to Turkish, 110–15;
    respect for Rwandan, 122; theories
    of, 19, 22n3, 34, 78. *See also* Blue in
    Green; nation (-state); nationalism;
    nation-building
Spook Who Sat By the Door, The (Film,
    1973), 150, 203–5. *See also* African
    Americans; conspiracy; fantasy; film
state. *See* nation (-state)
state of exception, 20, 40, 47, 51n5
statistics, 54, 61–64, 172, 185, 188, 224. *See
    also under* knowledge, production of
Stealth bomber; 87, 143. *See also* B2; F117
Stealth technology, 138–43, 146n10, 146n11
Stockholm syndrome, 185
Stocking, George, 155
structural-functionalism, 240, 258
Strauss, Leo, 10–11
Sudan, 3, 62, 155. *See also* Africa
Sulaymaniyah, 108

Tambiah, Stanley, 16n6
Taussig, Michael, 16n6
Teixeira de Macedo, 93
Tel Aviv, 113. *See also* Israel; Middle
    East
terrorism/terrorists; al-Qaeda, 79;
    classification of, 32, 33, 71, 86, 118, 120,
    121, 202, 205; in Colombian rhetoric,
    53, 58, 60, 64; in Iraq, 18, 338; links to
    NGOs, 21; logic of, 150, 281; War on
    Terror, 182, 193, 198, 201, 206, 207n9.
    See also al-Qaeda; Bush, George W.;
    categorization; insurgency/insurgents;
    September 11, 2001; War on Terror
Tet offensive, 185, 187–90, 192n7. *See also*
    Vietnam War
third world, 209–11
Tolstoy, Leo, 8, 76
torture, in French counterinsurgency, 171,
    173, 193–94; of Hutu Rebels in U.S.
    investigation, 121–23; in Iraq War, 184,
    274, 294 338, 342n3, U.S. use during
    War on Terror, 4, 56, 196, 200–3, 206, in
    Vietnam, 184
training, in ethics: 274; of the U.S. military
    by anthropologists, 263–64
translator, 121, 299; anthropology's role as,
    211; as an importance source of cultural
    knowledge in Iraq war, 304–6, 310n9.
    See also anthropologists; interpreters;
    phraselator
Trouillot, Michel-Rolph, 210
trust, 318; between anthropologists and
    subjects, 160, 163–64, 166, 239, 243;
    between Iraqis and U.S. military, 299,
    303–5, 310n9–10
Turkey, 12, 24, 76, 86, 105–15, 115n8, 227
Turks, 105–15, 237–38
Turna, Burak, 105, 106

Uçar, Orkun, 105, 106
Uganda, 86, 117–121
Unger, Roberto, 14
United Nations (UN), 76, 114, 135n1;
    opposition to U.S. invasion of Iraq, 120;
    peacekeeping forces in Haiti, 18, 39–41;
    rumored takeover of Amazon, 90, 98;
    World Food Programme, 220; world
    order, 9, 10, 19, 22n2, 27. *See also* Blue
    in Green

United States, 3, 8, 22, 68, 76, 85, 262, 290, 312, 337, 349; Civil War, 9; Department of Homeland Security, 123, 206n4, 291; domestic effects of the War on Terror, 194–206; engagement with Haiti, 20, 39–44, 46–49, 51n7; extradition of Hutu Rebels, 119–23; role in the Israeli-Palestinian conflict, 125–35; spectral role in Haiti, 39–50; State Department, 119–21; U.S./Brazil relations, 90, 98–100; U.S./Turkey relations, 105, 111–12; seeking asylum in, 123; U.S./Rwanda relations, 117–23; vs. the "Third World," 210–11. *See also* American power; citizens/citizenship; passports; Pax Americana

U.S. Agency for International Development (USAID), 15n3, 174, 257

U.S. Air Force, 207n7, 261, 301; development of airborne weaponry, 139–44, 146n11; in first Gulf War, 143–44

U.S. Army, 106, 108, 333, 347, 351; behaving (un)ethically in Iraq, 273–76 311, 313–24; development of the HTS, 231–34, 261; in Iraq war, 17, 73, 75, 218, 228; interactions with Iraqis, 297–308, 309n1, 309n4; in the future, 199; in Vietnam War, 169, 174–75, 187–91. *See also* Counterinsurgency Field Manual, the; HTS; Pentagon; U.S. military

U.S. House Un-American Activities Committee, 233

U.S. Marine Corps, 169, 171, 175, 182, 191n3, 196, 201, 241, 273–75, 276, 281, 282, 325n6, 343–45, 347–54, 354n1; in Afghanistan, 267; behaving ethically in Iraq, 273–76; Intelligence Agency, 261; interactions with Iraqis, 297–308; YouTube video of Marine killing a puppy, 337–38. *See also* Counterinsurgency Field Manual, the; U.S. military

U.S. military, 1–14, 241, 280, 281 313, 347; anthropology/ethnography of, 1–3, 5–11, 262, 293; cultural turn of, 1–7, 15n2, 175, 196, 209, 234, 249–250, 276–77, 279–91, 298–308, 340, 341; employment of social scientists in, 1–4, 8, 68, 151, 154, 160–65, 174, 209–13, 239–43, 244n2, 257, 263–71; 280, 285, 291–93; engagement in Latin America, 94, 99,

101, 102n3; failures of interventions, 68, 76, 82n3; film as training tools for, 150, 173, 193–96; policies and practices during the War on Terror, 14n1, 68–72, 80–81, 138, 194–206, 207n7, 260, 290, 299, 338; as portrayed in Turkish media, 105–10; presence in Haiti, 41–49; spending, 134, 136n3, 137, 198, 206n3, 206n4; theorists, 2, 14n1. *See also* American power; counterinsurgency; cultural training; ethics; security

U.S. Naval Observatory, 92

U.S. Navy, 92, 298, 302, 328

U.S. power. *See* American Power; U.S. military

U.S. weapons industry, 87, 138–45, 146n12; role in the Israeli-Palestinian conflict, 125–35. *See also* B2; F-117; stealth technology

University of Chicago, 5, 6–8, 13, 14, 15n4, 16n5

uprising, 188, 253–54; African American in the U.S., 203–5; Haitian, 44, 47; in Iraq against the British, 238; in Palestine, 125–35; in Japanese internment camps, 160; in the Maldives, 23. *See also* colonialism; insurgency; intifada

Valley of the Wolves: Iraq (film), 105–14

Vann, John Paul, 174

Vela, Evan, 311, 314–5, 317–18, 322–24, 325n7

Viet Cong, 185, 187–90, 232

Vietnam, 257, 288, 322, 345. *See also* Sahlins, Marshall

Vietnamese: soothsayers, 247; violence towards, 150, 180–90 191n2, 327–30, 337

Vietnam War, 179–90, 194; and aircraft, 139, 146n6; anthropological critique of, 12–13; antiwar movement, 204–5, 328–29; impact on American society, 144; lessons learned, 69–70 196; as a low-intensity/counterinsurgency conflict, 174–75, 209, 239, 312, 353; Project Camelot, 163, 174, 280, 291; strategies of winning, 150; Thailand Affair, 163, 291. *See also* CORDS; pacification; Phoenix Program; Tet Offensive

Vine, David, 293

violence, 108, 110, 112, 121, 176, 191n4, 274, 275, 282, 291, 340, 343; in

Afghanistan, 1; against tourists, 117–19; in colonial conflicts, 81; as form of legitimate coercion, 20–21, 78, 80; in Haiti, 40–42; in Iraq, 1, 221, 228, 274–75, 300; in Israeli-Palestinian conflict, 125–35; in the Maldives, 24–26; in *The spook who sat by the door,* 204–5; study of, 2, 3, 7, 11, 16n6, 19; targeting civilians in Colombia, 53, 54–57, 61–65; in Uganda, 86; U.S. Media coverage of (in Palestine), 13235; U.S. sponsored during the War on Terror, 196, 197, 201–2, 211, 270, 312; during Vietnam War, 180–88; 327–30, 337. *See also* Afghanistan, conflict in (2001–); Blue in Green; Iraq War (2003–); insurgency; terrorism; uprising

Walton, Jeremy, 86

War on Terror, the, 138, 145, 150, 235, 279, 280; American power during, 6, 12, 21, 85–87, 117, 120–23, 150, 195–206; and Brazilian fears of invasion, 89–103; impact on anthropology, 291–93, 294n2, impact on U.S. domestic policy,

195–206, 207n10; and Islamic extremism, 33; rhetoric of, 60, 69, 338

War Relocation Authority (WRA), 150, 156, 157, 159, 255

Warner, Michael, 109

Wax, Dustin, 149–51, 182

Weber, Max, 8, 20, 21, 67, 76–77, 79, 333

West Bank, 86, 125–34, 135n1–2

Whitehead, Neil, 16n6

Wilson, Woodrow, 9, 10

Winter Soldier, 325n6, 327–34, 339–41, 342n7, 352, 354n11

women, 106, 115n6, 162, 181, 189, 193, 194, 282, 319, 341, 352; in U.S. military, 290–307; as victims of violence, 228

World Bank, the, 114

World War I, 9, 73, 183, 236, 237

World War II, 137, 139, 145n2, 173, 340, 350; internment of Japanese Americans during, 150–61, 162, 164, 252; relative peace, decolonization post, 7, 10, 20, 46, 49; U.S. anthropologists during, 1, 12, 150, 159–61, 164, 246–60

Zizek, Slavoj, 7, 110